EPHESOS

Metropolis of Asia

HARVARD THEOLOGICAL STUDIES
41

HARVARD
THEOLOGICAL
STUDIES

CAMBRIDGE, MASSACHUSETTS

EPHESOS
Metropolis of Asia

An Interdisciplinary Approach to Its
Archaeology, Religion, and Culture

Edited by
Helmut Koester

DISTRIBUTED BY
HARVARD UNIVERSITY PRESS
FOR
HARVARD THEOLOGICAL STUDIES
HARVARD DIVINITY SCHOOL

Harvard Theological Studies 41

First Harvard Divinity School printing in 2004; second HDS printing, 2010.

Book design and typesetting at the *Harvard Theological Review*
Managing Editor: Tamar Duke-Cohan
Editorial Assistants: Laura Nasrallah, Rebecca Lesses, Greg Schmidt Goering, and Anthony Rivera
Cover Art: The Tetragonos Agora and Theater from *Archaeological Resources for New Testament Studies* slide series
Cover Design: Jim Gerhard
Harvard Theological Studies Series Editors: Allen D. Callahan, John B. Carman, David D. Hall, Helmut Koester, Jon D. Levenson, Francis Shüssler Fiorenza, Ronald F. Thiemann

Library of Congress Cataloging-in-Publication data

Ephesos metropolis of Asia: an interdisciplinary approach to its archaeology, religion, and culture / edited by Helmut Koester.
    p.   cm. — (Harvard theological studies: 41)
    Includes most of the papers presented at a symposium organized by Harvard Divinity School and cosponsored by the Harvard University Departments of Classics and Fine Arts, March 1994.
    Includes bibliographical references and index.
    ISBN 0-674-01349-2 (Pbk.: alk. paper)
    1. Ephesus (Extinct city)—Civilization—Congresses.
2. Excavations (Archaeology)—Turkey—Ephesus (Extinct city)—Congresses. 3. Ephesus (Extinct city)—Religion—Congresses. 4. Rome—Religion—Congresses. I. Koester, Helmut, 1926– . II. Harvard Divinity School. III. Harvard University. Dept. of the Classics. IV. Harvard University. Dept. of Fine Arts. V. Series: Harvard Theological Studies; no. 41.
DF261.E5E7 1995
939'.23—dc20   95-39808
                                            CIP

Manufactured in the U.S.A.   AF 1-7093

CONTENTS

Illustrations

[*]Permission to reprint the illustrations marked with an asterisks has kindly been granted by the Austrian Archaeological Institute in Vienna. We are also grateful for permission to base the map attached to this volume on O. Oberleitner's map, originally published in *IvE*.

+Permission to reprint this photograph has kindly been granted by the estate of the late Erol Atalay, Austrian Archaeological Institute, Vienna.

Abbreviations

ACO	Acta conciliorum oecumenicorum
AJA	*American Journal of Archaeology*
AJP	*American Journal of Philology*
ANRW	*Aufstieg und Niedergang der römischen Welt*
AnzWien	*Anzeiger der Akademie der Wissenschaften in Wien*
ARW	*Archiv für Religionswissenschaft*
ASAtene	*Annuario. Scuola Archeologica di Atene e delle Missioni Italiane in Oriente*
ATLA	American Theological Library Association
BCH	*Bulletin de correspondance hellénique*
BCHSup	Bulletin de correspondance hellénique supplement
BerMatÖAI	*Berichte und Materialien des österreichischen archäologischen Instituts*
DIA	Deutsches archäologisches Institut
DOP	*Dumbarton Oaks Papers*
EPRO	Études preliminaires aux religions orientales dans l'empire romain
FC	Fathers of the Church
FiE	*Forschungen in Ephesos*
GRBS	*Greek, Roman, and Byzantine Studies*
HSCP	*Harvard Studies in Classical Philology*
HTR	*Harvard Theological Review*
IG	*Inscriptiones Graecae*
IGRR	*Inscriptiones Graecae ad res Romanas pertinentes*
IstMit	*Istanbuler Mitteilungen*
IvE	*Inschriften von Ephesos*
IvM	*Die Inschriften von Magnesia am Maeander*
JAC	*Jahrbuch für Antike und Christentum*
JBL	*Journal of Biblical Literature*
JdI	*Jahrbuch des deutschen archäologischen Instituts*
JHS	*Journal of Hellenic Studies*

JÖAI	*Jahreshefte des österreichischen archäologischen Instituts*
JRomS	*Journal of Roman Studies*
JTS	*Journal of Theological Studies*
LCL	Loeb Classical Library
LIMC	*Lexicon Iconographicum Mythologiae Classicae*
LSJ	Liddell-Scott-Jones, *Greek-English Lexicon*
MDAI.A	*Mitteilungen des deutschen archäologischen Instituts. Athenische Abteilung*
NovT	*Novum Testamentum*
NovTSup	Novum Testamentum Supplements
NTS	*New Testament Studies*
ÖAI	Österreichisches archäologisches Institut
ÖAW	Österreichische Akademie der Wissenschaften
OGIS	W. Dittenberger, *Orientis Graecae inscriptiones selectae*
PG	Migne, Patrologia Graeca
PO	Patrologia orientalis
PIR	*Prosopographia Imperii Romani*
PW	Pauly-Wissowa, *Realenzyklopädie des klassischen Altertums*
PWSup	Pauly-Wissowa, *Realenzyklopädie des klassischen Altertums*, Supplement volumes
RAC	*Reallexikon für Antike und Christentum*
RArch	*Revue archéologique*
SBAW.PPH	Sitzungsberichte der bayerischen Akademie der Wissenschaften. Philosophisch-philologische und historische Klasse
SBT	Studies in Biblical Theology
SIG	W. Dittenberger, *Sylloge inscriptionum Graecarum*
SNTSM	Society of New Testament Studies Monographs
TAPA	Transactions of the American Philosophical Association
ZPE	*Zeitschrift für Papyrologie und Epigraphik*

Short Titles

Alzinger, *Architektur*

Wilhelm Alzinger, *Augusteische Architektur in Ephesos*, vol. 1 (Sonderschriften des ÖAI 16; Vienna: ÖAI, 1974).

Alzinger and Neeb, *Pro Arte Antiqua*

Wilhelm Alzinger and Gudrun Christa Neeb, eds., *Pro Arte Antiqua: Festschrift für Hedwig Kenner* (2 vols.; Sonderschriften des ÖAI 18; Vienna: Koska, 1985).

Aurenhammer, *Skulpturen 1*

Maria Aurenhammer, *Die Skulpturen von Ephesos: Idealplastik 1* (*FiE* 10.1; Vienna: ÖAW, 1990).

Aurenhammer, *Skulpturen 2*

Maria Aurenhammer, *Die Skulpturen von Ephesos: Idealplastik 2* (*FiE* 10.1; Vienna: ÖAW, forthcoming).

Bammer, "Architekturfassaden"

Anton Bammer, "Elemente flavianisch-trajanischer Architekturfassaden aus Ephesos," *JÖAI* 52 (1978–80) Beibl.

Bammer, Fleischer, and Knibbe, *Führer*

Anton Bammer, Robert Fleischer, and Dieter Knibbe, *Führer durch das archäologische Museum Selçuk-Ephesos* (Vienna: ÖAI, 1974).

Benndorf, *Zur Ortskunde und Stadtgeschichte*

Otto Benndorf, *Zur Ortskunde und Stadtgeschichte* (*FiE* 1; Vienna: Hölder, 1906).

Duncan-Jones, *Economy of the Roman Empire*

Richard Duncan-Jones, *The Economy of the Roman Empire: Quantitative Studies* (2d ed.; Cambridge: Cambridge University Press, 1982).

Engelmann, "Zum Kaiserkult in Ephesos"

Helmut Engelmann, "Zum Kaiserkult in Ephesos," *ZPE* 97 (1993) 279–89.

Ettlinger, *Conspectus*

Elisabeth Ettlinger et al., eds., *Conspectus formarum terrae sigillatae Italico modo confectae* (Materialien zur römisch-germanischen Keramik 10; Bonn: Habelt, 1990).

Fleischer, *Artemis von Ephesos*

Robert Fleischer, *Artemis von Ephesos und verwandte Kultstatuen aus Anatolien und Syrien* (EPRO 35; Leiden: Brill, 1973).

Fleischer, "Fries des Hadrianstempels"

Robert Fleischer, "Der Fries des Hadrianstempels in Ephesos," in Egon Braun, ed., *Festschrift für Fritz Eichler zum 80. Geburtstag* (Vienna: ÖAI, 1967) 23–71.

Friesen, *Twice Neokoros*

Steven Friesen, *Twice Neokoros: Ephesus, Asia and the Cult of the Flavian Imperial Family* (EPRO 116; Leiden: Brill, 1993).

Heberdey, "Vorläufiger Bericht 1904"

Rudolf Heberdey, "Vorläufiger Bericht über die Ausgrabungen in Ephesos 1904," *JÖAI* 8 (1905) Beibl.

Heberdey, Niemann, and Wilberg, *Theater*

Rudolf Heberdey, Georg Niemann, and Wilhelm Wilberg, *Das Theater in Ephesos* (FiE 2; Vienna: Hölder, 1912).

Hennecke-Schneemelcher, *NTApoc*

Edgar Hennecke and Wilhelm Schneemelcher, *New Testament Apocrypha* (2 vols.; Philadelphia: Westminster, 1963).

Jobst, "Bau- und Bildkunst"

Werner Jobst, "Zur Bau- und Bildkunst der Spätantike in Ephesos," in Alzinger and Neeb, *Pro Arte Antiqua*, 2. 195–206.

Jobst, "Embolosforschungen I"

Werner Jobst, "Embolosforschungen I," *JÖAI* 54 (1983) Beibl. 215–19.

Kandler, Karwiese, and Pillinger, *Lebendige Altertumswissenschaft*

Manfred Kandler, Stefan Karwiese, and Renate Pillinger, eds., *Lebendige Altertumswissenschaft: Festschrift für Hermann Vetters* (Vienna: Holzhausen, 1985).

Karwiese, "Koressos"

Stefan Karwiese, "Koressos—ein fast vergessener Stadtteil von Ephesos," in Alzinger and Neeb, *Pro Arte Antiqua*, 2. 214–25

Keil, *Führer*

Josef Keil, *Führer durch Ephesos* (4th ed.; Vienna: Rohrer, 1964).

Keil, "XII. vorläufiger Bericht"

Josef Keil, "XII. vorläufiger Bericht über die Ausgrabungen in Ephesos," *JÖAI* 23 (1926) Beibl. 265–70.

Knibbe, "Ephesos, nicht nur die Stadt der Artemis"

Dieter Knibbe, "Ephesos, nicht nur die Stadt der Artemis. Die 'anderen' ephesischen Götter," in Sencer Şahin, Elmar Schwertheim, and Jörg Wagner, eds., *Studien zur Religion und Kultur Kleinasiens: Festschrift für Karl Friedrich Dörner zum 65. Geburtstag* (2 vols.; EPRO 66; Leiden: Brill, 1978) 2. 489–503.

Knibbe, *Parthermonument*

Dieter Knibbe, *Das "Parthermonument": (Parthersieg)altar der Artemis (und Kenotaph des L. Verus an der Triodos)* (*BerMatÖAI* 1; Vienna: Schindler, 1991).

Knibbe, *Der Staatsmarkt*

Dieter Knibbe, *Der Staatsmarkt: Die Inschriften des Prytaneions* (*FiE* 9.1; Vienna: ÖAW, 1981).

Knibbe, *Via Sacra I*

Dieter Knibbe, Gerhard Langmann, et al., *Via Sacra Ephesiaca I* (*BerMatÖAI* 3; Vienna: Schindler, 1993).

Knibbe, *Via Sacra II*

Dieter Knibbe, Hilke Thür, et al., *Via Sacra Ephesiaca II* (*BerMatÖAI* 7; Vienna: Schindler, 1995).

Knibbe and İplikçioğlu, "Neue Inschriften aus Ephesos VIII"

Dieter Knibbe and Bülent İplikçioğlu, "Neue Inschriften aus Ephesos VIII, " *JÖAI* 53 (1981/82).

Knibbe, Engelmann, and İplikçioğlu, "Neue Inschriften aus Ephesos XII"

Dieter Knibbe, Helmut Engelmann, and Bülent İplikçioğlu, "Neue Inschriften aus Ephesos XII," *JÖAI* 62 (1993).

Langmann and Scherrer, "Bericht. Ephesos. Agora"

Gerhard Langmann and Peter Scherrer, "Bericht. Ephesos. Agora," *JÖAI* 62 (1993).

MacMullen, *Roman Social Relations*

Ramsay MacMullen, *Roman Social Relations* (New Haven: Yale University Press, 1974).

Magie, *Roman Rule*

David Magie, *Roman Rule in Asia Minor* (2 vols.; Princeton: Princeton University Press, 1950).

Miltner, "XXII. vorläufiger Bericht"

Franz Miltner, "XXII. vorläufiger Bericht über die Ausgrabungen in Ephesos," *JÖAI* 44 (1952) Beibl.

Mitchell, *Anatolia*

Stephen Mitchell, *Anatolia: Land, Men, and Gods in Asia Minor* (2 vols.; Oxford: Clarendon, 1993).

Oberleitner, *Funde aus Ephesos und Samothrake*

Wolfgang Oberleitner, Kurt Gschwantler, Alfred Bernhard-Walcher, and Anton Bammer, eds., *Funde aus Ephesos und Samothrake* (Kunsthistorisches Museum in Wien, Katalog der Antikensammlung 2; Vienna: Uebereuter, 1978).

Oster, "Ephesus as a Religious Center"

Richard E. Oster, "Ephesus as a Religious Center under the Principate, I," *ANRW* 2.18.3 (1990) 1661–1726.

Outschar, "Monument des Memmius"

Ulrike Outschar, "Zum Monument des C. Memmius," *JÖAI* 60 (1990) 57–85.

Price, *Rituals and Power*

Simon R. F. Price, *Rituals and Power: The Roman Imperial Cult in Asia Minor* (Cambridge: Cambridge University Press, 1984).

Reisch, Knoll, and Keil, *Die Marienkirche*

E. Reisch, F. Knoll, and Josef Keil, *Die Marienkirche* (*FiE* 4.1; Vienna: Hölder, 1932)

Rogers, *Sacred Identity of Ephesos*

Guy M. Rogers, *The Sacred Identity of Ephesos: Foundation Myths of a Roman City* (London/New York: Routledge, 1991).

Rumscheid, *Bauornamentik*

Frank Rumscheid, *Untersuchungen zur kleinasiatischen Bauornamentik des Hellenismus* (2 vols.; Beiträge zur Erschließung hellenistischer und kaiserzeitlicher Skulptur 14; Mainz: Zabern, 1994).

Scherrer, "Augustus"

Peter Scherrer, "Augustus, die Mission des Vedius Pollio und die Artemis Ephesia," *JÖAI* 60 (1990).

Schneider, *Bunte Barbaren*

Rolf M. Schneider, *Bunte Barbaren* (Worms: Wernersche Verlagsgesellschaft, 1986).

Thür, "Arsonoë IV"

Hilke Thür, "Arsinoë IV, eine Schwester Kleopatras VII. Grabinhaberin des Oktogons von Ephesos? Ein Vorschlag," *JÖAI* 60 (1990) 43–56.

Thür, *Hadrianstor*

Hilke Thür, *Das Hadrianstor in Ephesos* (*FiE* 11.1; Vienna: ÖAW, 1989).

Vetters, "Vorläufiger Grabungsbericht 1980"

Hermann Vetters, "Ephesos: Vorläufiger Grabungsbericht 1980," *AnzWien* 118 (1981).

Vetters, "Vorläufiger Grabungsbericht 1981"

Hermann Vetters, "Ephesos: Vorläufiger Grabungsbericht 1981," *AnzWien* 119 (1982).

Vetters, "Vorläufiger Grabungsbericht 1982"

Hermann Vetters, "Ephesos: Vorläufiger Grabungsbericht 1982," *AnzWien* 120 (1983).

Vetters, "Vorläufiger Grabungsbericht 1983"

Hermann Vetters, "Ephesos: Vorläufiger Grabungsbericht 1983," *AnzWien* 121 (1984).

Vetters, "Vorläufiger Grabungsbericht 1984 und 1985"

Hermann Vetters, "Ephesos: Vorläufiger Grabungsbericht für die Jahre 1984 und 1985," *AnzWien* 123 (1986).

Wilberg, *Der Viersäulenbau auf der Arkadienstrasse*

Wilhelm Wilberg, *Der Viersäulenbau auf der Arkadienstrasse* (*FiE* 1; Vienna; Hölder, 1906) 132–40.

Wood, *Discoveries at Ephesus*

John T. Wood, *Discoveries at Ephesus* (1877; reprinted Hildesheim: Olms, 1975).

Preface

In March 1994, archaeologists from the Austrian excavations at Ephesos met with American scholars at Harvard Divinity School for a "Symposium on Ephesos." The symposium was organized by Harvard Divinity School and cosponsored by Harvard University's Departments of Classics and Fine Arts. Participants were not only archaeologists, but also scholars of the classics, history of religions, New Testament studies, and the history of ancient Christianity. This volume brings together the papers that were presented at the symposium.

The discoveries of the Austrian excavations at Ephesos have been published extensively in the pertinent channels of the Austrian Institute of Archaeology and the Austrian Academy of Arts and Sciences, as well as in numerous monographs and Festschriften. Very little, however, has so far appeared in English language publications. This volume will therefore help to make some of the results of these excavations more readily accessible to the English speaking public. It would be impossible, of course, to discuss in a single four-day symposium and present comprehensively in one volume all of the results of a hundred years of archaeological work in Ephesos, although the first essay of this volume will serve to give a general overview of the entire archaeological site and its findings. Otherwise, the archaeological essays in this book present some of the more interesting and often controversial results of recent investigations: the sacred processional way of Artemis, the Hadrianic Olympieion and the Church of Mary, the so-called Temple of Domitian, and the heroa of Androklos and Arsinoë. Bibliographical references, which each of the contributors provided, will also assist scholars and students in further exploring the results of the excavations at this important site and the problems of interpreting these discoveries.

The Harvard Ephesos Symposium and the publication of its contributions, however, are designed to serve a far more ambitious goal. The editor and the contributors want to present a new model for "biblical archaeology." Biblical archaeology can no longer be limited to the archaeology of the Holy Land and to the paths of Jesus of Nazareth, nor should it seek to trace the footsteps of Paul in Asia Minor and Greece or unearth the remains of the Seven Churches of the Book of Revelation. Rather, interdisciplinary discussions of scholars from various fields should help to achieve a better understanding of the social, cultural, and religious environment of the world of the Bible: not only the ancient Near East, but also the Greco-Roman world of the New Testament and early Christianity. In the field of New Testament studies, the Holy Land of Israel is but a memory of first beginnings; Asia Minor and Greece quickly became the centers of the new religious movement. Ephesos, the metropolis of Asia, was the center of the early Christian missionary enterprise—as much as half of the writings of the New Testament may have originated from it (most of the letters of Paul, Luke's Gospel and the Acts of the Apostles, the Pastoral Epistles, and—from nearby Patmos—the Book of Revelation). A better understanding of the culture and religion of this important city will contribute to a fresh interpretation of these writings. If students of the New Testament wish to benefit from archaeological scholarship, they must become better acquainted with nonliterary materials unearthed by others, and they must participate in the process of interpretation.

For the last several years, my colleague David Mitten, professor of classical archaeology at Harvard University, and I have brought our seminar in "Archaeology and the World of the New Testament" to Ephesos in order to give students in the study of religion the opportunity to discuss their seminar papers on site. Members of the Ephesos excavation team of the Austrian Archaeological Institute generously shared their expertise in these on-site seminar sessions, as well as repeatedly extending their hospitality to us.

My sincere thanks go to all those who have contributed to this volume and to its production: to those who participated in the Symposium on Ephesos and enriched it with their comments and questions; to the Austrian colleagues who have patiently assisted in the editorial process; to all contributors who willingly adjusted the length of their essays to the limitations of space; to Tamar Duke-Cohan, managing editor of the Harvard Theological Review, and to her staff, especially Laura Nasrallah, Rebecca Lesses, Greg Schmidt Goering, and Anthony Rivera, who never tired in the often difficult task of editing and composition; to Patrick Santana for the production of the map of Ephesos; and to Dr. Harold W. Rast, director of Trinity Press International in Valley Forge, PA, for his willingness—even on short notice—to publish this book in the series Harvard Theological Studies.

In gratitude for all that we have learned in this collaborative effort, this book is dedicated to our friends at the Austrian Archaeological Institute in Vienna on the occasion of the centenary celebration of excavations at Ephesos.

Helmut Koester
Harvard University
16 August 1995

The City of Ephesos

FROM THE ROMAN PERIOD TO LATE ANTIQUITY

Peter Scherrer
Österreichisches Archäologisches Institut

Both the religious upheaval of the fourth century CE, which eventually made Christianity the religion of the Roman state, and social and economic changes deeply affected the design of public space and the architectural style of cities under Roman imperial power. Ephesos provides a particularly clear example of this, since serious earthquakes necessitated extensive rebuilding. A hundred years of intensive excavations that the Austrian Archaeological Institute has conducted have furnished much evidence for the study of such changes.[1]

1. I am grateful to my colleagues on the Ephesian excavation team, whose generosity has allowed me to refer to the results of recent and still unpublished work on the site. I also want to thank Helmut Koester and his colleagues for organizing the Ephesos Symposium at Harvard Divinity School, which was a forum for further stimulating discussions. For more detailed information, literature, maps, and photographs, see my forthcoming book, *Beiträge zur ephesischen Topographie und Stadtentwicklung von den Anfängen bis Theododius I* (Vienna: ÖAI, forthcoming). For general reference, see Dieter Knibbe, "Ephesos: Geschichte," PWSup 12 (1970) 249–97; and Wilhelm

Glen Bowersock has demonstrated that pagan cults in Asia Minor
existed into the sixth century CE,[2] This was only the case, however,
when pagan cult centers were located well away from the administra
tive centers of the state and the Christian hierarchy. The council of
431 CE and its acts presuppose that Ephesos was no longer a pagan
city. In addition, of the twenty or so churches and buildings assumed
to be churches that have been discovered up to this time, only a few
can be dated to the early fifth century with certainty.[3] Archaeological
evidence suggests that during this time pagan temples and shrines
were either destroyed or transformed into buildings serving the Christian cult. The inscription of Demeas,[4] who boasts that he had taken
the daemon Artemis from its site (probably the Gate of Hadrian [map
no. 38]) and replaced it with a Christian cross, may be typical of the
zeal of Ephesian Christians. This gate marked the Triodos,[5] an area
of great religious significance, because here, at the southern end of
the Marble Road,[6] the Processional Way to Ortygia—the mythical
birthplace of Artemis—branched off the Plateia, as the sacred way
was called in antiquity.[7]

The Urban Development of the Hellenistic and Roman City

Although the development of the city in archaic and classical times
cannot be discussed in detail here, several settlements preceded Hellenistic and Roman Ephesos. In the early Bronze Age a settlement

---

Alzinger, "Ephesos: Archäologie," PWSup 12 (1970) 1588–1704. A summary
of the present status of the excavations can be found in Ekrem Akurgal, *Ancient Civilizations and Ruins of Turkey* (7th ed.; Istanbul: Net Turistic Yayinlar,
1990) 142–70, 378–84.

2. Glen W. Bowersock, *Hellenism in Late Antiquity* (Ann Arbor: University of Michigan Press, 1990) 1–13.

3. This statement is based more on the lack of modern investigation than
historical evidence. See, however, Stefan Karwiese's discovery in 1993
("Ephesos," *JÖAI* 63 [1994] Grabungen 21–24) of an early Christian church
in the northwestern edge of the stadium (map no. 21).

4. *IvE* IV 1351; the date of this inscription is uncertain.

5. Knibbe, Engelmann, and İplikcioğlu, "Neue Inschriften aus Ephesos
XII," 123–24 no. 13.

6. Hilke Thür, *Hadrianstor*, 129 no. C.

7. See *IvE* II 422a, 454; VI 2298a; VII 3013, 3071, 3080.

existed on the hill now known as Mount Ayasoluk,[8] between the Kaÿstros River to the north and a deep bay to the south, which originally separated this hill from Panayirdağ (Mount Pion).[9] The Lydian town, which is well attested in literature, and the city founded near the Artemision by King Kroisos have not yet been located. Ancient Koressos, an archaic Greek settlement founded under the legendary leadership of the Attic prince Androklos, was probably located on the opposite, southern side of the bay on the northwestern promontory of Panayirdağ.[10] Another village, probably Smyrna, was recently discovered in the area of the later Tetragonos Agora (map no. 30), where Gerhard Langmann's excavations revealed houses that were in use from the late eighth or early seventh centuries BCE.[11]

Few traces have been found of the new Hellenistic city, which Lysimachos established in approximately 290 BCE in the valley between Bülbüldağ (Lepre Akte) and Panayirdağ. The course of the city wall is known (except for the west slope of Panayirdağ), as is a smaller Hellenistic agora in the area of the later Tetragonos Agora,[12] and a street linking this agora with the harbor (map no. 32).[13] A second agora, located further to the west, is mentioned in an inscription and was probably the place where most of the administrative

8. This Turkish designation is a distortion of the Greek *agios theologos*, the name for the location of the Church of St. John. The ancient name of the hill was probably "Ephesos"; see Benndorf, *Zur Ortskunde und Stadtgeschichte*, 52.

9. Excavations conducted in 1990 in the area directly in front of the medieval castle have shown this; see Selahattin Erdemgil and Mustafa Büyükkolançı, "1990 yılı Efes-Ayasuluk tepesi prehistorik kazısı," in *XIII. Kazı sonuçları toplantısı II, Çannakkale, 27–31 mayis 1991* (Ankara: T. C. Kültür Bakalığı Anitlar ve Müzeler General Müdürlüguü, 1992) 265–81.

10. Even if no walls were unearthed, excavations around the so-called Macellum (map no. 18) near the stadium and the *Felsspalttempel* ("rock-crack temple"; map no. 16) affirm the existence of a settlement no later than the archaic period; see Karwiese, "Koressos," 2. 214–25; Helmut Engelmann, "Beiträge zur Topographie," *ZPE* 89 (1991) 286–92.

11. Information regarding these excavations can be found in the yearly reports in *JÖAI*, especially since vol. 61 (1992).

12. For preliminary reports, see n. 11 above.

13. For the location of the harbor, see the contribution of Heinrich Zabehlicky in this volume.

buildings were located.[14] The theater was built at the site of its Roman sanctuary on the west slope of Panayirdağ (map no. 26).[15]
Under Augustus, Ephesos was made capital of the province of Asia,
the small plateau between Bülbüldağ and Panayirdağ was chosen as
the new center of the Roman city. The complex of buildings at this
site has become known as the State Agora[16]; the oblong central area,
measuring 160 m by 58 m (map no. 56), however, should be understood as a temenos.[17] In contrast to the Tetragonos Agora, no honorary inscriptions or statue bases were found here, and the surrounding
stoas did not contain shops or rooms. In the western portion of the
open area, a small temple with a peristasis of 6 by 10 columns was
built (map no. 58). Wilhelm Alzinger identified it as a temple of Isis,
built at the time of the second triumvirate under the influence of
Cleopatra VII[18]; Bernard Andreae believed it was a temple of Dionysos
in honor of Marc Antony[19]; and Werner Jobst interpreted it as the
Sebasteion.[20] In my opinion, this is the temple that Octavian dedicated to the *conventus civium Romanorum* ("assembly of the Roman
citizens") for Divus Julius and Dea Roma in 29 BCE, when Ephesos
became the capital of Asia.[21]

14. *IvE* IV 1381.

15. Heberdey, Niemann, and Wilberg, *Theater.*

16. For the interpretation of the complex of buildings at this site, see Peter
Scherrer, "Augustus," 98–99; for a detailed description and different interpre-
tation of the temples, see Werner Jobst, "Zur Lokalisierung des Sebastion-
Augusteum in Ephesos," *IstMit* 30 (1980) 241–60.

17. The distinction between forum and temenos and the characteristic fea-
tures of both types of public places have been discussed recently by Johannes
Eingartner, "Fora, Capitolia und Heiligtümer im westlichen Nordafrika," in
Hans-Joachim Schalles, Henner von Hesberg, and Paul Zanker, eds., *Die römische
Stadt im 2. Jahrhundert n. Chr.: Der Funktionswandel des öffentlichen Raumes:
Kolloquium in Xanten vom 2. bis 4. Mai 1990* (Xantener Berichte 2; Cologne/
Bonn: Habelt, 1992) esp. 217.

18. Wilhelm Alzinger, "Das Regierungsviertel," *JÖAI* 50 (1972–75) Beibl.
283–94.

19. Bernard Andreae, *Odysseus: Archäologie des europäischen Menschen-
bildes* (Frankfurt: Societats-Verlag, 1982) 69–90.

20. Werner Jobst, "Zur Lokalisierung des Sebastion-Augusteum in Ephesos,"
248–59.

21. Dio Cassius *Hist.* 51.20.6.

In the Augustan period, the new political center emerged north of the temenos as the Prytaneion (map no. 61) and the Bouleuterion (map no. 63) were constructed. A three-sided peristyle, with a double foundation at its western end (map no. 62), occupied the space between these two buildings; the cults of Artemis and Augustus were probably celebrated here.[22] This combination of the powerful city goddess and the Roman emperor symbolized Ephesos's existence as both a nominally free city and a part of Rome and its new world order. In a layer of late-antique debris in the nearby Basilike Stoa (map no. 64), Wilhelm Alzinger found the head of a statue of Augustus with the *corona civica* and an inscription,[23] which prove that the Sebasteion was established as early as 25 BCE.

The three-aisled Basilike Stoa, which replaced the older one-aisled stoa of the temenos, was built in the space between the administrative buildings and the temenos of Divus Julius and Dea Roma and was dedicated in 11 CE to Artemis, Augustus, Tiberius, and the city of Ephesos.[24] At the eastern end of the stoa, monumental statues of Augustus and Livia were set up, and traces suggest that other members of the imperial family, such as Germanicus, were also honored here. The extremely wide intercolumniate space was somewhat reduced by the extension of the Ionic capitals with boukrania; this may indicate that cultic activities for the Julio-Claudian family took place here rather than any market activity.[25] The monumental building complex symbolizes the unification of foreigners and Roman citizens as residents of the free city of Ephesos. Imperial propaganda is the dominating element in this area: the temenos for Divus Julius and the Basilike Stoa take up the largest and most central spaces. It is no

22. Scherrer, "Augustus," 98–101. Miltner ("XXII. vorläufiger Bericht," Beibl. 293) called it the "state altar," while Wilhelm Alzinger (*Architektur*, 55–57) claimed that these foundations were a double temple of Divus Julius and Dea Roma.

23. Wilhelm Alzinger, "Ephesiaca," *JÖAI* 56 (1985) 62; *IvE* III 902.

24. *IvE* II 404; for new fragments, see Knibbe, Engelmann, and İplikcioğlu, "Neue Inschriften aus Ephesos XII," 148–49 no. 80.

25. Knibbe and İplikcioğlu, "Neue Inschriften aus Ephesos VIII," 135 no. 142; Wilhelm Alzinger, "Ephesiaca," *JÖAI* 56 (1985) 99–101. Engelmann ("Zum Kaiserkult in Ephesos," 279–89) discusses inscriptions that were recently discovered.

coincidence that at this time the imperial freedman C. Julius Nikephoros gave money for the sacrifices to Roma and Artemis at the
altar of Hestia before the year 27 BCE and later assumed the prytany
for life.[26] The monumental gate erected by Mazaeus and Mithridates (map
no. 34) between 4 and 2 BCE demonstrates the dominance of the
imperial freedmen in Ephesian politic. This structure occupies the site
of the original Triodos, the most holy intersection of the *Via Sacra*
with the Processional Way to Ortygia. Statues of Augustus, his designated heirs Gaius and Lucius Ceasar, and their parents looked down
upon those who were passing through this gate.[27] In antiquity, the
portion of the sacred way leading from the Triodos through the valley
between Bülbüldağ and Panayirdağ to the government center was called
the Embolos, now commonly called Curetes Street (map no. 27).[28] At
the time of Augustus, Curetes Street was an ancient burial site with
graves lining both sides of the *Via Sacra*.[29] A late Hellenistic heroon
(map no. 43), which Hilke Thür supposed to be the Tomb of Androklos,[30] may have marked this uninhabited area as early as the late
second century BCE. C. Memmius, a grandson of Sulla, was given a
luxurious sepulcher at the upper end of the Embolos (map no. 52),[31]
while an octagonal structure adjacent to the Tomb of Androklos is
now identified as having been built for Arsinoë IV, the sister of
Cleopatra VII, who was murdered in Ephesos in 34 BCE (map no.
44).[32] C. Sextilius Pollio, builder of both the Basilike Stoa and an

26. *IvE* III 859 and 859a; for a better reconstruction of 859a, see Helmut
Engelmann, "Ephesische Inschriften," *ZPE* 84 (1990) 92–94. That Julius
Nikephoros changed his name from *Ceasaris libertus* ("freedman of Caesar")
to *Augusti libertus* ("freedman of Augustus") indicates a date of 29 BCE for the
commencement of this building complex, while the inscriptions of the *curetes*
on the walls of the Prytaneion show that this building was finished approximately twenty to twenty-five years later; see Dieter Knibbe, *Der Staatsmarkt*,
93; Alzinger, *Architektur*, 53–55.
27. *IvE* VII 3006, 3007.
28. Ibid., V 2000; VI 2117; VII 3008, 3059.
29. Knibbe, *Via Sacra I*, 9–15.
30. In this volume, see Hilke Thür's contribution.
31. Ulrike Outschar ("Zum Monument des C. Memmius," *JÖAI* 60 [1990]
57–85) presents a new and convincing reconstruction.
32. Thür, "Arsinoë IV," 43–56.

aquaeduct, was buried in a tomb (map no. 59) built into the western front of the terrace that formed the façade of the temenos of Divus Julius (the State Agora); the tomb faced Curetes Street. It is possible that Mazaeus and Mithridates were also buried in annexes of their gates, as a grave inscription of Mithridates, found nearby, in the pavement of the Marble Road near the theater, indicates.[33] During the reign of Tiberius, more probably in 23 CE than during the Lydian twelve city earthquake, which occurred six years earlier, a serious earthquake struck Ephesos.[34] This earthquake greatly influenced the future expansion of the city. It seems that constructions on the lower slope of Bübüldağ, most likely late Hellenistic private houses, were devastated. The space thus gained, however, was only partly at the disposal of new inhabitants, because much of it was reserved for public buildings, as I shall later discuss in the context of the temples of Sarapis and Domitian. Near the Embolos, semiofficial, state apartments, the so-called Slope Houses 1 and 2, were constructed to serve for meetings not open to the public at large. This interpretation, an alternative to the view that these houses were luxurious private dwellings, seems particularly convincing with regard to the lower parts of Slope House 2—the property of a priest of Dionysos, T. Flavius Furius Aptus. The ground plans of apartments 6 and 7, which he and his family owned, clearly support use for official as well as residential purposes. As long as a decade ago, Werner Jobst was already able to suggest that a hospitium, probably used for guest accomodation, existed there.[35]

After the earthquake of 23 CE, the new Tetragonos Agora was the most important building project undertaken. It was a square with an open courtyard measuring 112 m in length, far exceeding its Hellenistic predecessor in size and magnitude. Most recent excavations and architectural investigations show that its two-aisled stoa had an upper

33. *IvE* III 851.
34. Alfred Hermann ("Erdbeben," *RAC* 5. 1104) has collected the literary sources concerning these earthquakes. Another earthquake in Ephesos has traditionally been dated to 29 CE; this date, however, seems late for our case; see the investigation presented by Susanne Zabehlicky-Scheffenegger in this volume.
35. Werner Jobst, "Ein *hospitium* im Hanghaus 2 von Ephesos," in Kandler, Karwiese, and Pillinger, *Lebendige Altertumswissenschaft*, 200–203.

story on all four sides.[36] As a result of the construction of the
Tetragonos Agora, the Marble Road, leading from the north to the
Triodos, had to be moved to the east; thus, the Gate of Mazaeus and
Mithridates no longer served as a triumphal arch on the side of the
Triodos, but became the south gate of the Tetragonos Agora. The
canal system under this gate had to be reconstructed in order to prevent the rain water flowing down the Embolos from flooding the
agora. An equestrian statue of Claudius, which Roman citizens set up
in 43 CE, reveals that the Tetragonos Agora must have been officially
opened by that time. The date at which it was finished is fixed by the
dedication of the hall forming the eastern upper story to Artemis,
Nero, and Agrippina.[37] The function of this hall, which was accessible from the Embolos by a staircase at its southern end (only one
vaulted gate near its north end allowed access from the Marble Road)
is unclear.[38] Recent excavation work has shown that a crosswall separated the northernmost part of the hall and that in this part the floor
level was raised.[39] If we interpret this section as being a tribunal, the
hall may have been identical to the auditorium mentioned soon after
200 CE in the vicinity of the Celsus Library (map no. 35),[40] and could
have been used for trials and other purposes of proconsularic assemblies.

During the time of Nero, the city expended its resources not only
to complete the upper story of the Tetragonos Agora, but also enlarged the theater for the growing assembly of the people, restruc-
tured the stadium to its monumental shape, and erected a customs

36. This is contrary to previous opinions, which assumed that an upper
story only existed on the east side; see Wilhelm Wilberg, *Die Agora* (*FiE* 3;
Vienna: Hölder, 1923) 4–10 and the illustrations of his reconstruction on p.
5 fig. 4, and p. 87 fig. 149; Alzinger (*Architektur*, 48–49) provides a summary
of research that supports this older opinion.
37. *IvE* VII 3003.
38. Gerhard J. Lang, "Zur oberen Osthalle der Agora, der 'Neronischen
Halle' in Ephesos," in Kandler, Karwiese, and Pillinger, *Lebendige Altertumswissenschaft*, 176–80.
39. According to Stefan Karwiese's excavations recorded in Vetters, "Vorlä
ufiger Grabungsbericht für 1984 und 1985," 80–81 fig. 5.
40. *IvE* VII 3009; Helmut Engelmann, "Celsusbibliothek und Auditorium
in Ephesos," *JÖAI* 62 (1993) 111 n. 16.

building for fisheries.[41] Ephesos also must have had more than one gymnasium in the earliest imperial periods. One was most probably located in the area near the State Agora, later called the Upper Gymnasium (map no. 65). The other served the purposes of the *gerousia* and was probably a predecessor of the Theater Gymnasium (map no. 24).[42] Apart from some possible repairs to the Basilike Stoa at the time of Nero,[43] major building activities in the area of the State Agora did not commence until the Flavian period, when the city received its first neokorate. Houses west of the temenos for Divus Julius and Dea Roma were dismantled in order to make room for the construction of a terrace that would support the Temple of the Flavian Sebastoi (map no. 53), surrounded by a pseudoperipteros with eight to thirteen columns.[44] The Embolos was paved in 94/95 CE, probably for the first time.[45] Water from the Marnas and Klaseas rivers was brought into the city with pipelines that fed at least half a dozen nympheia; one was built south of the State Agora (map no. 66).[46] The Tomb of Sextilius Pollio (map no. 59) was renovated or rebuilt for the first time into a fountain.[47] Opposite the new temple terrace, the proconsul C. Laecanius Bassus built a beautiful Hydrekdocheion (map no. 60).[48] The Ephesian citizen Ti. Claudius Aristion was a donor for the impe-

41. *IvE* II 411; VII 4123 (stadium); Ia 20 (customs building).

42. Engelmann ("Zum Kaiserkult in Ephesos," 288–89) provides an overview of the inscriptions that may indicate the existence of a gymnasium near the State Agora. Newly found inscriptions mention the Gerousia's own gymnasiarchs as early as the reign of Tiberius. See Knibbe, Engelmann, and İplikçioğlu, "Neue Inschriften aus Ephesos XII," 116–19 no. 8–10. The Theater Gymnasium in its present, second-century form is not constructed according to the insula system used in the Roman imperial period; its orientation may correspond to an earlier building period.

43. A partly erased dedicatory inscription to Nero (*IvE* II 410) belongs to the (newly added?) western chalcidicum.

44. For a good history of research and an extensive interpretation of the complex, see Friesen, *Twice Neokoros*.

45. *IvE* VII 3008.

46. Ibid., II 404.

47. Ibid., II 413, 419; Anton Bammer, "Elemente flavianisch-traianischer Architekturfassaden aus Ephesos," *JÖAI* 52 (1978–80) 67–80.

48. *IvE* III 695.

rial temple, where he served as high priest and neokoros.[49] He also financed the construction of the water pipe that came into the city from Tire, two hundred and ten stadia (about twenty miles) west of Ephesos, and led to the so-called Fountain of Trajan on the Embolos (map no. 49),[50] in addition to another fountain near the street coming from the Magnesian Gate (map no. 67).[51]

The construction of the Embolos seems to have been finished at the end of Trajan's reign or at the beginning of Hadrian's. In 114 CE, a propylon was set up near the Fountain of Trajan to honor the emperor,[52] and a little later the new Triodos Gate (map no. 38), already mentioned above, was constructed at the southern end of Marble Road. P. Quintilius Varius Valens and his family built a public bath on the northern side of the Embolos (map no. 40)[53] with a latrine in the adjacent insula to the west (map no. 39).[54] In front of the bath complex, a small votive temple was dedicated to Artemis, Hadrian, and the demos.[55]

At this time, honorary sepulchers were once again built in the lower Embolos area. A sarcophagus originally set up there, but later dragged behind the Hellenistic heroon (map no. 43), contained the skeleton of a man about sixty years old. The portrait head of his tomb statue shows the diadem of an imperial high priest of Asia.[56] The famous orator T. Claudius Flavianus Dionysos was buried under the flight of stairs leading to the Neronic Hall of the Tetragonos Agora.[57] The most famous tomb is the reconstructed building known as the Library of Celsus. It was erected by the proconsul Ti. Julius Celsus

49. See Friesen, *Twice Neokoros*, 45–48.
50. *IvE* II 424; VII 3217.
51. Ibid., II 424a.
52. Ibid., II 422.
53. Ibid., II 500.
54. Ibid., II 455; archaeologists and guides often incorrectly designated the insula a brothel.
55. This building has been wrongly identified as the second neokorate temple of the city; it was never a functioning temple and was completed at least ten years before Ephesos received its second neokorate in 129/130 CE.
56. These finds will be published by Hilke Thür in cooperation with Maria Aurenhammer, Ulrike Outschar, Egon and Susanne Reuer, and myself.
57. *IvE* II 426; VII 3047.

Polemaeanus about 110 CE and completed by T. Claudius Aristion approximately ten years later. The richly ornamented sarcophagus of Ti. Julius Celsus Polemaeanus stood in a sepulchre below a two-story brick building with a marble façade, which was endowed as a library. The glamour of the reconstructed façade and Friedmund Hueber's discovery of its curvature[58] have distracted scholars from the fact that the library blocked the Processional Way to Ortygia. It is more likely, however, that this road already had a dead end, because the so-called Sarapeion (map no. 33),[59] even if traditionally dated later, must have been constructed in the early second century CE as well. On the southern side of this sanctuary, a giant temple is situated exactly on the site of the former road. Eight monolithic columns of 14 m height support its porch. The vaulted roof is constructed with huge wedge-shaped limestone blocks.[60] Excavations during 1991 and 1992[61] will make it possible to complete a reconstruction of the two-storied, one-aisled stoas built in the Corinthian order around the square courtyard, which is approximately 70 m in length. The rear walls of the ground floor were disguised by marble revetments. The absence of stone slabs as floor coverings and the unfinished ornaments of the temple frieze prove that construction was terminated before completion. The absence of a dedicatory inscription makes dating difficult, but close architectural similarities between these stoas and those of the Harbor Gymnasium, finished in 92/93 CE, suggest successive construction

58. Friedmund Hueber, "Beobachtungen zur Kurvatur und Scheinperspektive an der Celsusbibliothek und anderen kaiserzeitlichen Bauten," in *Bauplanung und Bautheorie in der Antike* (Diskussionen zur antiken Bauforschung 4; Berlin: DAI, 1983) 175–87.

59. Josef Keil's identification is based on circumstantial evidence and is hardly conclusive. See Josef Keil, "Das Serapeion von Ephesos," in *Halil Edhem hatıra kitabı I* (Türk Tarih Kurumu Yayınalarından 7.5; Ankara: Türk Tarih Kurumu Basimev, 1947–48).

60. The ground plan and architectural design of this temple were explored during Josef Keil's excavations before and after World War I; see Rudolf Heberdey, "IX. vorläufiger Bericht über die Ausgrabungen in Ephesos 1913," *JÖAI* 18 (1915) Beibl. 77–86; Josef Keil, "XII. vorläufiger Bericht," Beibl. 265–70.

61. Preliminary results are reported in Gerhard Langmann and Peter Scherrer ("Ephesos," *JÖAI* 62 [1993] Grabungen [1992] 14–16).

work by the same craftsmen.[62] Like the Library of Celsus, which was built at approximately the same time, the eastern stoa shows a curvature that is evident in the slightly different heights of the architectural fragments and the curved surface of the stylobate.

As a consequence of the construction of this temple complex, the Triodos was moved up the hillside to the south and east and placed at the end of Marble Road. Because of this, the Library of Celsus occupied the most prestigious site in the city, since the processional road to Ortygia began nearby, at the back of the altar (map no. 36) that was situated opposite the Gate of Mazaeus and Mithridates. The space between this altar and the Library of Celsus was soon filled with new buildings, which may also have been monuments to heroes.[63] Thus, by the beginning of the reign of Hadrian, the entire area from the Temple of the Flavian Sebastoi through the Embolos, down to the Sarapeion, was filled with temples, nympheia, baths, honorary tombs, and gates; private dwellings along the main streets more or less disappeared.

A new city district was subsequently created to the north of the street that was later called the Arkadian Street (map no. 5). This area was originally a swamp, but would become the site of the largest buildings of Ephesos. At the eastern end of the harbor basin, which in the Hadrianic period was surrounded by jetty walls on all sides,[64] the Harbor Baths (map no. 8) and the Harbor Gymnasium (map no. 9)[65] were built, perhaps on the solid ground of a former island. Ti. Claudius Aristion, together with a circle of illustrious friends, was sponsor and inaugurator of these complexes during the year of his prytany (92 CE) and his service as scribe of the demos (93 CE).[66] A

62. Further comparisons show that artisans from Aphrodisias planned and executed the work; see Wolf-Dieter Heilmeyer, "Korinthische Normalkapitelle," *Römische Mitteilungen*, Ergänzungsheft 16 (1970) 97–99.

63. More tomb inscriptions found in this area support this opinion; see, for example, *IvE* VI 2109; Knibbe, Engelmann, and İplikçioğlu, "Neue Inschriften aus Ephesos XII," 134 no. 33.

64. See the contribution of Heinrich Zabehlicky in this volume.

65. In antiquity, the baths were referred to as the Baths of the Emperor (or Emperors) (*IvE* IV 1104, 1155); the gymnasium was known as the Gymnasium of the Emperors or similar names (*IvE* III 621, 633, 661).

66. *IvE* II 427, 461, 508.

huge open space called the Xystoi, surrounded on all sides by three-aisled porticoes, was attached to the eastern side of the gymnasium (map no. 10). These buildings, with a total dimension of 200 m by 240 m, served both sports and philosophy; they may have been originally designed to serve as a place for the Olympic games, for which there is evidence from the time of the emperor Domitian.[67] Building activity seems to have been halted after the assassination of the emperor and was resumed in 129/130 CE, during the time of the second Ephesian imperial neokorate. C. Claudius Verulanus Marcellus and his wife Scaptia Philippe donated the marble panels for the walls of at least one of these porticoes,[68] and the prytanis Dionysios Nikephorou gave some precious marble columns.[69]

During the reign of Hadrian, while the Harbor Baths complex was still being completed, another large building was begun on its northern side. This was the Temple of Hadrian as Zeus Olympios, the second imperial neokorate temple of Ephesos (map no. 15).[70] This complex has not yet been sufficiently explored. The temple itself was oriented north-south and was surrounded by four porticoes, of which only the southern portico (map no. 14), measuring 263 m in length, has been uncovered. The Church of Mary (map no. 13) was later built into the western part of this portico.

During the reign of Antoninus Pius and his adopted sons, M. Claudius P. Vedius Antoninus Phaedrus Sabinianus was a distinguished sponsor of building activities.[71] Because of his numerous donations he received the title of *ktistes*, or founder of the city.[72] Some of the building activities that he promoted are known only through honorary inscriptions that do not detail the buildings or their function. It is clear, however, that he rebuilt the Bouleuterion,[73] adding statues of

67. Friesen, *Twice Neokoros*, 117–41; *IvE* IV 1089, 1104, 1124, 1125, 1155.
68. *IvE* II 430.
69. Ibid., III 661.
70. Karwiese, "Koressos," 214–25.
71. *IvE* VII pp. 88–90 lists his family tree, *cursus honorum* ("fixed sequence of public offices"), and donations.
72. Ibid., III 727; VI 2065; VII 3075.
73. Ibid., II 460.

the imperial family,[74] and established a bath-gymnasium complex (the Vedius Gymnasium [map no. 19]) north of the stadium in Koressos, which was dedicated in 146/147.[75] During the same period, another group of Ephesian donors built the East Gymnasium near the Magnesian Gate (map no. 69). The columns of the courts of both gymnasia feature composite capitals that are nearly identical in detail; they were apparently built by the same architectural school.[76] With these two new buildings five gymnasia were available to the citizens of Ephesos.[77] A sixth gymnasium was built in the beginning of the second century near the Artemision[78] either in addition to an older structure or as its replacement.[79]

After this boom in construction in the midsecond century, there are no records of major architectural donations in the city for the remainder of this century, except for foundations for the imperial cult. The so-called Parthian Monument, erected after the death of Lucius Verus (169 CE), is an interesting and controversial building. Its original location is still debated. Most recently, the insula north of the Temple of the Flavian Sebastoi opposite the State Agora[80] and the altar of Artemis at the lower end of the Embolos[81] were claimed as locations

74. Ibid., II 285a (Faustina); V 1505 (Lucius Verus).

75. Ibid., II 431, 438.

76. On the rivalry between the sponsors of the East Gymnasium and the Vedius Gymnasium and the emperor's intervention on behalf of Vedius, see ibid., V 1491–93.

77. The most recent study is that of Fikret Yegül, "The Bath-Gymnasium Complex in Asia Minor during the Imperial Roman Age" (Ph.D. diss., Harvard University, 1975).

78. *IvE* VII 3066; see also III 938, 938a; IV 1143; V 1500.

79. Ibid., V 1618.

80. A list of the locations at which parts of this monument were found is provided in Oberleitner, *Funde aus Ephesos und Samothrake*, 66, 91. Schneider (*Bunte Barbaren*, 125–28) suggested a location north of the Temple of the Flavian Sebastoi, because he dated the terrace façade not to Flavian times as did Anton Bammer (*Architektur und Gesellschaft in der Antike* [2d ed.; Vienna: Böhlau, 1985] 124–25) and Friesen (*Twice Neokoros*, 72–75), but connected it to the Parthian monument by dating and contents.

81. Werner Jobst, "Embolosforschungen I," Beibl. 215–19; idem, "Zur Standortbestimmung und Rekonstruktion des Parthersiegaltares von Ephesos," *JÖAI* 56 [1985] 79–82; Friedmund Hueber ("Der Embolos, ein urbanes Zentrum von Ephesos," *Antike Welt* 15 (1984) 11 and n. 9) already doubted this with

for the Parthian Monument. The most outstanding donor during the last decades of the second century was the famous orator T. Flavius Damianus, who completed the Baths of Varius by installing a room for imperial worship.[82] Damianus's most significant donation is the building of a vaulted stoa for the *Via Sacra*.[83]

In the period from the Severan dynasty to the middle of the third century, a series of larger buildings were constructed. Some are known only through dedicatory inscriptions.[84] T. Flavius Menander rebuilt an old Hydreion directly opposite the tomb of Memmius (map no. 25).[85] In Koressos, at least the south stoa of the Olympieion was repaired or altered around the time of Caracalla (211–217 CE).[86] The so-called Macellum (map no. 18) opposite the stadium must have been an (imperial) cultic site with a courtyard surrounded by halls and a central monument of 20 m in diameter with sixteen niches.[87] The building activities of M. Fulvius Publicianus Nikephoros, the last great donor of Ephesos for more than a hundred years, took place during the reign of Severus Alexander or Maximinus Thrax. His halls contained areas reserved for different corporations of artisans; these may have stood along the Koressian part of the Plateia.[88]

The Reorganization of Ephesos from the Fourth to the Early Fifth Centuries CE

The elimination or Christianization of pagan monuments was not the primary motivation for the large-scale building activities and architectural renovations of the fourth century. With major earthquakes and the devastation caused by Gothic plunderers, the prosperity of the

good reason. For a compromise position, see Dieter Knibbe, *Parthermonument*, 5–18.

82. *IvE* VII 3080.

83. See Dieter Knibbe's contribution in this volume.

84. See, for example, the architraves that originally belonged to long halls of streets or courtyards (*IvE* VII 3001, 3002).

85. Ibid., II 435.

86. Karwiese, *Die Marienkirche*, 14–15.

87. Keil, "XII. vorläufiger Bericht," 250.

88. Dieter Knibbe, "Der Asiarch M. Fulvius Publicianus Nikephoros, die ephesinischen Handwerkszünfte und die Stoa des Servilius," *JÖAI* 56 (1985) 71–77.

city had begun to decline as early as the time of the emperor Gallienus, and the population also seems to have declined. The preference for settlement in the harbor plain finally resulted in a new city wall (map no. 6) which enclosed only the Koressos area between Arkadian Street and the Vedius Gymnasium, thus excluding the Hellenistic and early imperial city centers.

The latest, as yet unpublished excavations provide proof of an earthquake and an accompanying fire. These events cannot have happened later than the midfourth century, and were probably much earlier, during the time of Gallienus in 262 CE. The whole Tetragonos Agora collapsed and the halls of the so-called Sarapeion were also destroyed. The Slope Houses probably suffered the same fate, even if Hermann Vetters has dated the destruction of the Slope Houses to earthquakes between the years 358 and 369.[89] Literary sources attest to earthquakes at other sites at this time,[90] but confirmation of Vetter's hypothesis awaits a more detailed examination of the stratigraphic evidence. The letters of the emperors Valens, Valentinian, and Gratian, which were inscribed on the Octagon (map no. 44), also attest to earthquakes. The emperors complained about insufficient restoration work by the municipal authorities despite imperial financial aid.[91]

When a disastrous earthquake destroyed the Harbor Gymnasium, the Xystoi, and Harbor Baths, the entrance to the Harbor Baths was reconstructed as the *Atrium Thermarum Constantianarum* ("entrance hall of the baths of the sons of Constantine") with the use of boukrania from the Parthian Monument. Since one of the dedicatory inscriptions honors the emperor Constans,[92] the baths must have been in use again before the year 350 CE. The Harbor Gymnasium and the Xystoi were

89. Hermann Vetters, "Introduction," in Werner Jobst, *Römische Mosaiken aus Ephesos I: Die Hanghäuser des Embolos* (*FiE* 8.2; Vienna: ÖAW, 1977) 20, 23; but see also Clive Foss, *Ephesos after Antiquity: A Late Antique, Byzantine and Turkish City* (Cambridge, MA: Harvard University Press, 1979) 188. Stefan Karwiese ("Das Beben und Gallien und seine anhaltenden Folgen" in Kandler, Karwiese, and Pillinger, *Lebendige Altertumswissenschaft*, 126–31) provides good evidence for the earthquake of 262.

90. Ammianus Marcellinus 17.7.1 (358 CE); 26.10.15 (365 CE); Malalas 342 (368 CE).

91. *IvE* Ia 42.

92. Ibid., IV 1314.

never rebuilt, but a simple chapel was erected on top of the leveled debris, four meters above the original level of the palaestra.[93] Earthquakes also destroyed the Library of Celsus, except for its façade, which was utilized as the monumental back wall for a nympheion. Reliefs from the Parthian Monument showing important scenes of imperial propaganda were reused in the front wall of the nympheion. The inscription written in poetic meter in the first floor of the façade of the library mentions Stephanos,[94] who may have been the sponsor of the nympheion and other alterations in the center of Ephesos.[95] A further alteration in the façade of the Library of Celsus may aid in dating the nympheion: the inscription of the second statue from the north, which originally represented one of the virtues of Celsus, was replaced by the words Ἔννοια Φιλίππου ("positive mind of Phillipus"). This seems to refer to the Praefectus Orientis Flavius Philippus,[96] who died in the captivity of Magnentius in 351 CE. Since Constantius II had first thought that Philippus stayed with Magnentius of his own free will, the prefect fell into disgrace. In order to rehabilitate him after having learned the truth, Constantius II sent letters

93. The exact location can no longer be ascertained because the chapel and common houses were cleared by the first archaeologists, who were searching for the stratum of the older building. A short report about these excavations is included in Otto Benndorf, "Erzstatue eines griechischen Athleten" (*FiE* 1; Vienna: Hölder, 1906) 182–84, and in Benndorf's first excavation report, "Vorläufiger Bericht über die Ausgrabungen in Ephesos I," *JÖAI* 1 (1898) Beibl. 65, where he suggests a medieval date for these buildings without giving further proof for this opinion.

94. *IvE* 5 VII 5115.

95. This inscription may well refer to the same Stephanos who is honored in the epigram that was found in the Embolos (ibid., IV 1310). On the weak evidence that this inscription was found near a sixth-century consular statue (Jale Inan and Elisabeth Rosenbaum, *Roman and Early Byzantine Sculpture in Asia Minor* [London: British Academy, 1966] 157–58 no. 202 pls. 178/4 and 186/4–5), however, Miltner ("XXII. vorläufiger Bericht," 279–81) claimed the epigram for the base of this statue. A third inscription in poetic meter, honoring Stephanos as a proconsul, was found in the Byzantine structures of Mount Ayasoluk (Knibbe and İplikcioğlu, "Neue Inschriften aus Ephesos VIII," 142 no. 150).

96. Arnold H. Martin, John P. Martindale, and J. Morris, *Prosopography of the Later Roman Empire* (4 vols. in 3; Cambridge: Cambridge University Press, 1971) 1. 696–97, see Flavius Philippus no. 7.

to several cities in the east praising the loyalty of Philippus and ordered them to set up golden statues of the deceased. One of the bases
of these statues names Constantius Gallus as Caesar; from this we
learn that the whole episode must have taken place sometime between
351 and 354 CE.[97] Parts of the emperor's rulings were found in secondary use as pavement slabs of the Embolos near the Temple of
Hadrian, revealing that Ephesos must have followed suit.[98]

Relief slabs from the Parthian Monument were reused in at least
four nympheia, as well as the wells of the harbor area and Arkadian
Street. All these nymphea were supplied with water from the Marnas
river. An inscription shows that the proconsul of Asia, L. Caelius
Montius, who was in charge of the restoration of the Harbor Baths,
also restored the monumental surge tank at the end of the aqueduct
(map no. 66) southeast of the State Agora, in honor of the imperial
brothers Constans and Constantius II.[99] L. Caelius Montius may have
also contributed to other buildings that used water, including the one
in front of the Library of Celsus. Restoration of the water supply,
including baths, was evidently one of the principal concerns of this
period.

At this time, inscriptions honoring the emperor never contained
wording that might offend Christians, and were no longer similar to
the votive inscriptions customary since the time of Augustus, which
presumed the divine nature of the ruler. Of greater interest, however,
is the fact that public buildings of the highest prominence in the cult
of the emperors, such as the Parthian Monument, could be dismantled
and reused for new, officially sanctioned building purposes. Three
heads found in the Basilike Stoa—one of Augustus with a *corona
civica* and two heads from a monumental seated pair of Augustus and
Livia—were carefully marked with a cross on their foreheads.[100] The

97. This inscription is from Cythrae in Cyprus (Theodor Mommsen, ed.,
Corpus inscriptionum latinarum [Berlin: Reimer, 1873] III.1 214; Hermann
Dessau, ed., *Inscriptiones latinae selectae* [2d ed.; Berlin: Weidmann, 1962]
no. 738).

98. *IvE* I 41.

99. Ibid., IV 1316, 1317.

100. For the meaning of the cross on the forehead, see the literary and
archaeological examples in Gerhard Langmann, "Eine Kaisertaufe in Ephesos,"
JÖAI 56 (1985) 66.

Basilike Stoa seems to have escaped major earthquake damage until that time, but because of the uncertainty of the dating, it is impossible to know whether the building of a small Christian church into the western chalcidium of the stoa, opposite the imperial pair at its eastern end, is related to this Christian defacing of the statues.

No fixed or approximate date can be given to any building activity during the time of Valentinian and his co-rulers; during this time, major earthquakes shook Asia Minor every few years and the empire faced economic and political problems. Large-scale building activities were not resumed until the time of Theodosius I, when the old Tetragonos Agora was rebuilt under the name of "Foros Theodosianos."[101] Only the eastern portico and its upper story, the so-called Neronic Hall, survived major damage. On all other sides, the entire superstructure was rebuilt, but this rebuilding does not seem to have included an upper story anymore. Around 400 CE, the wealthy Christian Scholastikia sponsored the rebuilding of the Baths of Varius (map no. 40) on the Embolos. Parts of the Prytaneion, including its dedicatory inscription[102] were reused, indicating that it had been destroyed, probably by an earthquake, by that time. The fallen statues of Artemis, which were slightly damaged, were buried carefully; there is no sign of a willful Christian destruction as is often claimed.[103] Diverse inscriptions from the Prytaneion were used as building material in the Tetragonos Agora.[104]

Other buildings of the State Agora were also used as quarries. The north façade of the Temple of the Flavian Sebastoi was dismantled, and parts of it were reused as supports in the southern hall of the Tetragonos Agora.[105] Corinthian capitals in its northern stoa must

101. *IvE* V 1534.
102. Ibid., II 437.
103. For example, Franz Miltner, *Ephesos, Stadt der Artemis und des Johannes* (Vienna: Deuticke, 1958) 100–104. These statues are now the pride of the Efes Müzesi in Selçuk (inv. nos. 712, 717, 718); see Fleischer, *Artemis von Ephesos*, E46–E48.
104. *IvE* VII 3071 (pavement from the front of the Prytaneion); ibid., IV 1055, 1063, 1071, 1073 (votive inscriptions to Hestia Bouleia and lists of *curetes*).
105. Anton Bammer, "Elemente flavianisch-traianischer Architekturfassaden aus Ephesos," *JÖAI* 52 (1978–80) 84.

also have come from a first-century structure dedicated to the imperial cult, as is evident from their decorations, which include eagles
and dolphins; I suspect that these capitals come from the Temple of
the Flavian Sebastoi. It is clear that the rebuilding of both the Varius
Baths by Scholastikia and the Tetragonos Agora took place at the
same time, since both buildings not only incorporate spoils from the
Prytaneion, but share other reused material also.[106] The original use
of many other spoils incorporated in the reconstruction of the
Tetragonos Agora can be identified, but these details cannot be discussed in the framework of this paper.

The former center of the imperial cult, the State Agora, was abandoned except for the functionally redefined Basilike Stoa. Over time,
the once splendid buildings were surrounded by tenement constructions. In contrast, the old arterial street of the city that came from the
Magnesian Gate and passed the State Agora first on its southern and
then on its western side was completely reconstructed. The known
buildings here were unfortunately uncovered in the early period of the
excavations and were never examined in detail. Consequently, some
are inaccessible; for example an interesting late antique structure, which
John T. Wood, who excavated it before 1870, called a "basilika."
Other buildings also await reexamination: the nearby so-called Tomb
of Luke (map no. 68), which is probably an early Roman heroon,
later converted into a church or memorial chapel; the surge tank,
often called the Hydreion (map no. 66), which Caelius Montius repaired; and what is probably a fountain in the vicinity (map no. 67).
(The latter two are now covered by a modern road and have already
been mentioned above.) The fountain near the Tomb of Sextilius Pollio
(map no. 59), where some late antique repair work was found,[107] may
have been refurbished at this time with the statues of the blinding of
Polyphemos by Odysseus,[108] which once belonged to the pediment of
a temple of unknown location.

106. For example, parts of *IvE* II 256, which mentions the family of
Germanicus, were found in the Baths of Scholastikia (near the front stair of
the Temple of Hadrian) and in the walls on the side of the street leading from
the north gate of the Tetragonos Agora to the theater.

107. This unpublished information was kindly provided by Anton Bammer,
who took part in the excavations there and did the restoration work.

108. Bernard Andreae, "Die Polyphem-Gruppe von Ephesos," in Kandler,

The so-called Gate of Herakles was probably built in the midfifth century at the upper end of the Embolos (map no. 51).[109] The street and the buildings lining it were adorned or repaired with spoils from the area of the Prytaneion, in particular, columns that are inscribed with yearly lists of priests; for this reason, the Austrian archaeologists named this "Curetes Street." The Hellenistic heroon (map no. 43) at the lower Embolos was converted into a fountain surrounded by slabs engraved with crosses.[110] While the Octagon and the Tomb of Memmius survived earthquakes and religious turmoil unscathed, sepulchers along the Embolos that stood in the way of new buildings were destroyed. The altar between the Library of Celsus and the Gate of Hadrian was completely leveled and a magnificent stoa with a mosaic floor was built in its stead; unfortunately, only traces of this building have survived.[111] The so-called Temple of Hadrian (map no. 41) was also reconstructed. In front of the building, the proconsul Nummius Aemilianus replaced a statue of the tetrarch Maximian with a statue of Theodosius, once-exiled father of the emperor.[112] The frieze that was placed into the pronaos of the building shows scenes from the founding legends of Ephesos, such as the wild boar hunt of Androklos and the routing of the Amazons by Herakles and Dionysos. Franz Miltner has interpreted a final slab as depicting Theodosius surrounded by the ancient gods.[113] Theodosius's inclusion in the final panel indicates that he was regarded as the new founder of Ephesos. After the completion of the rebuilding of the area of the Embolos from the Gate of Herakles to the nympheion at the Library of Celsus,

Karwiese, and Pillinger, *Lebendige Altertumswissenschaft*, 209–11 pl. 24. A restored copy can now be found in the Efes Müzesi in Selçuk.

109. Anton Bammer ("Ein spätantiker Torbau aus Ephesos," *JÖAI* 51 [1976–77] Beibl. 119–22) claims that this gate was established in 459 because the dedicatory inscription includes the name Fl. Konst[. . . .] (*IvE* II 587), whom he identifies with the proconsul of this year. Jobst ("Bau- und Bildkunst," 201) supports this dating based on stylistic arguments.

110. See Hilke Thür's contribution in this volume.

111. Jobst, "Embolosforschungen I," 231–36.

112. *IvE* II 306.

113. Miltner, "XXII. vorläufiger Bericht," 271–72; see also Fleischer, "Fries des Hadrianstempels," 23–71; and Jobst's summary ("Bau- und Bildkunst," 201).

an inscription rightly called the Embolos "the magnificent ground of the city."[114]

Under Arkadios, who ruled the eastern part of the empire from 395 to 408 CE, the rebuilding of the city continued with the repair of the theater; the northern analemma wall had collapsed as a result of earthquakes. Its completion was duly celebrated with epigrams about the responsible proconsul Messalinus.[115] With the new entrance next to the stage building and the broad staircase in front of the theater, a new architectural concept was realized. Once again parts of the façade of the Temple of the Flavian Sebastoi and materials generally believed to have originated from the grand altar in front of the Artemision were used both for the repair of the theater and in order to pave the square in front of it.

The street leading from the theater to the harbor (map no. 5) was enlarged into an avenue of 11 m in width with porticoes 5 m wide on both sides; it was named Arkadian Street in honor of the emperor.[116] It was illuminated by candelabra at night. A magnificent monument with four columns was built in its center[117]; these have been interpreted as a memorial for the four evangelists.[118] It is not yet possible to draw conclusions about the largely unexcavated area between Arkadian Street and the Tetragonos Agora. The only known monument is the Gate of Medusa at the western end of the street, which began at the west gate of the Tetragonos Agora. With its width of 14 m, this was the broadest street in Ephesos (map no. 32). Palm leaf ornaments fixed to the sides of the capitals of the Gate of Medusa correspond exactly to those at the Gate of Herakles. This indicates that the gates must be dated to the same time and demonstrates that

114. *IvE* IV 1300.
115. Ibid., VI 2043, 2044. Another epigram for his lost statue (IV 1307) was found in the Embolos.
116. Ibid., III 557.
117. It apparently owes its present shape to restorations that were made in the sixth century. An epigram on the columns honors Frontinus as an outstanding builder (ibid., IV 1306).
118. Wilberg, "Der Viersäulenbau auf der Arkadianstrasse," 132–40. Another four-column monument, dated to the time of Theodosius II, is known only from its capitals; see Jobst, "Bau- und Bildkunst," 200 pl. 4 nos. 1–2.

in the early Byzantine period the harbor region was still integrated into the municipal area and was widely restored.

More than twenty churches—the most important architectural documentation of Christianity in Ephesos—are already known. Two of the most important are the predecessor of the domed basilica of the Justinian period, built over the tomb of St. John the Theologian (map no. 78) and the cemetery church in the Grotto of the Seven Sleepers (map no. 71), built perhaps for St. Timothy; literary evidence locates his tomb on the Panayirdağ.[119] Both churches were built as memorials outside of the city in ancient cemetery areas, and both can be dated to a time before the Council of Ephesos of 431 CE.[120]

Not much is known of the other churches; details about their ground plans, decorations, and functions cannot be given. The buildings known or presumed to have been churches are scattered throughout the city; all of them are small, except for the recently excavated basilica in the East Gymnasium[121] and the episcopal Church of Mary (map no. 13, see below). The acts of the Council of Ephesos, which mention the closing of several churches,[122] confirm that various churches served the different neighborhoods of the city. It is significant that when the predecessor building of a church is known, it is a public or pagan building. One of these is a church that was built into the Sarapeion.[123] A large basilica was built into the sekos of the Artemision.[124] Churches were built into the palaestrae of at least two of the five Ephesian bath-gymnasium complexes. A small church stood in the Harbor Gymnasium on top of the rubble of the fourth-century earthquake. The

119. *Acta Timothei* (May 8); see also *Synaxarium Constantinopolitanum* (May 8).

120. Franz Miltner, *Das Coemeterium der Sieben Schläfer* (*FiE* 4.2; Vienna: Rohrer, 1937); Georgios A. Soteriou, et al., *Die Johanneskirche* (*FiE* 4.3; Vienna: ÖAI, 1951).

121. Vetters, "Vorläufiger Grabungsbericht 1981," 71–72; idem, "Vorläufiger Grabungsbericht 1982," 116–17; idem, "Vorläufiger Grabungsbericht 1983," 215; idem, "Vorläufiger Grabungsbericht für 1984 und 1985," 84.

122. For further information, see Vasiliki Limberis's contribution in this volume; also see Cyril Alex. *Ep.* (Mansi *Consiliorum Collectio* 4.1242).

123. Rudolf Heberdey, "IX. vorläufiger Bericht über die Ausgrabungen in Ephesos 1913," *JÖAI* 18 (1915) Beibl. 86–87 figs. 28 and 30.

124. Anton Bammer, "Die Geschichte des Sekos im Artemision von Ephesos," *JÖAI* 62 (1993) Beibl. 167–68.

large basilica built into the East Gymnasium has already been mentioned; its importance is demonstrated by the geometric mosaics covering the entire floor of the naves, the aisles decorations with opus
sectile of Numidian marble, and donors' inscriptions from deacons on
candelabra that were found lying on the floor. This church may be
dated to the fifth century, but whether this area was already situated
outside of the city limits at the time the church above the Hellenistic
city walls was erected cannot be determined; if it was outside the
city, the church was constructed as a cemetery church.[125] The construction of churches in gymnasia can perhaps be explained by the
fact that gymnasia served not only athletics and philosophy but also
included installations for the imperial cult.

The church discovered by Stefan Karwiese[126] in 1993 in the substructure of the main entrance to the northern terrace of the stadium
served as a cemetery church, at least in later times. An inscription,
found in secondary use as a corner stone of a house wall in the
Koressian part of the Plateia, half way between the theater and the
stadium, mentions that this part of the Plateia was newly paved up to
the House of the Archangel Gabriel[127] and may thus refer to this
newly located church. Memorial churches built into such places as
stadia or gymnasia may commemorate places of martyrdom.

The Church of Mary was built into the southern portico of the
gigantic Hadrianic Olympieion after its destruction in approximately
400 CE. Its large marble blocks were not reused elsewhere but burned
on the spot in lime kilns. On the basis of stratigraphic evidence,
Stefan Karwiese has argued that this church could not have been built
until the last quarter of the fifth century—that is, at least a generation
after the Council of Ephesos.[128] It is evident that this late date causes
numerous problems, which cannot be discussed here in detail. The
Council of Ephesos took place in a church that was called the "Great

125. During excavations that Gerard Seiterle conducted, tombs were found
near the Magnesian Gate, which were simply and imprecisely labelled "late
antique." See Vetters, "Vorläufiger Grabungsbericht 1981," 70.
126. A preliminary report will be forthcoming in *JÖAI*.
127. Knibbe and İplikçioğlu, "Neue Inschriften aus Ephesos VIII," 125 no.
124.
128. See his contribution to this volume.

Church" or the "Church of Saint Maria Theotokos"[129] and also in the episcopal palace. At the time of the council, had only the episkopeion been built? Did the meetings therefore simply take place in the portico of the Olympieion? The use of various spoils in the building of the church and the dating of the church itself awaits further investigation.[130]

Conclusion

As early as the time of Constantius II, Christian concerns motivated building plans, although it is not clear to what extent building activity was determined by the needs that arose after major earthquakes. Major reconstructions commenced in the time of Theodosius, and most of the buildings utilized spoils from older pagan cult facilities of the imperial era. The imperial edicts of 391 and 392, which prohibited pagan cult and terminated sacral laws, made such reuse possible.[131] These edicts therefore had enormous economic impact. Without the utilization of an immense quantity of spoils from older sacred buildings, which the edicts made possible, the revival of Ephesos would hardly have been possible. The traditional image, moreover, that late antiquity was a time of decline can hardly be confirmed by the interpretation of the archaeological evidence from Ephesos, which demonstrates the restoration of Ephesos from a Hellenistic-Roman metropolis to a Byzantine-Christian center.

129. An inscription from the time of Justinian reveals its name as "Saint Maria Theotokos and always Virgin" (*IvE* VII 4135).
130. Perhaps the most appropriate statement at this time is what Benndorf (*Zur Ortskunde und Stadtgeschichte*, 104) has already said: "It [the Church of Mary] poses enigmas that the excavations we have just started will only be able to solve imperfectly, because of the great lack of structural elements."
131. *Codex Theodosius* 16.10.10–12.

Urban Development and Social Change in Imperial Ephesos*

L. Michael White
Oberlin College

Perspectives on a Panorama of Change

The modern visitor to Ephesos has the opportunity to view an ancient city as it was, without the intrusion of modern life and modern architecture. This is the case with very few other archaeological sites. The archaeological work at Ephesos is one of the great gifts of this century. The stark character of the ancient ruins, however, may be deceptive to the modern onlooker who cannot also see the ancient city as a panorama of change. One sociologist has put it this way:

> When we examine the magnificent ruins of classical cities we
> have a tendency to see them as extraordinarily durable and per-

*The research for this article was completed with the help of a fellowship from the National Endowment for the Humanities, whose support is greatly appreciated. I also express appreciation to Professor Helmut Koester for his counsel, encouragement, and suggestions in the directions of this research and in the final form of the article.

manent—after all, they were built of stone and have endured for centuries. But this is mostly an illusion. We usually are looking at simply the *last* ruins of a city that was turned to ruin repeatedly. And if the physical structures of Greco-Roman cities were transitory, so too were their populations—cities often were almost entirely depopulated and then repopulated, and their ethnic composition often was radically changed in the process.[1]

My task, therefore, is to depict that panorama of change in Roman Ephesos through the media of archaeology and social history. It is important to understand the environment and the life of this city during a key period when the Hellenistic East changed first to Roman and then to Christian cultural dominance. The process of change reflected in these shifts is part and parcel of the topic at hand. How does one measure the change?

I suspect that scholars have too typically thought of the changes in Roman cities such as Ephesos only in terms of political and religious categories. Some features of the change may be seen in this way, especially as we move from imperial to Byzantine rule. Ramsay MacMullen has noted, however, that not much truly changed if one looks at the broader social panorama before and after the time of Constantine. Religious ideas alone are not sufficient for articulating precisely how the change came about. It is difficult to explain the balance between continuity and change that one finds in the fourth and fifth centuries without resorting to some scheme that involves a massive crisis or shift in public orientation. The traditional approach used to account for this picture of the change, similar to E. R. Dodds's *Pagan and Christian in an Age of Anxiety*, typically looks to the third century as an age of crisis and decline that made the shift possible.[2]

1. Rodney Stark, "Antioch as the Social Situation of Matthew's Gospel," in David Balch, ed., *Social History of the Matthean Community: Cross-Disciplinary Approaches* (Minneapolis: Fortress, 1991) 197.

2. E. R. Dodds, *Pagan and Christian in an Age of Anxiety: Some Aspects of Religious Experience from Marcus Aurelius to Constantine* (1965; reprinted New York: Norton, 1970). Dodds employed Gilbert Murray's notion of a "failure of nerve" in Greek religion (*Five Stages of Greek Religion* [New York: Columbia University Press, 1925] 155–63), caused in part by devastating political and social setbacks, which produced the profound sense of crisis in the third century. He then argued that Christianity triumphed because it had

Leading up to Dodds is a long development of this basic scheme, ranging from the disparaging assessment of social decline in Edward Gibbon to the typically Christian triumphalism of ideas over social environment in Adolf Harnack.[3] Is this the panorama of change seen in the urban life of Ephesos? The fortunes of Ephesos did not merely rise and fall with Roman rule. Unlike other major cities of the eastern empire, such as Corinth, Ephesos flourished, even during that critical period of transition—what some have labeled "crisis"—of the third and fourth centuries. Nor does it seem to have experienced some of the paroxysms of change in the fifth century as a result of Christian rule, as seen in Antioch or Alexandria. To be sure, Ephesos did face challenges and undergo changes in social makeup and religious life. Thus, one of the questions we should begin to consider, given the wealth of new data now made available by the excavations and publications of the Österreichisches Archäologisches Institut, is how this transition might have come about. I would like to propose some observations on both the character of that process of change and some potential methods for analyzing it. To this end, I suggest that one should not view the so-called Hellenization, Romanization, and Christianization of Ephesos as distinct cultural phases that were deposited in neat sedimentary layers. They were, instead, part of an integral process of social change,

a more satisfying set of reponses to the anxiety and anomie of this age of crisis. For challenges to the idea that such a notion of crisis existed, see Peter Brown, "Approaches to the Religious Crisis of the Third Century," in idem, *Religion and Society in the Age of St. Augustine* (London: Faber, 1972) 74–80; idem, *The Making of Late Antiquity* (Cambridge, MA: Harvard University Press, 1978) 45–46; Ramsay MacMullen, *The Roman Government's Response to Crisis* (New Haven: Yale University Press, 1976) esp. 168–73; idem, *Paganism in the Roman Empire* (New Haven: Yale University Press, 1981) 135–37. While this question is beyond the scope of the present study, its implications and assumptions must be kept in mind for future discussions.

3. On Gibbon, see esp. G. W. Bowersock, et al., eds., *Edward Gibbon and the Decline and Fall of the Roman Empire* (Cambridge, MA: Harvard University Press, 1977); Jaroslav Pelikan, *The Excellent Empire: The Fall of Rome and the Triumph of the Church* (San Francisco: Harper & Row, 1987). On Harnack, see L. Michael White, "Adolf Harnack and the 'Expansion' of Early Christianity: A Reappraisal of Social History," *Second Century* 5 (1985/86) 97–127.

each one building on and through the others, while the city itself underwent an organic process of urban development. The urban pan-orama of ancient Ephesos was an involving cultural ecosystem

The "Romanization" of Ephesos

Thanks to the Romans, stated a notable writer of the Antonine period, "the world is at peace through their agency; so much so that we are able to travel the highways and sail the seas wherever we wish without fear."[4] This is a remarkable statement of the success of Romanization, especially coming from a provincial who grew up near Ephesos in the middle of the second century. If one looks out from the theater at Ephesos toward the ancient harbor, however, Irenaeus's sense of Rome's imperial reach becomes imaginable. Moreover, the characteristic sentiments within the statement above come from imperial propaganda, since the *Res Gestae* of Augustus, *pax* ("peace") and *libertas* ("freedom") were slogans for the "benefits of Empire."[5] During the middle of the second century, Ephesos experienced an unprecedented building boom. Whatever its renown and glory had been in previous times, Ephesos took its recognizable urban shape from this building program under the Flavian and Antonine emperors. In later usage *libertas* was transformed as imperial *liberalitas* ("generosity"); the bestowing of benefits had become the new cardinal virtue of Romanization.[6] This new ethos, however, resulted in the creation of

4. Irenaeus *Adv. haer.* 4.30.3; my translation.
5. The *Res Gestae Divi Augusti* was set up as the decree of the *koinon* of Asia to celebrate the birthday of Augustus as the beginning of the new year. Enacted some time in the second decade of the first century CE, the decree was consciously published as imperial propaganda by being set forth as monumental inscriptions in several major cities of Asia. For the text, see *Res Gestae Divi Augusti* (LCL; trans. Frederick W. Shipley; 1924; reprinted Cambridge, MA: Harvard University Press, 1967). On the propaganda value, see J. Rufus Fears, *Roman Liberty: An Essay in Protean Political Metaphor* (Indiana University Distinguished Research Lectures; Bloomington: University of Indiana Press, 1980) 15–17. As Fears points out, a consolidation of various types of imperial propaganda would continue to function in rhetorical usage down to the time of Constantine. Erich Gruen, however, has suggested that much of the ideological weight of the slogan *Pax Romana* accrued under later emperors.
6. See Fears, *Roman Liberty*, 20–21, 26 n. 5.

a pluralistic environment, especially in the old Hellenistic cities of the East.

From this perspective, then, the quotation is even more striking, since it comes from the Christian bishop Irenaeus of Lyons, who had grown up in Asia under Hadrian and Pius and witnessed persecution during the reign of Marcus Aurelius.[7] For Irenaeus, no less than for the imperial propagandists, this sense of Rome's benefits carried religious implications and assumptions. This further raises the question of what is meant by the term "Romanization," especially in discussing cities such as Ephesos. Far too often scholars have taken the same imperial propaganda as empirical fact.

The term "Romanization" derived its technical significance through the work of Theodore Mommsen.[8] For Mommsen, the legal structures of Roman rule gave shape to life and pervaded the conquered territories in a consistent manner. The *Res Gestae* of Augustus was displayed as overwhelming evidence of this centrifugal force.[9] Hence, Romanization is typically described in terms of Roman law and administrative organization, imperial building programs, and the use of Roman names and dress, all establishing their impact predominantly under Augustus. Subsequent emperors merely carried on the program, with greater or lesser success, until the period of crisis. MacMullen observes that if building programs were direct indicators of an imperial agenda to overlay the provinces with a veneer of Roman culture, then it is striking that the amount of expenditure in the relatively underdeveloped West was exceeded a hundredfold in the already urbanized and Hellenized East.[10] I shall return to this point later, since MacMullen does not further develop the implications of this important distinction.

7. Irenaeus *Adv. haer.* 4.30.3. Irenaeus is usually thought to have come from Smyrna because of his association with Polycarp. The key text is a letter from Irenaeus to a certain Florinus from the region of Asia preserved in Eusebius *Hist. eccl.* 5.20.5–7.

8. Thus, among others, Theodore Mommsen, *Römisches Staatsrecht* (3 vols.; Leipzig: Hirzel, 1981–88). See Ramsay MacMullen, "Notes on Romanization," *Bulletin of the American Society of Papyrologists* 21 (1984) 161–77, reprinted in idem, *Changes in the Roman Empire: Essays on the Ordinary* (Princeton: Princeton University Press, 1990) 56–66.

9. McMullen, "Notes on Romanization," 161–62.

10. Ibid., 163.

In his discussion, MacMullen suggests that the "*capacity*"—his term and emphasis—for Romanization was largely a product of wealth and access to both Roman resources and technical skill. Hence it was largely an urban phenomenon and limited to the upper crust of local societies; it never really penetrated the rural areas and the lower register. In the West in particular, but equally in rural parts of Africa or Asia Minor, the actual success of Romanization was limited at best. In explaining why this might have been so, MacMullen suggests that it was less a function of conscious resistance or hostility—and even less of overt nationalism—than a function of indifference, a reluctance to change when there were no compelling social stimuli at work, such as social mobility or wealth.[11]

In addition to MacMullen's point about the generally urban character and more or less voluntary process of acculturation, one is struck by the contrast of its effects in the West over against the East. In the example of Roman Britain—even where one finds extensive imposition of Roman building programs and social organization—upon the departure of the Romans and the arrival of the "barbarians," archaeological evidence indicates a rapid change in the nature of the material culture in only a generation or two.[12] In effect, even among seemingly Romanized Britons the acculturation did not take hold. The same kind of observation has been made regarding other regions of the western empire, such as the differences between urban Carthage—and the more Romanized environs of Africa Proconsularis—and the rural areas of Numidia.[13]

When discussing Romanization, then, one deals primarily with a phenomenon of urbanization among a population that already had diverse social contacts. It was a process that relied upon a previous layer of acculturation, especially Hellenization. In other words, what

11. Ibid., 175, 177.
12. For the archaeological evidence, see esp. Charles Thomas, *Christianity in Roman Britain to AD 500* (Berkeley: University of California Press, 1981) 482.
13. As suggested by W. H. C. Frend, *The Donatist Church: A Movement of Protest in Roman North Africa* (Oxford: Clarendon, 1952). Compare the recent study by James C. Russell, *The Germanization of Early Medieval Christianity: A Sociohistorical Approach to Religious Transformation* (New York: Oxford University Press, 1994).

scholars have typically called Romanization may be different from region to region depending on the particular nature and pace of inter-action between local cultures and the pluralistic nature of Roman rule. Our traditional picture of Romanization is in fact derived from the eastern and previously Hellenized part of the empire, and it is a phenomenon of internal social change through urbanization rather than merely cultural overlay. It is more characteristic of previously Helle-nized cities and the populations they attracted. Hence Ephesos and the other major urban centers of the Aegean rim are of special interest in studying this phenomenon. To return again to the example of Irenaeus, the Greek from Asia who went to Rome and Gaul, one notes that the area where he lived and continued to write in Greek had been a Hellenistic outpost before expansion of the Rhone valley trade corri-dor under the Romans.[14] Irenaeus's move to Gaul may reflect contin-ued social contacts with the Aegean urban centers and may also suggest how Christians and other "foreign" cults came to move into the Rhone valley area less by conversion than by broader social patterns and migration.[15]

14. This is especially true of Massilia. Strabo *Geog.* 4.1.4 reports that there was an *Ephesieion* at Massilia (modern Marseilles). Presumably this means a temple to the Ephesian Artemis where a typically Ephesian cycle of festivals was celebrated. This understanding is supported by Strabo's claim that the image of Artemis there was a copy of a famous statue brought from Ephesos itself at the foundation of the city. It must be supposed, therefore, that this sanctuary and its religious calendar were brought to this Phocaean and later Hellenistic outpost by an enclave of immigrants from Ephesos, but at what period this occurred remains unclear. On the colonization from Ephesos, see Irad Malkin, *Religion and Colonization in Ancient Greece* (Leiden: Brill, 1987) 69–72; idem, "Missionaires païens dans la Gaule grecque," in idem, *La France et la Méditerranée* (Leiden: Brill, 1990) 42–52. He suggests at least two distinct waves of colonization prior to the Hellenistic period.

15. See above n. 7. By way of comparison, the cult of Mithras in the same region of Gaul seems to have been spread by eastern provincials who moved to Gaul and were connected (either by slavery or by other means, such as clientellage) to local social networks. There is little or no evidence of an influence for the diffusion of Mithraism through the military in this region, since Gaul was not heavily garrisoned. Eventually some names of local Gallic origin appear. Some of the individuals were of relatively high social standing. The prosopographic analysis for the known Mithraic inscriptions is discussed in Vivienne J. Walters, *The Cult of Mithras in the Roman Provinces of Gaul*

Urban Change in Ephesos

Between the end of the first century and the end of the fourth, Ephesos experienced important social, political, and religious changes. Yet throughout this period Ephesos remained "the first and greatest metropolis of Asia" (πρώτης καὶ μεγίστης μητροπόλεως τῆς Ἀσίας), as the headings of numerous inscriptions reveal its own public presentation. How Ephesos accommodated this change while surviving the vicissitudes that beset other cities is important for understanding its history.

Recent studies have emphasized the relative stability of Roman rule in the Hellenistic East, and especially in Asia Minor during the third and fourth centuries and even beyond, while in the West, urban centers were diminishing in size and wealth due to "constriction of markets" and a resultant "deterioration of commerce."[16] MacMullen notes:

> Ephesos flourished. . . up to 614, thanks to its connections with
> a well-maintained road system, to say nothing of maritime trade;
> and the *vitality of exchange* that shows in the recently revealed
> commercial section that paid for the gilded ceilings of the new
> baths, the main avenue's lighting system,. . . [and other urban
> building programs].[17]

Despite some notable local disasters, such as the plagues of the late second and midthird centuries, the economic indicators are relatively constant and are certainly measurable. They are seen through outlays for art, public benefactions, building programs, foundations, and, most common of all, inscriptions. Moreover, looking to the role of public bequests and building programs, Ephesos remains "demonstrably healthy" and at least in schematic terms not much had changed even by the fourth and fifth centuries.[18] Eventually, wealthy Christian bene-

---

(EPRO; Leiden: Brill, 1974) 31–37. See also L. Michael White, *Building God's House in the Roman World: Architectural Adaptation among Pagans, Jews, and Christians* (Baltimore: Johns Hopkins University Press, 1990) 47–59 (esp. 56).

16. See the regional survey of Ramsay MacMullen, *Corruption and the Decline of Rome* (New Haven: Yale University Press, 1991) 15–35, and further bibliography cited there.

17. Ibid., 34.

18. Ibid., 36. Especially for this later period see the work of Clive Foss,

factors would gradually take over the role and position of their earlier religious and civic counterparts, the Ephesian elite, as one hears of Christian "negotiators" (πραγμάτεις) and bankers or gold dealers.[19] The urban growth of Ephesos is a key to this process of change. Strabo noted: "The city, because of its advantageous situation in other respects [than the harbor], grows daily and is the largest market (*emporium*) in Asia on this side of the Taurus."[20] Similarly, Philostratos, ostensibly quoting a speech of Apollonius of Tyana, observed:

> Ephesus. . . a city which took the beginning of its race from the purest Attic [stock], and which grew in size beyond all other cities of Ionia and Lydia, and stretched herself out to the sea, outgrowing the land on which she is built, and is filled with studious inhabitants, both philosophers and rhetoricians, thanks to whom the city owes her strength not to her cavalry, but to the myriads of humans in whom she inculcates wisdom.[21]

This latter comment is particularly noteworthy, since it reflects on the physical growth and the population of the city, and since, despite its ostensible setting, it comes after the second century. This growth of Ephesos, although inaugurated under the Julio-Claudian emperors, did not commence until the end of the first century under Domitian, when Ephesos replaced Pergamon as the neokoros ("temple warden") of the imperial cult. The urban growth shifted gears smoothly after the *damnatio memoriae* of Domitian and developed rapidly under Trajan and Hadrian. It is also worth noting that this is the same period during which Acts was probably written and Christianity grew in Ephesos.

Foreigners at Ephesos: Two Snapshots

The complex and incremental quality of the sort of change that one finds at Ephesos makes assessment difficult. Much like the gradual nature of other evolutionary processes, such change involves multi-

---

Ephesus after Antiquity: A Late Antique, Byzantine, and Turkish City (Cambridge, MA: Harvard University Press, 1979).

19. *IvE* VI 2263, 2271.

20. Strabo *Geog.* 14.1.24 (LCL; trans. Horace Leonard Jones; 8 vols.; London: Heinemann and New York: Putnam's, 1919) 6. 231; adapted.

21. Philostratos *Vit. Ap.* 8.7.8 (LCL; trans. F. C. Conybeare; 2 vols.; London: Heinemann and New York: Macmillan, 1912) 2. 319; adapted.

faceted lines of stimuli, response, habituation, and adaptation. Catching a glimpse of one moment is rather difficult; the cumulative effect, however, is easier to grasp. Thus I shall start by marking off some limits—a window of change in the life of Roman Ephesos—by calling to mind two snapshots of life there some three centuries apart. The first comes from the well-known account of Acts 18:24–19:41, which purports to recount Paul's first sojourn in Ephesos around the mid-50s CE. In the light of current New Testament scholarship, it is difficult to use Acts as a historical source for reconstructing actual events of Paul's day.[22] Using Acts uncritically as evidence for the social and religious situation in Ephesos during the midfirst century will prove misleading at the very least. The details of the story provide more information about the author's own situation or circumstances.

Current scholarship generally locates Luke-Acts in an urban context,[23] and at least one recent study has suggested placing its composition in Ephesos itself, sometime around the turn of the second century.[24] Scholars often suggest that the details of Acts 18–20 come from firsthand knowledge of life at Ephesos at that same time. In particular, the episode recording the silversmiths' riot (Acts 19:23–44) yields a number of such details.[25] Paul's "friendship" with sympathetic asiarchs (Acts 19:31) has received the bulk of the attention,[26] but one should note the role of the *grammateus* ("clerk") of the city

22. See the discussion by Gerd Lüdemann, *Early Christianity According to the Traditions in Acts: A Commentary* (Minneapolis: Fortress, 1989) 1–18. The basic view is that of Ernst Haenchen, *The Acts of the Apostles* (1971; reprinted Oxford: Blackwell, 1982).

23. See Philip Esler, *Community and Gospel in Luke-Acts: The Social and Political Motivations of Lucan Theology* (SNTSM 57; Cambridge: Cambridge University Press, 1987) 14, 30, although Esler himself argues for a location in Antioch on the Orontes (p. 231 n. 36).

24. Peter Lampe, *Die Lokalisation der Lukas-Leser* (Tübingen: Mohr/Siebeck, 1992).

25. G. H. R. Horsley, "Silversmiths at Ephesos (*I.Eph.* VI. 2212)," *New Documents Illustrating Early Christianity* 4 (1979) 7–10.

26. See, for example, Ernst Haenchen (*The Acts of the Apostles*, 574), who argues persuasively that the portrayal of the asiarchs as attracted to Paul's teaching is not likely to be historical.

and the reference to its neokorate status (Acts 19:35). One senses a uniquely Ephesian character to the narrative. The reference to the city as "neokoros of Artemis" sounds as if it were an accepted and long-established label. Yet the first attested occurrence of the term at Ephesos, either in epigraphic or numismatic remains, comes from the time of Nero.[27] Thus, at best it would seem to have been a new accolade for the city in Paul's day; at worst, if one posits a date later in Nero's reign, the phrase would not yet have been operative. Dating this phrase to the time of Nero is problematic, however, since the neokorate status was usually reserved for local versions of the imperial cult, and only became more commonplace in Asia toward the end of the first century. Ephesos did not receive its first imperial neokorate until the time of Domitian, in 89, but after the *damnatio memoriae* the neokoros was recast as honoring Vespasian.[28] A neokorate designation earlier than that under Domitian is not attested.[29] In other words, the phrase "neokoros of Artemis" probably does not date to the days of Paul, although it was likely known by the time of the writing of Acts nearer the turn of the second century. While "neokoros of Artemis" may have become a civic slogan under Nero, prior to its more typical appearance later in Ephesos for the imperial cult,[30] the setting reflected in Acts seems anachronistic, even if it does suggest direct knowledge of Ephesos at a later date.

I have argued recently that Acts portrays characterizations and conventions of urban life at the time when it was written as part of its peculiar interpretation of the process of expansion of the Christian

27. Oster, "Ephesus as a Religious Center," 1702, based on Stefan Karwiese's dating of numismatic evidence to as late as ca. 65 CE, compare "Ephesos: C. Numismatische Teil," PWSup 12 (1970) 330. See also Richard Oster, "Note on Acts 19:23–41 and an Ephesian Inscription," *HTR* 77 (1984) 233–37; idem, "Numismatic Windows into the Social World of Early Christianity: A Methodological Inquiry," *JBL* 101 (1982) 215–16; idem, "Ephesian Artemis as an Opponent of Early Christianity," *JAC* 19 (1976) 30–31.

28. *IvE* II 232–43.

29. See, for example, *IvE* VI 2053–56, which comes from the granting of the third neokorate in 211 CE.

30. As discussed by Magie, *Roman Rule*, 2. 1432–34; see Price, *Rituals and Power*, 64–68.

movement.[31] A crucial factor in each of the episodes in Acts 16–21 is Paul's encounter with numerous foreigners, who like himself have moved into urban centers. In the section concerning Ephesos, for example, one finds the disciples of John the Baptist (Acts 20:1–7), the synagogue community—specifically Apollos from Alexandria (Acts 18:24; 19:8, 33)—and Paul's own co-workers, including Prisca and Aquila from Corinth (Acts 18:19) and Gaius and Aristarchus from Macedonia (Acts 19:29). It seems to me that the riot is portrayed in large measure as a reaction against these non-Ephesian elements. This reaction is stereotyped in the response of the crowd (Acts 19:33–34), when the Jewish leader Alexander tries to address the people; the fact that the crowd recognized him as a "Jew"—that is, a foreigner— prompts their reaction. Given this tone in Acts, one may begin to ponder the ostensible role of the friendly asiarchs who advised Paul. Where do they come from and why do they show such favor to foreigners? Whatever might have really happened in Paul's own day, the author of Acts seems to think that the perceptions of locals concerning the foreignness of Paul, other Jews, and on the whole the earliest followers of the Christian movement is a key issue.

Another snapshot, from roughly the same area of town, is set approximately three centuries later. Somewhere along the later Arkadian Street there stood an inscription on a largish marble plaque (nearly 2 m square),[32] beginning with what appears to be the opening of a letter: "Abgar Ukkama, Toparch, to Jesus, the good savior,[33] who has appeared in the city of Jerusalem. Greetings." It is indeed a version of the apocryphal correspondence between Abgar and Jesus, also known from Eusebius.[34] On epigraphic grounds, the inscription is dated to the fifth or sixth century.

---

31. See L. Michael White, "Visualizing the 'Real' World of Acts 16: Toward Construction of a Social Index," in idem and O. Larry Yarbrough, eds., *The Social World of the First Christians: Essays in Honor of Wayne A. Meeks* (Minneapolis: Fortress, 1995) 234–61.

32. The inscription is published as *IvE* I 46.

33. Perhaps σώτηρ should be translated simply as "healer."

34. See Eusebius *Hist. eccl.* 1.13.6–10.

A parallel version of this text was found at Philippi, also in epigraphic form from a roughly comparable date.[35] These two epigraphic versions are textually related and show some divergence from the text in Eusebius. Yet another copy in epigraphic form was found at Ankyra.[36] This suggests that the epigraphic version had a separate transmission from the literary tradition of Eusebius.

One need not assume that this inscription primarily served an apotropaic function, as is usually proposed.[37] Instead, it may be suggested that the public display reflects an early attempt by Christians in the postpagan era to employ the known form of imperial decrees in support of an emergent Christian identity. Perhaps it was meant to stand prominently along or near the old processional route, now reoriented to ecclesiastical ends for the council of 431 CE. It would have been read as a royal decree in the form of a letter according honors to Jesus. The public representations suggested in this case reflect a significant change of status for the Christian movement in Ephesian society from that suggested above for Acts. As confirmed by a royal decree, Jesus is no longer a despised foreigner. Yet, the very form used to establish this claim still employs the standards, conventions, and assumptions of the old epigraphic ideology of imperial days. In Ephesos and other major Aegean cities one could hardly miss the pronouncements of eastern kings, now living as "friends of

35. See Denis Feissel, *Recueil des inscriptions chrétiennes de Macedoine* (BCHSup 8; Paris: Boccard, 1983) no. 222, but known since the early part of this century.

36. See Stephen Mitchell, "Regional Epigraphic Catalogues of Asia Minor: Reports," *Anatolian Studies* 27 (1977) 92–96 (no. 37).

37. This idea is based on Procopius (*De bello* 2.12.26), who in the sixth century describes the legend regarding its eventual display on the city wall of Edessa when the town was under siege. Reliance on the Procopius text may also underlie the later terminal date assigned to the inscriptions from Ephesos and Philippi. This is still the assumption of Feissel (see n. 35 above) and others going back to the work of F. Hiller von Gaertringen and M. von Oppenheim, "Höhleninschrift von Edessa mit dem Briefe Jesu an Abgar," *Sitzungsberichte der Berliner Akademie der Wissenschaften, Philosophische-historische Klasse* (1914) 817–828, as followed by W. Bauer in Hennecke-Schneemelcher, *NTApoc*, 1. 439; cf. Alain Desreumaux, *Histoire du roi Abgar et de Jésus* (Brussels: Brepols, 1993) 56.

Rome" and benefactors of the cities.[38] These two snapshots reflect a
significant change in the perception accorded to the Christian presence at Ephesos. Given the form of the latter, however, one may also
ask how much has really changed.

Charting Changes in the Urban Landscape

As suggested above, the notion of Romanization at Ephesos faces
some problems. In terms of urban building programs, the great growth
of Ephesos occurred after Domitian and continued through the Antonine
period. The remainder of this study begins to analyze some aspects of
the social change that occurred with and through this phase of urban
development. Subsequent developments of the later third to fifth centuries were predicated on this middle phase. Instead of assuming a
simple process of Romanization, then, one must chart more carefully
the archaeological and historical evidence from Ephesos for its own
process of urban development, focusing on three areas: the role of
local demographics, the pace and scale of its urban building programs, and the changing social location of "foreigners" or immigrants
as motivating forces of urban development.

Demographic Indicators

By the middle of second century CE, Ephesos was the most prosperous and important city in the eastern empire, with the exception of

38. For comparable decrees by client kings and petty potentates from the
eastern empire and from demonstrable historical contexts in Aegean cities,
note the following cases: from the early empire, the Thracian king Roemitalkes
and his son Kotys and grandson Raskouporis at Philippi (*BCH* 56 [1932] 203)
and Athens (*IG* III 552–53); Pythodoris, wife of Polemon, king of Pontos at
Athens (*OGIS* 376) and Smyrna (*OGIS* 377); Herod of Judaea and his family
members at Delos (*OGIS* 417) and Athens (*OGIS* 414; *IG* II² 3440–41, 3437–
439; see also *OGIS* 363); and Antiochos III and IV of Commagene at Athens
(*OGIS* 405–6; see also 383, 410). From the second century, one finds Prince
C. Julius Antiochos Epiphanes Philopappos, a grandson of Antiochos IV of
Commagene and a friend of Plutarch at Athens (*IG* II² 3112, 1759, 4511,
3451; see Plutarch *Quaest. conv.* 628a; idem, *Quomodo adulator* 27). Similarly at Ephesos the role of such foreign nobility is seen in the inscription of
C. Julius Agrippa, the son of C. Julius Alexander Rex (a descendant of Herod
the Great through the line of Tigranes V of Armenia), commemorating his

Alexandria. It was also one of the largest, and the building programs of the Flavian and Antonine periods seem to reflect marked growth commencing with the reign of Domitian. However, in the typical use of the term "Romanization" one tends to assume an imposition from the top of the hierarchy onto an otherwise fairly static population. Is this view warranted?

The total population of Ephesos in the second and third centuries is usually estimated at approximately 200,000 to 225,000, based on a demos—in this case, the male citizenry—of approximately 40,000.[39] Based on the usual population figures for the Roman Empire, Ephesos is then only behind Rome (approximately 800,000 to 1,000,000) and Alexandria (approximately 300,000) in size. It was slightly larger than Antioch, Pergamon, or Smyrna, and about double the size of Miletos and Sardeis.[40] Not all the population lived within the city proper, since these figures assume the extramural or "country" (*chora*) districts attached to the city.[41] There are two further questions for analysis: Are these numbers accurate, or at least representative? More significantly, was the size of the population relatively constant?

One can only guess regarding the first question. Many of the traditional discussions of population, including those of Beloch, were based on the exaggerated numbers found in ancient historical literature. J. C. Russell severely criticized these estimates, and on the basis

---

benefactions to the city in the second century (*IvE* V 1537; see no. 85 in the appendix below).

39. T. R. S. Broughton, "Asia," in Tenney Frank, *An Economic Survey of Ancient Rome* (6 vols.; Baltimore: Johns Hopkins University Press, 1938) 4. 813. The size of the demos is based on a reference to Aurelius Barenius having fed 40,000 citizens in the early third century. Compare the comment of Galen (*De naturalibus facultatibus* 5.49) regarding his native city of Pergamon: "If then our citizens number as many as 40,000; so also if you add their wives and slaves, you will find yourself admitting that you have increased to more than 120,000 people" (quoted in Broughton, "Asia," in Frank, *Economic Survey*, 4. 812).

40. Broughton, "Asia," 4. 812–15. These figures were typically drawn from the pioneering work of Julius Beloch, *Die Bevölkerung der griechisch-römischen Welt* (Leipzig: Hinrichs, 1886) 242.

41. See Richard Duncan-Jones, *The Economy of the Roman Empire*, 259–61. For Asia, see also A. H. M. Jones, *Cities of the Eastern Roman Provinces* (2d ed.; Oxford: Clarendon, 1971) 77–79, 302–5.

of urban space, using a model of population density, argued that these numbers must have been much smaller. For Ephesos he suggested a total population in the early Roman empire of 51,000, while only Smyrna, at 90,000, was a larger Asian city.[42] One must question the use of urban space as an accurate measure of population, since the crucial factors in the equation are the habitable area and the density figure. Russell had calculated the habitable area of Ephesos at 345 hectares with a density value of 147.8 people per hectare (2.47 acres). The actual physical extent of the habitable areas of most of these ancient cities is not clear from archaeological evidence. The value of his hypotheses regarding density is also questionable. Russell had calculated the density of Rome at 200 people per hectare with a total population of only 350,000 at its peak under Augustus—"by medieval standards, a relatively crowded city."[43] In contrast, MacMullen suggests that the actual population density of Rome was perhaps 200 per acre—nearly 2.5 times more dense—and maybe more.[44] The estimates of density for a number of Roman towns based largely on the archaeological evidence suggest that people were much more crowded than Russell thought. The estimates for the walled area of Ostia, for example, range from 300 to 840 per hectare (or approximately 120 to 340 per acre).[45]

With regard to the population of Ephesos, one could easily increase Russell's figure to 125,000 to 170,000 simply by recalculating the density along the lines suggested by MacMullen.[46] Recent archaeo-

42. Josiah Cox Russell, *Late Ancient and Medieval Population* (TAPA 48.3; Philadelphia: American Philosophical Society, 1958) 80–81. Russell's estimates are consistently lower than those of Beloch. For example, Russell estimates an Alexandrian population of 216,000 in the first century and 122,000 by the fourth (p. 79). On other early attempts at demographic calculation, see Tim G. Parkin, *Demography and Roman Society* (Baltimore: Johns Hopkins University Press, 1992) 58–66; for the case of Alexandria, see p. 64.

43. Russell, *Late Ancient and Medieval Population*, 65.

44. Ramsay MacMullen, *Roman Social Relations*, 63. For the density data, he cites Beloch, *Bevölkerung der griechisch-römischen Welt*, 410.

45. See the discussion of Duncan-Jones, *Economy of the Roman Empire*, 276.

46. That is, using Russell's figure of 345 hectares but a density value of either 147.8 per acre or 200 per acre. Still, one would not suspect that the

logical work suggests a wider geographical distribution of the population at Ephesos including outlying village districts in the Kaÿstros Valley.[47] Russell's estimate of the habitable area is also too low. The population of Ephesos was more than 180,000—and probably slightly larger than Pergamon—with a free adult male population of approximately 28.6% of the total.[48] Several recent studies of historical demographics suggest that at 180,000 to 200,000 such an urban population far exceeds anything in European history until modern times, with rare exceptions, such as Alexandria or Rome.[49] Was this population static in size and makeup?

Ancient sources indicate that Ephesos grew appreciably in size under Roman rule because of its prestige and geographic position.[50] The bulk of these references come from the second and third centuries CE. When did this population boom occur? Specifically, how should it be correlated with the changing picture of the urban development of Ephesos? How does population growth occur? Another comment by Philostratos provides a useful correlation: "All men are carried there as to their native land, and no one is so senseless and inclined to deny the obvious that the city is the common treasury of Asia and her resource in need, and no one is so carping as to criticize

population density of Ephesos was quite as high as that at Rome, given what is presently known about the layout of the city.

47. On population groups in surrounding villages, see below n. 84.

48. See Duncan-Jones, *Economy of the Roman Empire*, 259–60, 264 n. 4.

49. See Peter N. Stearns, *European Society in Upheaval: Social History since 1750* (2d ed.; New York: Macmillan, 1975) 63–65 (for a substantial bibliography on the modern period, see pp. 340–41). The majority of recent discussions in historical demography are based on studies from early modern Europe, see esp. E. A. Wrigley, "A Simple Model of London's Economic Importance in Changing English Society and Economy 1650–1750," in idem and Philip Abrams, eds., *Towns in Societies: Essays in Economic History and Historical Sociology* (Cambridge: Cambridge University Press, 1978) 295–309; Jan de Vries, *European Urbanization 1500–1800* (London: Routledge, 1984). For an application of this discussion of population scale to a Roman city, see esp. Willem Jongman, *The Economy and Society of Pompeii* (1988; reprinted Amsterdam: Gieben, 1991) 27–52, 74–77.

50. In addition to the passages quoted above from Strabo and Philostratos, see also Aelius Aristides *Or.* 14.1, 24; and Dio Chrysostom *Or.* 40.11.

the city's expanse."[51] Philostratos thus links the rise of Ephesos as the preeminent city of Asia with the city's growth both in physical expanse and in population. Moreover, Philostratos observes that foreigners were migrating there in appreciable numbers, as to a new homeland.

Given mortality and fertility rates in ancient Roman cities, it is unlikely that large cities were able to maintain a constant population—much less to grow—without substantial infusions from outside population sources.[52] The key example of this process is, of course, the city of Rome itself, which grew to unprecedented proportions compared to any city in the ancient world of Europe or the Mideast.[53] In the case of Rome, however, this process occurred much earlier, in the first century, and is correlated with what may be called the Romanization of the Italian towns.[54] Population growth must have been the result of the movement of people either from other cities or from the countryside.[55] The three key factors that determine the size and composition of a population in demographic studies are fertility (birthrate), mortality (deathrate), and migration.[56] Most studies of ancient populations have concentrated on projecting life expectancy and the ratio of births to deaths based on the available evidence, largely epigraphic, for the age of individuals at death.[57] There are, however, some difficulties associated with the nature of this evidence—

51. Philostratos *Vit. Soph.* 1.23 (LCL; trans. Wilmer Cave Wright; London: Heinemann and New York: Putnam's, 1922).

52. Russell (*Late Ancient and Medieval Population*, 73–79, 139–41) argues that the population of the Roman world, including the city of Rome itself, generally was in decline from the first to the fourth centuries and until the beginning of the medieval period. This view is no longer generally accepted, but his observations are worth noting for their relevance to the difficulty in maintaining a steady population level.

53. This is one of the main thrusts of the studies by Keith Hopkins, *Conquerors and Slaves* (Cambridge: Cambridge University Press, 1978) 1–98; and idem, *Death and Renewal* (Cambridge: Cambridge University Press, 1983) 69–118.

54. See Peter Brunt, *Italian Manpower* (Oxford: Oxford University Press, 1971).

55. See MacMullen, *Roman Social Relations*, 55–60.

56. Parkin, *Demography and Roman Society*, 72.

57. For the epigraphic discussions, see esp. Franz Georg Maier, "Römische Bevölkerungsgeschichte und Inschriftenstatistik," *Historia* 2 (1953/54) 318–

which comes mostly from funerary monuments—and whether it is generally representative for statistical purposes.[58] More recently, attention has shifted to the evidence of alimentary foundations as a way of calculating age groups within civic populations.[59] Reliable statistical information regarding migration patterns has been even more difficult to derive. Migration is a key factor, especially in dealing with urban population growth; it may also have a significant impact on the overall age and gender composition of a population.[60] Among immigrant groups the proportion of males might increase significantly, as is indicated among Greek immigrants to Miletos in the third and second centuries BCE.[61]

It is likely that the usual net population change[62] rate for the Roman world was negative, more in the range of −0.5% per annum because of an excess mortality, where deaths exceeded births.[63] It is estimated that infant mortality was especially high: approximately 33%

51; Richard Duncan-Jones, "City Population in Roman Africa," *JRomS* 53 (1963) 85–90.

58. Parkin, *Demography and Roman Society*, 4–26. See also n. 61 below.

59. See Richard Duncan-Jones, "Human Numbers in Towns and Town-Organizations of the Roman Empire: The Evidence of Gifts," *Historia* 13 (1964) 199–208.

60. Ibid., 72, 176 n. 11, 135.

61. Ibid., 99. Based on epigraphic evidence, the ratio of males to females in this immigrant population was approximately 3:1 and the ratio of adults to children was about 5:2. In other words, where in a typical population one would assume that the distribution would be approximately 50% adult (evenly split male and female) and 50% children (and perhaps slightly more children than adults), this case yields an adult male component of nearly 55% with the remainder split between adult females (approximately 18%) and children (approximately 27%). Needless to say, such a composition would seriously affect birthrates as well.

62. Parkin (*Demography and Roman Society*, appendix B, tables 11–12) simply uses the term "growth ratio" based on the standard demographic tables. This "growth ratio" is ultimately more complex, since it is a function of the births and deaths (based on the probable age structure of the total population) and the gross reproductive rate (based on the number of females of childbearing age). My use of the term "net population change" assumes Parkin's discussion of the basic population structure for the Roman world; see pp. 67–90, esp. 86–89.

63. Ibid., 89. In general, it seems that the normal fertility rate in premodern European societies was roughly constant, owing in part to patterns of nursing

of all children born within the first year, and by the fifth year approximately 50% had died.[64] In other words, on average less than half of all children born lived until puberty and entered the reproductive pool. In some cases, the normal ratio of births to deaths might have been as low as −1.0% per annum.[65] Hence, assuming a relatively stable population base, it would appear overall that the population was actually shrinking or, at best, barely holding constant, depending on which excess mortality rate one adopts. These calculations do not take into account the extraordinary mortality rates accruing from wars, particularly invasions, or periods of famine or plague.[66] Under imperial rule, cities like Ephesos were faced with the need to stimulate population growth.

To imagine their dilemma let us assume that the population of Ephesos began at only 100,000, half of the traditional estimate but still a very large urban center by ancient standards. The ancient sources indicate that it grew impressively; perhaps it doubled over the period of time—by approximately 150 CE[67]—to reach the traditional esti-

---

and lactation. Up until ca. 1650–1750, however, the birthrate never exceeded the mortality rate. Medieval population in Europe remained fairly constant as a result of limited geographic mobility and a roughly even birth to mortality ratio per year. This ratio was usually in the range of 30–40 births to deaths per 1000. Consequently, in the medieval period the *net population change* (that is, the resultant ratio of births to deaths) on an annual basis was usually nil. Compare Stearns, *European Society in Upheaval*, 63–65; and Parkin, *Demography and Roman Society*, 75–87.

64. Ibid., 93. On the impact of this level of mortality, see Peter Brown, *The Body and Society: Men, Women, and Sexual Renunciation in Early Christianity* (New York: Columbia University Press, 1988) 5–17; Hopkins, *Death and Renewal*, 201–55.

65. This is the figure suggested by Hopkins (ibid., 69–74), who recognizes that this figure emphasizes the picture of the negative population growth and the concomitant need for replacement in order to achieve the monumental growth of Rome. The lower figures come in part from the suggestions of lower fertility rates, especially in Italy and cities in general, as posited by Brunt (*Italian Manpower*, 140–45).

66. The province of Asia faced two devastating plagues at about this same time, one later in the second century and the other in the 260s. See below n. 109.

67. The dates used here are meant to be merely representative for purposes of setting up demographic projections. This date reflects the midpoint of the

mates of 200,000. Positing an average annual net population change of –1.0%, consistent with that proposed for other Roman cities of the time,[68] the base population would decline over a century to only 36,603. An average influx of 2,578 people per annum would therefore be necessary to double the population in 100 years (that is, starting at 50 CE). Taking Parkin's more cautious net population change rate of –.05% per annum, one would still need on average an annual influx of 1,769 new residents to double the population in a century.[69] At a flat net population change rate of 0% per annum—the stable population proposed for the medieval period—an influx of 1,000 new residents per annum would be necessary.

In terms of the basic demographic discussions, two other points remain. First, these calculations assume that the age and gender structure of the immigrant population are generally the same as that of the base population. This, however, may not always have been the case, especially in situations where the influx represents a predominantly male labor force or military veterans. In such circumstances, the actual net influx per annum would have to be even higher since the net reproductive rate of the influx group would be lower than that of the base population, while the mortality rate would remain relatively constant.

Second, given an overall negative net change in the base population and the concomitant influx of new residents to achieve growth, over time the new residents and their descendants become an increasing percentage of the total population. For example, using the raw calculations above at a net population change of –1.0% per annum, the residents who immigrate to Ephesos—and their descendants—would reach half of the total population (50.3%) in only 33 years and at 100

---

second century, when substantial population growth seems to be suggested by the literary sources noted above. Chronological elements, however, must be checked against other archaeological evidence. Thus, the actual limits might better be set at approximately 80 to 180. See below.

68. See Hopkins, *Conquerors and Slaves*, 96–98; the figures are also used by Willem Jongman based on Rome and Pompeii; see *The Economy and Society of Pompeii*, 65–96.

69. These calculations are based on average figures per year and do not attempt to contend with annual fluctuations. As a result, the actual influx figures would most likely be marginally higher.

years would be 81.7% of the total population of 200,000. Using the more conservative net population change rate of –0.5% per annum, the immigrants and their descendants would reach half of the total population (50.2%) in 50 years and at 100 years would be 69.7% of the total population of 200,000. These gross growth models suggested for second- to third-century Ephesos not only require a substantial influx of immigrants, but will also have a considerable impact on the overall ethnic makeup of the city. It may clarify why attitudes toward "foreigners" were a topic of concern, as reflected in the two snap-shots of Ephesian life noted above.

These general findings are summarized in table 1 below for four models of urban population change, assuming a base population of

Table 1

Doubling the Urban Population
Model Calculations of Demographic Change

Population	Model 1 Roman 1	Model 2 Roman 2	Model 3 medieval	Model 4 early modern
Base population (at year 0)	100,000	100,000	100,000	100,000
Net population change rate per annum (births-deaths per 1000)	–1.0%	–0.5%	0 (even)	+0.5%
Influx rate per annum	2,578	1,769	1,000	274
Parity point (year base/influx even)	at year 33 (influx = 50.3%)	at year 50 (50.2%)	at year 100 (50%)	———
percent of total influx (at year 100)	81.7%	69.7%	50%	17.7%
Total population (at year 100)	200,000	200,000	200,000	200,000

100,000 that doubles in a century. Models 1 and 2 represent the most common net population change rates suggested for the Roman imperial period. Model 3 represents the common rate for the stable population of the medieval period; model 4, for the rapid growth of the early modern period. The graphs in figure 1 represent the two models of the Roman period and show the growth curve and intersection points for the two groups, the indigenous population (or base) and the immigrants (or influx). The graphs in figure 2 show the relative proportion of the total population for the same two groups as a function of time.

The figures project the order of magnitude of population change, rather than an actual population estimate for Ephesos. Future discussions of the actual population of Ephesos in imperial times must await further archaeological work. The actual rate of influx to Ephesos annually must have been relatively high in order to sustain a pattern of net population growth over a relatively long period of time.

Building Correlations

While there are a variety of ways to evaluate the process of urban development, probably the most discernible—both to moderns and to the ancients—is through architecture or building programs. Hence, I am interested in how quickly the old Hellenistic city of Ephesos, which had been founded under Lysimachos in the third century BCE, came to look more like the Roman city of Ephesos, and how rapidly it grew in size. Scholars have typically assumed that the growth of Ephesos, as with other cities of the Greek world, occurred as a uniform and rather rapid process under the early emperors, beginning with Augustus.

For the present discussion, however, it is important to note the relatively late date at which most cities in the Aegean rim went through Roman architectural development. Such courses of architectural development, albeit with local variations, may be observed at Corinth, Athens, Thessaloniki, Miletos, Sardeis, Aphrodisias, and even Pergamon. This observation calls to mind another penetrating insight from MacMullen, who said, "in Roman history the salient fact in the earlier

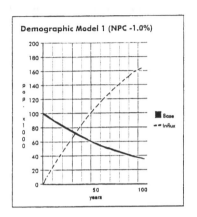
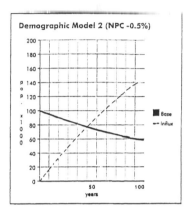

Figure 1: Demographic Models of Roman Population Change
(Refer to Table 1; Total population = Base +Influx)

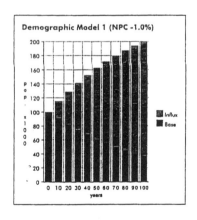
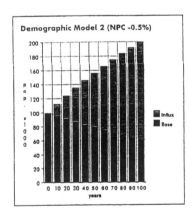

Figure 2: Relative Proportions in Roman Demographic Models
(Refer to Table 1)

half appears to be the assembling of an empire, and in the latter half the decorating of it."[70] At least outside of Italy, urban development of the empire was a product of this "latter half."

In applying this perspective to Ephesos, one must ask whether the process of urbanization as seen through architectural development also suggests these phases. The following chart, a summary compilation of numerous archaeological and epigraphic sources, will help to organize the evidence.[71]

Table 2

The Urban Development of Ephesos under Roman Rule
(organized by period and region)

Regional Sectors:	*Sponsors or Benefactors:*
1. Temple of Artemis	R = Emperor or provincial official
	[* = projects by different emperors]
2. State Agora - Magnesian Gate	L = Local citizen(s) of Ephesos
	(includes civic dedication)
3. Embolos - Marble Road	A = Asian noncitizen (including
	asiarchs)
4. Theater - Harbor	P = Resident foreigners (other than
	provincial officials)
5. North Stadium Street - Koressian Gate	

70. Ramsay MacMullen, "Roman Elite Motivation," *Past and Present* 88 (1980) 3–16, reprinted in idem, *Changes in the Roman Empire*, 19; see also 13–24.

71. Dieter Knibbe and Wilhelm Alzinger, "Ephesos vom Beginn der römischen Herrschaft in Kleinasien bis zum Ende der Principatszeit," *ANRW* 2.7.1 (1979) 748–830; Keil, *Ephesos*; and Broughton, "Asia," 4. 719–53. A helpful chart for the city at the time of Vibius Salutaris (ca. 103 BCE to 4 CE) is given by Rogers, *Sacred Identity of Ephesos*, 128–35. I have generally followed the regional divisions suggested by Rogers, based on his useful correlation of the city plan with the processional route. Since this is a simplified table, I shall not try to list current bibliography for each building; I have tried, however, to take into account the recent archaeological work of the Austrian excavators as much as possible.

Sector   New Building   Edifice Renovated

Period 1: Late Republican (133–31 BCE)

2. Bouleuterion   L
   Tomb of Luke   L
   Temple of Divus Julias
      and Dea Roma   L
3. Monument of Memmius   L

Period 2: Julio-Claudian (31 BCE–81 CE)

	sponsor or benefactor		*sponsor*
1.		Temenos of the	
		Artemision	R
2. Basilike Stoa	R		
Prytaneion	R?		
Peristyle with double			
monument	R?		
Tomb of Sextilius Pollio	L		
		Temple of Dea Roma and	
		Divus Julius	
3. Shops of lower Embolos	L?		
Slope Houses 1 & 2			
Octagon			
Heroon of Androklos			
West Gate of Tetragonos Agora			
Gate of Mazaios			
and Mithridates	R		
Doric Stoa of Marble Road	R		
4.		Theater (completion)	R
so-called Palace		Theater (renovation)	R*
of Proconsul (?)	R		
Harbor Gate	R		
5.		Stadium	L(P?)

Period 3: Flavians and Antonines (81–212 CE)

sponsor or benefactor		*sponsor*	
1.		Temenos of Artemision	R*
		Temenos of Artemision	R*
		Temenos of Artemision	R*
2.		Magnesian Gate	R?
		East Gymnasium	
State Agora	L		
Monumental Fountain	L		
Temple of the Flavian Sebastoi			
Hydrekdocheion	L	Prytaneion	L/A
Odeion	A	Bouleuterion	L/A
Fountain of Domitian	L		
(=Memmius Monument)			
3.		Paving of the Embolos	L
Fountain of Trajan	L		
Smaller Temple of Artemis			
(=Temple of Hadrian)	L/R		
Baths of Varius	L		
Latrines	L	Slope Houses 1 & 2	
Library of Celsus	P		
Second Neokorate Temple?		West Gate of	P
Sarapeion		Tetragonos Agora	
4.		Theater	A/P
		(additions/analemma)	
"Xystoi"	L	Paving of "Stoa of	
(=Verulanus Hall)		Verulanus"	L
		Decoration of "Bankers'	
		Stoa"	P
Harbor Baths			
Harbor Gymnasium			P
Olympieion (includes so-called			
Market Basilica, later known as Church of			
Mary or Church of the Councils)			R

5. Macellum

	Paving Square of	
	Koressos	A
Vedius Gymnasium	A	
Aquaeduct of Marnas		

The urban landscape of Ephesos owes its basic layout to the Augustan age, but its real development occurred in the second century, as shown by the sheer number of buildings either constructed or renovated during period 3 (from Domitian through the Antonines). It is also notable that the construction in period 2 tends to be either civic dedication or a grant by the emperor or one of his officials, including imperial freedmen. There is a lull between the building activities of Nero, the last Julio-Claudian, and the next phase, which began under Domitian. The pace of urban development in Ephesos quickened markedly under Trajan and Hadrian; it continued under the Antonines before another lull in the later third century prior to the renewed building activities of the fourth and fifth centuries. If one were to consider the size of the buildings or projects involved, and hence also some indication of relative costs, the gap between periods 2 and 3 would widen further in terms of the overall impact on the shape of the urban landscape.[72] A good example is the way in which the corner where the Embolos intersects Marble Street (at the southeast corner of the Tetragonos Agora) came to be dominated by new architecture in period 3. The Library of Celsus, built by a non-Ephesian during a local initiative at the time of Trajan, overshadows both in height and in style the older Gate of Mazaios and Mithridates, the imperial freedmen of the Augustan period. Similarly, the region to the northwest of the theater (regions 4 and 5) was taken over by the construction of three monumental complexes: the Harbor Gymnasium and the Harbor Baths, both begun under Domitian, and the Olympieion complex, built under Hadrian.

72. This observation is based on a general estimate only from the perspective of the ground plans of the new buildings in period 3. A more systematic measurement based on ground plane size, combined with a calculation based on the height of buildings, would not only confirm this observation, but I suspect would widen the gap.

Especially under Hadrian and the Antonines, some of the acceleration in building projects may have resulted from imperial initiatives. During Flavian rule, even though there was a lull in urban development at Ephesos itself, an imperial plan for urban centralization was begun; it linked the main cities to one another through new road and communication networks, thus creating a higher level of prosperity for the urban dwellers.[73] Trajan's program of urbanization created further centralization by integrating elements of imperial administration with the traditionally autonomous local councils.[74] Yet this change in provincial administration did not thwart local initiatives; instead, it seems to have stimulated them, as evidenced by the number of cases involving disputes, accusations, and competition among the main cities of Asia.[75] The implications for the status, wealth, and mobility of local individuals from Ephesos and Asia will become apparent later in this discussion.

Hadrian sought to stimulate building programs further by making his own personal presence felt; according to Dio Cassius, he "aided the cities. . . with supreme munificence (μεγαλοπρεπέστατα). . . and he assisted practically all of them, giving to some a water supply, to others harbors, food, public works, money, or various honors, each according to its own need."[76] Thus, Hadrian dealt directly with local groups, such as the council of Ephesos and the *koinon* of Asia, when he visited Ephesos and the surrounding cities.[77] Hadrian's policy of fostering such programs—which he and others called Panhellenism— was to encourage local decurions and assist them in acting as civic benefactors.[78]

---

73. Magie, *Roman Rule*, 1. 566–76.

74. Ibid., 1. 595–99; see also Rogers, *Sacred Identity of Ephesos*, 13–14.

75. Fergus Millar, *The Emperor in the Roman World (31 BC–AD 337)* (Ithaca: Cornell University Press, 1977) 435, 438–40.

76. Dio Cassius *Hist.* 69.5.2. (LCL; trans. Earnest Cary; 9 vols.; London: Heinemann and Cambridge, MA: Harvard University Press, 1954) 8. 435.

77. *SIG* 839; see also Magie, *Roman Rule*, 1. 612–22.

78. Anna S. Benjamin, "The Altars of Hadrian in Athens and Hadrian's Panhellenic Program," *Hesperia* 32 (1963) 57–86. A classic case is the wealthy T. Claudius Herodes Atticus from Greece, the patron of much of the contemporaneous urban building at Athens and Corinth. Flourishing under Hadrian and Pius, he was adlected to the Senate and served for a time as *corrector* of

Hadrian and the early Antonines continued a practice begun under Trajan of promoting local Greek and Asian aristocrats into public office and eventually the Senate in recognition of their civic benefactions at Ephesos and like cities. The sponsors of the building projects in period 3 at Ephesos are local benefactors, whether citizens or noncitizens of Ephesos, and their gifts significantly outnumber direct imperial grants. Thus, while imperial initiatives were still at work, local interests were clearly being stimulated to decorate the expanding landscape of urban Ephesos in the second century. Both wealth and motivation were necessary for this enterprise. Public adornments, particularly inscriptions and honorific statues, increase significantly during this same period and are a function of the display of wealth as well as civic pride. The peak of surviving epigraphic evidence comes from the later second century; and although such evidence diminishes, it does not disappear in the third and fourth centuries during the shift to Christian rule. The degree to which this epigraphic habit reflects the influence of Roman tastes and forms suggests that in a city like Ephesos the pace of influence in urban life for both locals and foreigners was relatively later than one may have previously supposed.[79] What is significant about this enterprise at Ephesos is the degree to which non-Ephesians appear in the record. The archaeological data corroborate the general scale of the demographic growth outlined in the previous section. The magnitude of the building programs also required a substantial work force, both in skilled artisans and labor. Moreover, the style and scale of such buildings required an influx of materials and perhaps new building techniques, not to mention the economic resources to secure such skills, labor, materials, and land.

Asia. Herodes Atticus also built a bath at Alexandria Troas at a cost of 7,000,000 drachmae (Magie, *Roman Rule*, 1. 626). See also Paul Graindor, *Un Milliardaire antique: Hérode Atticus et sa famille* (Cairo: Société Anonyme Egyptienne, 1930); W. Ameling, *Herodes Atticus* (2 vols.; Hildesheim: Olms, 1983); J. L. Tobin, "The Monuments of Herodes Atticus" (Ph.D. diss., University of Pennsylvania, 1991).

79. On the proliferation of inscriptions and papyri in terms of the social implications of Romanization, see Ramsay MacMullen, "The Epigraphic Habit in the Roman Empire," *AJP* 103 (1982) 233–46 and the bibliography cited there.

Epigraphic Evidence

Based on both raw demographic projections and building programs, it appears that there was a substantial influx of new population to Ephesos in the second and third centuries. Analyzing the prosopographic data for foreigners at Ephesos will be the basis for this part of the discussion. While one may ultimately want to consider literary sources, such as Aelius Aristides, Dio Cassius, Lucian, or Paul, this study looks at indicators left behind in stone, beginning by sketching out the broader categories for such a prosopography.

The first category, that of persons in imperial service, includes higher ranking imperial officials, such as proconsuls, procurators, and correctors, as well as military officers and their detachments, imperial freedmen or other petty bureaucrats, and members of the imperial family. A large number of the inscriptions from Ephesos come from this category. The sojourn for such individuals would have typically been of specified or limited duration. In a few cases, however, one finds that such officials decided to remain in Ephesos or return there after retiring from the imperial service. Such individual cases should also be listed as permanent immigrants.[80]

The second category is that of asiarchs and high priests and priestesses of Asia who are not originally from Ephesos. Because of Ephesos's importance in the *koinon* of Asia, especially after the time of Domitian, there were increases in these two honorific offices, especially among non-Ephesian decurions from the other major cities of the *koinon*. These people must have visited Ephesos at times and in some cases were benefactors; it is probable that many of them also had business dealings or interests in Ephesos as a trade center. They often tended to remain loyal to their own hometowns, where they were local civic leaders and public benefactors. One should therefore

---

80. These are given in the catalogue of category 3 in the appendix: Afranius Flavianus, probably from Italy, who served as proconsul of Asia in 103 CE and was later granted Ephesian citizenship (no. 99 [*IvE* II 430]); Aurelios Chryseros, an imperial freedman of the third century who settled in Ephesos with his wife and children (no. 103 [*IvE* VI 2219]); a man (whose name is lost) designated as *Romanos*, honored with a funerary monument by his wife Claudia (given the clear designation for him, one is led to guess that she may have been of local Ephesian stock; see no. 100 [*IvE* VI 2235b]).

include in this category anyone known as asiarch or high priest or priestess of Asia who seems to have maintained permanent residence ~~elsewhere~~ ~~or has no available epigraphic record~~ at Ephesos.[81] In this regard evidence suggests that the imperial cult at Ephesos served as a centralizing force in the provincial organization. Of 138 high priesthoods known from epigraphic evidence, 74% were held by men and 26% by women, but only about 33% to 35% of the total, male and female, were held by Ephesians. Moreover, the number of high priesthoods that women and non-Ephesians held seems to have increased during the second and early third centuries.[82] The neokorate status of Ephesos within the provincial imperial cult, commencing in 89 CE, therefore, seems to have facilitated the interaction of numerous local aristocrats from other cities, many of whom did not become permanent residents at Ephesos.

The third category, that of persons not in imperial posts, is in some ways the most interesting, and is thus the focus for the remainder of this discussion. An epigraphic catalogue for this group is included in the appendix. This group reflects in more direct ways individuals who actually resided in Ephesos and participated in its public life, although some, such as the several victors at the Artemisia noted in this list, were presumably in Ephesos on a temporary basis. Significant

81. A good example are the husband and wife, Alkiphron and Juliane, of Magnesia on Meander (*IvM* 158). They served as priest and priestess of Asia in approximately 54–59 CE, under Nero. The inscription indicates that Juliane was the first woman to hold the office. This was prior to the establishment of the provincial imperial cult in Ephesos proper in 89 CE. Compare T. Claudius Pheseinos and his wife Stratonike from Teos (*IGRR* IV 1571) who likewise served as high priest and priestess in the provincial cult of the emperors in approximately 89/90; they were followed in the office by their daughter Claudia Tryphaina, who like them continued to hold local offices at Teos (see *IvE* II 232; in this study, see appendix, no. 43).

82. For much of these data I am indebted to an unpublished paper by Steve Friesen, "Networks of Religion and Society at Ephesus: Men and Women in the Provincial Highpriesthood," presented at the annual meeting of the Society of Biblical Literature, 1992. On the offices of high priest and priestess of Asia, see R. A. Kearsley, "Some Asiarchs of Ephesos," *New Documents Illustrating Early Christianity* 4 (1987) 46–55; and idem, "A Leading Family of Cibyra and Some Asiarchs of the First Century," *Anatolian Studies* 38 (1988) 43–45.

cases come from those individuals, families, or groups who actually resided in Ephesos on a more permanent basis. This does not preclude the possibility that some of them moved on from Ephesos or traveled and returned to Ephesos.[83] As mentioned earlier in connection with Irenaeus, there was a sizable enclave of Christians from Asia in both Rome and southern Gaul.

This catalogue lists one hundred seventeen inscriptions for different "foreigners" who identify themselves as such in some way; with cross references, the total number of inscriptions is one hundred eighty-three. The catalogue has been arranged geographically according to the place of origin of the persons or groups. The total number of individuals represented is one hundred fifty; in addition, there are nine groups recorded. At least three of the inscriptions seem to refer to enclaves of ethnic Phrygians or Pisidians residing in Ephesos or its satellite villages of the Kaÿstros Valley.[84] Two others reflect Jewish enclaves, one of which is called οἱ ἐν Ἐφέσῳ Ἰουδέοι ("the Jews of Ephesos") while the other seems to be a Jewish youth organization

83. A comprehensive prosopographic catalogue, therefore, would also include a fourth category, that of Ephesians who are known to have moved elsewhere, but this is extraneous to the present discussion on the social makeup of Roman Ephesos. Nonetheless, evidence for movement away from Ephesos is valuable, since it further attests to the need for immigration in order to maintain or increase the overall population. It may also reflect the complex network of relationships operative in the early imperial period, especially among Roman citizens of provincial origin. An example of this fourth category is M. Claudius P. Vedius Antoninus, a decurion of Ephesos who held the offices of asiarch and high priest of Asia (*IvE* III 732, VI 2039). Although already a Roman citizen, he embarked upon an equestrian career (*IvE* III 726) and apparently emigrated. Within another generation his family had achieved senatorial rank, and his grandson Phaedrus Sam(b)inianus was posted as quaestor of Cyprus (*IvE* VII 4110). Nonetheless, the family seems to have maintained some ties with Ephesos (see *IvE* V 1492–93), and his wife left a bequest to the city, for which she was granted an honorific statue from "the fatherland" (*IvE* VII 3077). The Ephesian sophist and civic benefactor T. Flavius Damianus was also a member of this family by marriage (*IvE* III 672). Compare the senator under Trajan, M. Arruntius Claudianus, originally from Xanthos, who is honored at Ephesos, although he may be only an occasional resident (*IvE* III 620; see *IvE* I 27; in this study, see the appendix, no. 74).

84. Appendix, nos. 69–71 (*IvE* VII 3256, 3252, 3254), all referring to the villages of Almura or Magnola.

(νεωτέροι) from Hypaipa.[85] There are also ethnic enclaves or merchant associations from Berytus,[86] Tyre,[87] and Italy,[88] and a guild of Dionysiac artisans (τεχνῖται) from Teos.[89] Unfortunately, there is little indication of the size or makeup of such groups. It is interesting, however, that almost all these inscriptions come from contexts where the group is honoring an individual for beneficence.

Among the individual cases little is heard from members of the laboring classes; a few seem to be craftsmen or artisans and their families.[90] Some cases reflect individuals who may have originally traveled to Ephesos for other reasons, such as the Gallic equestrian and the imperial freedman who married local Asian women and were eventually buried at Ephesos.[91] Some immigrants advanced through the ranks of local Ephesian culture, such as the Karian Chrysaor, son of Bacchios, apparently a noncitizen who was enrolled in the list of *curetes*, special priests of the civic cult of Kybele and Artemis.[92] Nonetheless, the vast majority of the inscriptions where foreign origin is discernible come from members of the upper classes. This fact should not be altogether surprising since the epigraphic habit was primarily an élite medium. It is noteworthy, however, that a large proportion of individuals use the Roman trinominum, which indicates citizenship. It suggests that the impulse to move to Ephesos was especially strong among those who had already accommodated socially to Roman administration. Nonetheless, one should not assume that only those from higher social backgrounds were part of the pattern of immigration. The evidence of the groups noted above suggests that there was a kind of social pyramid, and that ethnic enclaves and groups relied heavily on the networks of support from those of the

---

85. See appendix, nos. 88–89 (*IvE* V 1677, VII 3822).
86. Appendix, no. 90 (*IvE* VI 2215a).
87. Appendix, no. 4 (*IvE* III 614).
88. Appendix, no. 97 (*IvE* II 409, III 658, 800, VI 2058).
89. Appendix, no. 23 (*IvE* I 22).
90. Appendix, nos. 78–80 (*IvE* II 510, 516, VI 2237c); while the first two clearly seem to be Greek artisans, the third may be a dealer in marble and is a Roman citizen.
91. Appendix, nos. 55 (*IvE* V 1553) and 103 (*IvE* VI 2219), respectively.
92. Appendix, no. 68 (*IvE* IV 1028–29).

patronal classes. In other words, for each aristocratic foreigner, one may expect a network of clients or other dependents.[93]

It is striking how many of the immigrants are from other regions of Asia Minor. The corridor of Galatia, Mysia, and Lydia is heavily represented, especially along a route of cities including Ankyra, Dorylaion, Akmoneia, Thyateira, and Hypaipa. Of the one hundred fifty individuals in the third category, forty come from this area alone. The second largest body of immigrants comes from Karia and next from Phrygia and Pisidia. When plotted on a map, it appears that there were some well worn routes to Ephesos that included both the physical and social pathways. The nearby cities of Magnesia, Nysa, Tralles, and Hypaipa, all of which were tied socially and economically to Ephesos, show the intersections of these broader pathways, while the next tier of urban centers, including Pergamon, Akmoneia, and Sardeis seem to be important way stations for the process. A good example is T. Flavius Montanus from Akmoneia, the high priest of Asia who subvented the enlargement of the theater under Trajan. His family and descendants continued to be prominent in Ephesos throughout the second century, and their ties to Akmoneia also continued.[94] A similar case is the family of the asiarch T. Claudius Polydeukes, an equestrian from Magnesia on Meander who received numerous honors at Ephesos in the Antonine period. He was granted Ephesian citizenship, and members of his family eventually held the offices of *agonothetes* and *grammateus* of the city.[95] One of the best known cases is that of the family of T. Julius Celsus Polemaeanus, originally from Sardeis, who was elected to the Senate under Trajan and served as procurator of Asia. The family resided in Ephesos, where Celsus was posthumously honored by his son Aquila with the construction of the library that still carries his name.[96]

---

93. The case of T. Claudius Pheisinos and Stratonike from Teos is one of several individuals known from Teos (see appendix, nos. 23, 42–45) and includes the Dionysiac artisans (see n. 87 above). This guild also honors patrons from its hometown who are now in Ephesos (appendix, no. 23, *IvE* I 22).

94. Appendix, nos. 12–15 (*IvE* III 854, 698, 714).

95. Appendix, nos. 32–34 (*IvE* III 642, II 472, III 676, I 22–23; see *IvM* 187–88).

96. Appendix, nos. 36–39 (*IvE* VII 5101–107, 5112). See n. 72 above.

A good example of the social and geographical movement of these individuals is offered by the family of C. Antius Aulos Julius Quadratus. The family was of Galatian royal ancestry and originally from Ankyra, but it came to have ties through migration and intermarriage to Pergamon, Sardeis, Akmoneia, Tralles, Hypaipa, Mylasa, and Samos. They eventually became citizens of Ephesos.[97] Aulos Julius Quadratus himself was elected to the senate and served as consul under Trajan. He was a leading benefactor and citizen of Sardeis, Pergamon, and Ephesos. The family continued to serve in prominent local offices at Ephesos beyond the year 200. Two of Quadratus's cousins, Julius Amyntianus and A. Julius Amyntas, likewise of Ankyran royal stock, are probably from the side of the family that also produced C. Julius Severus through the lineage of Julia Severa of Akmoneia.[98] They were also related to the family of T. Celsus and Aquila Polemaeanus.[99] C. Julius Severus himself was admitted to the tribunate under Hadrian and served as proconsul of Achaia; later he served as corrector of Bithynia.[100] These cases indicate that Ephesos, as an imperial urban center, attracted local aristocrats from Asia Minor and their clients, retainers, and other economic dependents. This provides a good ex-

97. Appendix, nos. 4–9 (*IvE* III 614, 930, VII 3033–34, V 1538, III 980, IV 1122; see *IGRR* IV 1687, 1729). See also the family tree at *IvE* III 980.

98. Appendix, no. 5 (*IvE* III 930). For C. Julius Severus, see *IGRR* III 173 and *PIR*[2] J 573. Julia Severa is well known as a municipal female archon and imperial priestess at Akmoneia under Nero. While she was from the Galatian royal line, her husband, Lucius Servenius Capito was an equestrian from an Asian colonial family. Their son, L. Servenius Cornutus, was elected to the Senate under Nero, and C. Julius Severus, another descendent, was admitted to the tribunate under Hadrian. Julia Severa is also noted for having donated a building that became the Jewish synagogue at Akmoneia. See White, *Building God's House*, 81–82; and idem, "Finding the Ties that Bind: Issues from Social Description," in idem, ed., *Social Networks in the Early Christian Environment: Issues and Methods for Social History* (Semeia 56; Atlanta: Scholars Press, 1991) 18–20. See also Levick, *Roman Colonies in Southern Asia Minor*, 98–105. M. Julius Severus, probably also a relative, appears as a public benefactor at Philippi; see G. Kasarow, "Inscriptions et antiquités de la Macédoine occidentale," *BCH* 47 (1923) 288–89.

99. See PW 10 (1919) 168–70 (= no. 83); 544–46 (= no. 183); *PIR*[1] I.176; C. S. Walton, "Oriental Senators in Service of Rome: A Study of Imperial Policy down to the Death of Marcus Aurelius," *JRomS* 19 (1920) 38–49.

100. See Magie, *Roman Rule*, 1. 626; *PIR*[1] S 104, 375, 405; *IGRR* III 173.

ample of the social networks of Roman rule, where links exist throughout the social register and from provincial cities to Ephesos itself.[101] A slightly different case, but no less significant for the urban development of Ephesos, is that of C. Vibius Salutaris,[102] an Italian equestrian whose father may have had earlier ties to the Italian merchants association in Ephesos. Having been posted in Mauretania in his earlier career, he eventually settled in Ephesos in approximately 104 CE and was granted citizenship after he made a foundation bequest to the city. The stipulations of this bequest are recorded in a lengthy inscription from the theater and reflect close ties to the public religious processions that celebrate the city's history and sense of sacred identity.[103] The processions, charitable distributions, and collection of statues, for which Salutaris made dedications, not only expressed important links to the civic cult of Artemis, but also integrated elements of the imperial cult. Thus, the alimentary foundation of Salutaris plays on the role of civic benefactor as preserver of sacred identity. Among Salutaris's circle of friends, one may note both the old leading families of Ephesos and those newly arrived. Arruntius Claudianus, Afranius Flavianus, Aquila Polemanus, and Julius Quadratus were his contemporaries, friends, and patrons.[104] The benefactor had patrons, too, and yet his beneficence earned him a kind of peerage.

Conclusion

For C. Vibius Salutaris, the urban development of Ephesos offered a chance for acceptance and advancement. Through civic benefaction he could move beyond the social status to which he might otherwise be limited in his own native context. Salutaris's case is not a tradi-

101. Compare the case of the Lycian family of Licinnia Falvilla from Oenoana as discussed by MacMullen, *Corruption and the Decline of Rome*, 75–79. Some of the individuals in her family tree are provincial or imperial officials, while a number of the marriages reflect direct ties to Ephesian notables.

102. Appendix, no. 98 (*IvE* I 27–35). See Rogers, *Sacred Identity of Ephesos*, 80–115.

103. Ibid., 16–18.

104. Ibid., 14. See nn. 80 and 83 above. For a case in which Salutaris calls Arruntius Claudianus a "friend and patron," see *IvE* III 620.

tional example of Romanization; he was, after all, already Romanized before coming to Ephesos. He was drawn to Ephesos, however, as were the others noted in this study. Together they rebuilt the city with overshadowing architecture and lavish public decoration. They, too, could be called "founders" of the city.[105] The fact that Ephesos provided such an open environment for this reciprocal exchange provides evidence for its success in growth and urban development as well as further social change. The dates of this social change coincide with both demographic shifts and urban building programs. Indeed, they are integrally related.

Through further archaeological work and analysis it will perhaps be possible to detect more subtle lines of social connections and the way in which they influenced the development of Ephesos in the second and third centuries and beyond. One would expect that specific ties to other cities of the region for trade, production, and labor will prove significant evidence.[106] The influence of immigration from other regions of Asia Minor, notably Ankyra, may also be detected in some of the architectural traditions of what is sometime called the Hellenistic revival of the second-century building programs.[107] At the same time, it will inevitably throw into sharper relief the social background of the second sophistic and literary revival that one sees with figures like Plutarch, Dio, and Lucian. Indeed, Lucian was a notable "foreigner," like Plutarch's friend and protégé, Philopappos.[108] In the final analysis, scholars must rethink how religious changes are inte-

105. The epithet *ktistes* is common in building and other honorific inscriptions, even among the non-Ephesians.

106. See the article on pottery production and trade by Susanne Zabehlicky-Scheffenegger in this volume.

107. Regarding architectural development, see Sarah Macready and F. H. Thompson, eds., *Roman Architecture in the Greek World* (London: Society of Antiquaries, 1987); and Susan Walker and Averil Cameron, eds., *The Greek Renaissance in the Roman Empire* (London: Institute for Classical Studies, 1989).

108. Regarding the literary and intellectual environment, see esp. G. W. Bowersock, *Greek Sophists of the Roman Empire* (Oxford: Clarendon, 1969) 17–58; C. P. Jones, *The Roman World of Dio Chrysostom* (Cambridge, MA: Harvard University Press, 1978); idem, *Culture and Society in Lucian* (Cambridge, MA: Harvard University Press, 1991). See also n. 38 above.

grated into this mix, for both the persistence of Hellenism and the emergence of Christian social groups were by-products of the urban development and growth—or the so-called Romanization—of imperial Ephesos.[109]

109. See G. W. Bowersock, *Hellenism in Late Antiquity* (Ann Arbor: University of Michigan Press, 1990) 1–28. For a suggestion on how demographic shifts could lead to religious transformation, see R. Stark, "Epidemics, Networks, and the Rise of Christianity," in White, *Social Networks*, 159–75.

Appendix: Foreigners in Imperial Ephesos, An Epigraphic Catalogue

Catagory 3: Persons Not in Imperial Posts
[Totals: $N^{inscriptions}$ = 117 (183); $N^{persons}$ = 150; N^{groups} = 9]

IvE No.	Date/CE	Persons/Groups	Origin/Ethnogeography	Position/Occasion at Ephesos	Other References
A. Bithynia and Pontus/Northern Aegean					
1. I 20	54–59	L. Fabricius Vitalius with list of contributors	(Samothrakeion)	honors for building fishery and customs house	
2. V 1627	2d/3d?	L. Calpurnius Calpurnianus	Prusa, Bithynia	a student, honored with funerary monument by father and mother, T. Calpurnius Quintianus Africanus and Politta	
3. IV 1117 ?		Dionysios	Amastris (Pontus)	(statue of) victor in boxing at Ephesian Olympiad	
B. Galatia/Mysia/Lydia					
4. III 614	94–105	C. Antius Aulos Julius Quadratus	Ankyra via Pergamon (with ties to Sardeis)	consul eparch; honored at Ephesos by Laodicea (Syria) honors at Didyma (by Tyrians)	*IvE* VII 3033, V 1538 III 980, VII Ξ34 *IvD* 151

	Date	Name	Place / Marriage	Office	References
4a.		Julia Tyche (mother of above)	Pergamon		*IGR* IV 1687
5. III 930	117–38	A. Julius Amyntianus and Aulos Julius Amyntas (son/father; also cousins of Quadratus, above)	Ankyra via Tralles (?)	agoranomos	*IvE* III 685
6. VII 3034		Julia Polla (sister of Quadratus)	married T. Fl. Apellas from Hypaipa (ties to Mylasa)	agonothete and panegyriarch	(*IvE* III 980) *IvE* III 989a, VII 3034, IV 1122, III 980 *IG* II² 2959
7. III 980	ca. 180–93	Flavia Polla (daughter of Julia Polla, above)	married M. Julius Damianus (from Mylasa)	priestess, kosmeteira	*IvE* I 47.20 *IG* II² 2959
8. III 980	ca. 200	Ulpia Demokratia (grandaughter of Flavia Polla, above)	Mylasa remarried at Samos	kosmeteira	*IGR* IV 1729
9. III 980		Claudia Crateia Veviane (daughter of Demokratia, above)	Ephesos	prytanis and archiereia	*IvE* I 47
10. II 436–37	210–11	T. Fl. Menander and T. Fl. Lucius Hierax (brothers or father/son)	Hypaipa (also Alexandria)	building of Hydreion	*IvE* III 801, VII 3244
11. III 895	ca. 209–20	T. Flavius Herodes Papio and wife, Sempronia Secunda Papiane	moved from Hypaipa	theoros at Olympia	(*OGIS* 712)

12. VI 2037 102–12	T. Flavius Montanus	Akmoneia (Lydia)	dedication of construction in theater by "high priest of Asia, sebastophant, and agonothete"	*IvE* V 2061–63, I? 498 *IG* IV 643, 1696
13. III 854 102–12	T. Flavius Soter, (brother of above) and sons, T. Fl. Rufus Flavianus and T. Fl. Montanus	Akmoneia (Lydia)	honorific for imperial freedman, M. Ulpius Glyptus; given with sons	
14. III 698 late 2d	T. Fl. Montanus Maximillianus (later descendents of above family)	Akmoneia (Lydia)	proconsul; honored by asiarch, Rupillius Alexander	*IvE* 714
15. III 714 late 2d	L. Rupillius Alexander and his wife Po. Aelia Tyndiana	Akmoneia? (Lydia)	asiarch archiera	
16. VI 2300a ?	Petronius Longus	Blaundos, Lydia (near Akmoneia)	funerary monument by son, Petronius Eurythmos	
17. III 688 54–59	C. Julius Kleon, son of Fabia Kleona; and Alexander, son of Menander	Eumeneia, Lydia (near Akmoneia)	Alexander, now resident in Ephesos honors his "friend" Kleon, as tribune and son of archiera of Asia, Fabia Kleona (also of Eumeneia)	
18. III 821 ?	Cornelius Apollinarius and Aurel. Rufus	Apollonia on the Rhyndakos (Mysia)	city representative who paid honors at Ephesos to the procurator, [—]	
19. III 897 217–18	[—], mother of M.	Thyateira?	statue of woman; honored by son	

No.	Date	Name	Provenance	Honors / Notes	Sources
		Aurelius Apuleius Agathokles	(Lydia)	victor at Artemisia in Hypaipa; declaration of agonothete, Aur. Alexander on behalf of demos and council of Ephesos	
20. VII 3813	3d	Aur. Serapion, a musician (kitharist)	Thyateira (Lydia)	honors to [—] as adiatorix prytaneis; dedicated to Hestia, Clarian Apollo, Sopolis, and "all the gods"	*IvE* III 667, (for Sopolis, see *IvE* II 128, IV 1077, 1233)
21. V 1558	?	*koinon* of Galatia	(Galatia)		
22. 1060	3d	Favonia Flaccilla and Favonius Flacillus	*koinon* of Asia, Asia		
23. I 22	138–60	T. Aelius Alcibiades	Nysa and Teos	honored by Dionysiac technitai (from Teos)	
I 23a.		P. Aelius Pompeianus Paeon	represents "citizens of Side, Tarsus, and Rhodos"	in above honors	
I 23b.		Aristides, son of Aristides	represents Perge and Pergamon	in same	
24. III 615	1st?	M. Antonius Pythodorus (descendent of Chairemon and Pythodorus)	Tralles and Nysa	honored by demos for benefaction	*CIG* II 2945
25. III 615a	?	Kallinoe (mother of Chairemon of Nysa? see above)	Tralles	priestess	
26. IV 1147	?	Julius Tryphonianus comic play(write?)	Tralles	pythia, and in honor of his office of Kaisareus	

	Ref	Date	Name	Place	Description
27.	VII 4340	3d ?	[—]ius Secundinus, Platonic philosopher	Tralles	statue in his honor by his teacher, Coilios Marcellinus
28.	VII 3850	2d	C. Octavius Eutyches and Munatius Dionysius, the sons (?) of Aelia Eutyche	Ephesian Hypaipa	joint funerary monument at Hypaipa to honor them and their wives and children after them
29.	VII 3854	3d	Aur. Croesus, son of Dionysius	Hypaipa	an agoranomos; commemorates purchase of komarchia See *IvE* VII 385? VII 3857–858
30.	VII 3856	272/73	Aurelius Marcus, son of Publius Athenagoras	Ephesian Hypaipa	commemorates purchase of komarchia at Hypaipa
31.	VII 3906	1st	C. Stertinius Aquilla and his wife, Stertinia Eirene	Hypaipa	a freedman and freed- woman of C. Stertinius Maximus or C. Stertinius Orpex (a freedman) from Ephesos, apparently residing in Hypaipa *IvE* VII 4123
32.	III 642	140–60	L. Claudius Charidemus Philometor (brother of T. Cl. Polydeuces Marcellus)	Magnesia on Meander	asiarch and agonothete; See *IvE* I 22–23 honored as benefactor by deme and council of Ephesos
33.	II 472	140–60	T. Cl. Polydeuces Marcellus (brother of above; sons of T. Cl. Charidemus; nephew of T. Cl. (Polydeuces)	Magnesia on Meander (Magnesia on Meander) (Magnesia on Meander)	*grammateus* of Ephesos; *IvE* I 22, 23 asiarch and equestrian *IvM* 188 asiarch *IvM* 187

No.	Reference	Date	Name	Location	Description
34.	III 676		T. Fl. Metrodoros	Magnesia on Meander	statue base from theater
35.	IV 1134	2d–3d	Aur. Septimius Stratonikus	Philadelphia (Lydia)	victor in boxing at Olympia
36.	VII 5101–4	105	T. Julius Celsus Polemaeanus	Sardeis	procurator of Asia; *IvE* VII 5106–7 senator; Library of Celsus built in his honor by son, T. Julius Aquila Polemaeanus
37.	VII 5101 VII 5107	105	T. Julius Aquila Polemaeanus, (son of above)	Sardeis	procurator; senator
38.	VII 5104–5	100–5	Julia Quintilla Isaurica (daughter of above)	Sardeis	dedications to father in building of Library of Celsus
39.	VII 5112	ca. 100	[—] Scribonianus	Sardeis?	uncle of Celsus Polemaeanus, commemorated in dedication of Library of Celsus building
40.	VII 3809	3d	Aur. Reginus, an athlete	Sardeis	decree of agonothete, *IvE* VII 3813 Aur. Moschion (son of asiarch), as victor in wrestling at the Artemisia at Hypaipa

C. Caria/insulae Aegeae (Ionia)

No.	Reference	Date	Name	Location	Description
41.	III 618	ca. 140	[—] Aristokrates	Keramos	archiereus of Asia and *CIG* II 2987b agonothete
42.	III 643c	1st–2d	T. Cl. Italicus and Claudia Tertulla	Teos and Italy (?)	*grammateus* *IGR* IV 1567 priestess *IvE* II 266, 280

No.	Name	Place	Description	Citation
43. II 232 89/90	T. Cl. Pheisinos, husband of Stratonice; and father of Claudia Tryphaina	Teos	archiereus of Asia	IGR IV 1571; IvE II 232a, 233, 237, 238, 240
44. III 659 3d	M. Cornelius Aurelius Zeno, son of M. Corn. Aur. Theodoros and Fl. Demetria Flacilla	Teos	archiera of Teos honorific in Sarapeion	
45. V 1562 mid-3d	Flavius Zotikos	(Teos) Teos	senator honors his wife with statue	IGR IV 1576
45a.	Claudia (wife of above?)	Rhodos and Sardeis	daughter of T. Cl. Hermias and Aelia Pythia; sister of T. Cl. Draco and Sosipatra; descendent of Caninia Gargonilla	CIG II 3109 IGR IV 1127; Sardeis VII.191 (IvE VII 3065) IvE III 892
46. III 673 138–60	T. Fl. Hypsikles	Rhodos	honored by son with statue	IvE V 1548
47. V 1487 128–29	L. Erastus	islands (Rhodos?)	Hadrian's ship captain; urging Ephesos to grant citizenship	
48. V 1488 128–29	Philokyrios	islands (Rhodos?)	same as above	
49. V 1658 ?	[—]	Knidos	funerary inscription (? by a spouse and children)	
50. III 907	Priskos, son of Dioneikos	Didyma? Paros	from a list of leuko-phorountes in Theater Gymnasium	IvE III 907. 907.8 907.15
51. II 426 117–38	Sokrates T. Kl. Flavianos	Miletos Miletos	sarcophagus	

No.	Date	Name	Place	Description
52. III 686	mid-2d	Dionysios, sophist M. Julius Aquila, son of T. Julius Damianus and Aelia Acilia	Miletus	archiereus of Asia and agonothete
			Miletus	asiarch also honored at *IvE* III 689 Ephesos (as fellow priestess of Ionians)
53. VII 3047	117–38	Kl. Eutychos	Ephesos?	honors from demos and council for T. Kl. Flavianos Dionysios (above) as governor; given by his patron, Kl. Eutychos
54. II 235	late 1st	T. Cl. Charmos	Klazomenai (Karia)	equestrian; dedication *IvE* II 234, 236–42 on behalf of his city to deified Vespasian on occasion of first neokorate; through asiarch, T. Cl. Aristion
55. V 1553	1st/3d	[—], wife of an equestrian, Vetulanius Sabinianus, and mother of Vetul. Augureinus	*koinon* of Asia? Gaul (husband) (note: intermarriage since wife is from Asia)	funerary dedication to wife, as "archierea of Asia"
56. IV 1258	?	[—]	Aphrodisias	votive to unnamed god
57. V 1530	2d	T. Cl. Diogenes may be son of L. Ant. Cl. Dometinus	Aphrodisias? Aphrodisias	asiarch?; building of *IvE* III 810 "New Marnas" aquaeduct; asiarch; *PIR*² 193 gymnasiarch perpetual

58. VI 2944	2d	T. Cl. Attalos, also son of Cl. Dometinus	Aphrodisias?	archiereus of Asia; senator *PIR²* 172
59. VII 4109	ca. 200	T. Cl. Attalos Melior Kleo[—], (either the same as above, or his son)	Ephesian	asiarch of prytaneion and *grammateus* of demos of Ephesos; made a dedication on behalf of demos and council to family of Septimius Severus
60. III 793	ca. 85–96	Publius (Chareisios?)	Aphrodisias	honorific statue for him
61. I 11	117–38	Kallikrates, son of Diogenes	Aphrodisias	an athlete, statue of honor
62. I 12	2d	Aur. Achilleus	Aphrodisias	athlete
63. III 674	138–60	T. Flavius Paulinus	Kibyra? (Karia)	asiarch *IGR* IV 911, 9⊐
64. IV 1392	?	C. Julius Adrastos	Karian-Phrygian	public document
65. III 703	?	Charmides, son of Charmides and Charmides, son of Pereites	Trapezopolis (Karia)	honorific statue on *IvE* III 703a street to L. Peducaeus Fronto, procutor
66. VI 2067	117–38	M. Ulpius Damas Catullinus	Trapezopolis (Karia)	statue in honor of *MAMA* 6.60 archiereus of Asia and agonothete
67. II 241	90/91	T. Julius Damas Claudianus	koinon of Asia (Trapezopolis?)	archiereus of Asia, mentioned in honors from city of Tmolos on occasion of first neokorate
68. IV 1028	mid-2d	Chrysaor, son of Bacchios	of Karian descent	named in list of *IvE* IV 1029 *curetes*

D. Phrygia/Pisidia/Lykia/Pamphylia/Lykaonia

69. VII 3256 ?	"the Phrygians dwelling in Almura"	Phrygia	honors for [—] (with indications of a cult of Men?)	IvE VII 3260, 3262, 3253
70. VII 3252 ?	P. Aelius Menekrates; L. Verius Bassus, archon of "the dwellers" (that is, resident foreigners)	Phrygia? or Karia?	a foundation for mysteries of Demeter and of Men	IvE VII 3254, (below)
71. VII 3254 ?	Menekrates, son of Artemidoros, and his son Menekrates; and Melition, son of Hermolaos	Phrygia or Caria?	funerary honors given by "those dwelling in Almura (or Magnola)"	IvE VII 3253
72. IV 1246 ?	[—], and priest, Glaukos Menekrates	?	dedication of buildings for temple precincts to an unnamed god (Sarapis? or —)	
73. IV 1137 ?	T. Aelius Aurelius Beryllus, flutist	Aizani (Phrygia)	statue base in theater	
74. III 620 ca. 95–105	M. Arruntius Claudianus	Xanthos (Lykia)	honored by Vibius Salutaris (see below), as "friend and patron"	IvE I 27
75. IV 1238 ?	civic leaders: C. Flavonius Anicianus Sanctus, et al.	Pisidian Antioch (Kolonia)	statue of Tyche Soteira dedicated to Ephesos	
76. VI 2202 2d?	P. Aelius Flavianus Apollodorus	Aspendos, Pamphylia	funerary monument to him as philologos, given by his brother, P. Aelius Flavianus Zoilus	
77. VI 2211 ?	Julianos [—] and	Savatra, Lykaonia	father, a priest of Savatra,	

| | | son, Anemnatos | | gives funerary monument for son, a philologos in Ephesos | |

E. Ins. Kyklades/Achaia

78. II 510	14–31	Agatharchos, son of Pionius, a sculptor	Samos	statues of Tiberius	*IvE* II 510a
79. II 516	?	Athenaios, son of Dionysios, sculptor	Paros	small statue of Attis	
80. VI 2237c	?	Tib. Cl. Trophimus and wife, Marmarion	Paros ?	funerary monument by two sons, Paparion [*sic*] and Julius	
81. VI 2287a 1st BCE?		Metrodora; Demetrius and Dionysius Symmachos (brothers)	Paros Achaia	funerary monument	
82. III 640 ca. 125–50		T. Claudius Atticus Herodes	Athens and Marathon	honorific statue	
83. VI 2243	?	Cn. Cornelius Epaphroditus and Cn. Cornelius Glaucus	Corinth	a trainer; funerary monument set up by brother (?)	
84. II 526	?	G. Klaudios Korinthios with G. Iulios Iulianos	Corinth?	statue of Nike on Embolos	See *IvE* II 52▮

F. Armenia/Syria/Judaea

85. V 1537	2d	C. Julius Agrippa, son of C. Julius Alexander, *rex* (a descendant of Herod the Great through line of Tigranes V of Armenia)	Armenia; Judaea	honorific for benefaction in theater
86. IV 1251	?	an archisynagogos	?	honors?

No.	Date	Name	Origin	Description
87. V 1676	4th–(?)	Marcus Mussius, Jewish	?	funerary monument
88. V 1677	4th–(?)	Julius [—], Jewish	?	funerary monument by wife, Julia, and children, with honors as archiiatros by Jewish community of Ephesos οἵ ἐν Ἐφέσῳ Ἰουδέοι fragmentary found at Hypaipa See *IvE* III 622 IV 1161–167 VII 4350
89. VII 3822	4th–(?)	an organization (?) of Jewish "Youths"? (νεώτεροι, literally "youngers, juniors")	?	
90. VI 2215a	?	Berytians (in Ephesos?)	Berytos	relief of Ktetos of Berytos greeting seated figure of Asia Berytia
91. V 1539	ca. 170–73	Hadrianos, sophist (composer)	Tyre	epigram from Artemesion in honor of his patron, Cn. Claudius Severus (consul in 173), who was married to a daughter of Emperor Marcus Aurelius
92. III 668		Fl. Apollinarius	Syria	shipbuilder

G. Egypt/Kyrenaiaka

No.	Date	Name	Origin	Description
93. VII 3005	2d	Ischyrion and Isidoros	Alexandria	honored for construction of stoa in Tetragonos Agora (later granted Roman citizenship)
94. IV 1264	?	—	Alexandria	relief of Homonoia between

No.	Date	Name	Place	Description	Citation
95. IV 1121	?	P. Aelius Serapion	Alexandria	Ephesian Artemis and Alexandrian Sarapis; statue of victor in stadium at Ephesian Olympiad	
96. III 789	?	P[—], "eclectic philosopher"	Alexandria	honored by boule and demos	

H. Italy/Gaul/North Africa

No.	Date	Name	Place	Description	Citation
97. II 409	44	merchant's association (conventus civium Romanorum qui in Asia negotiantur)	Italy	dedication to Claudius	*IvE* III 658, 80] VI 2058
98. I 27	104	G. Vibius Salutaris	Gaul and Italy	honorific for establishing foundation (set up on theater wall)	(honorific statue̅) *IvE* I 28–35
98a. I 37	104	G. Vibius Salutaris		Latin text of honors for same	
98b. I 36 a–d	104	G. Vibius Salutaris		statues of gods set up at same	
99. II 430	103, 131	Afranius Flavianus	Italy?	proconsul of Asia; later granted Ephesian citizenship; friend of Vibius Salutaris	*IvE* I 27.341–4̅
100. VI 2235b	?	[—] and his wife, Claudia	Rome?	husband designated *Romanos* ("Roman citizen"), gives funerary monument for wife	
101. III 920/ 920a	?	Aurelius Italicus, M. Aurelius Italicus (father and son, or brothers)	Italian ?	eirenarch and agoranomos honors for both	

No.	Ref	Date	Name	Designation	Notes
102.	II 511	14–31	Boetos, a sculptor	Carthage	statue of Tiberius
103.	VI 2219	3d	Aurelios Chryseros	?	imperial freedman; now resident; funerary monument by wife, Vennia Capitoleine, and their children — See *IvE* II 511a; *IvE* VI 2261

I. Other/miscellaneous

No.	Ref	Date	Name	Designation	Notes
104.	II 574	?	Zotikos (son of?)	"Asiatikos" (a toponymic?)	graffito from agora
105.	III 909a		Apolla	"of Phygelos" (a toponymic?)	from a list of names in the market hall
106.	III 901	94 or 97/98	Euthenos	"Scythian"	from a list of molpoi in in the theater

At Home in the City of Artemis

RELIGION IN EPHESOS IN THE LITERARY IMAGINATION OF THE ROMAN PERIOD

Christine M. Thomas
Society of Fellows, Harvard University

Reading the ancient novels is both pleasurable and promising as a point of departure for a study of the literary image of Ephesos in the Roman period.[1] Geographic description (*ekphrasis*) is a significant ingredient in the assortment of literary devices that lend these works their appeal. Ephesos, as a physical location and a network of civic institutions, figures prominently in two of the five novels that are preserved more or less completely: Xenophon's *Ephesiaka* and Achilles Tatius's story of Leukippe and Kleitophon. Moreover,

---

1. The five "canonical" novels, so called because we have nearly complete manuscript copies of them, and some of the fragments have recently been translated with useful introductions in B. P. Reardon, *Collected Ancient Greek Novels* (Berkeley: University of California Press, 1989). For a more extensive collection of the fragments, with new editions of the Greek texts, see Susan A. Stephens and John J. Winkler, *Ancient Greek Novels: The Fragments: Introduction, Text, Translation, and Commentary* (Princeton: Princeton University Press, forthcoming).

these novels are a compelling snapshot of the religious imagination of the eastern Roman Empire; religion forms an inextricable part of their fabric.[1] Since the pleasure of reading ancient novels was what made them marketable, one can safely assume that the attitudes depicted in them are widespread and generic, meant to attract and entrance, rather than to provoke, and to create a common ground against which to present the events of the story. In this sense, the novels are a reliable index of "popular" religious attitudes,[3] and indeed the two novels with the highest number of references to Ephesos can also be characterized as among the more popular. The *Ephesiaka* is unsophisticated in its plot devices—although it may be an epitome[4]—and its Greek inelegant. Achilles Tatius wrote a more refined work; but its existence on six or so papyri, dating from the late second through the

2. Reinhold Merkelbach, in his influential but much-criticized *Roman und Mysterium in der Antike* (Munich: Beck, 1962) views these novels as allegorizations of mystery initiations: they have both a literal level and a "Mysteriensinn," which alludes to the details of mystery cults and would be understood by the initiate only. For reviews, see Morton Smith "Reinhold Merkelbach, *Roman und Mysterium in der Antike*," *Classical World* 27 (1964) 378, and Hans Gärtner on the *Ephesiaka* in particular ("Xenophon von Ephesos," PW 2. 18 [1967] 2055–89, esp. 2074–80). I follow B. P. Reardon's response to this hypothesis ("The Greek Novel," *Phoenix* 23 [1969] 291–309): because both the mysteries and the novels are metaphors for human life, connections exist between them. For Reardon, the novels are myths about personal identity in a Hellenistic world in which the social identity provided by the polis has broken down.

3. "Popular" is not intended here as a class designation. There is little hard evidence that the readership of the novels was any different than that of other literary works; given the low level of literacy and the high cost of manuscripts, it is unlikely that the audience of the novels extended beyond the social élite (see the discussion below). Regardless of who read them, and despite their sophistication, novels do not exhibit the literary pretensions of other sorts of ancient literature, and are "popular" in this sense.

4. The *Ephesiaka* may be an epitome. The reference in the Suda numbers the volumes of the *Ephesiaka* at ten, whereas our version has only five. Books three and four, moreover, are remarkably short. See Karl Bürger, "Zu Xenophon von Ephesus," *Hermes* 27 (1892) 36–67; and Gärtner, "Xenophon," 2072–74; against this thesis, see Tomas Hägg, "Die Ephesiaka des Xenophon Ephesios: Original oder Epitome?" *Classica et Mediaevalia* 27 (1966) 118–61. On the Greek style, see Gärtner, "Xenophon," 2070–72.

fourth century CE, demonstrates its broad dissemination. Three of these six fragments are from codices, an indication, at least into the third or fourth century CE, of a work with less literary pretension than those written on scrolls.[5] In the *Ephesiaka*, Ephesos is necessary to the plot. Xenophon's wealthy and privileged young sweethearts are themselves Ephesian, and their tale is one of their return—*nostos*, to use the Homeric term—to their home in Ephesos, after they are separated and carried around the Roman Empire in a series of shipwrecks, pirate attacks, and sales into slavery. Leukippe and Kleitophon, the protagonists in Achilles Tatius, initially have no tie with Ephesos. One of them was born in Tyre, the other in Byzantion. Similar to Xenophon's heroes, they spend much of the novel in a series of Mediterranean mishaps, the resolution of which takes place in the law courts of Ephesos, with some help from Artemis and her worshippers.

The prominent appearance of Ephesos in these two novels is initially surprising. The novels typically focus on colorful climes; exotic locales with a radically different cultural history, such as Egypt, were certain to attract an audience, and they appear as a matter of course in this literature. Ephesos, however, had been part of the Greek world for the better part of a millennium, and, as a provincial center of administration in the Roman Empire, was presumably part of the everyday world of the Greek reading audience. Were there aspects of the religious image of Ephesos that were particularly marketable, that is, successful at attracting an ancient audience? As will be shown, Ephesos appears in the novels not as a land of sojourn, but as the desired destination; bustling and glamorous, it is nevertheless a Greek polis, a haven of Greek identity, serving as a contrast to the more exotic locations in the novels.

A glance into the nonnovelistic Greek literature of the Roman period demonstrates surprising uniformity in the presentation of Ephesos. Historians, philosophers, and orators alike repeat the same anecdotes and characterizations of the city. It is undoubtably for this reason that

5. William H. Willis, "The Robinson-Cologne Papyrus of Achilles Tatius," *GRBS* 31 (1990) 73–102. On parchment codices in general, see Eric G. Turner, *The Typology of the Early Codex* (Philadelphia: University of Pennsylvania Press, 1977) 35–42, 89–97.

novelists wove Ephesos into the fabric of their works. Part of the pleasure of reading them is recognizing what one already knows; the authors played on preexisting assumptions to create audience appeal. Three complexes of *topoi* seem the most evocative of the specifically religious dimension of Ephesos's profile in literature of the Roman period: the image of Artemis, the inviolability of her temple, and the appearance of Rome on the religious horizon of this literature, which, as will be seen, is more of an absence than a presence. With each of these topics, one limns the imaginative component of the identity of Ephesos—not so much what Ephesos represented historically during this period of time, as what people thought it represented. I shall return to the theme of the interplay between this literary image and what can be reconstructed of the religious life of Ephesos from archaeological evidence, as well as to the role the city itself played in the process of creating its image.

Certain limits shape this study. Only Greek literature falls within its scope; Greek is the language of the novels and the language of the city of Ephesos. Although Latin sources at times enter the notes of this article, no claim is made to offer a complete study of that literature. Second, even the earliest Christian sources from this period have been left out of consideration, since that topic is treated elsewhere in this volume. A search of the root Ἐφεσ- throughout the authors on the CD-ROM database of the *Thesaurus Linguae Graecae* formed the basis of more extensive investigation of the texts.[6] The appendix lists the authors culled by this search and the raw number of references found in each.

The ability to define religion and religious attitudes clearly is assumed by this essay, but not taken for granted. The topics broached are, of necessity, simultaneously also social and political, since in antiquity few aspects of "secular" life did not carry a "religious" dimension. Conversely, precisely because one cannot define what religion is not in ancient society, it is almost impossible to define just what it is; it is both everywhere and nowhere. I have tried, in what follows, to keep this dialectic in view, realizing that this lack of clear boundaries is one of the aspects of ancient society that modern researchers may never be able to understand completely.

6. TLG Data Bank Texts (Irvine: University of California, 1992) CD ROM #D.

The Image of Artemis Ephesia

It is not surprising that Artemis figures prominently among the references to the city of Ephesos and things Ephesian in this sample of Greek literature. What is remarkable is the proportion of these references. In the non-Christian literature of the first century BCE to the fourth century CE, there are approximately five hundred and twenty-four references to Ephesos and things Ephesian on the CD-ROM database of the *Thesaurus Linguae Graecae*. Some one hundred and seventy-five are incidental references to Ephesos that tell little about the literary image of the city or its religious import; among these are the mere name of the city as a travel destination, or the adjective Ἐφέσιος as the ethnic component of a proper name, for example, the very popular Ἡράκλειτος Ἐφέσιος, "Herakleitos the Ephesian." Once these types of references are excluded from the count, however, fully one-third of the passages referring to Ephesos or things Ephesian refer to the goddess, her sanctuary, or her cult personnel.

Martin Nilsson and H. Gärtner[7] noted long ago that the *Ephesiaka* of Xenophon harmonize the Ephesian goddess with the attributes of Artemis more widely disseminated in Greek mythology. This is doubtless true, and a signal example of this conflation occurs early in the novel. The two young protagonists, Anthia and Habrokomes,[8] see each other for the first time at a "local festival of Artemis" (τῆς Ἀρτέμιδος ἐπιχώριος ἑορτή)[9] involving a procession from the city to her sanctuary "seven stades" away. All of the local girls of marriageable age (παρθένους) and the local boys entering military training (ἐφήβους) are required to take part in the ritual. The offerings and sacrificial victims[10] lead the procession, then come the torches, baskets, and

7. Gärtner, "Xenophon," 2058–59; Martin P. Nilsson, *Griechische Feste von religiöser Bedeutung, mit Ausschluß der attischen* (Leipzig: Teubner, 1906) 244–46.
8. Abrokomes is also attested. The name appears as Ἀβροκόμης, Ἁβροκόμης, and Ἀβροκόμας in the manuscripts. For discussion, see Gärtner, "Xenophon," 2060.
9. Xenophon *Ephesiaka* 1.2.2.
10. Ibid., 1.2.4; " . . .first the sacrificial victims, the torches, the baskets, and the incense; then horses, dogs, hunting equipment. . . " (πρῶτα μὲν τὰ ἱερὰ καὶ δᾷδες καὶ κανᾶ καὶ θυμιάματα· ἐπὶ τούτοις ἵπποι καὶ κύνες καὶ σκεύη κυνηγετικά). I disagree with Graham Anderson ("Xenophon of Ephesus: An Ephesian Tale," in Reardon, *Ancient Greek Novels*, 125–69, esp.

incense, followed by horses, dogs, and hunting equipment. After this, the contingent of young women follows, with Anthia at the head of the group. She in dressed in what seems to be her everyday attire:

> She wore a purple tunic down to the knee, fastened with a girdle and falling loose over her arms, with a fawnskin over it, a quiver attached, and arrows for weapons; she carried javelins and was followed by dogs. Often as they saw her in the sacred enclosure the Ephesians would worship her as Artemis. And so on this occasion too the crowd gave a cheer when they saw her, and there was a whole clamor of exclamations from the spectators; some were amazed and said it was the goddess in person; some that it was someone else made by the goddess in her own image.[11]

This is a classic portrait of the virgin huntress. It bears little resemblance to the cult statues of Artemis Ephesia, in which the goddess is portrayed with a headdress (a *polos* or sometimes a mural crown), heavily figured necklaces, multiple round protuberances between the necklaces and waistband,[12] and a tightly wrapped skirt with tilelike

---

129) in his translation of τὰ ἱερά as "sacred objects"; "sacrificial victims" seems the most conventional interpretation.

11. Xenophon *Ephesiaka* 1.2.6–7, translated in Anderson, "Xenophon of Ephesus," 129; ἐσθὴς χιτὼν ἁλουργής, ζωστὸς εἰς γόνυ, μέχρι βραχιόνων καθειμένος, νεβρὶς περικειμένη, γωρυτὸς ἀνημμένος, τόξα ὅπλα, ἄκοντες φερόμενοι, κύνες ἑπόμενοι. Πολλάκις αὐτὴν ἐπὶ τοῦ τεμένους ἰδόντες Ἐφέσιοι προσεκύνησαν ὡς Ἄρτεμιν. καὶ τότ᾽ οὖν ὀφθείσης ἀνεβόησε τὸ πλῆθος, καὶ ἦσαν ποικίλαι παρὰ τῶν θεωμένων φωναί, τῶν μὲν ὑπ᾽ ἐκπλήξεως τὴν θεὸν εἶναι λεγόντων, τῶν δὲ ἄλλην τινὰ ὑπὸ τῆς θεοῦ πεποιημένην. The MS reads περιποιημένην, resulting in a number of conjectures. I follow the emendation of Antonius D. Papanikolaou, ed., *Xenophontis Ephesii Ephesiacorum Libri V* (Bibliotheca scriptorum Graecorum et Romanorum Teubneriana; Leipzig: Teubner, 1973) 3.

12. Robert Fleischer, in his various iconographic studies of the cult statue, resists the interpretation of the round protuberances as breasts. According to Fleischer, they are never worked in the dark stone in which the face, hands, and toes are presented on some statues of the Ephesian Artemis, thus they do not represent a naked part of the goddess's body, but rather a removable piece of her clothing (Fleischer, *Artemis von Ephesos*, 74–88; idem, "Artemis Ephesia," *LIMC* 2. 1.755–63, esp. 763). Moreover, similar "breasts" appear on images of Zeus Labraundos, a male god in Anatolia (Fleischer, *Artemis von Ephesos*, 310–24). Fleischer notes that the interpretation of the round items as breasts

rectangular fields filled with animal motifs.[13] Even the aspect of Artemis as the πότνια θηρῶν, "mistress of the beasts," a designation found already in the *Iliad*, is somewhat attenuated in this portrait.[14] Instead of the deer that often accompany her (and sometimes also Artemis Ephesia), we have only the hunting dogs in this passage, and no other animals in her retinue.[15]

---

has gained currency chiefly since the Renaissance, and derives from two Christian sources: Minucius Felix *Octavius* 22.5; Jerome *Comm. in Eph.* praef. Fleischer cites ("Neues zu kleinasiatischen Kultstatuen," *Archäologischer Anzeiger* 98 [1983] 81–93, esp. 81–89) with limited approval Gérard Seiterle's suggestion, in an unpublished lecture given in 1978, that the protuberances are the testicles of bulls offered in sacrifice. Recently, Lynn LiDonnici argued ("The Images of Artemis and Greco-Roman Worship: A Reconsideration," *HTR* 85 [1992] 389–415) that, even if the items were not originally breasts, they may have been interpreted in this fashion in the later imperial period; despite her well-structured argument, the evidence—three statues on which the protuberences are presented with nipples, and the two literary passages cited above—remains slight. It is important that the only two literary references are Christian—not always the most reliable source for the attitudes of polytheists.

13. The three statues on display at the Ephesos Museum (Efes Müzesi) in Selçuk, Turkey, all follow this general pattern (Efes Müzesi inv. nos. 712, 718, and 717; Fleischer, *Artemis von Ephesos*, E 45–47). Fleischer considers the large Artemis (his no. E 45) to be the most faithful rendering of the cult statue. For all the possible variations in this general scheme, and for interpretations of the various elements of its iconography, see Robert Fleischer, "Artemis von Ephesos und verwandte Kultstatuen aus Anatolien und Syrien: Supplement," in Sencer Şahin, Elmar Schwertheim, and Jorg Wagner, eds., *Studien zur Religion und Kultur Kleinasiens: Festschrift für Friedrich Karl Dörner zum 65. Geburtstag* (2 vols.; Leiden: Brill, 1978) 1. 324–58, esp. 324–26; see also Fleischer, "Artemis Ephesia," 762–63. The statues probably vary so much in the details of Artemis's costume because it consisted of removable pieces of clothing and jewelry that were renewed year by year (idem, *Artemis von Ephesos*, 125, 132).

14. Homer *Il.* 21.470. Fleischer ("Artemis Ephesia," 755) claims that the earliest designation of Artemis Ephesia was Δεσποίνη Ἐφεσία ("mistress of Ephesos"); D. G. Hogarth found this inscribed on a sixth-century plaque from the Artemision (*Excavations at Ephesus: The Archaic Artemisia* [London: British Museum, 1908] 120, 138, 246, *non vidi*).

15. For the accompanying deer, see Homer *Od.* 6.102–9. Flanking deer were added to the cult image at Ephesos only in Roman times; this image appears for the first time on coins under Hadrian (Fleischer, "Artemis Ephesia," 763).

Achilles Tatius renders the same iconographic representation in the other novel in which Ephesos figures prominently. During one of the many attempted rapes in this novel, this one in Ephesos, Leukippe invokes Artemis. She cries out at Thersandros, her Ephesian attacker: "Tell me, aren't you afraid of your goddess Artemis? You rape a virgin in the virgin's own city? Lady goddess, where are your arrows?"[16] Artemis Ephesia would not be portrayed with arrows; again, the author seems to have in mind Artemis the huntress.

Although far removed from Xenophon's *Ephesiaka* in technique and sophistication, Heliodoros's novel, the *Ethiopika*, also makes a rough equation between Artemis Ephesia and the Artemis of more widespread Greek mythology. At one point in the narrative,[17] Charikleia tries to pass off herself and her sweetheart Theagenes as an Ephesian brother and sister who were shipwrecked in the course of their year of service to the sibling gods—she as a priestess of Artemis, and he as a priest of Apollo. According to Charikleia's story, the mishap occurred while they were traveling as divine ambassadors to Delos, for the annual festival of the two gods. The pairing of Artemis Ephesia with Apollo is somewhat surprising. Although both were worshipped at Ephesos into Roman times, according to present knowledge, their sanctuaries showed no close association,[18] unlike many

16. Achilles Tatius *Leukippe and Kleitophon* 6.21.2, translated in John J. Winkler, "Achilles Tatius: Leucippe and Clitophon," in Reardon, *Ancient Greek Novels*, 259; (οὐδὲ τὴν Ἄρτεμιν, εἰπέ μοι, τὴν σὴν φοβῇ, ἀλλὰ βιάζῃ παρθένον ἐν πόλει παρθένου; δέσποινα, ποῦ σου τὰ τόξα;). The text is Ebbe Vilborg, ed., *Achilles Tatius: Leucippe and Clitophon* (Studia Graeca et Latina Gothoburgensia 1; Stockholm: Almqvist & Wiksell, 1962).
17. Heliodoros *Ethiopika* 1.22.
18. Apollo appears in many contexts in Ephesos. A fifth-century BCE inscription attests Apollo Patroios, Ἀπόλλων Πατρώϊος (Oster, "Ephesus as a Religious Center, 1661–1728, esp. 1668). He is found alongside the μήτηρ ὀρεία ("mother from the mountains") of the sanctuary on the north slope of Panayirdağ (Mount Pion) (Knibbe, "Ephesos, nicht nur die Stadt der Artemis," 2. 489–503, esp. 493–94). According to Athenaios (*Deipnosophist.* 8 § 361e, citing Kreophylos), the founders of Ephesos erected a temple of Pythian Apollo near the harbor at the same time that they built one for Artemis near the agora; the Apollo sanctuary may turn out to be the unexcavated temple on an outcropping of rock northwest of the large second-century temple complex that later housed the Church of Mary. Another cult of Apollo was installed in the Prytaneion (map no. 61), the home of Artemis's association of *curetes*, in the early second century. See Knibbe, *Der Staatsmarkt*, 102–3.

cities in western Asia Minor, in which Apollo, Artemis, and Leto were worshipped side by side.[19] Moreover, to portray Charikleia as an Ephesian priestess of Artemis on her way to Delos is startling; that island was the birthplace of the goddess for the rest of the Greek world, but for Ephesos, the birth of the goddess took place in Ortygia, near Ephesos, and was celebrated there annually.[20]

This apparent lack of precision is usually explained as mere inaccuracy on the part of the novelists. Gärtner, for example, supposes that Xenophon had never seen a festival of the Ephesian Artemis at all, but merely invented a generic scene employing the characteristic aspects of Artemis.[21] Indeed, Heliodoros, Xenophon, and Achilles Tatius do not purport to be historians of religion, and doubtless their descriptions of the geographical backdrops of their works are written to provide local color rather than to explain the sites accurately. One must question, however, whether their portrayals are based on ignorance of the most basic features of Artemis Ephesia. Other more

19. At Klaros, fragments of massive statues of this divine trio can be viewed; inscriptions show that one of the temples was dedicated to Apollo and another to Artemis. At Letoon, three temples stand side by side. An inscription identifies one of them as being dedicated to Leto; the other two were probably dedicated to her children. According to Strabo (*Geog.* 14.1.20), one of the temples in Ortygia near Ephesos housed a statue group of Artemis, Apollo, Leto, and their nurse, Ortygia. It is presumably this statue group that is represented on Ephesian coinage under Hadrian (see Stefan Karwiese, "Ephesos, C: Numismatischer Teil," PWSup 12 [1970] 297–364, esp. 336). The divine twins were not generally worshipped together, however, before the archaic period (Walter Burkert, *Greek Religion* [Cambridge, MA: Harvard University Press, 1985] 219–20).

20. See Strabo *Geog.* 14.1.20. On the significance of Ortygia as the birthplace of Artemis, and its relationship with generic Greek myth, see Knibbe, *Der Staatsmarkt*, 70–73. Tacitus (*Annals* 3.61) tells of the response of Ephesos to an empirewide attempt by the Roman Senate to limit rights of asylum offered by temples. The Ephesian embassy arrived first. Although they stressed that the Ephesian Artemis was the sister of Apollo and daughter of Leto, they insisted that she had not been born on Delos, "as the rabble believed" (ut vulgus crederet), but that Leto bore the divine twins in Ortygia.

21. Gärtner, "Xenophon," 2059. J. Gwyn Griffiths, in contrast, sees in this early scene of the novel "the stamp of personal knowledge and affection" ("Xenophon of Ephesus on Isis and Alexandria," in Margreet B. de Boer and T. A. Edridge, eds., *Hommages à Maarten J. Vermaseren* [EPRO 68; 3 vols.; Leiden: Brill, 1978] 1. 409–37, esp. 411).

pedantic Greek authors of the Roman period, such as the antiquarians Pausanias and Strabo, also follow suit in deemphasizing the specifically Anatolian aspects of the Ephesian Artemis in the interests of harmonizing her and her cult with more generally held Greek values. Neither of these two authors fails to distinguish cult practices and the iconographic and mythological complexes particular to the cult of Artemis Ephesia. Strabo, for example, describes the eunuch priests of Artemis Ephesia, the *megabyzoi* (μεγάβυζοι). Apparently already in his day, they were not actively serving in Ephesos; he speaks of this institution in the imperfect, as a habitual practice of the past, and contrasts it with the aspects of the cult that still continue in force in his own day:

> They used to have eunuchs, whom they would call *megabyzoi*, and they would always be in search of people from other regions who were worthy of such an office, and would hold them in great honor. It was customary for virgins to serve as priestesses alongside them. Now, although some of the customs are practiced, some are not, but the temple remains a place of asylum now as before.[22]

For Strabo, the *megabyzoi* seem merely to be male equivalents of the virgin priestesses, alongside whom they served. The fact of their castration troubles him little; he emphasizes that this office signified a supraregional honor. All of this is apparently interpretation, either on the part of Strabo or his informants, for he is describing a practice that had fallen out of usage in his own time, and thus cannot research the issue personally.

Eunuch priests do appear, however, in related Anatolian cults. Well into the imperial period, the Magna Mater at Rome was served by eunuch *galloi*, a custom that the worshippers brought when they came

22. Strabo *Geog.* 14.1.23; my translation. ἱερέας δ᾽ εὐνούχους εἶχον, οὓς ἐκάλουν Μεγαβύζους, καὶ ἀλλαχόθεν μετιόντες ἀεί τινας ἀξίους τῆς τοιαύτης προστασίας, καὶ ἦγον ἐν τιμῇ μεγάλῃ· συνιερᾶσθαι δὲ τούτοις ἐχρῆν παρθένους. νυνὶ δὲ τὰ μὲν φυλάττεται τῶν νομίμων τὰ δ᾽ ἧττον, ἄσυλον δὲ μένει τὸ ἱερὸν καὶ νῦν καὶ πρότερον. Greek text and English translation are available in Horace Leonard Jones, ed., *The Geography of Strabo in Eight Volumes* (LCL; London and New York: Heinemann and Putnam's, 1917) 6. 228–29.

from Asia Minor to establish the cult.[23] Instead of quiet and honorable chastity, however, the contemporary Latin sources describe a frenzied and bloody rite of self-castration by means of which aspiring priests consecrated themselves to the goddess. The mythological counterpart of these eunuch priests was the unfortunate Attis, who castrated himself in a burst of insanity after being unfaithful to his lover, Kybele:[24]

> He [Attis] retrenched the burden of his groin, and of a sudden was bereft of every sign of manhood. His madness set an example, and still his unmanly ministers cut their vile members while they toss their hair (onus inguinis aufert / nullaque sunt subito signa relicta viri. / venit in exemplum furor hic, mollesque ministri / caedunt iactatis vilia membra comis).[25]

Strabo's domestication of these eunuch priests into an overall framework in which castration signifies not consecration, but chastity—a traditional value associated with Artemis—is also reflected in Pausanias. To this antiquarian, living two centuries later, the quaint personnel of the Ephesian Artemision are not the eunuch priests, but the Essenai (Ἐσσῆνας), the "entertainers" (ἱστιάτορας) of the Artemision, who remain chaste not because of corporal alteration, and not for life but only for the year of their service.[26]

23. According to Pliny, the priests of the Mother of Gods, called *galli*, castrated themselves with Samian pottery (*Hist. nat.* 35.46.165; Matris deum sacerdotes, qui Galli vocantur). Martial (3.81) also mentions castration by a Samian potsherd, the sacrifice of a *gallus* to Kybele.

24. This is the version that Ovid tells in his *Fasti* 4.223–44. Other versions attribute the self-castration to different causes.

25. Ovid *Fasti* 4.241–44 in James George Frazer, ed., *Ovid in Six Volumes: Fasti* (2d ed.; LCL; Cambridge, MA: Harvard University Press, 1989) 5. 207; see also 4.183–90 on the noise of the procession and howling of the eunuchs. Similarly, Juvenal describes a huge half-man, part of the chorus of the mother of the gods (matrisque deum chorus), who divested himself of his genitalia long ago with a potsherd, and is accompanied by a raucous musical procession (ingens semivir. . . mollia qui rapta secuit genitalia testa / iam pridem, cui rauca cohors, cui tympana cedunt; *Satires* 6.511–16).

26. Pausanias 8.13.1. Pausanias compares them with priests among the Mantinaeans, who are forbidden from entering the home of a private person and otherwise live in ritual purity, not even washing—this illustrates the difference between ritual purity and ordinary cleanliness. Inscriptions attest that

Evidence for the seeming suppression of the distinctly Anatolian elements of the cult of Artemis Ephesia, then, extends further than the novels. The identification of the "Anatolian" Artemis Ephesia with the "Greek" Artemis should give us pause; perhaps, instead of the product of careless research on the part of the novelists, it is part of a general and meaningful pattern of thought. In the case of Strabo and Pausanias, their information on current practice is doubtless accurate. Epigraphic evidence suggests that, as early as the midfourth century BCE, the *megabyzoi* were no longer eunuchs.[27] Much of the Greek world may have, by that time, forgotten that eunuchs once served at the Artemision, and more so, that the rite of castration it presupposed had any affinity with other cults of Anatolian goddesses.[28]

Although the novels in general may be poorly informed on specific cultic practices, it would have been surprising if Xenophon and Achilles Tatius had been completely unaware of the distinctive iconographic representation of Artemis of Ephesos. Sanctuaries specific to this goddess existed throughout the Roman Empire. Strabo knows of sanc-

---

the activities of these *essenai* at Ephesos included both the enrollment of new citizens and sacrifices to Artemis (*IvE* IV 1408; 1409; VI 2001 line 10; V 1448).

27. An inscription from Priene dating to 334–333 BCE reads: "[Megabyzos,] son of Megabyzos, temple warden of the Artemis in Ephesos" ([Μεγάβυζος] Μεγαβύζου νεωκόρος τῆς Ἀρτέμιδος τῆς ἐν Ἐφέσωι; F. Frhr. Hiller von Gaertringen, ed., *Inschriften von Priene* [Berlin: Reimer, 1906] 231, cited in R. A. Kearsley, "Ephesus: *Neokoros* of Artemis," in S. R. Llewelyn, ed., *New Documents Illustrating Early Christianity: A Review of the Greek Inscriptions and Papyri published in 1980–81* [6 vols.; North Ryde, NSW: Ancient History Documentary Research Centre, Macquarie University, 1992] 6. 203–6, esp. 205). *Megabyzos* seems to have functioned as a generic proper name for the successive generations of these officials; the term is Persian; LSJ s.v. Μεγάβυζος. On the personnel specific to the Artemision, see Fleischer, "Artemis Ephesia," 756, with bibliography; and Oster, "Ephesus as a Religious Center," 1721–22.

28. On the issue of the identification of the Ephesian goddess with Artemis, and on the cult of Artemis Ephesia specifically in the Roman period, see Oster, "Ephesus as a Religious Center," 1699–1726. For a wealth of epigraphic and archaeological information on the cult see also G. H. R. Horsley, "The Inscriptions of Ephesos and the New Testament," *NovT* 34 (1992) 105–68, esp. 141–58.

tuaries of Artemis Ephesia in Massilia and Iberia[29]; Pausanias additionally knows of sanctuaries in Corinth, Arkadia,[30] and in Skillus near Elis, the latter owing its foundation to the most illustrious of converts to the Ephesian Artemis, Xenophon the historian.[31] The archaeological evidence is even more broadly distributed: sanctuaries have come to light in Asia Minor, the Greek mainland, Italy, and the north coast of the Black Sea.[32]

The fact that images of Artemis Ephesia are widespread in the Roman world has great bearing on the issue of the general knowledge of the iconographic peculiarity of Artemis of Ephesos. Of the one hundred and fifty-four representations catalogued in the most recent work by Robert Fleischer,[33] most are relatively small, that is, inap-

29. The cult in Massilia was founded when the Phokaians, out to colonize the area, put in at Ephesos because an oracle ordered them to take on a guide from the Artemision. They brought along an Ephesian woman, Aristarcha, whom Artemis had commanded in a dream to sail with them and found her temple in the new colony. She became the first priestess (Strabo *Geog.* 4.1.4). For Hemeroskopeion near New Carthage in Iberia, see 3.4.6; for Emporion and Rhodos in Iberia, see 3.4.8.

30. For Corinth, see Pausanias 2.2.6 (the sanctuaries are in the agora, where most of the other temples are located); for Alea in Arkadia, see 8.23.1; for Megalopolis in Arkadia, see 8.30.6; at the latter, Pausanias saw an image of Artemis Ephesia in one of the rooms of the stoa containing the municipal government.

31. Pausanias 5.6.5; Strabo *Geog.* 8.7.5; Diogenes Laertius 2.51–52 ("Xenophon"). Xenophon himself narrates the story in the *Anabasis* (5.3.4–13). Skillus is located in Spartan territory outside of Elis, on the way to Olympia. Xenophon built a small temple replicating the Ephesian Artemision there, and installed a cult statue.

32. The temple of Artemis Ephesia in Sardeis is mentioned in a Hellenistic inscription found in Ephesos; the inscription recounts how members of a religious embassy from Sardeis were tried and executed in Ephesos for a perceived breach of piety (Dieter Knibbe, "Ein religiöser Frevel und seine Sühne: Ein Todesurteil hellenistischer Zeit aus Ephesos," *JÖAI* 46 [1961–63] Hauptbl. 175–82. In addition to Sardeis, Richard Oster ("Holy days in honour of Artemis," in G. H. R. Horsley, *New Documents* [1987] 4. 74–82, esp. 79–80) finds archaeological testimony of the cult of Artemis Ephesia at Smyrna, at Aphrodisias, near Dirmil in Karia, on Chios, in Macedonia, Rome, Berezan in the Ukraine, and Pantikapaion on the Crimean Bosphorus.

33. Fleischer, "Artemis Ephesia"; the earlier works are idem, *Artemis von Ephesos*; and idem, "Supplement."

propriate to stand as the cult image in a public sanctuary. A large-scale production of images for private worship must have existed. Moreover, these images, copies of the cult statue, are almost without exception from Roman imperial times, with the greatest reproduction in the second century,[34] precisely when the putatively ill-informed novelists would have been writing.

Fleischer catalogues one hundred and forty-two reliefs and statues, or fragments of them, in stone, terra-cotta, bronze, and lead[35]; of the sixty-two images that have any indication of a find site, thirty-six are from outside of Ephesos. The majority of these, twenty-two, were found in Asia Minor[36]; but examples also come from Italy, Massilia, Greece, the Cyrene, Egypt, and Palestine. The image of Artemis of Ephesos was, apparently, relatively widespread and well known throughout the empire. Whatever their city of origin, Xenophon and Achilles Tatius would have found it relatively easy to inform themselves about the appearance of Artemis of Ephesos. If the ancient lexicon known as the Suda is correct, and Xenophon also wrote a work entitled *Concerning the City of Ephesos* (Περὶ τῆς πόλεως Ἐφεσίων),[37] it is inconceivable that he had never seen the goddess's image.

34. Robert Fleischer, "Artemis Ephesia und Aphrodite von Aphrodisias," in Maarten J. Vermaseren, ed., *Die orientalischen Religionen im Römerreich* [EPRO; Leiden: Brill, 1981] 298–315, esp. 300.

35. The other items in his catalogues comprise coins, gemstones, and a bronze plate.

36. In Phrygia: Hierapolis, Laodikea on the Lykos, Hacılar, and Mossyna; in Ionia: Klaros, İzmir, Klazomenai, and Metropolis; Antioch in Pisidia; Tarsos in Kilikia; Prusias ad Hypium, Çapak near Cumaovası. Coins bearing the image of Artemis Ephesia, while unknown in the west, were also minted at sites all over the eastern Mediterranean; see the maps at the end of Fleischer, *Artemis von Ephesos*. As Fleischer points out, the coins may not indicate local shrines to Artemis of Ephesos, but social, political, and economic ties of the cities in question to Ephesos (p. 134).

37. Although compiled in the late tenth century, the Suda is based on earlier sources of varying reliability, some of them representing the best scholarship in antiquity. The phrase περὶ τῆς πόλεως Ἐφεσίων has sometimes been understood as an additional description of the novel: the text reads "Xenophon, the Ephesian, a historian: the *Ephesiaka*. It is a love story in ten books about Abrocomes and Anthia; and Concerning the City of the Ephesians; and others." (Ξενοφῶν, Ἐφέσιος, ἱστορικός· Ἐφεσιακά· ἔστι δὲ ἐρωτικὰ

The seeming confusion of the novelists on the iconographic level is matched, however, by a curious mixture of images from Ephesos itself. Representations of Artemis the virgin huntress are common at Ephesos.[38] The earliest coins of Artemis Ephesia, dating from the third century BCE, portrayed her as the short-skirted huntress. Only from the second century BCE onward does the well-known cult statue appear on the coinage of Ephesos. Beginning in that period, both the "Greek" Artemis and Artemis Ephesia continue to appear on various mintings into the late Roman Empire. Especially from the second century CE onward, new variants of the "Greek" Artemis appear: Artemis pulled by a span of deer, riding on a deer, or holding a torch.[39] The cult image of Artemis Ephesia is much earlier than these numismatic representations; because of various stylistic considerations, Fleischer dates the archetype to the seventh century BCE.[40] The fact that the coin series begins with the more generally Greek image suggests that in the Hellenistic period, the city of Ephesos itself actively encouraged the identification of its patron goddess with the most generic characterization of Artemis. Although the archaeological record demonstrates that the peculiar image of Artemis Ephesia remained beloved throughout the Hellenistic and Roman period, the novels themselves may be taken as evidence that Ephesos succeeded in its policy of identification.

βιβλία ι΄ περὶ Ἀβροκόμου καὶ Ἀνθίας· καὶ Περὶ τῆς πόλεως Ἐφεσίων· καὶ ἄλλα (text is Ada Adler, *Suidae Lexicon* [5 vols.; Stuttgart: Teubner, 1967–71] 3. 495). It is more likely that two independent works are in question here, since περὶ τῆς πόλεως Ἐφεσίων hardly characterizes the novel. See Gärtner ("Xenophon," 2057) for discussion and citations of older literature.

38. See the two works in the Ephesos Museum, Efes Müzesi inv. nos. 1572 and 2165 (Selahattin Erdemgil, Cengiz İçten, Ümran Yüğrük, et al., *Ephesus Museum Catalogue* [Istanbul: Hitit Color, 1989] 36, 19).

39. Fleischer, *Artemis von Ephesos*, 39–46; idem, "Artemis Ephesia," 758. On Artemis on coins in general, see Karwiese, "Ephesos," 352–54.

40. The symmetrically outstretched arms, closed legs, and wooden construction of a moderately sized statue, as attested by Pliny (*Hist. nat.* 16.79.213–15), all suggest this date (Fleischer, *Artemis von Ephesos*, 116–32). On some statues, the face, hands, and toes were made of dark stone or bronze to emulate the oiled wood of the cult image (pp. 75–76). The *polos* and veil on the Artemis Ephesia are probably Hittite in origin, and the type of cult statue embodied in Artemis Ephesia is widespread in western Anatolia (pp. 391–93; idem, "Supplement," 356).

The alignment of Artemis of Ephesos with the more generically Greek Artemis is not, however, restricted to the solely iconographic. In Pausanias and similar elements of cultic practice are interpreted in terms of ritual chastity. This employment of the Ephesian Artemis is also prominent in Achilles Tatius, which generalizes this characterization: Artemis of Ephesos is seen as the champion of chastity, not in ritual context, but in everyday behavior, that is, a supporter of chastity as a moral value, a conventional Greek attitude. This is close to the heart of the novels; each is a story of chastity vindicated, of the value of exclusive faithfulness to one's mate, despite all possible threats.[41]

Early in Achilles Tatius's novel, Artemis appears to Leukippe, the heroine, and offers her personal protection: "Do not be sad, you shall not die, for I will stand by you and help you. You will remain a virgin until I myself give you away as a bride. No one but Kleitophon will marry you."[42] True to her word, Artemis not only protects Leukippe, but at the conclusion of the novel,[43] provides her with a means of demonstrating her virginity, vindicating herself against slanderous accusations, and proving her fitness to marry the hero. The chastity ordeal takes place in the Artemision of Ephesos, where the priest of Artemis tells of a cave in a grove at the back of the temple, on the

41. On the sexuality represented in the novels, see David Konstan, *Sexual Symmetry: Love in the Ancient Novel and Related Genres* (Princeton: Princeton University Press, 1994); John J. Winkler, *The Constraints of Desire: The Anthropology of Sex and Gender in Ancient Greece* (London/New York: Routledge, 1990). In a typical scene, the newly married couple promises to die rather than live separated from one another: Xenophon *Ephesiaka* 1.11.5 "...that I will not live or look upon the sun if I am separated from you even for a short time" (Anderson, "Xenophon of Ephesus," 135) (ὡς ἐγὼ καὶ βραχύ τι ἀποσπασθεῖσα σοῦ οὔτε ζήσομαι οὔτε τὸν ἥλιον ὄψομαι).

42. Achilles Tatius 4.1.4, translated in Winkler, "Achilles Tatius," 222; Μὴ νῦν . . . κλαῖε. οὐ γὰρ τεθνήξῃ· βοηθὸς γὰρ ἐγώ σοι παρέσομαι. μενεῖς δὲ παρθένος, ἔστ' ἄν σε νυμφοστολήσω· ἄξεται δέ σε ἄλλος οὐδεὶς ἢ Κλειτοφῶν. As elsewhere in this novel, chastity is a more significant value for the woman. In the scene that is the counterpart to this one, it is Aphrodite who appears to Kleitophon, and promises to make him a high priest of the goddess of love (4.1.7). Kleitophon, in fact, loses his virginity before his marriage to Leukippe.

43. Achilles Tatius *Leukippe and Kleitophon* 8.6.

wall of which is hung a magical syrinx. The cave is forbidden except to women who are pure virgins. When a girl enters, the doors of the cave are closed behind her; if she is a virgin, the syrinx plays beautiful music, the doors of the cave open automatically, and the girl appears crowned with sprigs of pine. If not, a scream is heard, the crowd is bid to leave until three days later, when a virgin priestess opens the cave to find the syrinx cast on the ground, and no trace of the young woman. Leukippe's successful completion of this ordeal forms one of the climaxes of the novel's conclusion.

The conflation, on both the symbolic and iconographic level, of the features of the Ephesian Artemis with the more generally Greek characteristics of Artemis is widespread in Roman-period literature and was actively fostered by the city of Ephesos itself. This may run contrary to expectation, since the importance of the iconographic peculiarity of each of the gods can hardly be overestimated. Their visual appearances were a primary form of communication between them and their human worshippers; among other things, it was by knowing the image of a goddess that one could recognize her if she appeared in a dream. The *xoanon*, the cult image, of Artemis Ephesia, like those of other gods, was thought to have nonhuman origins. Pausanias attributes this image to the Amazons, those superhuman beings whom the founders of Ephesos drove away.[44]

In the literature, however, Ephesos, the city of the Ephesian Artemis, becomes a magnet for all lore about Artemis. This may have been true also in the religious imaginations of many inhabitants of the Roman Empire. Ephesos had provided, after all, the most opulent home on earth for Artemis. By the fourth century BCE, Himerios writes that, when dividing up the world with his sister, Apollo chose to dwell among the Greeks and gave Ephesos to Artemis as her inheritance.[45] In the novel of Achilles Tatius, Leukippe's father comes, at

---

44. Pausanias 4.31.8; see also 7.2.6–9.
45. Himerios *Or.* 60.3: "As far as this, when the leader of the Muses divided all the earth beneath the sun with his sister, although he himself dwells among the Greeks, he appointed that the inheritance of Artemis would be Ephesos." (ταῦτά τοι καὶ ὁ Μουσηγέτης τὴν ὑφ' ἥλιον πᾶσαν πρὸς τὴν ἀδελφὴν νειμάμενος, αὐτὸς μὲν οἰκεῖ παρ' ῞Ελλησιν, Ἀρτέμιδος δὲ ἀπέδειξε κλῆρον ὑπάρχειν τὴν ῞Εφεσον).

the conclusion of the novel,[46] to Ephesos as part of a sacred embassy. Artemis had appeared to his forces during their war against the Thrakians; they won the battle by her epiphany and duly brought her a sacrifice to acknowledge her help. Ephesos was the clear choice among sanctuaries, even though the epiphany is not said to have been specifically the Ephesian Artemis.

The novelists, as well as those who minted the early coinage at Ephesos, could imagine the Ephesian Artemis by means of other icons. The novels and the iconographic policy of the city were capitalizing on the body of lore about Artemis that was most widely known. This reimaging of the goddess of Ephesos intends as broad an audience as possible, which, in the world of the novels, translates into a larger readership.

Asylum at the Artemision

The temple of Artemis attracted the attention of Roman period authors and audiences for a number of reasons—for its size, antiquity, and beauty, as well as the collection of magnificent artworks in its precinct. The grandeur of the sanctuary is a theme hardly confined to the Roman period; already in classical literature, Ephesos had achieved this reputation.[47] One aspect of the temple, however, captured the imagination of Roman-period writers more than any other: the inviolability of the sanctuary.

Ensuring the security of the deposits of money at the sanctuary is one of the primary functions of a temple-state, such as the Artemision had been from early times. An oft-cited passage calls the sanctuary the "common bank of Asia" and the "refuge of necessity,"[48] a major

46. Achilles Tatius *Leukippe and Keitophon* 7.12.

47. See Pausanias 4.31.8; 10.26.6; 10.38.6; Strabo *Geog.* 14.1.23; Herodotos *Hist.* 2.148.

48. Aelius Aristides *On Harmony, to the Cities* 24; οὐδεὶς οὕτως ἀγνώμων... ὅστις οὐκ ἂν συγχωρήσειεν ταμεῖόν τε κοινὸν τῆς Ἀσίας εἶναι τὴν πόλιν καὶ τῆς χρείας καταφυγήν. This is oration 23 (Bruno Keil, *Aelii Aristidis Smyrnaei quae supersunt omnia*; vol. 2: *Orationes* XVII–LIII *continens* [Berlin: Weidmann, 1898] 32–54) or 42 (Wilhelm Dindorf, Aristides [3 vols.; Leipzig: Reimer, 1829] 1. 768–96). The deposits were officially recorded (Dio Chrysostom 31.54).

attraction of Ephesos, and the backbone of the trade of this harbor city. Even at those times when this reputation should have been shattered, such as pillaging of the temple by the oligarchy in the fourth century BCE,[49] and the notorious destruction of the temple by the arsonist Herostratos, the adage that the temple was inviolable continued to be repeated in the literary sources of all periods. It was the goddess's unusual absence that explained catastrophe: the temple went up in flames because it was the night of Alexander's birth, and Artemis had traveled north to assist.[50] A number of stories also circulated about how conquerors of the city itself would spare the temple out of piety toward the goddess. Both Polyainos and Aelian recount that when Kroisos was to march against the city, Pindaros the tyrant of the city advised the Ephesians to attach ropes from the gates and walls of the city to the columns of the temple of Artemis. According to Aelian, this was meant to extend the protection of asylum to the city itself, and Kroisos did spare the city.[51]

The security of the temple is praised even above its wealth. Dio Chrysostom claims that the Ephesians, although no wealthier than the citizens of any other city, would sooner strip off the clothing of the goddess than touch one of the deposits in her sanctuary:

49. According to Arrian (*Anabasis Alexanderi* 1.17.11), when Alexander overthrew the oligarchy that had been ruling Ephesos and reinstated the democracy, some of the abuses of the oligarchs were corrected. Those who had looted the temple were executed (τοὺς τὸ ἱερὸν συλήσαντας).

50. Plutarch *Alex.* 3.3. Hegesias from nearby Magnesia set forth this theory. According to the Ephesian μάγοι ("magicians") themselves, the event was a sign of disaster for Asia. Strabo also mentions the disaster (*Geog.* 14.1.22), as does Lucian (*Peregr. Mort.* 22.5).

51. Aelian *Var. Hist.* 3.26; "Pindaros advised the Ephesians to lay out ropes and attach them from the gates and the walls to the columns of the temple of Artemis, so that they would allow the city to be anathema to Artemis, and he thereby devised to confer the right of asylum to the city" (translation mine) (συνεβούλευεν ὁ Πίνδαρος Ἐφεσίοις ἐκδήσαντας ἐκ τῶν πυλῶν καὶ τῶν τειχῶν θώμιγγας συνάψαι τοῖς κίοσι τοῦ τῆς Ἀρτέμιδος νεώ, οἱονεὶ τὴν πόλιν ἀνάθημα ἐῶντας εἶναι τῇ Ἀρτέμιδι, ἀσυλίαν διὰ τούτων ἐπινοῶν τῇ Ἐφέσῳ); the text is Rudolph Hercher, ed., *Claudii Aeliani Varia Historia Epistolae Fragmenta* (Leipzig: Teubner, 1866). See also Polyainos *Strategemata* 6.50. Similarly, Xerxes set on fire most of the temples in the region, except the one at Ephesos (Strabo *Geog.* 14.1.5).

You know about the Ephesians, of course, and that large sums of money are in their hands, some of it belonging to private citizens and deposited in the temple of Artemis, not alone money of the Ephesians but also of aliens and of persons from all parts of the world, and in some cases of commonwealths and kings, money which all deposit there in order that it may be safe, since no one has ever yet dared to violate that place, although countless wars have occurred in the past and the city has often been captured. . . . They [the Ephesians] would sooner, I imagine, strip off the adornment of the goddess than touch this money.[52]

This service was also extended to debtors themselves, who could flee to the sanctuary in Ephesos to receive protection from their creditors, if they still had the means to make the journey.[53]

It is this extended provision of security, granted to all unjustly in danger of murder and imprisonment, that figures most prominently in the Greek literature of the Roman period. The image of Ephesos as a place of sanctuary, of asylum, is as common in works of fiction as it is in works of history. The right of asylum was said to originate in mythological times: the Amazons sought refuge in the sanctuary when they were pursued by Dionysos and, later, by Herakles.[54] Historical sources recount a respectable number of political figures—Roman, Greek, Egyptian, and others—who turned to Ephesos when their careers became unviable, and their continued existence threatened. Demetrios Poliorketes, the son of Antigonos Monopthalmos; the sib-

---

52. Dio Chrysostom 31.54–55 (LCL; trans. J. W. Cohoon and H. Lamar Crosby, eds.; 5 vols.; Cambridge, MA: Harvard University Press, 1940) 3. 59–61. ἴστε που τοὺς Ἐφεσίους, ὅτι πολλὰ χρήματα παρ' αὐτοῖς ἐστι, τὰ μὲν ἰδιωτῶν, ἀποκείμενα ἐν τῷ νεῷ τῆς Ἀρτέμιδος, οὐκ Ἐφεσίων μόνον, ἀλλὰ καὶ ξένων καὶ τῶν ὁπόθεν δήποτε ἀνθρώπων, τὰ δὲ καὶ δήμων καὶ βασιλέων, ἃ τιθέασι πάντες οἱ τιθέντες ἀσφαλείας χάριν, οὐδενὸς οὐδεπώποτε τολμήσαντος ἀδικῆσαι τὸν τόπον, καίτοι καὶ πολέμων ἤδη μυρίων γεγονότων καὶ πολλάκις ἁλούσης τῆς πόλεως. . . . οἶμαι πρότερον ἂν περιέλοιεν τὸν κόσμον τῆς θεοῦ πρὶν ἢ τούτων ἅψασθαι.

53. Plutarch *Moralia* 828 D. Characteristically, Plutarch advises that the asylum offered by Frugality (εὐτελείας) is better, since it exists everywhere.

54. Pausanias 7.2.7; the Ephesians defended the right of asylum at the sanctuary by citing this precedent (Tacitus *Annals* 3.61).

lings of Cleopatra; and Ptolemy XII Auletes all took refuge at the Artemision.[55] Larger groups also availed themselves of this right: the Roman settlers of Ephesos who were threatened during the Mithridatic uprising fled to the altar of Artemis.[56]

The occasional abuses of these appeals for asylum, as in the case of other sanctuaries, led to tragic accounts that were retold in colorful detail. Athenaios tells of Eirene, the devoted courtesan of Ptolemy, the son of Philadelphos, who fled with him to the temple of Artemis when the Thracians were trying to kill him. Their pursuers murdered both in the temple precinct; she clung to the doorknockers on the doors of the temple and, like a sacrificial victim, splashed the altar with her blood as she died.[57] The Roman and Italian settlers in Ephesos endured a similarly gory end. Mithridates ordered their slaughter while he passed through Ephesos (88 BCE); the Ephesians killed them as they fled to the Artemision for sanctuary, not even sparing those who were clasping the images of the gods and goddesses (συμπλεκομένους τοῖς ἀγάλμασιν).[58]

These tales of horror spring out of a concrete temporal context. Such desperate pleas for safety rose out of the political turbulence of the Hellenistic and Republican periods. Ephesos was an important

55. Demetrios fled to Ephesos after his father's death, and went on to have a lively political career (Porphyry *Chronica* 3.3; 6.1). Dio Cassius claims that Antony killed the siblings (ἀδελφοί) of Cleopatra when they sought refuge at the Artemision (48.24.2). Perhaps he has in mind Arsinoë, whom Josephus claims was killed by Antony at the temple of Artemis in Ephesos; according to Josephus (*Ant.* 15.89), Cleopatra had her younger brother poisoned. Appian seems to preserve the most accurate account: Arsinoë was received by the *megabyzos* in Ephesos as a queen, for which Antony later wished to punish him; Arsinoë was killed not in the temple of Artemis in Ephesos, but at the temple of Artemis Leukophryne in Miletos (*Bell. civ.* 5.9). According to Dio Cassius (39.16.3), despairing of a return to the throne, Ptolemy XII went to Ephesos, spending time in the sanctuary (παρὰ τῇ θεῷ διητᾶτο). This was temporary; with the support of the Romans, he returned to his native land.

56. Appian *Mithridatica* 23 (88).

57. Athenaios *Deipnosophist.* 13 § 593b.

58. Appian *Mithridatica* 23 (88). This is one of many similar abuses, such as at the Asklepieion in Pergamon, at Kaunos, and many other locations on the coast of Asia Minor.

arena of world affairs during this period.[59] By the middle of the Roman imperial era, when most of our sources were composed, these events were in the distant past; yet they lingered on in historical memory, and spread abroad the characterization of Ephesos as the last hope of desperate individuals, a haven of possible security for those battered by fate.

A novelist like Achilles Tatius was quick to exploit this *topos*. In his work, the asylum offered by the Artemision in Ephesos becomes a full-blown plot device. Although the two protagonists do not come from Ephesos, it is in that city that they experience their *anagnorisis*, as they encounter and recognize each other. The author explains the practice of asylum in a passage imitating the antiquarians:

> From ancient days this temple had been forbidden to free women who were not virgins. Only men and virgins were permitted here. If a nonvirgin woman passed inside, the penalty was death, unless she was a slave accusing her master, in which case she was allowed to beseech the goddess, and the magistrates would hear the case between her and her master.[60]

Whatever the outcome of the case, according to Achilles Tatius, no harm would come to the suppliant: "If the master had in fact done no wrong, he recovered his maidservant, swearing that he would not bear a grudge for her flight. If it was decided that the serving girl had a just case, she remained there as a slave to the goddess."[61]

The Artemision itself provides both of the innocent lovers sanctuary against false accusations: Kleitophon is wrongly convicted of the murder of his beloved, and, as we have seen, Leukippe faces the slander that she has not successfully withstood the various assaults on her chastity. The protection offered by the goddess becomes the salvation of the two young people. The cultic complex surrounding

---

59. For the history of Ephesos from its acquisition by Rome in 133 BCE through the Roman civil war and beyond, see Dieter Knibbe and Wilhelm Alzinger, "Ephesos vom Beginn der römischen Herrschaft in Kleinasien bis zum Ende der Principatszeit," *ANRW* 2.7.2 (1980) 748–830.

60. Achilles Tatius *Leukippe and Kleitophon* 7.13.2–4, translated in Winkler, "Achilles Tatius," 267.

61. Achilles Tatius *Leukippe and Kleitophon* 7.13.3, translated in Winkler, "Achilles Tatius," 267.

Artemis intervenes in the plot with a concreteness and vividness that rivals the action of any of the characters.

In the course of Kleitophon's trial, he has accused Melite, an Ephesian woman and his reputed paramour, of having a hand in the murder. Although he did not kill the girl and he knows that Melite is also innocent, he accuses her because he believes that Melite has framed him. As a convicted criminal, Kleitophon is subject to giving evidence under torture. He is about to be hung up and stretched out when someone is seen approaching the chambers. It is the priest of Artemis, who arrives in the courtroom crowned with laurel to announce that an embassy to the goddess (θεωρίας τῇ θεῷ) has arrived. All punishments must cease until the ambassadors have completed their sacrifice. A moratorium is set on Melite's trial.[62]

The leader of the foreign embassy happens to be Leukippe's father, Sostratos, who has come to sacrifice to Artemis because her appearance during a battle in his home region of Byzantion gave his forces the victory. Artemis also appeared to Sostratos personally and promised that he would find his lost daughter and Kleitophon in Ephesos. When he finds Kleitophon but no Leukippe, and learns that the trial is for the murder of his beloved daughter, his faith wavers. Kleinias, Kleitophon's friend, reassures him: "Courage, Father; Artemis does not lie. . . . Don't you see how she just saved this man too, snatching him from the torturers as he hung in the ropes?"[63]

At that moment, a temple attendant comes to the chamber to announce that a foreign woman has just sought asylum at the Artemision. Kleitophon and Leukippe's father immediately recognize from the attendant's description that it must be Leukippe, who is not dead after all. The oracle of Artemis turns out to be true: she has kept both young people safe. When the guards come to escort Kleitophon from the courtroom back to jail, a crowd, now happily praising Artemis, blocks their way until the priest of Artemis gives a personal guarantee that he will keep Kleitophon and present him when the trial is scheduled to continue. The two lovers are happily reunited in the

62. Achilles Tatius *Leukippe and Kleitophon* 7.12.
63. Achilles Tatius *Leukippe and Kleitophon* 7.14.6, translated in Winkler, "Achilles Tatius," 268.

precinct itself, and enjoy the hospitality of the priest of Artemis until all of their troubles are resolved. Achilles Tatius also plays with the motif of the abuse of asylum, a theme prevalent among the historians of the Roman period. When Kleitophon and Leukippe meet their legal adversary, Thersandros, in the Artemision, the man strikes Kleitophon and draws blood. Kleitophon launches a long, tragic monologue (τραγῳδῶν ἐνέπλησα βοῆς τὸ ἱερόν):

> Whither further may we flee violence? Where may we seek shelter? To whom of the gods after Artemis? We are attacked in the very temples; we are struck in the sanctuaries! . . . Even to the wicked the temples' security gives refuge, but I who never a wrong have done, a refugee of Artemis, am knocked about at her own altar, while the goddess (alas!) looks on. . . . This sacred floor is stained with human gore. Who makes such libation to the goddess?[64]

The abuse of the rights of asylum at Greek temples in general is a widespread *topos* in history and tragedy. Achilles Tatius was hoping to give his audience the pleasure of recognizing this, and the motif also lends his narrative a specifically Ephesian flavor, since many of the stories of butchered supplants concerned this city.

In Kleitophon's monologue, one finds yet another *topos*, that of the misuse of the right of the asylum by the guilty. Achilles Tatius employs this motif again when Thersandros accuses the high priest of Artemis of sullying the reputation of the temple by admitting the two lovers into the sanctuary: "A murderer and adulterer, living in the house of the goddess of purity! Oh, an adulterer dwelling with the Virgin! . . . You have made. . . the home of Artemis a bedroom for

---

64. Achilles Tatius *Leukippe and Kleitophon* 8.2.1–3 translated in Winkler, "Achilles Tatius," 270; Ποῦ φύγωμεν ἔτι τοὺς βιαίους; ποῖ καταδράμωμεν; ἐπὶ τίνα θεῶν μετὰ τὴν Ἄρτεμιν; ἐν αὐτοῖς τυπτόμεθα τοῖς ἱεροῖς· ἐν τοῖς τῆς ἀσυλίας παιόμεθα χωρίοις. . . . καὶ τοῖς μὲν πονηροῖς αἱ τῶν ἱερῶν ἀσφάλειαι διδόασι καταφυγήν, ἐγὼ δὲ μηδὲν ἀδικήσας, ἱκέτης δὲ τῆς Ἀρτέμιδος γενόμενος, τύπτομαι παρ' αὐτῷ τῷ βωμῷ, βλεπούσης, οἴμοι, τῆς θεοῦ. . . . μεμίανται τὸ ἔδαφος ἀνθρωπίνῳ αἵματι. τοιαῦτα σπένδει τίς τῇ θεῷ. The manuscripts read αὐλαίας instead of ἀσυλίας, but as this yields no good sense, and the scribal error is easy to explain, I follow Vilborg's emendation here (Achilles Tatius, 8.2.1–3).

adulterers and whores."[65] Apollonios of Tyana launches a similar criticism when he complains of the thieves, robbers, and kidnappers present in the Artemision; he laments that the Ephesians have allowed the temple to become "a den of robbers" (τὸ γὰρ ἱερὸν τῶν ἀποστερούντων μυχός ἐστιν).[66] Jesus' remark about the temple in Jerusalem many years earlier, itself a citation of Jeremiah's complaint (Jer 7:11), shows that the relevance of this *topos* was broader than individual religious traditions in antiquity (Mark 11:17 and parallels).

In the *Ephesiaka*, the Ephesians Habrokomes and Anthia ultimately thank Artemis for their survival and reunion, although a host of gods, each appropriate to the locality in which any given episode of the story is played out, have a hand in their preservation.[67] At the close of the novel, Anthia and Habrokomes return to Ephesos, pray and sacrifice to Artemis, and set up an inscription in honor of the goddess "commemorating all of their sufferings and adventures" (καὶ γραφὴν τῇ θεῷ ἀνέθησαν πάντων ὅσα τε ἔπαθον καὶ ὅσα ἔδρασαν).[68]

Similarly to their fictional depiction in Achilles Tatius, the Ephesians themselves saw to it that the inviolability of the temple remained effective. Appian tells that Antony arrested the *megabyzos* for offering sanctuary to Arsinoë from her sister Cleopatra while she was in Ephesos, but popular outcry led Antony to release the priest.[69] The right of asylum at times became a political issue. Strabo tells that the

65. Achilles Tatius 8.8.10–11, translated in Winkler, "Achilles Tatius," 275. φονεὺς καὶ μοιχὸς παρὰ τῇ καθαρᾷ θεῷ· οἴμοι μοιχὸς παρὰ τῇ παρθένῳ.... ἡ τῆς Ἀρτέμιδος οἰκία μοιχῶν γέγονε καὶ πόρνης θάλαμος.

66. Apollonios *Ep.* 65.

67. On the remarkable polytheism expressed by this text, see Gärtner's comments ("Xenophon," 2068–69). He rightly attributes the appearance of so many divinities as a sign of Xenophon's desire to avoid, at any cost, a monotonous narrative. Although the lovers meet at one of the festivals of Artemis, it is the oracle of Apollo at Kolophon that commands them to marry; the oracle foretells that Isis will be their savior (Xenophon *Ephesiaka* 1.6).

68. Xenophon *Ephesiaka* 5.15.2.

69. Appian *Bell. civ.* 5.9. Hilke Thür has recently proposed that the octagonal heroon near the Celsus Library at Ephesos may have been the tomb of Arsinoë; the skeleton inside the sarcophagus was that of a girl of around twenty, and the structure, for which no inscription has been found, dates stylistically to between 50 and 20 BCE ("Arsinoë IV," 43–56); see also her contribution in this volume.

spatial limits of asylum often changed. Alexander extended it for one stadion; Mithridates extended it an arrow's flight from the corner of the roof, a little more than a stadion; Antony doubled this distance, including part of the city in it. Augustus, in turn, limited this extension, since, according to Strabo, it put the city in the power of criminals.[70] Although this consideration may have served as partial motivation for Augustus's action, limiting the right of asylum in any way was an imposition on the independence of the city and its sanctuary.[71] The right of asylum, and the security of the Artemision, were political and economic services that Ephesos was able to offer to Greeks and Romans alike, by dint of the relatively independent temple estate and hierarchy. This continued to be respected under the empire; although Augustus limited the geographical extent of the temple temenos, he did strengthen its estate by the return of some of its properties.[72]

Widespread knowledge of the asylum offered by Artemis served the fame and prosperity of the city, attracting a number of wealthy and important figures, many of them aristocratic political refugees. All services need advertisement, however; the treatment of the historians shows how accounts of past events could carry forward the message. The *Ephesiaka* reflect one way in which the temple complex itself played a part: it provided a location in which votive dedications could laud the services of the goddess. Given the status of Ephesos as a city of harbor and markets, these accounts would be spread abroad by travelers, merchants, and visitors to Ephesos, as well as by Ephesians who traveled abroad. The novelists tapped into this existing body of lore. The *topos* not only gave the reader pleasure in the fulfillment of their expectations; it was also an ingredient expedient for structuring the plots of tales of adventure and rescue. The city's fame lent an aura to the novelists' stories, and the stories themselves ensured that the city's reputation would continue to live on.

70. Strabo *Geog.* 14.1.23.
71. See Knibbe, *Der Staatsmarkt*, 75. It was presumably their desire to maintain this independence that led the Ephesians to turn down Alexander's offer to rebuild the Artemision after its fourth-century destruction by fire (Strabo *Geog.* 14.1.22); Alexander required only that they record his generosity on an inscription.
72. *IvE* Ia 19B b4; VII 3501; 3502.

Roman Presence in Ephesos

In the previous two sections, which treated different aspects of the cult of Artemis, literary, historical, and archaeological data roughly corresponded, demonstrating that the portrait of Ephesos among Greek authors of the Roman period reflected what was happening in the world of real events that took place in Ephesos, and the policies of the city itself. With regard to Roman presence at Ephesos and specific changes in the religious life of Ephesos in the Roman period, archaeological and epigraphic evidence draws a different picture of the city than do the literary sources in Greek. If Latin authors had also been included in the survey, Rome would have figured more prominently. For example, Dio Cassius, a Roman citizen engaged in writing a history of Rome, gives the only detailed information about the imperial cult in Ephesos in Greek literature. He tells of the temples of Divus Julius (ἥρωα Ἰούλιον) and Dea Roma in Ephesos, which were erected in the time of Augustus. Significantly, the cult was not meant for the local inhabitants, but for Romans living in the provinces; Pergamon was the home of the cult of Augustus and Roma for the inhabitants of the province of Asia, or foreigners (τοῖς. . . ξένοις, Ἕλληνάς σφας ἐπικαλέσας), as Dio Cassius calls them— it is Caesar who calls them "Hellenes."[73] If the identification is secure, the double-cella podium temple near the Prytaneion in the upper agora could well be the temples of Roma and Divus Julius mentioned by Dio (map no. 58).[74] In addition to the architectural evidence, the proximity of this temple to the so-called Basilike Stoa on the north

73. Dio Cassius 51.20.7. Dio Cassius tells of corresponding cults for the province of Bithynia: the cult of Augustus and Roma was at Nikomedia, and the cult of Roma and Divus Julius, for Romans, was in Nikaia (51.20.6–7). On the early imperial cults in Asia, see Friesen, *Twice Neokoros*, 7–28.
74. Friesen also accepts this (*Twice Neokoros*, 11 n. 21). The architectural details, stylistically and technically, would fall into the late first century BCE. See Wilhelm Alzinger, "Das Regierungsviertel," *JÖAI* 50 (1972–75) Beibl. 230–99, esp. 250–54; and the diagrams in Anton Bammer, "Zu ÖJh 50, 1972–1975 Beibl. 242 ff. 249 ff.," *JÖAI* 51 (1976–77) Hauptbl. 57–58. On the question of the cult in general, see Ronald Mellor, *ΘΕΑ ΡΩΜΗ: The Worship of the Goddess Roma in the Greek World* (Hypomnemata: Untersuchungen zur Antike und zu ihrem Nachleben 42; Göttingen: Vandenhoeck & Ruprecht, 1975) 56–59.

side of the State Agora (map no. 61) would speak for this identification. Monumental statues of Livia and Augustus were found in the east end of this structure.[75] Dio Cassius also circulates the tale that Caligula did not grant imperial temples under his name either to Ephesos, Smyrna, or Pergamon, since his desired position of honor in these cities had been preempted by Artemis, Tiberius, and Augustus, respectively.[76]

These meager references pale by the sheer size of the archaeological remains of the imperial cults in Ephesos. Aside from the numerous inscriptions, monumental building complexes dot the city. Far larger than the double Temple of Divus Julius and Dea Roma, the Temple of the Flavian Sebastoi, as it is known from inscriptions, stands on its massive artificial terrace to the southwest of the upper agora (map no. 53). Steven Friesen has recently argued that this was dedicated in approximately 89 or 90 CE, during the reign of Domitian, although the plural form Sebastoi and fragments of a massive statue of either Titus or Domitian[77] suggest that the temple was dedicated to more than one of the Flavian emperors.[78] Last, the large second-century temple complex (map no. 15) north of the Harbor Baths (map

75. Alzinger, "Regierungsviertel," 260–65; Fritz Eichler, "Die österreichischen Ausgrabungen in Ephesos im Jahre 1966," *AnzWien* 104 (1967) 15–28, esp. 18–20.
76. Dio Cassius 59.28.1. Tacitus (*Annals* 4.55–56) tells of a similar incident in 23 CE under Tiberius; the right to build him a temple fell to Smyrna. Ephesos was rejected because of Artemis, and Miletos because of Apollo.
77. For the identification as Titus, see Georg Daltrop, Ulrich Hausmann and Max Wegner, *Die Flavier: Vespasian, Titus, Domitian, Nerva, Julia Titi, Domitilla, Domitia* (Berlin: Mann, 1966) 26, 86, 100, pl. 15b. The fragments (İzmir Müzesi inv. no. 670) were moved from the İzmir Museum in the early 1990s, and are now on display in the Ephesos Museum (Efes Müzesi) in Selçuk. In addition to the arm and head on display, parts of marble feet and fingers have also been found; these are in storage.
78. See Friesen, *Twice Neokoros*, 29–49. Scholars agree that the temple was completed under Domitian; at issue is which emperor granted permission to build it. Friesen argues that Domitian granted it, and that it was completed nine years into his reign, a sufficient period of time both for the embassies required to secure permission from the emperor and for the construction of the temple itself. David Magie (*Roman Rule*, 1. 572; 2. 1432–34) believes that Vespasian granted permission.

no. 8), the south stoa of which later became the Church of Mary, was probably the second neokorate temple dedicated to Hadrian, who was greeted in Ephesos as Zeus Olympios. Stefan Karwiese, who is excavating the complex, has called the temple complex the Olympieion.[79] Literary sources do not present the religious life of Ephesos as immune to political considerations in other eras. Many of our authors write about the erection of statues of other rulers in the Artemision itself. After the defeat of Athens at Aigospotamoi, the Ephesians put up statues of Lysander and other Spartans such as Eteonikos and

79. See Stefan Karwiese, *Erster vorläufiger Gesamtbericht über die Wiederaufnahme der archäologischen Untersuchung der Marienkirche in Ephesos* (Vienna: ÖAW, 1989); idem, "Der Numismatiker-Archäologe," *JÖAI* 56 (1985) Hauptbl. 99–108, esp. 105–8. Although little is left of the architecture—even the foundation blocks of the temple were removed in the fifth century by Christians—one capital of the temple can be viewed on site today, and massive geisa fragments from the south stoa of the complex were found in 1991. The architectural style of these pieces is not inconsistent with a Hadrianic dating. C. P. Jones ("The Olympieion and the Hadrianeion at Ephesos," *JHS* 113 [1993] 149–52) has questioned whether this structure is the Olympieion mentioned by Pausanias (7.2.9), although he agrees that it may be the second neokorate temple dedicated to Hadrian. Jones believes that the building mentioned by Pausanias may not refer to the neokorate temple, but rather to a sanctuary of Zeus, which must have existed in Ephesos well before the second century CE, and could not then be the same as the Church of Mary complex. What Pausanias meant by "Olympieion" is unclear, since the term is not otherwise attested for Ephesos; he writes that the heroon of Androklos is located on the path that passes by the Olympieion and leads to the Magnesian Gate (κατὰ τὴν ὁδὸν τὴν ἐκ τοῦ ἱεροῦ παρὰ τὸ Ὀλυμπιεῖον καὶ ἐπὶ πύλας τὰς Μαγνήτιδας). Identifying the Olympieion with this large temple complex is at least a reasonable possibility: excavations along the sacred way have demonstrated that there were two ways to the Magnesian Gate from the Artemision, one passing to the east of Panayirdağ, and one passing to its west. The latter was the less frequented, since, according to initial deep soundings on the northwest and southwest slopes of the hill carried out in 1992 by John C. Kraft and İlhan Kayan, the harbor of Ephesos partially surrounded the western half of the hill into the first century CE. The path leading around the west of Panayirdağ would have then been marshy until around the second century, when the large temple structure in question would have been constructed. Perhaps precisely for this reason, Pausanias specifies that the road he has in mind is the one that passes by the Olympieion, since it would have been the less usual and the newer route to the Magnesian Gate.

Pharax in the sanctuary (ἱερόν) of Artemis. They later set up statues of Konon and Timotheos "beside the Ephesian goddess" (παρὰ τῇ Ἐφεσίᾳ θεῷ) [80] During the time of the Macedonians, the Ephesians placed a statue of Philip in the temple.[81] We do hear about Roman statues in Ephesos in our literary sources: after the uprising under Mithridates, one of the actions for which the Roman government punished the Ephesians was their destruction of the statues of the Romans that had been set up in their city.[82] The epigraphic record, however, again suggests that Roman presence in the religious life of Ephesos was more visible than the literary sources would lead one to conclude. The Salutaris inscription of 104 CE, for example, provides for the display of statues of Trajan, Plotina, the Roman Senate, the equestrian order, the Roman people (*plebs*, δῆμος in the inscription), and Augustus in a procession through the city which was repeated on a nearly biweekly basis throughout the year.[83]

Major changes in the cult of Artemis, well-documented in the epigraphic and archaeological record, also pass without mention in the literary sources. In the novel of Achilles Tatius, when Kleitophon escapes from the house of Melite, he wanders on the streets of Ephesos during the festival of Artemis. There are drunken people everywhere; "all night long a crowd filled the entire agora."[84] The author does not clarify which of the two agoras he has in mind. The lower, Tetragonos Agora near the harbor was older, but the State Agora had stronger connections with the cult of Artemis in the Roman period. It is there

80. Pausanias 6.3.16.
81. Arrian *Anabasis Alexanderi* 1.17.11. This statue was torn down by the oligarchy that ruled Ephesos in the fourth century BCE.
82. Appian *Mithridatica* 21; they were also punished for their impious treatment of Roman gifts in the temple of Artemis (61).
83. The Roman statues, which appear in the front of the procession, are grouped with Ephesian images: the image of the Senate is grouped with the Ephesian *boule* and Artemis, the equestrian order with the Ephesian *ephebeia* and Artemis. Among the thirty-one statues in the procession, nine represent Artemis (Rogers, *The Sacred Identity of Ephesos*, see esp. the table on pp. 84–85, and the text of the inscription on pp. 158–62). Rogers interprets the Salutaris bequest as a way of placing the reality of Roman rule into perspective by incorporating and subordinating the new rulers to the Greek past.
84. Achilles Tatius *Leukippe and Kleitophon* 6.3.

that we find the lists of the *curetes*, an important association charged with organizing and supporting the festivals of Artemis.[85]

The scanty reference to Roman presence in Ephesos by Greek authors should be coupled with another characteristic of this literature: a conservatism and nostalgia for the Greek past. This can be demonstrated in works both of fiction and of history in this period. In the novels, a blind eye is cast toward anything Roman[86]; emphasis is placed on the municipal offices and institutions of the Greek polis, and Ephesos becomes the desired destination of the homesick characters. The *Ephesiaka* show remarkable specificity in geographic references to lower Egypt and to Ephesos and its surroundings. Although geographic data about other locations range from peculiar to impossible, most scholars argue for the compelling detail and substantial accuracy of the geographic knowledge of the Nile delta. Yet the heart of the novel lies in Ephesos, the homeland of the protagonists; because of this, J. Gwyn Griffiths has argued that the *Ephesiaka* may have been written by an expatriate Ephesian living in lower Egypt.[87]

85. See Knibbe, *Der Staatsmarkt*, esp. 74–79, 96–100. The association of *curetes* is also attested in the Hellenistic period; in one inscription (*IvE* IV 1389), the *curetes* are among the influential individuals recommending an applicant for Ephesian citizenship. Knibbe argues that the transfer of the *curetes* from the Artemision to the Prytaneion during Augustan times corresponded with a reduction of their responsibilities from the political and cultic to the cultic alone.

86. On the emphasis of the novels on standard Greek institutions, see Suzanne Saïd, "The City in the Greek Novel," in James Tatum, ed., *The Search for the Ancient Novel* (Baltimore: Johns Hopkins University Press, 1994) 216–36. On realism in the novels, see E. L. Bowie, "The Novels and the Real World," in B. P. Reardon, ed., *Erotica Antiqua* (Bangor, Wales: n.p., 1977) 91–96.

87. Gärtner ("Xenophon," 2059) admits that, at first view, the geographic references to Ephesos and its surroundings, as well as to the Nile delta, are striking in their exactitude, but he believes that these details could have been gleaned from Herodotos and geographic handbooks. Griffiths ("Xenophon of Ephesus on Isis," 426–37) believes this is true for the Ephesian data, but argues for the eyewitness nature of the upper Egyptian information. Henri Henne ("La géographie de l'Égypte dans Xénophon d'Éphèse," *Revue d'Histoire de la Philosophie et d'Histoire Générale de la Civilisation* 4 [1936] 97–106) notes that, although Xenophon mentions many cities in his work, in Egypt he names even the smaller towns, including some that are otherwise unattested.

Aside from the young characters' predictable longing to return to the city of their parents,[88] Xenophon also includes vignettes that highlight the ties to Ephesos. In the course of her travels, Anthia encounters Eudoxos, an Ephesian doctor shipwrecked on the way to Egypt, he too is trying in every way possible to return to Ephesos, even applying to the local aristocracy for the money for his journey. Anthia tries to talk with him every day, "since he reminded her of the people back home."[89] The religious institutions of their home city also bind them. When Anthia requires an oath from the doctor, he must swear "by their ancestral goddess, Artemis."[90] Similarly, at the outset of the story Anthia swears her fidelity to Habrokomes, her husband and fellow Ephesian, by "the goddess of our fathers, the great Artemis of the Ephesians."[91] The local divinity stands for the homeland and all that it encompasses.

Achilles Tatius characterizes Ephesos in a manner that is even more striking. Since Ephesos is not the homeland of the characters, nothing compels the author to include it in his novel. Little of the significant action of the novel takes place in Tyre, the home of Kleitophon, or in Byzantion, home of Leukippe, which are both on the fringes of the Greek world. It is in Ephesos that the reunion of the lovers takes place, and it is the Greek institutions of Ephesos, her law courts and temple, that effect the vindication of their suffering.

The novels respond to Roman presence by failing to place it at center stage. Although exact dating is difficult, there is no question

88. As they depart from Ephesos on their journey, the parents call out "May the Ephesians receive you again safe and sound, and may you recover your beloved homeland" (translation mine) (Xenophon *Ephesiaka* 1.10.10; ὑμᾶς ἀνασωθέντας ὑποδέξαιντο Ἐφέσιοι, καὶ τὴν φιλτάτην ἀπολάβοιτε πατρίδα). In a later passage (2.1.2), the young pair cries out in desperation to their parents and their beloved country, as at many other points. Griffiths ("Xenophon of Ephesus on Isis," 417–18) collects still more references in the text which show that "attachment to the polis [that is, Ephesos] is a very warm element" in the novel.

89. Xenophon *Ephesiaka* 3.4.3, translated in Anderson, "Xenophon of Ephesus," 149.

90. Xenophon *Ephesiaka* 3.5.5, translated in Anderson, "Xenophon of Ephesus," 150.

91. Xenophon *Ephesiaka* 1.11.5, translated in Anderson, "Xenophon of Ephesus," 135.

that the novels were written in the Roman world. In passing, Xenophon mentions Perilaus, the eirenarch of Kilikia,[92] an office that is only attested after 116 or 117 CE.[93] Habrokomes is also brought before the prefect of Egypt in Alexandria,[94] impossible in a world before Augustus. Although Achilles Tatius speaks anachronistically of satraps, a Persian term, the papyri, which range in date from the second to the fourth century, provide a secure dating in the high imperial period.[95]

In the other sources of the period, the same conservatism and love of the past is revealed in the selection of topics. The gap between what was taking place in Ephesos in the second century and what was written about Ephesos during the same period is considerable. In the Roman era, the periods of Ephesian history most often narrated were the time of its foundation, the military actions of Alexander and his immediate successors, and the encounter between Greece and Rome during the Republican period. These were the events that formed the world in which the audience of these works lived. The response of Greek authors to the fact of Roman dominance was not, apparently, to describe it, but to question what chain of events allowed Rome to come to power in the first place.

For the novels, Ephesos remained a bastion of the normal Greek world, a center of order in the course of the unsettling events that perturbed their characters. This is no less true for the historian. In Polyainos's narration of Kroisos's attack on Ephesos, the Lydian king spares the city of Ephesos because he fears the goddess.[96] This event took place long before the second century CE, when Polyainos began writing. The purpose of telling this story in a world in which Greek cities live under foreign domination is to present the image of Ephesos

92. Xenophon *Ephesiaka* 2.13.3.
93. An inscription found not far from Ephesos (Anderson, "Xenophon of Ephesus," 146 n. 13) attests to this. The office was widespread in Asia Minor, including Ephesos (Magie, *Roman Rule*, 1. 647, 2. 1514–15).
94. For example, Xenophon *Ephesiaka* 3.12.6.
95. Willis, "Achilles Tatius," 75–76.
96. Polyainos *Strategemata* 6.50; Κροῖσος τιμῶν τὴν θεὸν ἐφείσατο τῆς πόλεως ὥσπερ ἀναθήματος. The text is from Edward Woelfflin, ed., *Polyaeni Strategematon Libri Octi* (Leipzig: Teubner, 1887).

as a safe haven, as a place where Artemis holds sway and offers her protection. The divergence between the literary sources and the archaeological record regarding the presentation of Rome is striking. On the previous two topics, it was shown that city policy and literary production agreed, first in presenting Artemis of Ephesos as a Greek goddess, and then in emphasizing and preserving the role of the city as a place of asylum. Both of these goals were essentially conservative and retained characteristics that had long been part of the city's life: its Panhellenism and its independence as a Greek polis. The literary sources do not ignore Rome. The place of Ephesos in the religious imagination, however, remains anchored to the Greek past of this Roman-period city. This is not only true of the "escapist" literature of the novels; none of the Greek authors—neither the serious historian, nor the antiquarian, nor the novelist—dwelt on the religious innovations that Ephesos underwent during the Roman period. The stories people wanted to hear faced backward.

The prominent appearance of Ephesos in Xenophon's *Ephesiaka* and in Achilles Tatius's work may not be fortuitous. Xenophon and Lollianos may have been Ephesian, and the novelist Chariton, who may have written more than one work,[97] was from Aphrodisias. This, along with the accurate and detailed geographic descriptions of western Asia Minor in Xenophon and Achilles Tatius, and of Lesbos in Longos, suggests that much of the intended readership of the novels may have been located in the province of Asia.[98] Based on the content of the works, past scholarship assumed that the audience of the Greek novel consisted of women, young people, or a newly literate middle class. More recent scholars, employing papyrological evidence and studies of literacy in the ancient world, have argued that the readership of the novels was probably the same as that of other, more

97. *Metiochos* and *Chione*, two fragmentary novels, show affinities in language and style to *Kallirhoe*, which is explicitly attributed to Chariton. On Chariton as author of these three works, see Michael Gronewald, "Ein neues Fragment zu einem Roman," *ZPE* 35 (1979) 15–20; on *Chione*, see also Albrecht Dihle, "Zur Datierung des Metiochos-Romans," *Würzburger Jahrbücher für die Altertumswissenschaft*, n.s., 4 (1978) 47–55.

98. Ewen Bowie puts forward this argument ("The Readership of Greek Novels in the Ancient World," in Tatum, *Search*, 435–59, esp. 450–53); he envisages the readership as "the educated classes of *provincia Asia*" (p. 451).

highbrow, Greek literature—that is, from the élite and wealthy classes.[99] The same people who read the histories also read the novels.

What is surprising, if the novels did appeal primarily to an élite audience, is that the readers would then belong to the same classes that, in Ephesos, were building imperial cult temples, funding statues of Roman rulers, making dedications and offerings to them, and entering the Roman social orders as equestrians and senators. The cities of Asia Minor in particular coexisted harmoniously with Roman rule, benefiting from the imperial peace in a cultural efflorescence that expressed itself in the architectural and literary creativity of the second century. The profile of Ephesos in Greek literature suggests that the provincial élite lived in a delicate counterpoint between old and new. In the monuments of public display, prominent Ephesians were devising creative ways of living meaningfully in a Roman world; in the world of imagination, the profile of Ephesos and its Greek past lived on. For this audience, Ephesos provided a stable home city full of beneficent institutions which preserved the fictional characters about whom they read. The image of Ephesos in Roman-period literature reaffirmed basic Greek values and the belief in Greek independence of action.

Appendix

Occurrence of root Ἐφεσ-among Greek authors from the first century BCE to the fourth century CE, in decreasing order of frequency:[100]

99. Susan A. Stephens ("Who Read Ancient Novels?" in Tatum, *Search*, 405–18) has argued succinctly that the audience of the novel was no different than the readership of works such as Thucydides, that is, predominantly élite males. As she notes, the papyrological evidence suggests that, far from being common literature, copies of the novels may have been hard to procure. William V. Harris's recent study (*Ancient Literacy* [Cambridge, MA: Harvard University Press, 1989]) of literacy in the ancient world does not support either the notion of widespread literacy during the Roman period nor of a class of newly literate bourgeois who would have been a target audience for the novel (pp. 227–28). Harris estimates literacy in Rome and Italy during the imperial period at below fifteen percent, and less than five to ten percent in the western provinces (pp. 267, 272); he makes no such estimate for the east.

100. Some of the numerical counts are not entirely accurate, since, as in the case of Athenaios, multiple versions or epitomes exist for some works. Yet,

Athenaios	62
Xenophon of Ephesos	45
Aulus Herodianus	43
Philostratos	40
Strabo	39
Pausanias	36
Plutarch	34
Diodorus Siculus	27
Appian	20
Diogenes Laertius	20
Polyainos	18
Achilles Tatius	14
Galen and Pseudo-Galen	13
Lucian	13
Aelian	12
Arrian	10
Josephus	10
Aelius Aristides	8
Dio Cassius	8
Dio Chrysostom	8
Libanius	5
Dionysios of Halikarnossos	4
Oribasius Medicus	4
Porphyry	4
Apollonios of Tyana	3
Harpocration	3
Alexander of Aphrodisias	2
Dioscorides Pedanius	2
Himerios	2
Publius Aelius Phlegon	2
Antoninus Liberalis	1
Pseudo-Apollodoros	1
Apollonios the Sophist	1

considering the fragmentary preservation of ancient literature in general, it seemed advisable merely to present the numerical counts as they stand. Only cases in which the root appears as a component of a proper noun or adjective have been included.

Dictys of Crete	1
Epiktetos	1
Eutropios	1
Heliodoros	1
Iamblichos	1
Parthenios	1
Rufus Medicus	1
Sextus Empiricus	1
Sopater Rhetoricus	1
Suetonius	1

Ephesos in Early Christian Literature

Helmut Koester
Harvard Divinity School

In order to assess the information about Ephesos in early Christian literature, it is important to begin with the genuine letters of Paul and not with the well-known story of the riot of the silversmiths in Acts 19.

Paul mentions Ephesos for the first time in 1 Corinthians, written early in his stay at Ephesos, which, according to Acts 19:8–10, lasted two years and three months. The probable dates for this stay are from the fall of 52 to the spring of 55 CE, that is, after Paul's missionary activity in Macedonia, Corinth, and Achaia. Reconstructing the sequence of the letters that Paul wrote from Ephesos, as well as interpreting some parts of these letters, is problematic. There is no question, however, that these were turbulent and difficult years for Paul's ministry, not only with respect to events in Ephesos, but also with regard to his controversy with the newly founded church in Corinth.

Paul's Letter to the Galatians may have been the first letter[1] written from Ephesos,[2] but nothing about his stay in that city can be learned from this letter. 1 Corinthians however, was certainly written from Ephesos,[3] and contains several remarks that seem to reveal something about Paul's experience there. In 1 Cor 15:32, Paul remarks, "If after the manner of human beings I fought with beasts in Ephesos, what benefit is it to me?" This phrase has been interpreted either as a reference to an actual fight with wild beasts in the stadium[4] or as a metaphor for controversies with opponents.[5] While the former interpretation is unlikely, the latter is possible and would reveal that Paul had encountered serious challenges to his missionary activity. The phrase can also be interpreted in the context of the language of popular philosophy; here it is used in order to describe the struggle of the wise man against his desires and emotions.[6]

At the end of the letter, Paul discusses his travel plans, indicating that he intends to come to Corinth for a longer stay, traveling by way of Macedonia (1 Cor 16:5–7), but wants to remain in Ephesos until Pentecost (1 Cor 16:8). If Paul arrived in Ephesos in the fall of 52 CE, it is unlikely that he was already planning to leave in the following spring; 1 Corinthians is therefore better dated to the spring of the year 54. As the reason for the continuation of his stay in Ephesos, Paul points to further opportunities for missionary work, as well as

1. Apart from the generally accepted fact that Galatians was written before Romans, it is impossible to be certain about the time of the writing of Galatians relative to 1 and 2 Corinthians. See Hans Dieter Betz, *Galatians: A Commentary on Paul's Letter to the Churches in Galatia* (Hermeneia; Philadelphia: Fortress, 1979) 11–12. 1 Cor 16:1 indicates that Paul had written to the Galatians before the writing of 1 Corinthians ("Now concerning the collection for the saints: you should follow the directions I gave to the churches of Galatia").

2. Most scholars think that this is the most likely place of origin; however, "there is not the slightest hint in Galatians itself as to the place from which it was sent" (Betz, *Galatians*, 12).

3. Ephesos is mentioned explicitly in 1 Cor 16:8 as the city in which Paul stayed while he was writing the letter; see below.

4. *Acts of Paul* 7 developed the story of Paul's fight with the wild beasts in the stadium on the basis of this remark.

5. Hans Conzelmann, *1 Corinthians: A Commentary on the First Letter to the Corinthians* (Hermeneia; Philadelphia: Fortress, 1975) 264, 277–78.

6. Abraham Malherbe, "The Beasts at Ephesus," *JBL* 87 (1968) 71–80.

considerable resistance: "a great and effectual opportunity[7] has opened to me and there are many adversaries" (1 Cor 16:9). It is not possible to discern whether this resistance arose from Jews or Gentiles, or was caused by opposition within the newly founded Christian community. Other remarks in 1 Corinthians 16 reveal that the staff of the Ephesos campaign was sizable. Timothy, who was with Paul, was apparently sent to Corinth along with this letter (1 Cor 16:10). Apollos, formerly active in Corinth,[8] was in Ephesos (1 Cor 16:12), and Aquila and Prisca, as well as Stephanas,[9] Fortunatos, and Achaïkos (1 Cor 16:17), had come from Corinth to Ephesos (1 Cor 16:19). Moreover, the fact that Paul sends greetings "from the churches of Asia" (1 Cor 16:19) demonstrates that other churches had been founded in the province of which Ephesos was the capital.

Paul was not able to carry out his plan to leave Ephesos for Corinth after Pentecost of that year. The correspondence that is now preserved in 2 Corinthians must be dated in the period between the intended departure from Ephesos in the spring of the year 54 and Paul's actual departure for Corinth a year later. 2 Corinthians is a composition of several of Paul's shorter letters, written over a longer period of time.[10] During the year after the writing of 1 Corinthians, a new opposition to Paul had arisen in Corinth, instigated by foreign missionaries who had invaded the Corinthian church.[11] This forced Paul to write a letter to Corinth in defense of his own ministry, which is preserved in 2 Cor 2:4–7:4; he also visited Corinth briefly—crossing the Aegean Sea by boat—in the summer of 54. A second letter, written shortly after this visit, and preserved in 2 Corinthians 10–13, indicates that the personal visit only increased the tensions with the Corinthian church.

7. The Greek term for "opportunity" is θύρα, a term that Paul uses in the same way in 2 Cor 2:12. In both instances Paul speaks of an opportunity for the proclamation of the gospel.

8. 1 Cor 1:12; 3:4–6; 4:6. On Apollos, see also below.

9. Stephanas is called "the first-born of Achaia," who now has a house in Ephesos (1 Cor 16:15).

10. Gerhard Dautzenberg, "Der Zweite Korintherbrief als Briefsammlung: Zur Frage der literarischen Einheitlichkeit und des theologischen Gefüges von 2 Kor 1–8," *ANRW* 2.25.4 (1987) 3045–66.

11. See Dieter Georgi, *The Opponents of Paul in 2 Corinthians: A Study in Religious Propaganda in Late Antiquity* (Philadelphia: Fortress, 1985).

The remainder of the correspondence contained in this composite letter is made up of several brief letters (2 Cor 1:1–2:13 and 7:5–16; 8:1–24, 9 1–15) written from Macedonia in the summer of 55, after Paul had left Ephesos.

These later letters give evidence that Paul had meanwhile been in serious trouble (θλῖψις) "in Asia," and had even given up hope to escape with his life (2 Cor 1:8; ὥστε ἐξαπορηθῆναι ἡμᾶς καὶ τοῦ ζῆν). This implies that he had been imprisoned for a longer period during the winter of 54/55. Many recent scholars agree that this remark refers to an Ephesian imprisonment,[12] during which Paul also wrote the Letter to the Philippians—or several letters,[13] occasioned by the arrival of Epaphroditos, who had come from Philippi bringing financial support and by the delay of his return that a longer illness caused. At this time he also wrote the letter to Philemon, whose house was in Colossae. The physical proximity of Philippi and Colossae to Ephesos and the exchange of messengers make it likely that these letters were written from an imprisonment in Ephesos rather than Rome. Philippians and Philemon thus provide more information about the imprisonment in Ephesos.

Ephesos stands out as the place from which most of the Pauline correspondence originated—1 Corinthians, Philippians, Galatians, Philemon, and the major parts of 2 Corinthians. The remaining two genuine Pauline letters, namely his first letter (1 Thessalonians) and his last letter (Romans), were written in Corinth. There is no further mention of Ephesos in Paul's letters after his departure from the city. It is possible, however, that a letter survives that Paul wrote in Corinth to the church in Ephesos. This is certainly not the letter known as Ephesians[14] but a letter to Ephesos that has survived as chapter 16 of

12. This thesis was first convincingly argued by George Simpson Duncan, *Paul's Ephesian Ministry: A Reconstruction with Special Reference to the Ephesian Origin of the Imprisonment Epistles* (New York: Scribner's, 1929).

13. Wolfgang Schenk, "Der Philipperbrief in der neueren Forschung (1945–1985)," *ANRW* 2.25.4 (1987) 3280–3313; Helmut Koester, "The Purpose of the Polemic of a Pauline Fragment (Phil III)," *NTS* 8 (1961/62) 317–32; Lukas Bormann, *Stadt und Christengemeinde zur Zeit des Paulus* (NovTSup 78; Leiden: Brill, 1995) 109–18.

14. The Letter to the Ephesian is not a genuine letter of Paul's. Moreover, the address of this letter (ἐν Ἐφέσῳ) is missing in the best manuscript witnesses; see below.

Romans.[15] Here Paul sends greetings to Prisca and Aquila (Rom 16:4), his old associates from Corinth who had gone to Ephesos, according to 1 Cor 16:19 and Acts 18:18; a greeting to Epainetos, whom Paul calls the first-born of Asia (Rom 16:5), follows. Moreover, Romans 16:6–15 contains greetings to as many as twenty-three of Paul's fellow workers and personal acquaintances, who must have been located in Ephesos rather than in Rome, unless one assumes that there was a mass immigration of Ephesian Christians to Rome within less than a year after Paul's departure from that city. If Romans 16 was indeed a letter written to Ephesos, most likely as a cover letter for a copy of Romans that Paul sent to Ephesos, a wealth of additional information about the early Christian community in Ephesos is available. Not only are twenty-six names of individual Christians listed—there is no other early Christian church for which such information is available—but details about the Ephesian community also are included. There was a house church in the home of Prisca and Aquila (Rom 16:5a). As the first person converted, Epainetos obviously occupied a prominent position (Rom 16:5b). The first fellow worker mentioned after Epainetos is a woman named Maria (Rom 16:6). Next Junia and Andronikos, two fellow prisoners of Paul's, who hold the rank of apostle, are mentioned (Rom 16:7); this is also an important piece of evidence for the existence of a female apostle. A number of other persons are designated as engaged in some work as ministers of the church, among them again several women (Tryphaina, Tryphosa, Persis, and Julia). Of the twenty-six names, one is Semitic (Maria), nineteen are Greek, and six Latin; of these six Latin names, however, three belong to people who are certainly Jews (Prisca, Aquila, and Junia), while only two of the Greek names designate Jews (Andronikos and Herodion).[16] The fact that only a total of six persons named can be identified as Jews—two of these were Paul's fellow workers from Corinth, and another two identified as "apostles before me"—points to a largely

15. See, among others, J. J. MacDonald, "Was Romans xvi a Separate Letter?" *NTS* 16 (1969/70) 369–72; Wolf-Henning Ollrog, "Die Abfassungsverhältnisse von Röm 16," in Dieter Lührmann and Georg Strecker, eds., *Kirche: Festschrift für Günther Bornkamm zum 75. Geburtstag* (Tübingen: Mohr/Siebeck, 1980) 221–44.

16. Paul calls these συγγενεῖς μου, which cannot mean "relatives," but rather designates people of the same ethnic origin.

Greek, gentile constituency of the church in Ephesos.[17] Since all of these names appear in their simple form, without praenomina and cognomina, it is almost impossible to draw any conclusions with respect to their social status and citizenship. I believe it unlikely that those mentioned held Roman citizenship, and those who had come to Ephesos only recently were not even Ephesian citizens.

Ephesos in the Deutero-Pauline Letters

Ephesos appears in the prescript of Ephesians. It is certain, however, that this letter was neither written by Paul nor was it addressed to Ephesos. The letter is addressed to "the saints and faithful in Christ Jesus"[18]; but the designation "in Ephesos" is missing in the oldest and most valuable textual witnesses.[19] What is generally called the Letter to the Ephesians is actually a letter directed to all churches, written at the end of the first century CE. Its place of origin is unknown.[20] Ephesos is mentioned again several times in the Pastoral Epistles, 1 and 2 Timothy and Titus. These three deutero-Pauline letters were composed not earlier than the end of the first century, but probably as late as the fourth or fifth decade of the second century. Although all names of places and persons in these letters may be fictional, the author may have relied upon a tradition about Paul's activities in Greece, Macedonia, and Asia after his Roman imprisonment.[21] Traditionally, Rome claimed Paul as her martyr, but this claim can be

17. For the analysis of names in Pauline letters and a comparison with the fishermen's inscription from Ephesos (*IvE* I 20) see G. H. R. Horsley, *New Documents Illustrating Early Christianity* (6 vols.; North Ryde, NSW: Ancient History Documentary Research Centre, Macquarie University, 1989) 5. 95–114.

18. Eph 1:1; Παῦλος ἀπόστολος Χριστοῦ Ἰησοῦ διὰ θελήματος θεοῦ τοῖς ἁγίοις τοῖς οὖσιν [ἐν Ἐφέσῳ] καὶ πιστοῖς ἐν Χριστῷ Ἰησοῦ.

19. MSS 𝔓⁴⁶ ℵ* B* 6. 1739 Marcion.

20. A number of manuscripts have a subcriptio that informs the reader that the letter was written from Rome. This only reflects the later assumption that all so-called imprisonment letters of Paul were written from Rome.

21. It is true that the Pastoral Epistles do not mention an earlier imprisonment in Rome. This cannot be used, however, as an argument against the existence of a tradition that reported later activity of Paul in the East. Whether this tradition is based upon historically reliable information is another matter.

questioned, and the information about places and persons contained in these letters—although the letters themselves are pseudepigraphical—could be valuable if it points to a tradition about a second stay of Paul in the East after his Roman imprisonment. The question of the situations assumed in the Pastoral Epistles, however, is extremely complex and cannot be discussed in this context.[22]

For the purposes of this study, it can be said with certainty that 1 and 2 Timothy presuppose that Timothy is staying in Ephesos: "I have asked you to remain in Ephesos when I traveled to Macedonia" (1 Tim 1:3). It is also assumed that Onesiphoros and his house are in Ephesos and that he has provided useful services there for the church (2 Tim 1:16–18). Alexander, a coppersmith in Ephesos, is mentioned in this context as one who had done much harm to Paul and against whom Timothy is asked to be on his guard (2 Tim 4:14–15); an Alexander is also mentioned in Acts 19:33, a Jew who is informed about the riot of the silversmiths and prepares to give a speech, but never actually opens his mouth.[23] Finally, Paul says that he had sent Tychikos to Ephesos, and that Timothy should bring the coat and the books and parchments that Paul had left in Troas (2 Tim 4:12–13)— a request that would make sense if Paul was thought to be imprisoned in Philippi at the time of the composition of this letter.[24] In any case, whatever is said in the Pastoral Epistles about Ephesos reveals that at the beginning of the second century a Pauline tradition connected with Timothy existed in Ephesos. In the Pastoral Epistles, Timothy functions as a superior church leader who is passing the Pauline tradition to other churches and church leaders.[25] It is not impossible that

22. See Martin Dibelius and Hans Conzelmann, *The Pastoral Epistles* (Hermeneia; Philadelphia: Fortress, 1972) 1–5, 126–28.

23. It is unclear why Luke inserted this episode. On this problematic passage, see Ernst Haenchen, *The Acts of the Apostles: A Commentary* (Philadelphia: Westminster, 1971) ad loc.

24. On the question of Paul's imprisonment and martyrdom in Philippi, see Helmut Koester, "Paul and Philippi," in idem and Charalambos Bakirtzis, eds., *Paul and Philippi: A Symposium* (Valley Forge, PA: Trinity, forthcoming).

25. 1 Tim 4:14 presents Timothy as one who has received his office through the laying on of hands by the prebytery; in 2 Tim 1:6 it is Paul himself who has ordained Timothy. On the laying on of hands, see Dibelius and Conzelmann, *Pastoral Epistles*, 70–71.

the Pastoral Epistles already know of the tradition of Timothy as bishop of Ephesos; this, however, is explicitly mentioned for the first time by Eusebius.[26]

Ephesos in the Acts of the Apostles

Luke, the author of Acts, intended to write the chapter about Paul's activity in Ephesos (Acts 18:18–20:1) as the last and most splendid event in the missionary activity of the apostle. His sources presented formidable obstacles, however, because they reported that a Christian community had already been founded in Ephesos by Apollos and that there was also a group of followers of John the Baptist in that city— two reports that Luke felt he could not ignore. The result is a rather complex composition.

The report about the activities of the learned Alexandrian Jew Apollos (Acts 18:24–28) may rely on trustworthy information that was perhaps advertised by a group of Apollo's followers at the time of Luke. The references to Apollos in 1 Corinthians[27] suggest that Apollos later appeared in Corinth,[28] probably coming from Ephesos; he must have returned to Ephesos when Paul wrote 1 Corinthians, because Paul says at the end of the letter that he had urged him repeatedly to travel to Corinth (1 Cor 16:12).[29] Paul does not denigrate the work of Apollos and recognizes him as a Christian teacher in his own right, but it is also clear from Paul's remarks that rivalry existed between Apollos and him. Luke's report in Acts reveals that there was already a Christian community in Ephesos, founded by Apollos, before Paul began his missionary activity there.

---

26. "Timothy is related to have been the first appointed bishop of the diocese of Ephesos" (Eusebius *Hist. eccl.* 3.4.5). Eusebius continues by naming Titus as the first bishop of Crete, however, suggesting that this information is dependent upon the Pastoral Epistles.

27. 1 Cor 1:12; 3:4–6, 22; 4:6.

28. This is also attested in Acts 19:1 ("while Apollos was in Corinth").

29. On the problems of the expression "but it was not the will (for him to come to Corinth)," see Conzelmann, *1 Corinthians*, on 1 Cor 16:12. Does this formulation and the fact that Apollos is not mentioned in the greetings of 1 Cor 16:19–21 imply that Apollos was not present when 1 Corinthians was written?

It is difficult to find corroborating evidence for Luke's report of a group of followers of John the Baptist in Ephesos. Rivalry between the disciples of John and the disciples of Jesus probably existed in Palestine at an early date and is confirmed in a number of stories about John the Baptist in the synoptic gospels.[30] The Gospel of John, written at the end of the first century CE, includes several polemical passages that argue against the belief that John the Baptist was the messiah.[31] Such a sect may well have existed in Ephesos at Luke's time, if not as early as the arrival Paul.[32]

Using a lost composition that described Paul's activities in Ephesos, Luke begins with a travel report of Paul's trip from Corinth to Syria and Caesarea (Acts 18:18–21); Paul, together with Priscilla and Aquila, sails from Kenchreae in order to go to Syria (Acts 18:18). Their first stop is in Ephesos. The source Luke used here must have reported that Paul left Priscilla and Aquila in Ephesos (Acts 18:19) and continued to sail to Caesarea. Luke, however, inserted a brief report about Paul's visit to the synagogue and his preaching to the Jews[33]— a typical Lukan feature. They ask Paul to stay, but he declines and promises to return (Acts 18:20–21). In this way, Luke was able to

30. Mark 2:18–22 // Matt 9:14–17 // Luke 5:33–38; see also the materials used in the discussion about John the Baptist in Matt 11: 7–19; Luke 7:24–35. See esp. Walter Wink, *John the Baptist in the Gospel Tradition* (SNTSMS 7; Cambridge: Cambridge University Press, 1968).
31. John 1:15, 19–34; 3:25–30; 4:1; 5:33–35.
32. The historicity of the report about disciples of John the Baptist in Ephesos is debated; see Haenchen, *Acts of the Apostles*; Conzelmann, *Acts of the Apostles*, on Acts 19:1–7; Ernst Käsemann, "The Disciples of John the Baptist in Ephesos," in idem, *Essays on New Testament Themes* (SBT 41; London: S.C.M., 1964) 136–48.
33. This is evident from the fact that the text first, following the source, reports that Paul left Priscilla and Aquila "there" (Acts 18:19a); but then Luke inserts that Paul went to the synagogue (Acts 18:19b–21a; κατήντησαν δὲ εἰς Ἔφεσον, κἀκείνους κατέλιπεν αὐτοῦ, αὐτὸς δὲ εἰσελθὼν εἰς τὴν συναγωγὴν διελέξατο τοῖς Ἰουδαίοις). Acts 18:21b–22 resumes the source with "and he set sail from Ephesos; and he came to Caesarea." Because of this insertion by the author of Acts, the "there" (αὐτοῦ) of verse 19b is left dangling; it now suggests the impossible scenario that Priscilla and Aquila stayed at the port while Paul went to the synagogue. See Conzelmann, *Acts of the Apostles*, on Acts 18:19–21.

present Paul as the first preacher in Ephesos, only later including the
report about the presence of Apollos and the disciples of John the
Baptist.

In reproducing information about Apollos from his source, Luke
reports faithfully that Apollos was teaching correctly about Jesus, but
he adds the historically unlikely note that he knew only the "baptism
of John" (Acts 18:25c), thus connecting the information about Apollos
with that about the disciples of John. Conveniently, Priscilla and Aquila
are already there to correct this error.[34] Duly instructed about correct
Christian preaching, Apollos is dispatched to Achaia (Acts 18:24–
28).[35] Once more, Luke reveals unwittingly that a Christian community founded by Apollos existed in Ephesos before Paul's missionary
activity in that city, but he then eagerly adds that "when [Apollos]
wished to go to Achaia, the brothers and sisters encouraged him"
(Acts 18:27).[36]

Luke now has to deal with the problem of the presence of a sect
of John the Baptist in Ephesos. Apollos is safely in Corinth (Acts
19:1a); and Paul, arriving in Ephesos, learns that there are some disciples who had not received the Holy Spirit, because they had only
been baptized with the baptism of John. Paul rebaptizes them without
delay and the Holy Spirit immediately comes upon them so that they
speak in tongues (Acts 19:1b–7). A concluding note, saying that they
were only about a dozen people, assures the reader that this rival sect
was so small that it did not pose any real threat.

Luke's next imperative is to create the space needed for a description of Paul's successful ministry in the capital of Asia. Little historical information, however, can be gleaned from Luke's narrative. The

---

34. Acts 18:25c, together with verse 26, in which Priscilla and Aquila
instruct Apollos in "the way of God," are evidently Lukan insertions; see
Käsemann, "The Disciples of John in Ephesos," 144. The note about Apollos
knowing only abut the baptism of John is secondary. Unlike the report about
the disciples of John the Baptist (see below), nothing is said about a baptism
of Apollos with the Spirit, as this would have been awkward after the description of Apollos as a man "fervent with the Spirit" (18:25a; ζέων τῷ πνεύματι).
See Conzelmann, *Acts of the Apostles*, on Acts 18:25.

35. "Luke avoids a meeting between Apollos and Paul (but contrast 1 Cor
16:12)" (Conzelmann, *Acts of the Apostles*, on Acts 18:27).

36. Ibid.

duration of Paul's activity—three months in the synagogue (Acts 19:8) and two years in the hall of Tyrannos (Acts 19:9–10)—may have come from Luke's source. Everything else is either legend or a reflection of the situation in Ephesos in Luke's time—that is, approximately 100 CE. Luke projected the separation from the synagogue and the hostility of the Jews, both accomplished facts at his own time, back to the time of Paul. Paul understood his apostolic mission as one to the Gentiles, and there is no indication in his letters that he always preached first in the synagogues and left them for mission to the Gentiles only after hostilities arose. The letter to the Ephesians, preserved in Romans 16,[37] moreover, argues for a largely gentile Ephesian community, although here as elsewhere Paul has Jewish apostles and fellow workers, and there were Jewish members of the communities he founded. The existence of two rival religious organizations—the Jewish synagogues and the Christian churches—is characteristic of Luke's time, one or two generations later, rather than the time of Paul.

Furthermore, three episodes are recounted that describe Paul's ministry: first, Paul's miracle working, healing diseases even through his aprons and handkerchiefs (Acts 19:11–12); second, rivaling magicians, the sons of the Jewish high priest Skevas, fail when they try to use Jesus' and Paul's name for their exorcism (Acts 19:13–17); third, the newly won believers and even some of the magicians bring and burn their magical books (Acts 19:18–20). All three episodes are typical stories of the competition in the religious market place. They do not characterize either the situation in Ephesos[38] or the methods of Paul's missionary practices. Contrary to his self-presentation in his letters, Paul is here the stereotype of the successful magician or divine man. It is unlikely that the case of the seven exorcist sons of the Jewish high priest Skevas rests on local traditions, neither is there any high priest of that name attested, nor is it probable that seven sons of a Jerusalem high priest could be found in Ephesos.

The story of the riot of the silversmiths (Acts 19:23–40), in contrast, reflects the milieu of Ephesos and attests to Luke's knowledge

37. See the discussion of Romans 16 above.
38. The reference to magic in Ephesos reveals some local color, however; see Conzelmann, *Acts of the Apostles*, 157 and the literature cited in n. 3.

of the Ephesian political and religious situation. The cult of the Ephesian Artemis, because of which the city proudly called itself the "temple keeper" (Acts 19:35, νεωκόρος),[39] the production of small silver *naiskoi* with the statue of Artemis for sale to visitors of the famous temple (Acts 19:24),[40] the existence of the office of asiarch (Acts 19:31),[41] and the mention of the "scribe of the demos" (Acts 19:35) as the most powerful Ephesian official[42] are typically Ephesian features. This, however, does not prove that the story is historical. On the contrary, Paul's own letters reveal that he was in mortal danger at the end of his Ephesian stay, indeed imprisoned for some time and fearing for his life. Luke says nothing about that because the information is of no interest to his story. While Luke knows that Paul intended to depart for Macedonia (Acts 19:21–22), his primary interest is in the description of the serious threat that the Christian mission poses to the pagan cult, not at the time of Paul but at his own time.

Pliny's letter to Trajan about the Christians, written in the year 112 CE, demonstrates that the spread of the Christian faith began to constitute a serious threat to the regular temple cult and ritual: sacrifices at the temples had been neglected and the sacrificial meat found no buyers.[43] It is not unlikely that Luke, who wrote at about the same time, knew about analogous threats to the normal performance of the

39. This term is regularly used for cities that were host to a provincial temple for the cult of the Roman emperors, but it was used in Ephesos also with respect to the cult of Artemis; see Friesen, *Twice Neokoros*, 55–56.

40. It is unlikely that the designation "silver shrines" (ναοὶ ἀργυρεῖς) for the products of the silversmiths refers to small-scale models of the entire temple of Artemis; rather, the silversmith probably produced statues of Artemis standing in a simple, small naiskos.

41. The office of the asiarchs is widely attested in Ephesian inscriptions, but its function is not quite clear. The asiarchs were not connected with the cult of Artemis, but perhaps with the cult of the emperors and/or with the supervision of games. See Conzelmann, *Acts of the Apostles*, on Acts 19:31.

42. The "scribe" (γραμματεύς) mentioned here is the "scribe of the assembly of the people" (γραμματεὺς τοῦ δήμου) because the theater was the place for this assembly. A "scribe of the council" (γραμματεὺς τῆς βουλῆς) is attested for Ephesos, but it seems to have been a peculiarity of Ephesos that the scribe of the demos held a higher rank than the scribe of the council.

43. Plinius Secundus *Epistularum libri decem* 10.96.

cult of Artemis in Ephesos and to the sale of religious paraphernalia. This may have been the basis for the development of this narrative, which is fictional as far as Paul's ministry in Ephesos is concerned, but related to the actual situation at Luke's own time. Moreover, Pliny's letter reveals the Roman administration's increasing interest in the case of the Christians at the time Acts was written. Concern with the Roman reaction to a riot informs the speech of the scribe at the end of the story (Acts 19:40). Luke wants to demonstrate that the Christians are not the cause of such rioting and encourage local officials to enforce law and order in such a way that their responsibility to protect Christians is also upheld.

There is no relationship between this story—where Paul departs unscathed—and Paul's actual experiences in Ephesos—a long imprisonment and a trial that might have resulted in capital punishment. He must have become such a notorious troublemaker in this city that he did not dare to show his face there again, a fact reflected in the source used by Luke in Acts 20:14–17. On his return trip from Macedonia to Jerusalem, Paul did not dare to stop at Ephesos but sailed from Assos to Mitylene, and from there to Miletos by way of Chios and Samos, bypassing Ephesos (Acts 20:15). Luke explains that Paul's reason was his haste; he did not want to lose time since he wanted to be in Jerusalem on Pentecost (Acts 20:16). This is a poor explanation; waiting in Miletos for the Ephesian presbyters (Acts 20:17) would certainly have consumed more time than a quick stop in Ephesos.

Acts therefore does not reveal much about Paul's stay in Ephesos. Interesting information emerges, however, about the beginnings of Christianity in this city: the Jewish-Christian missionary Apollos, competing with disciples of John the Baptist, had begun a successful mission there before Paul's arrival. Luke also provides some insights into the formidable threat that the Ephesian Christian community presented to the established cult of Artemis at his own time. At the same time, Luke suppresses information about the diversity of the Christian community, although a number of competing Christian groups must have existed in the city by the turn of the first century, as Revelation, which was written in Patmos at about the same time, confirms.

Ephesos in the Book of Revelation

The author of Revelation includes Ephesos in the seven churches of Asia (Ephesos, Smyrna, Pergamon, Thyateira, Sardeis, Philadelphia, and Laodikeia) to which he is commanded (Rev 1:11) to address individual letters (Rev 2:1–3:22). The book was written by a prophet named John on the island of Patmos, to which he was exiled. His work is not pseudepigraphical; there is no reason to doubt that John was the real name of the author, and his home city may well have been Ephesos. This prophet John, however, is certainly not identical with Jesus' disciple John whose name later appears as the apostolic author of the Fourth Gospel and the three Johannine letters of the New Testament. The majority of scholars today date Revelation to the time of the emperor Domitian, although older materials may well have been incorporated into the text.[44]

The letter written to the church at Ephesos is the first of these seven letters (Rev 2:1–7). On the whole, it is full of praise for the church's labor and steadfastness and its rejection of false apostles and sees the church as unified except for the presence of a group the author calls the Nikolaites (Rev 2:6). This same group is referred to in the letter to the church in Pergamon (Rev 2:15). The author provides no further information about the character of this group. Later writers, beginning with Irenaeus and Clement of Alexandria, ascribe to the Nikolaites a heretical gnostic teaching and name as its founder the Nikolaos who appears on the list of deacons in Acts 6:5 and who is there characterized as a proselyte from Antioch.[45] Justin Martyr, however, who came to Rome from Ephesos, says nothing about this sect[46]; thus all later information is probably speculative.

John's letter to Ephesos is revealing for another reason. The language, theology, and spirituality of Revelation are completely different from that of Paul (and presumably Apollos), and John lives in a world of thought and language that differs markedly from that of the author of Luke-Acts. Paul, on the one hand, is a skilled writer, well-

---

44. For a survey of scholarship, see Otto Böcher, "Die Johannes-Apokalypse in der neueren Forschung," *ANRW* 2.25.5 (1988) 3850–98.

45. See Adolf Hilgenfeld, *Die Ketzergeschichte des Urchristentums* (Darmstadt: Wissenschaftliche Buchgesellschaft, 1963) 49–50.

46. Irenaeus probably did not find his information about the Nikolaites (*Adv. haer.* 1.26.3) in Justin's lost *Syntagma*.

versed in the style of the Greek diatribe; his theology is eschatological, but he refrains from apocalyptic speculations. Luke, on the other hand, writes a fairly elegant Greek and his biblical language and knowledge is that of the Septuagint, the Greek translation of the Hebrew scriptures; moreover, nothing in Luke's writings indicates that he is expecting an imminent cataclysmic eschatological event. The author of Revelation, however, uses a rather clumsy Greek that is heavily dependent upon Aramaic and often reflects the text of the Hebrew scriptures; his thought and theology are deeply steeped in the apocalypticism of postexilic Judaism.[47] It is difficult to imagine that he was addressing the same Greek-speaking, gentile, Christian church of Ephesos that Apollos and Paul had founded and that Luke—a contemporary of the prophet John—knew.

In his description of the Pauline mission in Ephesos, Luke makes an effort to present the church of Ephesos as a united Christian group. Acts 18:24–20:1 suggests that the real situation was very different. At the end of the first century, a variety of groups and sects existed in Ephesos: disciples of John the Baptist, a circle of Christians that claimed allegiance to Apollos, a church that derived its origin from Paul. To these groups one should add a prophetic conventicle, to which the prophet John sent his book from Patmos, and a sect called the Nikolaites. The congregation that Paul founded and that held on to the tradition of its founder is mentioned in the letter of Ignatius of Antioch to the Ephesians, but this congregation does not seem to have been the only—and perhaps not even the dominating—group of Christians in Ephesos.

Ignatius of Antioch and the Ephesian Christians

Some time during the reign of Trajan, only a few years after the writing of Acts, Bishop Ignatius of Antioch was traveling as a prisoner through Asia Minor on his way to Rome.[48] In Philadelphia, he

47. For the Jewish and Christian apocalyptic tradition of language and thought in Revelation, see Adela Yarbro Collins, "Early Christian Apocalyptic Literature," *ANRW* 2.25.6 (1988) 4665–4711.
48. On the date and the chronology of Ignatius's journey and letters, see William R. Schoedel, *Ignatius of Antioch: A Commentary on the Letters of Ignatius of Antioch* (Hermeneia; Philadelphia: Fortress, 1985).

had the opportunity to meet with Christians, and from there he seems to have dispatched messengers to the churches of Ephesos, Magnesia, and Tralles with the request to send delegations to Smyrna for a meeting there. After he had met these delegates, he wrote a letter to each of these communities. The letter to the Ephesian church is the longest of Ignatius's letters. It reveals that the Ephesian delegation to Smyrna was led by their bishop Onesimos—hardly the same person on whose behalf Paul had written to Philemon fifty years earlier[49]—whom Ignatius saw as the representative of the entire Ephesian church.

The governance of the Christian church of Ephesos by a bishop was a new phenomenon; Luke knew only of Ephesian presbyters. It is impossible to say to what degree the bishop controlled all Christian groups in Ephesos. Repeated admonitions in the letter to establish and preserve unity[50] seem to reveal that Ignatius had been informed of divisions; Ignatius also requests that the addressees be on their guard against false teachers.[51] He assumes, however, that the church in Ephesos knows about Paul and honors him, calling them "fellow initiates of Paul" and reminding them that Paul "had remembered them in every letter."[52] Ignatius takes for granted that Pauline teaching is normative for all the churches to which he writes.

Together with the church in Smyrna and its bishop Polycarp, the Ephesian church gave material support to Ignatius and also sent one of their members, Burrhos, to work as Ignatius's assistant and accompany him as far as Troas. Ignatius mentions the Ephesians explicitly in his letters to the churches in Magnesia, Tralles, Philadelphia, Smyrna, and Rome.[53] The support of the church in the capital of Asia was evidently significant to him.

49. Onesimos is mentioned in Ignatius *Eph.* 1.3; 2.1; 6.2. Since Onesimos was a common name, there is little chance that this was the Onesimos of Paul's Letter to Philemon; see Schoedel, *Ignatius of Antioch*, 43–44.

50. Admonitions to unity are found, for example, in Ignatius *Eph.* 3.2; 4; 5.

51. See Ignatius *Eph.* 6–7; 9; 16.2.

52. Ibid., 12.2. There are also several allusions to Paul's letters and quotations from them.

53. Ignatius *Mg.* 15.1; Ἀσπάζονται ὑμᾶς Ἐφέσιοι ἀπὸ Σμύρνης, ὅθεν καὶ γράφω ὑμῖν; idem *Trall.* 13.1; Ἀσπάζεται ὑμᾶς ἡ ἀγάπη Σμυρναίων καὶ Ἐφεσίων; idem, *Rom.* 10.1; Γράφω δὲ ὑμῖν ταῦτα ἀπὸ Σμύρνης δι'

The Apostle John and Ephesos

While Ignatius assumed that Paul was a recognized authority in Ephesos, there is no hint of the presence of the apostle John in Ignatius's letter to the Ephesians, nor is there any indication of the apocalyptic message of the prophet John who wrote Revelation. The absence of reference to either of these Johannine traditions in western Asia Minor is also striking in the letters of Polycarp, bishop of Smyrna during the period from Ignatius's visit at the time of Trajan until his martyrdom under Marcus Aurelius. Polycarp is a church leader in the tradition of Paul, to whom he referred explicitly,[54] and whose tradition he interpreted in a manner closely related to that of the Pastoral Epistles.[55] While it is likely that Polycarp knew the Gospels of Matthew and Luke,[56] it is certain that he did not know the Gospel of John. This lack of knowledge is especially significant if one considers P. N. Harrison's thesis that most of the *Letter of Polycarp* was not written until about 140 CE.[57]

The apologist Justin Martyr seems to have stayed in Ephesos some time before the middle of the second century. In his writings, he never refers to John or to the gospel attributed to him, while he uses Matthew and Luke frequently and also knows of Mark.[58]

The testimony of Papias, the bishop of Hierapolis during the first half of the second century,[59] is ambiguous. Papias does not reveal any

---

Ἐφεσίων τῶν ἀξιομακαρίστων; idem, *Phld.* 11.2; ἐν Τρωάδι, ὅθεν καὶ γράφω ὑμῖν διὰ Βούρρου πεμφθέντος ἅμα ἐμοὶ ἀπὸ Ἐφεσίων καὶ Σμυρναίων εἰς λόγον τιμῆς; idem, *Sm.* 12.1; ὅθεν καὶ γράφω ὑμῖν διὰ Βούρρου, ὃν ἀπεστείλατε μετ᾽ ἐμοῦ ἅμα Ἐφεσίοις, τοῖς ἀδελφοῖς, ὃς κατὰ πάντα με ἀνέπαυσεν.

54. Polycarp *Ep.ad Phil.* 3.2; 9.1.

55. Hans von Campenhausen, "Polykarp von Smyrna und die Pastoralbriefe," in idem, *Aus der Frühzeit des Christentums* (Tübingen: Mohr/Siebeck, 1963) 197–252.

56. See Helmut Koester, *Ancient Christian Gospels: Their History and Development* (Philadelphia: Trinity, 1990) 19–20; idem, *Synoptische Überlieferung bei den apostolischen Vätern* (TU 65; Berlin: Akademie-Verlag, 1957) 114–20.

57. P. N. Harrison, *Polycarp's Two Epistles to the Philippians* (Cambridge: Cambridge University Press, 1936).

58. Koester, *Ancient Christian Gospels*, 360–402.

59. The exact date of Papias's writings cannot be determined.

knowledge of John, although the quotations from his writings that are preserved in Eusebius[60] demonstrate that he was familiar with Mark and Matthew.[61] Although unable to find any reference to the Fourth Gospel in Papias's writings, Eusebius reports that Papias "used quotations from the First Letter of John."[62] Moreover, Eusebius says that Papias also "expounds a story about a woman who was accused before the Lord of many sins," a story that Eusebius does not attribute to John, where it is found in later manuscripts (John 7:53–8:11),[63] but to the Gospel according to the Hebrews.[64] Since no church father before the end of the fourth century attributed this story to John, Papias's knowledge of this story must arise from the apocryphal tradition of narratives about Jesus.

Eusebius's comments about the "two Johns," whom Papias knew, are intriguing.[65] These comments refer to a passage from Papias that Eusebius quoted verbatim:

> If ever anyone came who had followed the presbyters (τοῖς πρεβυτέροις), I inquired into the words of the presbyters, what Andrew or Peter or Philip or Thomas or James or John or Matthew, or any of the other Lord's disciples (τῶν τοῦ κυρίου μαθητῶν), had said, and what Aristion and the presbyter (ὁ πρεσβύτερος) John, the Lord's disciples (τοῦ κυρίου μαθηταί), were saying.[66]

Regarding the first John, Eusebius says that Papias "reckons him with Peter and James and Matthew and the other Apostles, clearly meaning the evangelist."[67] This John is doubtlessly the one who ap-

60. Eusebius *Hist. eccl.* 3.39.1–17.
    61. It is not clear, however, whether Papias's reference to Matthew, "who composed the sayings (τὰ λόγια)," refers to the extant Gospel of Matthew or to the synoptic sayings source, Q; see Koester, *Ancient Christian Gospels*, 166, 316.
    62. Eusebius *Hist. eccl.* 3.39.17; Κέχρηται δ' ὁ αὐτὸς μαρτυρίας ἀπὸ τῆς Ἰωάννου προτέρας ἐπιστολῆς.
    63. MS D, some Latin manuscripts, and the majority of the Byzantine manuscripts. It is missing in 𝔓[66.75] ℵ A B C L N T W Y 0141. 0211. 33. 565. 1241. 133. 1424. 2768 sy sa.
    64. Eusebius *Hist. eccl.* 3.39.17.
    65. Ibid. 3.39.5–6 (trans. Kirsopp Lake; LCL; 2 vols.; Cambridge, MA: Harvard University Press, 1959) 293.
    66. Ibid., 3.39.4; ET p. 293.
    67. Ibid., 3.39.5; ET p. 293.

pears in the list of the apostles, which Papias could have drawn from Mark or Matthew or from oral tradition. Eusebius's remark, "clearly meaning the evangelist," is unwarranted, because Papias does not name this John as one of the evangelists, together with Mark and Matthew, but as one of the Lord's disciples. The second John, Eusebius comments, is named by Papias "outside of the number of the Apostles putting Aristion before him and clearly calling him a 'presbyter.'" Then follows a remark that Eusebius does not draw from Papias:[68]

> This confirms the truth of the story of those who have said that there were two of the same name in Asia and that there are two tombs at Ephesus both still called John's. This calls for attention: for it is probable that the second (unless anyone prefer the former) saw the revelation which passes under the name of John.[69]

Moreover, Eusebius claims that Papias had actually heard Aristion and the presbyter John, an assertion not necessarily implied in the passage from Papias that Eusebius had quoted. A connection between Papias and John, the author of Revelation, may indeed exist, however: both are chiliasts, expecting the thousand-year kingdom of Christ, "set up in material form here on this earth."[70] Although Papias does not connect the presbyter John explicitly with Ephesos, one can reasonably assume that this John was indeed the author of Revelation.

Some memory of a John of Ephesos may have survived in the story that Clement of Alexandria tells about a young man, whom this John entrusted to the bishop (or a presbyter) of Smyrna and who then became the leader of a band of brigands.[71] There is no indication in Clement's report that this John was the evangelist[72]; moreover, the story may be based on an old tradition because there is no reference to Polycarp of Smyrna, and the designation "bishop" of Smyrna could

68. Ibid.
69. Ibid., 3.39.6; ET p. 293.
70. Ibid., 3.39.11. For the expectation of the thousand-year kingdom in Revelation, see Rev 20:2–7. Eusebius considers such belief and the traditions connected with it as "strange (ξέναι) parables and teachings of the saviour and. . . more mythical (μυθικώτερα) accounts" (3.39.11; ET p. 295).
71. Clement Alex. *Quis div. salv.* 42; quoted in Eusebius *Hist. eccl.* 3.23.5–19.
72. In Clement's story he is simply called "John the Apostle." In his introduction to the story, Eusebius quotes Irenaeus in order to make sure that this John is understood to be the "apostle and evangelist."

be Eusebius's interpretation of the original designation "presbyter" of Smyrna, that is, the story may come from a time before Polycarp became bishop of that city. If this is the case, the John of the old story was probably the prophet John who wrote Revelation.

Evidence therefore exists for a historical person, John of Ephesos, who was the author of Revelation. How did the apostle John, the assumed author of the Fourth Gospel, come to Ephesos, either as a second John of Ephesos; or how did he come to be identified with the original John of Ephesos? It seems to me that this identification is due to a fiction that Bishop Irenaeus of Lyon created. There is no trace of knowledge of this gospel in western Asia Minor. Neither Papias nor Polycarp reveal any acquaintance with it. The Gospel of John must have been written elsewhere, most likely in Syria or Palestine; it was brought to Egypt early in the second century, where gnostic theologians, especially the Valentinians, who later wrote the first commentaries on this gospel, used it extensively. By the middle of the second century, however, this gospel must have reached Asia Minor, where Irenaeus, a native of the area, became acquainted with it and took it to Lyon when he became bishop of the church in that city. Irenaeus was primarily responsible for introducing and defending the four-gospel canon of the New Testament. In order to lend greater authority to the Fourth Gospel, he identified its author with the well-known John of Ephesos and ascribed both the fourth gospel and Revelation to him.[73] This identification was even more important in view of the Quartodeciman controversy, as the Asian Christians could quote the Fourth Gospel in support of their special Easter praxis which differed from the Roman dating of Easter. In this context, Irenaeus, describing Polycarp's visit in Rome, states that Polycarp continued in his praxis "inasmuch as he had always done so in company with John the disciple of our Lord and the other apostles with whom he had associated."[74] It is evident that a personal association of Polycarp with any apostle is impossible, since according to Eusebius, Polycarp suffered martyrdom as late as 167 CE at the age of 84; if this is the case, he would have been born in 83. If Polycarp met any of the several Johns, it must have been the prophet John of Ephesos who

73. Irenaeus *Adv. haer.* 2.22.5; 3.3.4; 5.30.3.
74. Eusebius *Hist. eccl.* 5.24.16; see also 5.20.6.

wrote Revelation. One must then also associate this prophet John with the story of the John who met the heretic Kerinthos in a bath house.[75] The fictional identification of the author of the Fourth Gospel with the prophet John of Ephesos was successful, however. At the end of the second century, Bishop Polykrates of Ephesos, in his letter to Bishop Victor of Rome, speaks about "John, who leaned on the Lord's breast,. . . martyr and teacher, who sleeps at Ephesos."[76] By this time, there is no doubt that the church of Ephesos claimed that the tomb of John in their city was that of the author of the fourth gospel.

The *Acts of John*, written at the end of the second century, have also adopted this fiction. John arrives in Ephesos, coming from Miletos. He stays there and performs many miracles, even destroying the Temple of Artemis. He is then called to Smyrna, makes a long journey through many regions of Asia,[77] and finally returns to Ephesos for another stay. After a final worship service with his disciples, he goes outside the city, where a grave is dug for him, and lying down down in the grave, he dies. According to the *Acts of Paul*, Paul only makes a very brief visit to Ephesos. It seems that even the author of the *Acts of Paul* knew that Ephesos had now become the city of John, apostle and evangelist.[78]

Conclusion

From its very beginning in the middle of the first century, the Christian community of Ephesos exhibits a remarkable diversity. Literary testimonies demonstrate that this diversity continued well into the second century, spanning the entire spectrum from a prophetic-apocalyptic enthusiasm (witnessed in the Revelation of John) to the sacramental orientation of an episcopal church (advocated in the letter

75. Irenaeus *Adv. haer.* 3.3.4, which Eusebius quotes twice (*Hist. eccl.* 3.28.6; 4.14.6).

76. Eusebius *Hist. eccl.* 3.31.3.

77. Most of the report of this travel is lost.

78. There is no indication that this tradition of John, disciple and apostle, as it was brought to Ephesos, was in any way connected with a tradition of Mary, the mother of Jesus. The tradition of the ancient church is almost unanimous in the assumption that Mary stayed in Jerusalem, where she died.

of Ignatius of Antioch). Only two church leaders can be associated with Ephesos with absolute certainty: the apostle Paul and the prophet John, the author of Revelation. Indirect testimonies, however, suggest that the Alexandrian teacher Apollos was also one of Ephesos's earliest missionaries and that Paul's associate Timothy later occupied a leading position in this city after Paul's departure.

In his Acts of the Apostles, Luke first attempted to establish a particular Christian tradition as the single legitimate authority for Ephesos. Contrary to the information provided by his sources, he elevated Paul to the rank of founding apostle; Ignatius's letter to the Ephesians confirms that an appeal to Paul would find positive response in at least one of the several groups of Ephesian Christians. All known early Christian leaders who were active in Ephesos, however, were finally overshadowed by the authority of an apostle who had never been in that city and whose tradition did not arrive there until the second half of the second century: John the Evangelist. Once the Gospel of John had become known in western Asia Minor, it proved to be a powerful weapon for the Asian Christians in the Easter controversy. The prominence that Ephesos had achieved in the second century made it natural that the tomb of John would be located in the metropolis of Asia.

Via Sacra Ephesiaca

New Aspects of the Cult of Artemis Ephesia*

Dieter Knibbe
Österreichisches Archäologisches Institut

I n the year 112 CE, Pliny the Younger, governor of the province of Bithynia, sent a report to the emperor Trajan about the Christians,[1] whom he had encountered in his province: They met early

*This article presents a short summary of the results of my explorations, inspired by an inscription found in 1989 in which the the Gate of Mazaios and Mithridates is called a "triodos." The interpretation of this designation as well as the results of our 1991 excavations are published in Dieter Knibbe, Gerhard Langmann, et al., *Via Sacra Ephesiaca I* (*BerMatÖAI* 3; Vienna: Schindler, 1993). The publication of the results of the excavations conducted in 1992 and 1993 will appear shortly as Dieter Knibbe, Hilke Thür, et al., *Via Sacra Ephesiaca II* (*BerMatÖAI* 7; Vienna: Schindler, 1995). I want to express my warm thanks to Helmut Koester for the opportunity to present this report.

1. Pliny *Ep.* 10.96; as is well known, this letter and Trajan's response (*Ep.* 10.97) are the oldest extent pagan documents about Christianity. Trajan's response was, as a *constitutio principis*, the decisive legal decision throughout the empire. It decreed that Christians should not be investigated unless they were reported to the authorities. This decision was in effect until the reign of Decius in the midthird century CE, when the authorities of the Roman state took the initiative to investigate and arrest Christians.

in the morning before the sun rose, celebrating a common meal—the eucharist (εὐχαριστία) in the memory of the last supper of their Lord—and swearing oaths in which they promised not to wrong anyone. Pliny also reports that the Christian "superstition" had become so widespread that temples could no longer obtain the animals necessary for regular sacrifice. A similar report could have been written about the Christians in the neighboring province of Asia. In Ephesos, Asia's capital, however, the worship of Artemis—which was not very different from that of other pagan deities—continued to flourish. There were offerings of incense and, according to the bones found in the Artemision, sacrifices of a great variety of animals. On certain occasions, a series of bulls were offered to the goddess in bloody slaughter and, as the Swiss archaeologist Gerhard Seiterle[2] suggested, their testicles were fixed on the statue of Artemis. They are the "breasts" of the goddess—a theory repeatedly questioned by scholars.[3] This rite reveals the archaic concept that the power of the goddess was renewed in this way, so that she could in turn strengthen the world of nature and allow even the dead to receive a share of her vitality. Thus Artemis was not only the mistress of the earth's fertility, but also the protector of the dead, whom she visited from time to time in a procession on her sacred way around Panayırdağ (Mount Pion). This sacred way was originally a circular cemetery encircling the entire mountain; after King Lysimachos's founding of "Arsinoeia" (the later Nea Ephesos) on the west and south slopes of Panayırdağ in approximately 300 BCE, only the semicircular eastern and northern portion of this processional road continued to serve as a cemetery.

It is very likely that Panayırdağ was originally the property and realm of Kybele. What survived as her cult district, the Meter sanctuary on the rocky northwestern side of the mountain (map no. 72), is only a small remnant of her original realm of authority; that it was still active in the Roman imperial period is demonstrated by ceramic findings.[4] This cult area consists of a series of niches cut into the face

---

2. Gerhard Seiterle, "Artemis—die große Göttin von Ephesos," *Antike Welt* 10 (1979) 3–16.

3. Lynn R. LiDonnici, "The Images of Artemis Ephesia and Greco-Roman Worship: A Reconsideration," *HTR* 85 (1992) 389–416.

4. Josef Keil, *Führer*, 55–56 and pl. 26; see also 2 pl. 5.

of the rock, close to the modern asphalt road. The reliefs from these niches, now on display in the museum of Selçuk (inv. nos. 55, 74, 2256), show the enthroned goddess holding a tympanum and accompanied by Attis and her lion; her name appears in inscriptions as Μήτηρ ὀρείη Φρυγίη ("Phrygian Mountain Mother"). In some reliefs she is also accompanied by an old bearded man who may be interpreted as Ζεὺς πατρώϊος, known from the inscription on an archaic rock altar from the same cult area higher up on the hill above the niches of Kybele. He may have been the "Ancestral Zeus," the Phrygian Mother's junior paredros, who had been brought by the Ionian Greeks when they invaded the Ephesian region at the end of the second millennium BCE and settled somewhere in the Koressian district on the northern side of Panayirdağ above the sea. From archaic times to the Hellenistic period, the sea covered the entire plain west of the modern city of Selçuk to the southwestern slope of Mount Ayasoluk. There, another religious center had arisen early around a sweet water spring close to the shore and near a sacred tree; this is the origin of Artemis, a tree goddess and a timeless symbol of fertility. In spite of deep excavations that Anton Bammer conducted at the Artemision over many years, it has not yet been possible to understand fully the cultic activity that occurred at this site before the Lydian king Kroisos sponsored the erection of the first, so-called archaic Artemision (map no. 74). The excavations have shown the existence of two cultic sites, which were either devoted to two different deities or served two distinct ethnic clans for the worship of the same goddess. It is not possible to answer the question of whether these two cultic sites reflect the dualism of the Ionian Greek immigrants and the older population that Strabo (*Geog.* 14.1.21) called the Κᾶρες καὶ Λέλεγες ("Karians and Lelegians"). King Kroisos's decision to promote the goddess of Ayasoluk, who became Artemis in Greek interpretation, to the position of the first-ranking deity of the entire region was certainly a political one, as was his construction of a large marble temple for her, which covered over whatever past disharmony may have existed between rival shrines at this ancient holy site. Kroisos intended to unify this important region of his kingdom under the religious government of one mighty goddess.

Step by step, Kroisos's strong royal protection gave Artemis authority over the former kingdom of Kybele; the ancient *Via Sacra*, the way around the necropolis of Panayirdağ, was used as her triumphal way. She was also given the position of protector of the dead buried along this road—a role previously attributed to the Phrygian Mother. Altars at strategic locations established Artemis's claim to the *Via Sacra*. The most important of these was the point at which a road branched off the *Via Sacra* to Ortygia, the site promoted as the place of Artemis's legendary birth to Leto as the illegitimate daughter of Zeus. Each year on the sixth day of Targelion, or the sixth of May, her birthday was celebrated at Ortygia with mysteries,[5] offerings, and the dramatic representation of the scene of her birth by the *curetes*, who concealed the confinement of Leto from Zeus's legal wife Hera by banging on their shields. Different members of Ephesian society performed the role of the *curetes* every year, as inscriptions preserved in the Prytaneion reveal.[6] A banquet for all participants followed these performances.

Another altar stood near the Prytaneion (map no. 61), where the *Via Sacra*, ascending the valley between Bülbüldağ (Lepre Akte) and Panayirdağ, reached its highest point; it seems to have been a symbol of Artemis's victory (τρόπαιον) over the Phrygian Mother and all other goddesses and gods of Ephesos. Stones inscribed "altar of Artemis" (Βωμὸς τῆς ᾿Αρτέμιδος) demonstrate that a large number of altars originally stood along the *Via Sacra*, some larger, some smaller, designating stops on the route of the processions, during which Artemis was believed to communicate her power to the dead by visiting the tombs. Sacrifices at these altars conveyed her vitality and immortality to those who had died.

The Hellenistic king Lysimachos did not intend to found a "new" Ephesos, nor did he build the new city in order to improve the conditions of the old Ephesians, who were still living at the foot of Mount Ayasoluk near the Artemision. Rather, he followed the example of other successors of Alexander, especially the Seleucid kings of Syria, founding his own city, one that would no longer be under the domination of the mighty goddess and her powerful hierarchy of priests. He did not use the old name Ephesos for this city but called

5. Unfortunately, Strabo (*Geog.* 14.1.20) does not say anything about the nature of the mysteries that he mentions in his description of Ortygia.

6. On the Ephesian *curetes*, see Knibbe, *Der Staatsmarkt*, 70–76.

it "Arsinoeia" after his wife Arsinoë. Moreover, he invited to his new city settlers from Lebedos and Teos, as well as those of the old Ephesians who were willing to abandon their accustomed abode near the Artemision. The story that he forced them to leave their old homes by plugging the sewage systems so that the rain water would flood their houses is certainly unhistorical, although it reflects some actual events. Due to geological changes during the fourth century BCE, the ground water level had risen considerably in the ancient location of Ephesos and the Artemision. This also affected the Temple of Artemis, which had to be rebuilt on a higher level. The famous story of mad Herostratos, who burned the Temple of Artemis on the night on which Alexander the Great was born in order to earn immortal fame, is surely a clever fabrication. The pyrotechnic art of antiquity would not have enabled a single individual to torch a huge and well-guarded marble temple. Rather, Herostratos was useful; the priests of Artemis put him forward as a culprit in order to cover up their own conspiracy to burn the temple that Kroisos built, which was about to sink into a swamp and therefore needed to be replaced with a new structure. Herostratos was a useful scapegoat onto which to pin the charge of arson.[7]

If the old Ephesians refused to move into the new city of Arsinoeia, their fear may have been caused by the fact that they would have had to live on top of the cemetery along the ancient *Via Sacra*, although the graves of the old necropolis along its course had been covered with earth. The memory of the ancient tombs remained in the erection of heroa and cenotaphs near the altar of Artemis at the crossroads to Ortygia. When Lysimachos founded his new town, however, he did not realize that the worship of Artemis was already established within its walls from the beginning. No wonder, then, that after the king's death in the battle of Kouropedion (281 BCE), the name "Arsinoeia" disappeared and the new city assumed the name of the old metropolis of Artemis—Ephesos.

When Augustus decided to make Ephesos the capital of Asia and Romanize its architectural appearance, he encountered the same prob-

7. Stefan Karwiese, "Herostratos: Versuch einer Ehrenrettung," in T. Bakir, A. Cilingiroglu, and E. Doger, eds., *Erol Atalay Memorial* (Ege Üniversitesi Edebiyat Fakültesi Yayınları; Arkeoloji Dergesı Özel Sayı 1; İzmir: Ege Universitesi Basımevi, 1991) 89–95.

lem that had troubled Lysimachos three hundred years earlier: How was it possible to detach the city from the Artemision without committing an act of impiety against the goddess? Augustus restored to Artemis all property and rights that she had lost during the Roman civil war, hoping that this would gratify Artemis and that she would repudiate her claim to the domination of the city. His hope was in vain; Artemis's presence in the city was already firmly established in the Prytaneion, where she ruled the city together with Hestia Boulaia,[8] her ambassador within the walls of Ephesos. Artemis retained this position until she was finally deposed by Christianity.

Artemis's popularity began to decline, however, long before the edicts of Theodosius of 381 CE, which outlawed all pagan cults. As early as the second century CE, the old established religions began to lose their attraction. A wave of skeptical criticism swept over the ancient world.[9] While the educated classes turned to philosophy, the uneducated, if they had not become Christians, found their consolation in new religions of oriental origin, especially in the cults of Sarapis and Mithras, or they turned to other saving deities, who were as abundant as the number of human problems that they purported to solve. Even in the archaeological record, it is possible to observe the steps that were taken at this time in order to help Artemis in her struggle for survival.

Beginning in the second century CE, other gods and goddesses, who appeared to be more popular and helpful than Artemis, received the right to reside in the Prytaneion, the official religious center of the city. These included Demeter, the bringer of daily bread, and her daughter Kore; Sosipolis, the savior of the city; the μαντεῖος ("oracular sanctuary") of Clarian Apollo; and others. Together they attest to the decline of Artemis, who now also assumed functions that she did not have in earlier times. That she appeared in the role of Asklepios is evident at the end of the Parthian campaign of Marcus Aurelius and

8. The Prytaneion appears to have been the sanctuary of Artemis rather than of Hestia Boulaia. A large marble statue of Artemis was found in front of the building (inv. no. 712); it was perhaps felled by an earthquake at a time when her power had ended and when there was no longer any interest in reerecting the sculpture. Another statue was discovered in the Prytaneion itself, carefully buried by her last devotees (inv. no. 718). Both statues are now displayed in the museum of Selçuk.

9. See Knibbe, *Der Staatsmarkt*, 101–4.

Lucius Verus, when the two Roman legions, returning to the west, brought the plague with them. An oracle of Apollo, preserved in a hexametrical inscription, ordered the Ephesians to bring a gilded statue of Artemis to a sanctuary in the Hermous valley and to praise her glory with the singing of hymns; here the goddess appears as a nocturnal magician who burns waxen figurines as remedy against the plague.[10] In the year 162/63 CE, a vote (ψήφισμα) of the council and the people of Ephesos, confirmed by the Roman governor, ordered that the entire sacred month of Artemision should be free from all work.[11] Another inscription from approximately the same time reveals that the *hierokeryx* ("the sacred herald") of Artemis began to distribute offerings of oil on the sixth day of every month. This event formerly had taken place only once a year on the sixth day of Targelion (called the γενέσιοι ἕκται).[12] When the emperor Lucius Verus, who had spent some time in Ephesos during the Parthian campaign, died in Aquileia in the year 169, the Ephesians derived whatever glory they could from this event in order to enhance the status of their goddess Artemis. They built a cenotaph for Lucius Verus by enlarging the altar of Artemis at the crossroads to Ortygia (the "Triodos"[13] [map no. 36]) and thus claimed that the victory over the Parthians belonged to their goddess Artemis. Artemis, enshrined above, dominated whatever relief sculptures the new altar presented: the Parthians, other gods, large cities of the empire and even its capital Rome, the adoption of Fulvus Boionius Arrius Antoninus (later Antoninus Pius) by Hadrian together with the simultaneous adoption of Marcus Annius Verus and Lucius Ceionius Commodus (later emperors Marcus Aurelius and Lucius Verus) by Antoninus on 25 February 138, the apotheosis of Lucius Verus, and, at the lowest part of the monument, the cenotaph of the emperor. All of this was subordinated to Artemis.[14]

10. See Knibbe, Engelmann, and İplikçioğlu, "Neue Inschriften aus Ephesos XII," 130–32 no. 25.

11. *IvE* I 24.

12. See Dieter Knibbe, Helmut Engelmann, and Bülent İplikçioğlu, "Neue Inschriften aus Ephesos XI," *JÖAI* 59 (1989) Beibl. 171–72 no. 6.

13. An inscription found near the Gate of Mazaios and Mithridates confirmed that "Triodos" was the original name of this point; see above.

14. I have presented this interpretation of the so-called Parthian Monument in my *Via Sacra I*, 5–18.

The course of the *Via Sacra* from the Artemision to the city had to cross the lowland between Mount Ayasoluk and Panayirdağ, territory that had been a shallow bay of the sea when King Kroisos built the first Artemision in the first half of the fifth century BCE. By the beginning of the Hellenistic period, the water gradually withdrew westwards; the new land, however, was swampy, and, especially during heavy rains, the way between the Artemision and Ephesos was extremely difficult or completely flooded. Even today the plain west of Selçuk can turn into a lagoon after heavy rains; the traffic to and from Kuşadası was interrupted until the Turkish authorities built a new street on an elevated level approximately ten years ago. In ancient times, in addition to the rain, the rivers Marnas (present-day Degirmen) and Selinus (present-day Abuhayat) sometimes flooded the entire plain. Together with the high water level of the Kaÿstros River, this could lead to disastrous floods. The roads connecting the Artemision with Ephesos were originally nothing but sandy footpaths that had to be rebuilt after every rainy period. The excavations of 1992 and 1993 have shown that at approximately the beginning of the Roman imperial period, when the swampy ground was dry and sufficiently firm, the Ephesians began to construct roads plastered with small stones. The water problem, however, remained, even when the roads were rebuilt from time to time on a level that was higher than that of its predecessor. Only the construction of a sturdy highway of large limestone blocks, running on a dam of masonry above the high water level, solved the problem.

North of the *direttissima*—one of the porticoes built by Titus Flavius Damianus—and close to it, we found the "street in the Koressos" (πλατεῖα ἐν τῷ Κορησσῷ), which is mentioned in an inscription from the beginning of the third century CE. This impressive road connected Ephesos with the highway that led from Tralles and Magnesia in the south to Smyrna in the north. For hundreds of years, the Ephesians, although suffering from the difficulties of the road mentioned above, visited their goddess in the Artemision and followed the procession along the *Via Sacra* to Ortygia. At the end of the second century CE, however, Artemis no longer occupied first place in the competition with other gods and goddesses, who offered better answers to human problems, especially to the crucial question of life after death. Thus the people were no longer ready to endure uncomfortable conditions in order to worship Artemis. When rains came and the plain was flooded or muddy, they stayed at home. Perhaps because of a change in climate,[15] the water was often so high that people could not come, even if they so desired.

The rich Ephesian Titus Flavius Damianus, a well-known sophist, was the husband of the wealthy Vedia Phaedrina, a member of the famous family of the Ephesian Vedii whose benefactions are attested in numerous inscriptions through seven generations, from the beginning of the second century CE to the middle of the third century. Flavius Damianus intended to stay the decline in popularity of the cult of Artemis when he resolved to build a new road for the *Via Sacra*. Philostratos, a student of Damianus, described this effort: "He connected the sanctuary with Ephesos, leading the descending road[16] into it [the sanctuary] through the Magnesian Gates [map no. 70]. This portico, [constructed] entirely of stone [marble], was one stade long; the purpose of the building was that the sanctuary should not lack worshippers in case of rain." Philostratos also reports that this portico was built with a large amount of money (ἀπὸ πολλῶν χρημάτων) and that Damianus had it inscribed in honor of his wife.[17]

Archaeological remains between the Artemision and the stadium as well as on the eastern slope of Panayirdağ show that Damianus actually built two porticoes, one leading directly from the Artemision to the city (which I shall call the *direttissma* or *anodos* [ἄνοδος], "upward road"); it was marble and extended one stade from its beginning

15. This change may have been caused by the increasing deforestation that had gone on for many centuries in the effort to obtain wood for timberwork, ship building, and charcoal. This demand was increased even more by the construction of the large Roman baths that were heated day and night and thus consumed immense amounts of wood. As the hills and mountains had lost their forests, they were no longer able to retain the water, causing devastating floods at times of heavy rainfall.

16. κάθοδος can be translated "the returning road" or "the descending road."

17. Philostratus *Vit. Soph.* 2.23; Συνῆψε τὸ ἱερὸν τῇ Ἐφέσῳ κατατείνας ἐς αὐτὸ τὴν διὰ τῶν Μαγνητικῶν κάθοδον· ἐστι δὲ αὐτὴ στοὰ ἐπὶ σταδίου λίθου πᾶσα, νοῦς δὲ τοῦ οἰκοδομήματος μὴ ἀπεῖναι τοῦ ἱεροῦ τοὺς θεραπεύοντας ὁπόθ᾽ ὕοι.

near the temple.[18] Damianus built another portico for the sacred road (called the *kathodos* [κάθοδος]), which began at the Magnesian Gate and joined the *direttissima* at some point between the sanctuary and the northern entrance to the city. When John T. Wood began his exploration to locate the Artemision, he followed the remains of this portico. Large blocks of blue limestone forming squares with an inner diameter of 3.70 m lined the foot of Panayirdağ from the Magnesian Gate to approximately the depression between its two peaks. At this point, Wood left the remains of the portico and dug into the plain in a northeasterly direction along a street that was ten feet wider than the portico he had been following.[19]

Until 1991, no one knew what kind of building these limestone foundations supported; Wood thought that it might have been a wooden structure.[20] In 1991, I located as many blocks as I could find along the slope of Panayirdağ as well as in the plain west of Selçuk (see plan). I numbered these in two categories, according to whether they belonged to the *anodos* or the *kathodos*. I counted six sections for the *kathodos* (K I to K VI), with blocks on both sides of the modern road, and four sections for the *anodos* or *direttissima*. This enabled me to draft a geometrical map for portions of both roads.

In the following summer we opened a trench on the eastern side of Panayirdağ in section K IV. We found pillars of brick on top of the limestone blocks filled with remnants of opus cementicium. This led to the conclusion that the porticoes of Damianus were brick buildings over a limestone foundation, covered with barrel vaults.

The exploration of the foundations demonstrated that they were as deep as 5 m and were connected with strong walls on either side. This heavy and deep foundation was necessary because of the problematic hydrological situation mentioned above. We also found several predecessor roads, one on top of the other, separated by layers of sand that had been deposited by floods. A sarcophagus lay between two extant pillars of the stoa; it evidently had not been robbed in late

18. An analogy can be found in Pergamon, where the *via tecta* ("covered way") leading from the Asklepieion to the city also began as a marble portico.
19. Wood, *Discoveries at Ephesus*, 122.
20. Ibid., 120.

antiquity. The sarcophagus contained the bones of a woman approximately thirty-five years of age, buried together with her child of six months; anthropologists also found diminutive bone fragments, demonstrating that she was pregnant again at the time of her death. Archaeological finds in the sarcophagus suggest that she must have died in approximately the year 230 CE. The dating is based upon the following finds: a bronze mirror, a bronze capsule for cosmetic instruments, three unguentaria made of glass, two golden finger rings, two golden earrings, an unidentified object made of ivory, and many bone needles, apparently used to hold the linen cloth around the dead woman. After anthropological investigations, the bones were brought back to the sarcophagus and reburied.

Immediately behind the sarcophagus, which shows an uninscribed *tabula ansata* on its front side, we opened a barrel-vaulted grave house that contained the bones of twenty-three bodies. In contrast to the sarcophagus, which had been covered by later masonry and therefore escaped the grave robbers, the grave house had been robbed. Some pottery, glass pearls, and coins were found, which show that the grave house must have been in use at least from the time of the emperor Gallienus to the time of Arcadius (260–408 CE). To our surprise, we found no Christian artifacts; thus this grave house demonstrates that pagan religious activity survived into the fifth century.

In 1992, excavations were conducted on the northern side of Panayirdağ, where a group of supernumerary limestone foundation blocks were found. Their arrangement suggested that we had discovered the point at which the *direttissima* and *kathodos* met. We found the same situation that we had unearthed in the previous year in the excavations on the east side: foundation pillars of great depth that were connected by strong walls, obviously constructed in this way due to the same water problems. We also found several older street levels, one over the other, separated by strata of fine river sand. There was also evidence for the impressive older street—the πλατεῖα mentioned above—that was later replaced by a primitive street of broken bricks made firm with mortar; this was constructed when there was no longer any need for a connective highway to Smyrna. We found that the cemetery tradition survived even into later times when Artemis was no longer the protector of the necropolis along her *Via*

Sacra. The Stoas of Damianus were eventually destroyed by earthquakes and were not rebuilt because the goddess had died and her temple had become a quarry of marble. We found, however, that remains of the stoa had been used for the construction of grave houses on either side of the roadway. Even the foundations of the stoa were sometimes excavated and reused for primitive construction. Occasionally marble blocks were even taken from older, demolished grave buildings.

When the excavations ended in 1992, I was certain that we had found the junction of the *kathodos* and the *direttissima.* In 1993, in order to test and examine the results of the previous year, I started another trench approximately 100 m east of the trench that was dug in 1992. We found, from south to north, nearly the same situation: a late grave house covered with a brick vault and an opened late grave house of the same type with four burial places which were empty. Both grave houses were situated close to the stoa. We also found a burial place for gladiators, which dated to the second and third centuries CE. Funerary reliefs depicting gladiators with their weapons[21] were found in situ in niches of masonry blocks in which the *ostothekai* ("ossuaries"), or the dead may originally have been enshrined. Under the level of these graves and belonging to an older period, we discovered two large pithoi with the remains of burned human bodies—a horrible puzzle that still waits for the anthropologists.

We found a brick wall, the late primitive brick street, and under it once again the πλατεῖα mentioned above, as well as the foundations of a grave monument from the late Hellenistic period. We also found very late primitive graves, but nowhere did we discover any founda-

---

21. The reliefs show two heavily armed *murmillones* ("Thracian" gladiators), the upper part of their bodies naked, with a sword and a branch respectively in their bandaged right hands while the left hands hold helmets on large shields; and a *retiarius* (a gladiator fighting with net and trident) with his trident. The name of one of the *murmillones* is Palumbus, which means "wild cock pigeon," a name very common for gladiators after a famous gladiator from the time of Claudius (see Suetonius *Vita Claudii* 21). According to their general quality and to the letters of the inscriptions, the reliefs of the *murmillones* belong to the second century CE. The relief of the *retiarius* must be dated to the third century. A girl named Sarapiadis, whose mother ordered that the grave be made, may belong to the same social class.

tions for the *direttissima*. This implies that the stoa we had identified as the *kathodos* in 1992 was the *direttissima*, and that the junction of the two stoas is still unknown. The mistake of the 1992 excavation was that we had not measured exactly the direction of the stoa that we had designated as the *kathodos*; digging in an arbor of fig trees, we had no view of the foundation blocks of the *direttissima* east of the arbor. The purpose of the supernumerary foundation blocks, which we had supposed to be the junction of the *kathodos* with the *direttissima*, remains puzzling. One explanation could be that the *direttissima* had to detour in order to avoid an older cemetery area and that its direction was corrected by this construction. It will be the aim of future campaigns to use modern georadar methods in order to find the junction of the two parts of the *Via Sacra*.

How much do we know about the cult of Artemis? As I said in the beginning, her worship was not very different from that of other deities in pagan cults. Not every goddess had processions, however. In an earlier presentation of the evidence,[22] I have shown that not much is known about these processions. Three different types can be distinguished, however. First, processions from the Artemision around Panayirdağ occurred on certain days, which are unknown to modern scholars, probably during the ἱερομηνία, the holy month of Artemis which was called "Artemision." The wooden statue of Artemis, carved by Endoios, was probably carried on a four-wheel carriage, the ἀπήνη. The statue would have been dressed and adorned with the necessary care that was given to her in the imperial period by women of the high society in the city who served as κοσμητεῖραι τῆς θεοῦ ("adorners of the goddess").[23] The procession presumably stopped at the altars along the road, where worshippers sang, prayed, and made offerings. All who had participated were then invited to a common meal that took place after the procession, when Artemis had returned to her temple. Because of the nocturnal character of Artemis it can be assumed that these processions took place during the night; this is corroborated through coins which depicted Artemis with a torch. Artemis was also represented in this way on the reliefs of the so-

22. Knibbe, *Via Sacra I*, 28–32.
23. This title is found in many inscriptions, for example *IvE* III 742, 792, 875, 892, 980.

called Parthian Monument. Second, processions to Ortygia on the sixth of Thargelion[24] also took place. Third, in processions to the Artemision, the goddess represented by the most beautiful woman, returned from hunting accompanied by hunters, dogs, and a crowd of people.[25] The goddess appeared in this way here and sometimes on coins which depicted her in the more traditional Greek role of Artemis the Huntress. In the Asklepieion of Kos, a painting of Apelles depicted this procession.[26]

The processions founded in 104 CE by C. Vibius Salutaris have no relationship to the cult of Artemis. These processions were meant to honor a man who had become extremely rich in the service of the tax collectors—he was *portorium* and *decuma* of Sicily—and in his equestrian career. Returning to Ephesos as a private citizens, he did something that would make him immortal. In attempting to revive processions for Artemis for his own honor, Salutaris revealed the Greek nostalgia that still existed in a world that had become Roman.[27]

24. This date is provided by the Salutaris inscription (*IvE* I 27, lines 69, 225, 491). For Ortygia, see also Strabo *Geog.* 14.1.20.
25. Xenophon *Ephesiaka* 2.2–3.3.
26. Pliny *Hist. nat.* 45.93; see also Herondas *Mimiambi* 4.66.
27. See the valuable recent study by Rogers, *Sacred Identity of Ephesos.*

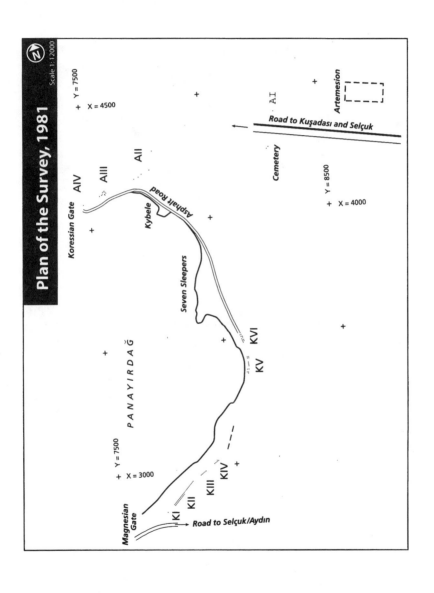

Plan of the Survey, 1981

Scale 1:12000

The Processional Way in Ephesos as a Place of Cult and Burial

Hilke Thür
Österreichisches Archäologisches Institut

The section in the center of Ephesos that excavators call Curetes Street (map no. 27)[1] is the inner part of the Processional Way.[2] This name arose from the columns of the Prytaneion[3] found there, bearing inscriptions honoring members of the order of *curetes*, although in antiquity the street or the quarter was probably called the Embolos.[4] This region is also near the old and new Triodos Gate,[5] the spot at which the ancient procession departed to the legendary birth-

1. Heberdey, "Vorläufiger Bericht 1904," Beibl. 76–77.
2. See Dieter Knibbe's contribution in this volume; see also idem *Via Sacra I*, 9–11, 28–32.
3. Franz Miltner, "XXII. vorläufiger Bericht über die Ausgrabungen in Ephesos," *JÖAI* 43 (1956–58) Beibl. 33. Regarding the building, see Alzinger, *Architektur*, 51–55. For the inscriptions, see Knibbe, *Der Staatsmarkt*.
4. Compare Jobst, "Embolosforschungen I," Beibl. 150–61, 212–15.
5. Gate of Mazaeus and Mithridates (map no. 34) and the Gate of Hadrian (map no. 38); see Knibbe, *Via Sacra I*, 55.

place of Artemis and Apollo.[6] This site acquired special cultic meaning as did all three-way intersections and crossings in antiquity. This paper presents an examination of the Curetes Street at three different points in time. I shall begin with the late Hellenistic period, specifically the end of the second century BCE, and subsequently explain one monument of every epoch in more detail.

Little is known about the appearance of Hellenistic Ephesos of the late second century BCE. The most significant structure from this time period was the city wall (map no. 17),[7] which was erected by Lysimachos and which is still well preserved at the top of Bülbüldağ (Lepre Akte). This wall, however, is difficult to trace on the smaller urban mountain called the Panayirdağ (Mount Pion).

Buildings dating back to the Hellenistic period are rare in Ephesos. At the Tetragonos Agora (map no. 30), several meters below the present-day ground level, for example, a small section of a hall of Hellenistic origin was excavated.[8] The stage building of the theater (map no. 26) has a construction phase dating to Hellenistic times,[9] and the stadium (map no. 21) may also have existed in Hellenistic times, perhaps as a wall structure built from earth. The public buildings essential for a town, such as the Bouleuterion and the Prytaneion, are thus far unknown for this period.

The Hippodamian city plan, a perpendicular grid system of streets of different width and rank,[10] originated during the period of the Hellenistic city foundation. It is significant that the Curetes Street does not conform to this grid system, but rather cuts diagonally across

6. Knibbe, *Der Staatsmarkt*, 70–73.
7. Josef Keil, "X. vorläufiger Bericht über die Ausgrabungen in Ephesos," *JÖAI* 15 (1912) Beibl. 185–96; Gerard Seiterle, "Die hellenistische Stadtmauer von Ephesos" (Ph.D. diss., University of Zürich, 1970); idem, "Ephesos. Lysimachische Stadtmauer," *JÖAI* 47 (1964–65) Grabungen 8–11; idem, "Das Hauptstadttor von Ephesos," *Antike Kunst* 25 (1982) 145–49.
8. Gerhard Langmann, "Grabungen 1989, Ephesos," *JÖAI* 60 (1990) Grabungen 28–30; idem, "Ephesos," *JÖAI* 61 (1991/92) Grabungen 1990/91, 5–6; idem and Scherrer, "Bericht. Ephesos. Agora," 12–14.
9. Heberdey, Niemann, and Wilberg, *Theater*, 90–93; Arnim von Gerkan, *Das Theater von Priene* (Munich: Schmidt, 1921) 90–93.
10. See Wolfram Hoepfner and Ernst L. Schwandner, *Haus und Stadt im klassischen Griechenland* (Wohnen in der klassischen Polis 1; Munich: Deutscher Kunstverlag, 1986) 15. 247–48.

it. The angle indicates both the way in which this street conformed to topographical conditions and its age, since it followed the same path as the Processional Way, which dates to the archaic period. In Hellenistic times, the Curetes Street was lined, at least partially, with structures that may have housed shops, trade offices, inns, and artisans' workshops. Remains of these structures are preserved at the south side behind the Octagon (map no. 44). A small well house in the northeastern corner of Slope House 2 (map no. 45) may already have been built at that time as well.

At the southwestern end of the Curetes Street lies a relatively well-preserved building of Hellenistic origin (map no. 43), which I shall describe in more detail below. In 1872, Ernst Curtius mentioned this building and named it a "city fountain."[11] In 1904, Rudolf Heberdey excavated this building[12] along with several adjacent structures: the gate building, that is, Hadrian's Gate[13] (map no. 38) at the western side, the Octagon[14] to the east, and a monument rebuilt in late antiquity as a workshop. Heberdey interpreted the building as a tomb or heroon. In contrast to the two neighboring buildings, it was not possible to reconstruct the original shape of the heroon. Due to the late antique decoration of the water basin in front of the building, it was identified as a Byzantine fountain. Its origin and interpretation have long been neglected, probably because of the lack of reconstruction. In 1988, when excavators found more architectural blocks from the heroon in Slope House 2, I began a systematic architectural investigation.[15]

The ruins of the building are preserved to a height of 4 m in the southeast corner, revealing a long rectangular ground plan. The long front side of the structure is interrupted in the middle, where it is recessed from the street, thus producing a U- or Π-shaped structure

11. Ernst Curtius, ed., *Beiträge zur Geschichte und Topographie Kleinasiens. Ephesus, Pergamon, Smyrna, Sardes* (Berlin: Vogt, 1872) 35.
12. Heberdey, "Vorläufiger Bericht 1904," Beibl. 70.
13. Thür, *Hadrianstor*.
14. See below pp. 178–82.
15. The investigative work was supported by the Österreichischen Fonds zur Förderung der wissenschaftlichen Forschung. The building will be published in Hilke Thür, *Das Heroon des Androklos am Embolos (FiE* 11.2; Vienna: ÖAW, forthcoming) with a contribution by Ulrike Outscher, "Keramische Evidenz zur Bauchronologie des Heroons." For the interpretation of the build-

(fig. 1). Measured at the base, the structure's total length is 10.35 m; the total depth is 5.8 m. The east and west wings of the front are 3.55 m long; the middle part is 3.26 m long and is recessed 2.3 m. The ground floor of the building has a solid core constructed of limestone ashlar, primarily of reused embossed square stones. As far as is visible, the blocks of the core are neither doweled nor clamped. The core is faced with a marble façade in the Doric order.

The story in Doric style is erected on a three-stepped substructure at the eastern, southern, and western sides of the building. On the northern side no steps are evident. An investigation of the foundation by means of trenches reveals that no three-stepped substructure existed at the front of the building. Moreover, there are no traces of the foundation of a staircase leading to the upper floor, although Josef Keil presumed that such a staircase existed.[16]

The superstructure of the first storey is evident both from the ground plan and from the ruin itself (fig. 3). The Doric façade is structured by pillars at the corners of the building. One base, preserved from the eastern wing, proves that the recessed middle part was also framed with pillars. A half-column divided the short sides of the building into two parts with a length of 2.45 m. Except for the corner pillars, the southern back side is not architecturally structured.

The last step of the substructure forms a bench that is decorated at the corners with lion paws. It serves as the stylobate for a richly profiled row of bases, which are 36 cm high. The decorated layer exists on all sides of the building, except at the recessed middle part. This profiled base is unexpected in a Doric order. The marble facing of the Doric order is secured with tie stones deep into the core. Orthostats (1.04 m high) were set up between the pillars and the half-columns. Following this layer is the crown molding of the orthostats, which is 30.5 cm high. The next layers are plain, measuring 90 and 30 cm. The last layer is only preserved at the southeast corner. The rest of the Doric storey must be reconstructed from architectural blocks not on the site. I speculate that another layer was added to the capital layer from the preserved blocks, which are 80 cm high.

---

ing, see Hilke Thür, "Der ephesische Ktistes Androklos und (s)ein Heroon an der Kuretenstraße," *JÖAI* 64 (1995) (forthcoming).

16. Keil, *Führer*, 112.

The capitals of the corner pillars are 37.5 cm high, have rich profiles, and are decorated with three flower rosettes. The total height of the Doric columns and pillars is 4.1 m; the proportion of the columns is 1 to 7. The Doric entablature follows the normal form. The metopes of the metope-triglyph frieze are decorated with different blossoms and rosettes, and partially with phiales. At the back of the building, however, they were undecorated.

The restoration of the middle part of the ground floor is problematic. The square-stone masonry in the recessed part is carefully developed; therefore, the present walls of this middle part must be the original structure. In contrast to the other sides of the building, however, they could not have been faced with the same marble façade. The comparison with the other sides proves that the surface of the core behind the marble blocks is not built as carefully as it was in the middle part. The traces of repairs to the Byzantine fountain that one would expect in the holes of the tie stones are missing. The fountain basin in the northern side of the building has the remains of marble flagstones 5 to 10 cm thick, which are set on the floor covering, also made from marble flagstone. They must have been set before or at the same time as the floor. Clamp holes for fastening them are preserved at the level of the base layer, and no traces of them exist above this level. In a 1988 trench, we found a 30 cm high layer of a red, very strong mortar under the floor flagstone. No Eastern Sigillata A pottery, which begins to appear in Ephesos at approximately 80 BCE,[17] exists in or beneath this water-resistant mortar layer. The marble wall covering seems to belong to the original structure of the building, as does a water channel leading from the backside through the core of the building, which could not have been cut secondarily through the core. The original shape of the water basin is unknown; at this time I am not able to identify the remains of the Hellenistic basin cornice.

Above the Doric ground floor, a second floor (fig. 2) was constructed in the Ionic order. Its ground plan matches the first floor, as

---

17. John W. Hayes, "Eastern Sigillata A," *Enciclopedia dell'arte antica, classica e orientale: atlante delle forme ceramiche* (2 vols.; Rome: Instituto della Enciclopedia italiana, 1985) 2. 9–26; Veronika Mitsopoulos-Leon, *Die Basilika am Staatsmarkt. Kleinfunde* (*FiE* 9.2; Vienna: Schindler, 1991) 86–93.

it too is U- or Π-shaped. The far side, which faced south, was closed off by a wall. Both the southeast and southwest corners end with pillars in the form of antae that continue to the north in a low wall like a cornice. This wall was covered by a profiled top, which continued up to the column in the middle axis of the eastern and western sides. The one remaining column of this site has partially unfinished fluting.

The pillars of the southern wall bore capitals decorated on three sides with rosettes; the profile of the capitals, which continues at the wall, is smaller and more detailed than the pillar capitals of the Doric order. The front of the second floor was constructed with an open colonnade in Ionic order (fig. 4). The Attic bases, columns, and capitals follow the normal form. The wider recessed middle was accentuated by a combination of columns and pillars, which bear an arch. On the back side of the blocks of the arch are half-rounded holes for the columns. The columns fitting into these holes have no fluting for a third of their circuit. One of the two half-column capitals from the order that framed the arch is also preserved.

The Ionic entablature consists of an architrave divided into three fasciae, a garland frieze, and a dental cornice. The architrave, whose fasciae are divided by an astragal, contains a crowning with an ovolo, a cavetto, and a fillet. The fruit garlands of the frieze are draped across the heads of bulls and deer. Beams supported the coffered marble ceiling. The nearly square compartments of the coffers were divided into central rhombi and four triangles. The panels are undecorated, except for the molding, a simple sloping fillet, which probably indicates the unfinished molding of an ovolo.

At the eastern, southern, and western sides the cover cornice of the building was formed by a dental cornice. The sima of the eastern and western sides is decorated with lion heads, partially perforated to allow rainwater to run out. The northern side, with its recessed middle part, led to a complicated resolution of the cover cornice. The side wings were crowned with a half-pediment; the half-tympanums were decorated with reliefs, which continued as a relief frieze in the recessed middle part. The middle was crowned with a second pediment; this tympanum was embellished with a shield. The inclination of this middle pediment was steeper than those of the half-pediments. Below the relief frieze, the dental cornice continued as a horizontal cornice without sima. The inclined geison with its sima continued as a crowning cornice above the relief frieze and divides itself at the inner corner into a second horizontal cornice without dentils and another inclined geison. On the ridge of the central pediment, a platform is produced for a pediment figure or a pediment akroterion. The blocks of the corner cornices also show beddings for corner akroteria or figures. The blocks of the eastern and western cornices have holes for fastening roof decorations, such as vases.

The height of the Ionic columns can be restored to 3.7 m; the diameter of these columns was 45 cm. Thus the ratio of column diameter to column height was about 1 to 8. The height from the Ionic floor to the top of the horizontal geison totaled 4.75 m; the height from the Ionic floor to the roof ridge measured 6.5 m. The total height of the entire building, measured from the level of the street, was slightly more than 13 m.

The heroon was designed as a free-standing building. Because of the lack of design of its posterior side, which was unstructured except for the corner pillars, and because the profiles and wall ashlar are primarily unfinished, it must be concluded that the posterior side was hardly visible.

In the second half of the first century BCE, the Octagon was built on the eastern side of the heroon at a distance of only 1.9 m.

At the western side lies a small rectangle (fig. 5) measuring approximately 4 m by 8 m, bordered at its western edge by a row of benches. The row consists of six blocks, with the four northern blocks bearing the letters K, Δ, E, and Π; these letters are builder's marks denoting the order of the benches. They were excavated in this sequence and thus at some point must have been rearranged in such a way that the normal alphabetical order was changed. The lengths of the benches vary between 80 cm to 100 cm; only the second bench from the south is shorter than average, measuring 58 cm. From the letter Π one can deduce that at least sixteen bench parts existed with a minimal length of approximately 15 m for the entire bench complex. In the south, at the end of the row, stands a bench with an armrest and a lion paw serving as a bench leg. It parallels the lion paws of the last step of the heroon substructure, which also formed a bench. The marble of the bench has the same striking blue veins as the Belevi marble, and the letters equal those on the other heroon blocks. The benches therefore may have belonged to the original equipment of the heroon. In late antiquity, a garland sarcophagus was buried in the small square between the heroon and the benches.[18]

The heroon was situated 5 m from the road; the fountain basin took up 2.5 m of that space. The northern side of the basin was erected over the wall of a channel that ran beneath the southern side of Curetes Street. The walls of the fountain basin were constructed of small pillars and parapets with late antique decorations of rhombi and crosses. Both the evidence of wear and the existence of lifting-holes at the inner sides of the blocks indicate that they were made from spoils. The parapet blocks stand on pedestal stones that have a similar profile to the *toichobate* ("wall profile") of the Doric order. Thus, the pedestal blocks probably belonged to the original fountain basin from the Hellenistic building phase.

Building inscriptions cannot, unfortunately, be used to date the building itself. Instead, the building technique of the heroon supplies the primary evidence for its dating. For example, the core of the base was constructed using the technique of pure ashlar masonry. The core of the adjacent Octagon, however, consists of opus cementitium. Excavators have proved that this new technique was used in Asia Minor beginning in approximately 50 BCE.[19] One can conclude, therefore, that the heroon was constructed before the Octagon and thus before the middle of the first century BCE. Further support for this terminus ante quem is provided by the channel that ran north of the heroon, which must have been built after it. This same channel, however, runs beneath and is older than the Octagon, which dates to 41 BCE.[20] From this, too, one can deduce for the heroon a construction date before the middle of the first century BCE. Moreover, the pottery found in trenches

18. See below pp. 186–87.
19. Compare John B. Ward-Perkins, "Building Methods of Early Byzantine Architecture," in David Talbot Rice, ed., *The Great Palace of the Byzantine Emperors* (Edinburgh: Edinburgh University Press, 1958) 85–86; Marc Waelkens, "The Adoption of Roman Building Techniques," in Sarah Macready and Frederick H. Thompson, eds., *Roman Architecture in the Greek World* (London: Thames & Hudson, 1990) 101.
20. See below pp. 178–82.

in the foundation level do not contain Eastern Sigillata A, which appeared in Ephesos after 80 BCE.[21] Ulrike Outschar, who made the pottery identification, hypothesized that the heroon was built between the middle of the second and the middle of the first century BCE.[22] This proposal can be further supported by the building decorations, including the Ionic capitals and the garland frieze. With their filigree, pointed egg elements of the echinus, and the graceful ranks at the pulvinus, the Ionic capitals of the building find parallels in the capitals of the Temple of Artemis in Magnesia on the Meander[23] and the Temple of Hekate in Lagina.[24] The beginning of construction at the Artemision has recently been dated to 190 BCE, and the Hekateion to 130 BCE.[25]

The thick and hoselike quality of the garland frieze (pl. 1) is comparable to that of the Opisthodomos of the Artemision in Magnesia.[26] Despite the compact overall design, the individual shapes of the fruits are in flat relief, consisting of grapes, leaves, pine cones, pomegranates, and flowers. The deer heads, with their strongly framed eyes and horns separated by a bulge, are similar in both cases. Also significant are the garlands of the column heads of the Smintheion in the Troas. The construction of this temple is generally dated to the second half of the second century BCE.[27] Notable also are the triglyphs which were done with "ears,"[28] a detail which, to my knowledge, no longer existed in early imperial times.

In the 1904 excavation report, Rudolf Heberdey mentioned "pieces of roughly cut frieze- and pediment-reliefs with battle scenes."[29]

21. See above n. 17.
22. See above n. 15.
23. Carl Humann, Julius Kohte, and Carl Watzinger, *Magnesia am Mäander: Bericht über die Ergebnisse der Ausgrabungen der Jahre 1891–1893* (Berlin: Reimer, 1904) 50–58; Rumscheid, *Bauornamentik*, 1. 25–28, 204–6; 2. 38–39, figs. 78, 3.4; 79, 3.4.
24. Arnold Schober, *Der Fries des Hekateions von Lagina* (Istanbuler Forschungen 2; Baden: Rohrer, 1933) 19–23; Rumscheid, *Bauornamentik*, 1. 132–39; 2. 33 fig. 72, 3–5.
25. The dating of the buildings is discussed by Rumscheid, *Bauornamentik*, 1. 25–28 (Artemision); 1. 132–39 (Hekateion).
26. Ibid., 1. 294; 2. 39 fig. 85.1.
27. Ibid., 1. 124–32, esp. 126; 2. 10 figs. 16.4, 17.9.
28. Ibid., 1. 313–14.
29. Heberdey, "Vorläufiger Bericht 1904," Beibl. 70.

Having discovered these unknown reliefs in the Selçuk museum, Hans Lauter subsequently presented three blocks and fragments of the frieze reliefs at the Archaeological Congress in Ankara in 1973.[30] The first relief (H 377 [fig. 6]) portrays a fight between a horseman and a foot soldier. The heavily armed horseman rides at a gallop from the right-hand side, that is, from an inner corner. His rival, apparently the loser of this battle, is a heavily armed foot soldier, shown in profile. He has sunken to his knees and tries to protect his face and body with a shield.

The second relief (H 376 [fig. 8]), which portrays a horseman, is broken at the lower right side. The horseman is represented in the type of Meleager or the Kalydonian boar hunt. Galloping toward the right side, the rider wears a short chiton with a belt at his waist and a short chlamys, which furls out behind him. The rider raises his right arm backwards to throw something, probably a lance. The intended target of his throw is not preserved.

The third relief (H 390 [fig. 9]) also shows a fragment of a foot soldier. Unfortunately, only the lower part of the figure, wearing a short chiton, is preserved. In 1983, two other reliefs were excavated at the western side of Slope House 2 (map no. 45).[31] They probably had already been excavated in 1904.

The fourth relief (H 374 [fig. 7]) belongs to a pediment and portrays a *biga* ("two horse chariot") and a foot soldier. The *biga*, dominating the left half of the picture, is driven by a charioteer as he heads toward the far left side of the relief. The driver of the chariot wears a long chiton and stands in the typical pose of charioteers. To the right of the *biga* is a heavily armed foot soldier facing in the opposite direction. This figure is fighting with an opponent on the far right of the picture; only one arm of this figure is preserved. The surface of the relief is in poor condition.

The fifth fragment of a relief (H 375 [fig. 11]) shows the upper part of the body of a heavily armed foot soldier with a shield. In 1991

30. Hans Lauter, "Ein republikanisches Triumphalmonument aus Ephesos," in Ekrem Akurgal, ed., *The Proceedings of the Tenth International Congress of Classical Archeology Ankara-Izmir 1973* (3 vols.; Ankara: Türk Tarih Kurunu, 1978) 2. 925–31 pls. 295–98.

31. See Maria Aurenhammer, "Arbeitsbericht 1983," in Vetters, "Vorläufiger Grabungsbericht 1983," 216–18 (pl. 10).

another relief was identified at the area of the Church of St. John. This sixth relief (H 380 [fig. 10]) represents a fight for a fallen person. The surface of the small left side of the relief block also has remains of a badly preserved picture. The block therefore must have belonged to a corner. The topside in a length of 51 cm oblique is worked out to the backside; a clamp leads to the backside. On a hillside, a fallen man is fatally wounded. He is presented in heroic nakedness without weapons. As a hero he is shown as a youth with short curly hair. At his left side, a man in a short chiton armed with an oval shield is fighting with a rival on the opposite side of the fallen figure. Because the block ends at this point, only the oval shield of the rival remains.

Heberdey presumed that the reliefs belonged to the tomb or heroon he had excavated between the Octagon and Hadrian's Gate. The material used, a distinctive blue-gray patterned marble, supports this possibility. Moreover, the reliefs fit perfectly into the reconstruction developed in recent years by means of a systematic building and stone investigation. It was even possible to determine the original places of the larger relief blocks in the building.

As mentioned earlier, the reliefs were part of a frieze that decorated the two pediment halves above a horizontal cornice and the recessed middle part. As mentioned earlier, block H 380 is a corner block. To the right another block must have been showing the fighter of whom only the oval shield is extant. Its position is definite because of the unique upper bearing, which is backwards oblique in the left part. The upper corner block of the preserved eastern inclined geison rested here; the lower bedding of 51 cm length equals the length of the oblique surface.

The longest preserved block (H 377), which is 1.85 m long, portrays a battle scene between a horseman and a hoplite. To the right it ends with a 15.5 cm wide joint that points forward, thus forming an inner corner. Only two possibilities exist for its original position in the building: the western side of the eastern wing (adjacent to the center part) or the western corner of the center part (adjacent to the eastern side of the western wing). Because of its length, the block could have fitted in beside block H 380; the relief pictures on the block exclude this placement, however, because the stone positioned here must have shown the warrior whose oval shield appears on H

380. Block H 377 can therefore only be placed in the second possible site—the western side of the center part. The position of the half-pediment relief (H 374) is derived from its angle of inclination. It belongs to the western half. The stone cut equals that of the eastern side, which means that the joint lay at the northern side. Its reconstruction in this position is also supported by the existence of a clamp hole.

The fragment H 376 presents a horseman with a waving coat. Because of the scene in this relief, it also cannot have bordered the battle scene around the fallen figure in H 380. Since the clamping differs, the possibility of its placement beside H 377 in the western inner corner is eliminated. Only two possible positions remain: the eastern end of the center or the northern block of the eastern side in the western wing. For thematic reasons which will be explained later, I prefer the first of the two positions.

The reliefs show a charioteer, a fallen figure in heroic nakedness, and both heavily and lightly armed soldiers. The heavily armed figure wears short chest armor ending in a straight line at the bottom. Under it appear two rows of *pteryges* ("leather flaps"). At the armholes the armor shows leather strips. Under the armor the figures wear a short chiton, and over the armor are bands of different materials. The heavily armed figure wears a helmet with cheek flaps, as well as forehead blades ending in volutes, a comb, and a forehead protection. The neck guard is a sideward-undulated brim. Petros Dintsis has named this type of helmet "pseudo-Attic."[32] The heavily armed hoplites are equipped with round shields.

The lightly armed figures, the horseman on block H 377, the hoplite on fragment H 390, and the figure on relief H 380 seem to wear only short chitons belted in the middle. Their headgear resembles a *pilos* helmet or a *kausia*, which can also appear in this shape. The warriors are equipped with oval shields in the scene in which they fight over a fallen soldier.[33] It is striking that the foes are clad and armed the

32. Petros Dintsis, *Hellenistische Helme* (Rome: Brettschneider, 1984) 119 ff.

33. For this type, see Michael Eichberg, *Scutum: Die Entwicklung einer italisch-etruskischen Schildform von den Anfängen bis zur Zeit Caesars* (Europäische Hochschulschriften Reihe 38.14; Frankfurt: Lang, 1987) 164–66.

same way. Their outfits match pictures on monuments of Hellenistic as well as high imperial times. Thus, neither the clothes nor the equipment provide hints of the ethnic origin of the fighters, nor can an exact date be gained. According to Petros Dintsis, however, the form of the pseudo-Attic helmet only existed until the beginning of the first century BCE.[34]

With regard to stylistic analysis, the simple if not primitive composition scheme of the reliefs catches the eye. The reliefs consist exclusively of single battle groups so separate from one another that, although they stand side by side, they do so without apparent relationship. A surprising amount of empty space exists between the warriors and the groups. Landscape elements are almost totally missing, with only small amounts of ground indicated below the figures. Since the actors are standing far apart, figures do not overlap; movements are basically parallel, while three dimensionality or even spacious illusion are not intended. The figures are flat, not even existing in half-relief; their plasticity is shallow. They are shown either in profile or in a front or back view. Three-quarter views are generally avoided, and where they do appear, they make an awkward, stiff impression. The fighters are peculiarly motionless. Their upper parts, even in a side view, are twisted in a front or back view. Limbs and weapons, however, are almost always basically parallel. Spatial reductions appear distorted. In oblique views the legs of the horses, especially the chariot horses, are graduated behind or above each other. In contrast to the simplifying and flattening reproduction of the figures, the calf muscles of the warriors and especially the muscles of the horses are strongly developed and distinctively reproduced.

In Hans Lauter's classification of the three reliefs known to him, he came to the conclusion that there were no real parallels either in Asia Minor or Greece to this "rough make, the disproportions, the awkwardness and distortions of the movements." He did, however, find one parallel in the reliefs of riders in the Apollo-Sosianus Temple in Rome. Consequently, he dates the Ephesian reliefs to the period 30 to 15 BCE and attributes them to either a triumphal monument for Octavian or an honorary monument for one of his supporters.[35] Al-

---

34. Dintsis, *Hellenistische Helme*, 118.
35. Lauter, "Ein republikanisches Triumphalmonument," 928–30.

though Lauter's interpretation was rejected by both Klaus Tuchelt[36] and Wolfgang Oberleitner,[37] the proposed dating and the suggestion that the reliefs were ordered by an Italian have in general been accepted.

A comparison with Hellenistic and late Hellenistic reliefs in Asia Minor has not yet been attempted. The reason may be that two diverse groups exist in Hellenistic relief art. The most prominent and well-known group contains the commissioned works of the dynastic Hellenistic ruling houses, the reliefs of the Pergamon altar,[38] and the sarcophagus of Alexander,[39] which are truly beyond comparison. In addition, there are a number of relief monuments from Asia Minor that are of lower quality. They are the commissioned works of private persons or cities.

Robert R. Smith[40] evaluated this second group correctly using the example of the frieze at the Artemision in Magnesia:

> Many figures have "lumpy," baroque-style muscles, ill-suited both to the scale of the figures and their manner of execution. . . . The frieze is poorly executed throughout, with frequently awkward and incompetent figures in repetitious groupings. However, this consistent lack of quality may not be due simply to incompetence—it was probably planned. On the building ca. 17 m above the ground, the frieze carving would have been sufficiently effective. Its stocky figures are well spaced and stand out at a distance. Better quality would have been of no purpose. The frieze H. 80 cm is treated merely as a course of the entablature (H. ca. 3.00 m), not much different in emphasis from the other

36. Klaus Tuchelt, *Frühe Denkmäler Roms in Kleinasien* (*IstMit* Beiheft 23; Tübingen: Wasmuth, 1979) 116–17.

37. Wolfgang Oberleitner, "Ein hellenistischer Galaterschlachtfries aus Ephesos," *Jahrbuch der Kunsthistorischen Sammlungen in Wien* 77 (1981) 86–88.

38. Heinz Kähler, *Der große Fries von Pergamon* (Berlin: Mann, 1948); Eva M. Schmidt, *Der große Altar zu Pergamon* (Leipzig: Seemann, 1961); Elisabeth Rohde, *Pergamon, Burgberg und Altar* (Munich: Beck, 1982).

39. Volkmar von Graeve, *Der Alexandersarkophag und seine Werkstatt* (Istanbuler Forschungen 28; Berlin: Mann, 1970).

40. Robert R. R. Smith, *Hellenistic Sculpture: A Handbook* (New York: Thames & Hudson, 1991) 181–86, 191–92.

elements. . . . The frieze is not more than a large figured moulding.[41]

Other Hellenistic friezes offer more parallels. The composition patterns of individual battle groups, placed alongside each other, and the resulting free space match a similar tendency, although to a lesser degree, in the friezes of the Temple of Apollo Smintheios in the Troas[42] and the Temple of Dionysos in Teos as well.[43]

A key element for the interpretation of the building is the figure of a horseman dressed in a short chiton with a chlamys that unfurls backwards (pl. 2). He corresponds well with a similar representation of the boar killing Androklos (pl. 3), the legendary founder of the city of Ephesos, on the relief-frieze of the small Temple of Hadrian (map no. 41) on Curetes Street. Strabo recorded that Androklos, son of King Kodros of Athens, was the leader of the colonists.[44] The historian Athenaios, who recorded the *Chronicle of Ephesos* by Kreophylos,[45] reported the legend that the colonists sent to the oracle in order to find a good place for settling. The oracle's answer was: "Where a fish will show and a boar will lead." Later, when fishermen were preparing their meal near the spring named Hypelaia and the sacred harbor, a fish and a piece of burning coal fell into dry brushwood, which then began to burn. The fire roused the sleeping boar, which began to flee. After the boar ran a long distance through the hills, Androklos killed the boar at the spot where the Temple of Athena now stands. There the colonists founded their city.

Pausanias also described the founding of the city and the death of Androklos:

> Androklos helped the people of Priene against the Carians. The Greek army was victorious, but Androklos was killed in the battle.

41. Ibid., 184; for the frieze of the Artemision, see Abdullah Yaylali, *Der Fries des Artemisions am Mäander* (*IstMit* Beiheft 15; Tübingen: Wasmuth, 1976).

42. Hans Weber, "Zum Apollo Smintheus Tempel in der Troas," *Istanbuler Mitteilungen* 16 (1966) 100–113.

43. Walter Hahland, "Der Fries des Dionysostempels in Teos," *JÖAI* 38 (1950) 66–109.

44. Strabo *Geog.* 14.1.3, 4, 21.

45. Athenaios *Deipnosophist.* 7.62 (ed. George Kaibel; Leipzig: Teubner, 1887) 361.

The Ephesians carried off his body and buried it in their own
land, at the spot where his tomb is pointed out at the present day
ʊʜ ʈʜⱷ ʟʊɑʈ ʟⱷⱥʟʟʜɴʛ ɍʜʜʜ ʈʜⱷ ⱳⱥʜⱷ ʜⱥⱥʜ ʜ ʜⱥⱥⱥ ʈʜⱷ ɳʟʜʜʜʜ ʜⱥʜ ʜ
the Magnesian Gate. On the tomb is a statue of an armed man.[46]

When the Temple of Hadrian[47] was repaired in approximately 300
CE, the frieze was built secondarily in its pronaos. The frieze could
be a quotation of the representation of the foundation legend from the
heroon of Androklos. On the frieze of the Temple of Hadrian the
running boar indicates that the rider is Androklos and that the frieze
retells the foundation legend.

The relief of the heroon is broken at the lower right side, and the
boar could easily be supplied at the missing part. The hypothesis that
the frieze at the Temple of Hadrian refers to a traditional prototype
is further supported by a coin from the time of the Antonines that
portrays a boar-hunting Androklos in exactly the same position.

If the relief at the heroon served as a prototype for the representation of the foundation legend, the frieze at the Temple of Hadrian
may provide other evidence. On that frieze, to the right of Androklos
and below the boar, is a warrior who has sunk to his knees. He holds
a dagger in his right hand and a shield in his left to protect himself
from an enemy coming from the right. Although he is shown as a
lightly armed soldier with a short chiton, his appearance is reminis-
cent of the hoplite on relief H 377. Because of the way in which the
blocks of the frieze were cut and reused in the temple, the figure of
the horseman must be missing, in comparison with the representation
on the heroon. The presence of this warrior leads to the conclusion
that the relief of the rider with the waving chlamys is Androklos near
the battle scene of the hoplite against the horseman.

Because the *biga* on the pediment relief portrays a single chariot,
this scene cannot be interpreted as a hint or cipher for chariot rac-

46. Pausanias 7.2.8. (LCL; trans. William H. S. Jones; 5 vols.; London:
Heinemann and Cambridge, MA: Harvard University Press, 1966) 3. 177.

47. Miltner, "XXII. vorläufiger Bericht," Beibl. 269–273; Nada Saporiti,
"A Frieze from the Temple of Hadrian at Ephesus," in Lucy Freeman Sandler,
ed., *Essays in Memory of Karl Lehmann* (Marsyas Supplement 1; New York:
New York University, 1964) 269–78; Fleischer, "Fries des Hadrianstempels,
23–71.

ing,[48] which as a funeral game would fit excellently into a heroon or tomb. Nor can the *biga* be interpreted as a hunting chariot because there is no object of a hunt. It is possible, however, to interpret it as a battle chariot, consistent with the event depicted behind it—combat activity from the period of colonization. Moreover, the relief showing the battle for the fallen figure may document an event of the foundation legend. From Pausanias, we know that Androklos fell in battle helping the people of Priene against the Karians. This scene could thus be interpreted as the heroic death of Androklos.

All of the authors of old travelogues supposed that the tomb of Androklos was located outside the city on the eastern side of Panayirdağ along the Processional Way, which is lined with many grave monuments.[49] Even the first excavator of Ephesos, the British railroad engineer John Turtle Wood, believed he had found the tomb of Androklos when he uncovered the ruins of a marble tomb in 1869. Thinking that he was following the description of Pausanias,[50] Wood followed the Processional Way from the Magnesian Gate to the north. He also looked for the Olympieion in this area outside the city but did not find it.

The probable site of the Olympieion has only been known since 1983, when Stefan Karwiese identified the ruins of a monumental temple on the north side of the Church of Mary as the Hadrianic temple of the imperial cult (map no. 15).[51] Although this temple complex was completely destroyed down to the substructure, the few extant remains of the colossal architectural blocks correspond well to a date in Hadrianic times.

Christopher P. Jones recently rejected the identification of the Temple of Hadrian with the Olympieion.[52] No evidence of an Olympieion earlier

---

48. Compare Karin Tancke, "Wagenrennen: Ein Friesthema der aristokratischen Repräsentationskunst spätklassisch-hellenistischer Zeit," *JdI* 105 (1990) 102–12.

49. Compare Knibbe, *Via Sacra I*, 9–13.

50. Wood, *Discoveries at Ephesus*, 126–27.

51. Karwiese, "Korressos," 2. 220–21, pls. 9, 10.

52. Christopher P. Jones, "The Olympieion and the Hadrianeion at Ephesos," *JHS* 113 (1993) 149–52.

than the reign of Domitian exists in literature, inscriptions, or coins. As support for his argument, Christopher Jones cited a coin from the time of Augustus with the legend: IOVI OLY[mpio] on it; for stylistic reasons Michel Grant ascribed this coin to a mint in Ephesos. More recent numismatic handbooks, however, do not ascribe this coin to Ephesos.[53]

Recent geological investigation explains why this site would have been chosen for a temple complex that required an especially large vacant area. Deep drillings west of the Church of Mary demonstrated that no mainland existed at this site in the first century CE. Because of the lack of larger vacant sites near the center of the imperial cult at the upper agora and the terrace of the Temple of Domitian (map no. 53), the newly gained vacant land on the coast, which was probably owned by the city, was chosen as the site for the Olympieion. The alternative proposal is that the Olympieion was positioned on the eastern side of Panayirdağ. This must be excluded as this area was inundated every year by the Marnas River. Dieter Knibbe's excavations at the Stoa of Damianus have proven this as well.[54]

A site for the Olympieion inside the city walls also demands that the Heroon of Androklos be sought within the city. A study of the ancient sources demonstrates that the κτίστης ("founder") is often buried within the city as a hero. Because his grave protected against enemies, as the old tradition maintained, assemblies took place and justice was administered at the grave of the founder.[55] It was the place of the cultic veneration of the hero. Every year a commemorative day may have been dedicated to a hero as well. His cult might include sacrifices and processions as well as athletic, equestrian, and poetic competitions. In addition to having his own priests, the hero may also have a cult site that was merely a statue or that took the form of a tumulus, temenos, tomb, cenotaph, or altar. The favorite

---

53. See, for instance, C. H. V. Sutherland, *The Roman Imperial Coinage* (rev. ed.; 10 vols.; London: Spink, 1984) 1. 34, fig. 472.

54. Compare Knibbe, *Via Sacra I*, 17.

55. See Roland Martin, *Recherches sur l'Agora grecques* (Études d'histoire d'architecture urbaines; Écoles française 174; Paris: Boccard, 1951) 194–200. Frank Kolb, *Agora und Theater: Volks- und Festversammlung* (Berlin: Mann, 1981) 7–8; Wolfgang Leschhorn, *Gründer der Stadt* (Stuttgart: Steiner, 1984) 98 ff.

place for the burial of the founder was the agora. Roland Martin gathered the names of twenty-seven heros buried upon an agora from ancient sources. It is interesting that twelve of these references are to graves of a mythical or historical founder.[56]

Most of the Processional Way from the Olympieion to the Magnesian Gate, the area to which Pausanias referred, has been excavated. In recent years, two monuments have been proposed as the tomb of Androklos: a complex on the hill lying west of the stadium (map no. 18) and a round substructure at Marble Street in front of the Library of Celsus (map no. 35).

The complex lying west of the stadium is a square structure surrounded by colonnades. In the center is a round substructure cut out of the rock.[57] At this time, nothing of the architecture of this round building has been identified. Pieces of the colonnades, however, were found both on the site and all over the city. The architectural decoration indicates a date at the beginning of the third century CE.[58] This dating corresponds with the existence of coins from Severan times that portray Androklos. In my opinion, however, it is difficult to equate this site with the description given by Pausanias. A visitor coming from the sanctuary on the way to the Magnesian Gate enters the city at the gate (map no. 20) beside the stadium. The visitor would reach this complex before he or she would reach or see the Olympieion, a pattern that contradicts Pausanias's description.

The second monument, the round substructure on Marble Street, also cannot be the tomb of Androklos, based on Friedmund Hueber's identification of a great deal of the architectural pieces originating from this structure. It was a monopteros and held waterworks.[59]

Do any other hints exist to strengthen the identification of the heroon with the tomb of Androklos? According to Pausanias the tomb stood on the road leading from the Olympieion (map no. 15) to the Magnesian Gate (map no. 70), and a statue of an armed man was on

56. Martin, *Recherches sur l'Agora grecques*, 200 n. 5.
57. Keil, *Führer*, 63–65; see also Karwiese, "Korressos," 2. 221.
58. Compare Thür, *Hadrianstor*, 95, pls. 155, 156.
59. Friedmund Hueber, "Bauforschung und Restaurierung am unteren Embolos in Ephesos," *Österreichische Zeitschrift für Kunst- und Denkmalpflege* 43 (1989) 141.

the tomb. If Pausanias passed through the city on this route, the heroon is situated nearly midway between the two aforementioned monuments. The statue of an armed man could have stood on the upper floor under the arch or on the top of the building on the ridge of the roof.

Near the heroon, in front of the Baths of Varius (map no. 40), a statue base with a dedication to Androklos has been excavated (pl. 4).[60] The inscription refers to the replacement of the statue of the founder Androklos at the time of Caracalla. Another inscription found on the street leading from the theater to the north refers to a donation of wine distributed by a *paraphylax* in a monument named AND-ROKLON[eion].[61] This Androkloneion must have had the equipment for seating a number of people. Such equipment is found at the heroon in the row of benches on the western side of the heroon and the way in which the last step was constructed as a bench.

Finally, a relatively poor inscription on two blocks belonging to the heroon itself must be included in the evidence. Two of the blocks of the horizontal cornice with dentils, arranged under the frieze, carry one letter each, an H and an N. These adjacent blocks could be completed to read KTIΣT]HN. This same form exists in the dedication to Androklos on the statue base from the Baths of Varius.

The evidence can be summarized as follows: a building exists between Hadrian's Gate and the Octagon that excavators thought was a heroon or tomb, and which is indeed a cenotaph or heroon, because of its architectural type, its decoration, including a garland frieze, sculptured relief-frieze, and its pediment. On the relief, the figure of the rider with a waving chlamys and the remains of a building inscription indicate the founder Androklos. Furthermore, the period of construction, which dates back to the end of the second century BCE, is consistent. The structure is therefore one of the oldest known buildings of the Hellenistic-Roman city. The topographical site at the traditional Processional Way, close to the agora, corresponds well with the sacred sites and legendary burial places of mythical city founders.

60. Helmut Engelmann and Dieter Knibbe, "Aus ephesischen Skizzenbüchern," *JÖAI* 52 (1978–80) 47 no. 81; *IvE* II 501 (sides A, C); *IvE* III 647 (side B).

61. Dieter Knibbe and Helmut Engelmann, "Neue Inschriften aus Ephesos X," *JÖAI* 59 (1989) 143–44.

In 133 BCE, when the last Attalid left his kingdom to the growing Roman Empire, the Greek cities on the western coast of Asia Minor nominally gained back their freedom.[62] What could be a more appropriate time in the history of Ephesos to reflect upon the founding of the city by Androklos, the son of a Athenian king, and to demonstrate this heritage with a raising of a monumental heroon?

Approximately a hundred years later, at the end of the Augustan era, several additional structures existed: the State Agora (map no. 56),[63] along with the Basilike Stoa (map no. 64),[64] the Prytaneion (map no. 61),[65] and the Augusteum (Double Temple) (map no. 62)[66] had become the new political center of the town. Then there was the temple (map no. 58)[67] in the State Agora, whose dedication is not clear. Following the road down, there is the Monument of Pollio, which was probably a tomb, and the adjacent fountain (map no. 59).[68]

At the upper end of Curetes Street, the Memmius Monument (map no. 52) was erected in honor of Memmius, the grandson of Sulla. The towerlike tomb and honorary structure have a square ground plan; in the elevation three sides are concave. These niches are covered by arches and framed with pilasters and corner columns. Above this storey, Anton Bammer has reconstructed an attic with pilasters and sculptured panels with figures between them.[69] In her investigations of the

---

62. Compare Magie, *Roman Rule*, 2. 955.

63. Franz Miltner, "XXI. Vorläufiger Bericht über die Ausgrabungen in Ephesos," *JÖAI* 43 (1956–58) Beibl. 27–36; Alzinger, *Architektur*, 51–55.

64. Alzinger, *Architektur*, 55–57; Anton Bammer, "Zu *ÖJH* 50, 1972–1975 Beibl. 242 ff. 249," *JÖAI* 51 (1976–77) Beibl. 56–59; and see Peter Scherrer's contribution in this volume.

65. Alzinger, *Architektur*, 49–51.

66. Ibid., 26–37; for the architecture of the building, see Elisabeth Fossel-Peschl, *Die Basilika am Staatsmarkt in Ephesos* (Graz: n.p., 1982).

67. Wilhelm Alzinger, "Ephesos: B. Archäologischer Teil," *PWSup* 12 (1970) 1601; for the interpretation of the temple, see Werner Jobst, " Zur Lokalisierung des Sebasteion-Augusteum in Ephesos," *IstMit* 30 (1980) 241–60; see also Wilhelm Alzinger, "Ephesiaca," *JÖAI* 56 (1985) 61–64.

68. Anton Bammer, "Das Denkmal des C. Sextilius Pollio in Ephesos," *JÖAI* 51 (1976–77) Beibl. 77–92.

69. Wilhelm Alzinger and Anton Bammer, *Das Monument des C. Memmius* (*FiE* 7; Vienna: Rohrer, 1971); Alzinger, *Architektur*, 16–20; Anton Bammer, "Die politische Symbolik des Memmiusbaues," *JÖAI* 50 (1972–73) 220–22.

stone ceilings of Ephesos, Ulrike Outschar has discovered numerous blocks of coffers, architraves, and friezes that certainly belonged to a second floor of the building.[70] She reconstructed a peripteral second floor and a pyramidal roof,[71] or a round finish with a garland frieze.[72] In the time of Augustus, the structures of the lower agora had also changed extensively. The south gate dedicated by Mazaeus and Mithridates (map no. 34)[73] was erected as a triumphal arch.[74] At the time of Claudius, the agora was shaped as a square with surrounding colonnades after the ground level had been increased by 2 to 3 m to the level that currently exists.[75] Because of this elevation, the west gate[76] could not have been Hellenistic, as it was previously generally considered, but must have been built at the time of Claudius.

Along Curetes Street the Slope Houses (map nos. 45 and 46) were built. Their oldest building phase dates back to the Augustan era. Directly east of the Androklos heroon, an octagonal tomb[77] was erected (see fig. 5). After the excavations in 1904, Wilhelm Wilberg developed a theory and reconstructed this octagonal tomb in a drawing[78] (fig. 12). Several architectural parts were taken to Vienna; since 1978 they have been rebuilt in the Ephesos Museum in Vienna.[79] In this reconstruction, a three-stepped substructure is placed on a square base faced with slightly concave marble orthostats. The northern front,

---

70. Ulrike Outschar, *Ornament und Fläche: Konstruktion, Gliederungsschema und Dekor römischer Steindecken in Ephesos* (Ph.D. diss., University of Vienna, 1989) 5–29.

71. Ibid., fig. Z 25.

72. Ulrike Outschar, "Zum Monument des C. Memmius," *JÖAI* 60 (1991) 57–85, 69 fig. 13; the garland frieze is published by Anton Bammer, "Ein Rundfries mit Bukranien und Girlanden," *JÖAI* 49 (1968–71) 23–44; see also Alzinger, *Architektur*, 43–44.

73. Wilhelm Wilberg, *Das Südtor* (*FiE* 3; Vienna: Hölder, 1923) 40–75.

74. Alzinger, *Architektur*, 9–16.

75. Langmann and Scherrer, "Bericht. Ephesos. Agora," 12–14.

76. Wilhelm Wilberg, *Das Westtor* (*FiE* 3; Vienna: Hölder, 1923) 18–39; Alzinger, *Architektur*, 45–48.

77. Alzinger, *Architektur*, 40–43, figs. 27–31; see also Hilke Thür, "Arsinoë IV," 43–56.

78. Heberdey, "Vorläufiger Bericht 1904," Beibl. 71–76.

79. Anton Bammer, "Kat. Nr. 86–104, Das Oktogon," in Oberleitner, *Funde aus Ephesos und Samothrake*, 2.95–98.

facing the street, is inscribed with two letters by the emperors Valens, Valentinian, and Gratian in Latin and Greek.[80] Above a crowning cornice lies another square step. The core of the square base is made of opus cementitium. Three more steps in octagonal form serve as the substructure and stylobate for the elevation. This consists of an octagonal core surrounded by an octagonal peristasis with eight columns. At the base of the massive core runs a bench with supports in the shape of lion paws. The upper part of the core is decorated with a boukranion frieze[81] and crowned with a two-fasciae architrave. The columns of the peristasis were of Corinthian order. The base had the normal Attic form; the columns had elaborate fluting. The capitals follow the standard form of the Corinthian order.[82]

The entablature of the peristasis consists of a three-fasciae architrave, crowned with a robust egg and dart pattern,[83] a decorated frieze, and a console cornice.[84] On the frieze, upright acanthus leaves alternate with griffins and open palmettos. Both the points of the leaves and the heads of the bird griffins serve as supports of blocked consoles. Curved consoles are arranged above the palmettos. The peristasis is covered by a marble ceiling[85] that also rests upon the wall architrave. The top side of the coffered blocks carries marks for a superstructure. Numerous step blocks indicate a roof constructed as a stepped

80. Heberdey, "Vorläufiger Bericht 1904," Beibl. 70–76; Adolf Schulten, "Zwei Erlässe des Kaiser Valens über die Provinz Asia," *JÖAI* 9 (1906) 40–70; *IvE* I 42, 43.

81. Rumscheid, *Bauornamentik*, 1. 163–64, 277, 294; 2. 19 no. 48.7 (pl. 42, 2.4).

82. Ibid., 1. 160–61; 2. 19 no. 48, 2 (pl. 41, 4) (with further references); Wolf D. Heilmeyer, *Korinthische Normalkapitelle: Studien zur Geschichte der römischen Architekturdekoration* (Mitteilungen des DAI, Römische Abteilung, Ergänzungsheft 16; Heidelberg: Kerle, 1970) 79–80, 86 n. 340 (pl. 21, 1).

83. Rumscheid, *Bauornamentik*, 1. 161, 254–57; 2. 19 no. 48, 3 (pl. 41, 5).

84. Henner von Hesberg, *Konsolengeisa des Hellenismus und der frühen Kaiserzeit* (Mitteilungen des DAI, Römische Abteilung, Ergänzungsheft 24; Mainz: von Zabern, 1980) 56–57, 62, 64–67, 179 n. 920, 182; Rumscheid, *Bauornamentik*, 1. 161–63, 278, 320; 2. 19 no. 48,5.

85. Outschar, "Ornament und Fläche," 30–31; Rumscheid, *Bauornamentik*, 1. 164, 331; 2. 19 no. 48.8–10.

pyramid in octagonal form. The top of the building was a sphere of marble.[86]

By comparing the architectural decoration of the building, primarily the Corinthian capitals, the frieze with the acanthus leaves, the cornice and the garland frieze, Edmund Weigand, Wilhelm Alzinger, Wolf-Dieter Heilmeyer, Henner von Hesberg, and Frank Rumscheid have dated the building to the years between 50–20 BCE.[87] Since it was first excavated, the Octagon has been interpreted as a tomb of honor or a heroon. In 1926 Max Theuer renewed examinations of the structure and found the conjectured grave chamber (fig. 13). Inside the square base is a simple vaulted room, which can be entered by a hidden small passage from the back side. At the time of the excavations, the undecorated marble sarcophagus, which had previously been opened by robbers, contained only a skeleton. The director of the excavation, Josef Keil, took the cranium for further investigations to the University of Greifswald in Germany. The investigations determined that the buried person had been a young woman up to 20 years old.[88] This result is especially significant. The privilege of a burial inside the city walls was granted only to members of the dynasties or to great benefactors of the city. If the buried woman had been a benefactor, an inscription listing her benefactions would be expected. No inscription, however, has been found.

Some years ago I discovered a solution to the mystery.[89] Flavius Josephus, Appian, and Dio Cassius provide information that is probably connected to this octogonal tomb.[90] The report narrates that the youngest sister of Cleopatra VII, named Arsinoë IV,[91] had been killed

86. One half of the sphere was excavated in 1983 in the northwest corner of Slope House 2.

87. Edmund Weigand, "Baalbek und Rom, die römische Reichskunst in ihrer Entwicklung und Differenzierung," *JdI* 29 (1914) 52–54; Alzinger, *Architektur*, 40–43; Heilmeyer, *Korinthische Normalkapitelle*, 79–80, 86 n. 340; Hesberg, *Konsolengeisa*, 56–57; Rumscheid, *Bauornamentik*, 1. 164–65.

88. Josef Keil, "XV. Vorläufiger Bericht über die Ausgrabungen in Ephesos," *JÖAI* 26 (1930) Beibl. 44.

89. See also Thür, "Arsinoë IV," 52–56.

90. Josephus *Ant.* 15.89; Appian *Bell. Liv.* 5.9.34; Dio Cassius *Hist.* 43.19.2.

91. Ulrich Wilcken, "Arsinoë 28: jüngste Tochter des Ptolemaios XII. Neos Dionysos, genannt Auletes," *PW* 2.1 (1896) 1288–89.

in Ephesos by Mark Antony in the year 41 BCE at the request of her sister. Arsinoë, who was then 15 to 17 years old, had fled to the shelter of the Artemision at Ephesos. Other references from ancient sources provide additional information. In 47 BCE Caesar awarded Arsinoë and her brother Ptolemy XIV sovereignty over Cyprus. In Alexandria the aristocratic party elevated her to the status of queen as an act of opposition against the unpopular Cleopatra. Later she fought against Caesar.[92] Caesar carried her along with his triumphal procession in Rome and afterwards set her free. She sought asylum at the Artemision in Ephesos, where the high priests received her as a queen. The next reference records her assassination in Ephesos.

The Egyptian aristocracy favored Cleopatra's younger sister Arsinoë. When Mark Antony came to Asia Minor in the winter of 42/41 BCE, he needed to form a good relationship with Egypt in order to be able to carry out the duties he accepted in Philippi to restore law and order in the eastern provinces. At this time he was free to enter into an alliance either with Arsinoë or Cleopatra. After he met with Cleopatra in Tarsus, however—an event well known from Plutarch's lively description[93]—Antony accepted the sovereignty of Cleopatra and guaranteed her throne. Arsinoë was assassinated at his order.

In concluding this section, I summarize briefly the main arguments for the identification of this tomb. In the center of the city of Ephesos is a grave monument that many scholars date to the years between 50 and 20 BCE, because of its architectural decoration. Literary tradition names 41 BCE as the year in which Arsinoë died. During the summer excavations of 1993, further investigations were undertaken in the lowest parts of the western slope houses. As a result, for the first time in years, this area was once again accessible. The bones of the skeleton from the sarcophagus were rediscovered; obviously the excavators had deposited them in the niches of the back wall of the grave chamber. The skeleton was almost complete with the exception of the missing neck vertebrae and the cranium, which had been taken to Greifswald for further investigation. Anthropologists Susanne and Egon

92. Dio Cassius *Hist.* 42; 39.1; 42.1; Caesar *Bell. Civ.* 3.112.10–11 and *Bell. Alex.* 23.2; 33.2.
93. Plutarch *Anton.* 26.4.

Reuer examined the bones and confirmed the results from Greifswald. The bones indeed belonged to the skeleton of a female individual who had died at the age of fifteen or sixteen. Although the exact date of Arsinoë's birth is not transmitted, she was the youngest child of Ptolemy XII; her brother, Ptolemy XIV, was born in 59 BCE. He was her father's youngest son.[94] Arsinoë therefore could not have been more than seventeen years old in 41 BCE. Thus the historical tradition and the results of archaeological investigation correspond perfectly.

Further indications of the owner of this grave monument are offered by the form of the building itself. As far as I know, the octagonal shape had never been used before as a funerary building. The octagonal form of the structure must be interpreted as an architectural reference to the middle part of the Pharos,[95] the world famous lighthouse of the native city of the Ptolemies. This shape is a symbol of the lineage and identity of the person buried in the grave. It is probable that Mark Antony intended to conceal Arsinoë's assassination by an honorable burial as far away from her native city as possible. The time frame in which this building was erected as well as the historical circumstances are both indications of the assassinated Ptolemaian princess Arsinoë IV.[96]

Additional investigations may dismiss doubts concerning the identification of the buried person. After the initial excavation years ago, the cranium belonging to this skeleton was probably added to the collection at the University of Greifswald. Unfortunately, the collection's inventory list identifying this cranium has since been lost. When the sarcophagus at Ephesos was recently reopened, however, anthropologists discovered a tooth. By means of this tooth, it may be possible to identify the corresponding cranium at Greifswald. Although no individual portrait of Arsinoë herself is known, several of her sister

94. Hans Volkmann, "Ptolemaios 36: Ptolemaios XIV. Philopator, jüngerer Sohn des Ptolemaios XII. Auletes," PW 23.2 (1957) 1759–60.

95. Hermann Thiersch, *Pharos. Antike, Islam und Occident: Ein Beitrag zur Architekturgeschichte* (Leipzig: Teubner, 1909); Thür, "Arsinoë IV," 54–56; most recently, Rumscheid (*Bauornamentik*, 1. 164 n. 578) provides references for the discussion of the derivation of the octagonal form.

96. Rumscheid (*Bauornamentik*, 1. 164) dates the architectural decoration to the third quarter of the first century BCE and expresses cautious agreement with the theory that this may be the tomb of Arsinoë.

Cleopatra have been found.[97] Thus an examination of the corresponding cranium may lead to an affirmation of the relationship of this individual to the family of the Ptolemies. Most of the buildings of Curetes Street discussed in this section were erected in the hundred years following the construction of Arsinoë's tomb. At Domitian Square (north of the Temple of Domitian) huge substructures were prepared in order to provide a large area for the first temple of the imperial cult, the Temple of Domitian, and its altar (map no. 53).[98] To the east of it, during Flavian times, the Fountain of C. Laecanius Bassus (map no. 60)[99] was built. The Pollio buildings were also reconstructed during this time. Marble Street and the Neronic Stoa (map no. 29)[100] were built in the area of the lower agora. The southern end of Marble Street was decorated with a gate structure marking the Processional Way to Ortygia, which departed from this spot. This gate, known in literature as Hadrian's Gate (map no. 38),[101] was dated to Trajanic-Hadrianic times due to its architectural decoration. Causing great changes in the urban architectural situation, the Library of Celsus (map no. 35),[102] adjacent to the south

97. Compare Helmut Kyrieleis, *Bildnisse der Ptolemaier* (Archäologische Forschungen 2; Berlin: Mann, 1975) 124, pls. 107–8.

98. Josef Keil, "XVI. Vorläufiger Bericht über die Ausgrabungen in Ephesos," *JÖAI* 27 (1932) Beibl. 51–60; Keil, *Führer*, 124–37; Wilhelm Alzinger, "Der Tempel des Kaisers Domitian," PWSup 12 (1970) 1649–50; Anton Bammer, "Architektur," *JÖAI* 50 (1972–71) Beibl. 399; idem, "Architekturfassaden," Beibl. 81–88 figs. 13–17; concerning the supporting figures on the terrace see Schneider, *Bunte Barbaren*, 125–28.

99. Elisabeth Fossel and Gerhard Langmann, "Das Nymphaeum des C. Laecanius Bassus," *JÖAI* 50 (1972–75) Grabungen 301–10.

100. Wilhelm Wilberg, *Die obere Osthalle* (*FiE* 3; Vienna: Hölder, 1923) 76–88. Gerhard Lang, "Zur oberen Osthalle der Agora, der 'Neronischen Halle' in Ephesos," in Kandler, Karwiese, and Pillinger, *Lebendige Altertumswissenschaft*, 176–80 pls. 20, 21.

101. Thür, *Hadrianstor*.

102. Wilhelm Wilberg, et al., *Die Bibliothek* (*FiE* 5.1; Vienna: Österreichische Verlagsgesellschaft, 1944); Volker Michael Strocka, "Zur Datierung der Celsusbibliothek," in Ekrem Akurgal, ed., *The Proceedings of the Tenth International Congress of Classical Archeology*, 2. 893–900; Friedmund Hueber and Volker Michael Strocka, "Die Bibliothek des Celsus: Eine Prachtfassade in Ephesos und das Problem ihrer Wiederaufrichtung," *Antike Welt* 6 (1975) 3–14.

gate of the agora, was built as a tomb and monument in honor of the proconsul of the Asian province. By the beginning of the second century at the latest Curetes Street was uniformly equipped on its northern side with colonnades and three splendid honorific constructions, namely, the Fountain of Trajan (map no. 49),[103] a Trajanic gate building decorating the entrance of a side road, and the so-called Temple of Hadrian (map no. 41).[104]

Several of the buildings just mentioned are connected to the name of one particular Ephesian.[105] His name as a high-ranking municipal official helps with the dating of the constructions; often he had personally donated the buildings, paying for them out of his own funds. This Tiberius Claudius Aristion[106] is known not only from numerous Ephesian honorary and building inscriptions,[107] but also from a letter written by Pliny the Younger,[108] who was assessor to a law suit against Aristion. The latter had apparently been cited before Emperor Trajan in Centumcellae (Civitavecchia) by envious people who accused him of having abused the people's benevolence in a suspicious manner. Tiberius Claudius Aristion successfully defended himself and was acquitted as a "a generous man and blamelessly popular" (*homo munificus et innoxie popularis*). His functions in the administrative and sacred spheres of Ephesos can be reconstructed from inscriptions.[109] In 88/89 and 90/91, he was *archiereus* ("high priest") of the state cult and from 89 to 91, he was neokoros. Because of these

103. Franz Miltner, "XXII. vorläufiger Bericht über die Ausgrabungen in Ephesos," *JÖAI* 44 (1959) Beibl. 326–46; Bammer, "Architekturfassaden," Beibl. 81–90.

104. Miltner, "XXII. vorläufiger Bericht," Beibl. 264–83; for references for the relief-frieze, see above n. 47.

105. The subject of this part of the paper will be published jointly in *JÖAI* 64 Beiblatt (forthcoming) by Maria Aurenhammer (portrait of the cult priest), Ulrike Outschar (pottery), Egon and Susanne Reuer (anthropology), Peter Scherrer (Tib. Claudius Aristion), and Hilke Thür (excavation report, sarcophagus).

106. *PIR*² 2.170 no. 788; 2. 170 no. 788; see also Peter Scherrer, "Tib. Claudius Aristion," *JÖAI* 64 Beiblatt (forthcoming).

107. *IvE* II 234, 235, 239, 424, 424a, 425, 425a, 461, 508; V 1489; VII 5101, 5113.

108. Pliny *Ep.* 6.31.3.

109. Compare Friesen, *Twice Neokoros*, 45–47.

offices, his functions would have related to the building of Domitian's temple complex. In 92/93 he held the top urban office of *grammateus* ("secretary of the people's council"). In this function his name was connected both to the building and the equipping of the Harbor Baths[110] and gymnasium (map nos. 8, 9). In an inscription in the "Imperial Hall"[111] he is named a prytanis; perhaps he also financed this hall.

Later, he built two large fountain buildings: the fountain on the road to the Magnesian Gate (map no. 67)[112] and the Fountain of Trajan (map no. 49),[113] both of which must be dated between 102 and 114 because of the imperial titles employed. In the inscription of the Fountain of Trajan he is called *tris Asiarches* ("thrice asiarch"). Aristion was also responsible for many building stages of the Aquaeduct of Marnas, which was finished in 113/114, as is known from a protective statute.[114]

Three honorary inscriptions to Tiberius Claudius Aristion mention the "many beautiful buildings" for which the city is indebted to him.[115] The last reference to his name occurs in the inscriptions of the Library of Celsus. He was commissioned by the son of Celsus, Tiberius Julius Aquila Polemaeanus, to finish the library.[116] The completion of this building is dated to a period between 117 and 123. Since Aristion's name does not appear after these dates, we can presume that he must have died by then. He was active for about thirty years as a great benefactor of the city.

This famous Ephesian, perhaps one of the richest men of his time, benefited his hometown greatly by holding several offices and donating numerous buildings, especially a water pipeline and two fountains. From his position we may conclude that he, too, was honored with an honorable burial within the town. I therefore propose that a discovery made in 1988 is related to this benefactor: Several years

---

110. Keil, *Führer*, 74–82.

111. *IvE* II 427; Otto Benndorf, *Eine Erzstatue eines griechischen Athleten* (*FiE* 1; Vienna: Hölder, 1906) 182.

112. Keil, "XII. vorläufiger Bericht," Beibl. 271–78; Anton Bammer, *JÖAI* 52 (1978–80) Beibl. 81–90; *IvE* II 424a.

113. See above n. 103; *IvE* II 424.

114. *IvE* II 424; VII 3217.

115. Ibid., II 425; III 638.

116. Ibid., VII 5101.

ago, at the western side of the Heroon of Androklos (fig. 5), a tree
was to be planted; just below the surface, however, workers struck at
the lld of a sarcophagus. When I began working on the heroon, I
remembered this sarcophagus and hoped to gain information about
the heroon through it. In 1988 I had both the lid and the sarcophagus
dug out. The lid had been pushed from its original position and was
broken. Between the sarcophagus and the lid was the plinth of the
statue of an official. The upper part of the sarcophagus was filled
with rubble. Ulrike Outschar conducted a pottery evaluation and concluded that this rubble filling and the rubble around the sarcophagus
were dated to the fifth or sixth century CE.[117]

For chronological reasons, therefore, the sarcophagus (fig. 14) could
not belong to the heroon since the half-fabricated garland sarcophagus was not made until the beginning of the first century CE. Moreover, the heroon had no grave chamber. As excavators emptied the
sarcophagus, a marble portrait of a head was found. It was deposited
into a corner with the face carefully placed downward. The realistic
portrait[118] is of high quality and portrays an old man of about sixty
years, with features reflecting the suffering of an aged person. On his
head, he wears a crown with five busts; the crown testifies that he
was a priest of an emperor cult. Unfortunately, the heads of the busts
are not preserved. Specialists on sculpture and portraits, including
Maria Aurenhammer, Kenan Erim, Paul Zanker, and Burt Smith suggested a date in Flavian to Trajanic times.

Excavators found several bones at the bottom of the sarcophagus.
Anthropologists Susanne and Egon Reuer determined that they were
the incomplete skeletons of two individuals, a man approximately
sixty years old and a boy three and a half years old; the two appear
to have been relatives. The old man suffered from arthritis and must
have been in great pain. An anthropological examination of the parts
of the cranium and the preserved lower jaw, in conjunction with a

117. The pottery will be published by Ulrike Outschar; see n. 105 above.
118. The portrait will be published by Maria Aurenhammer; see n. 105
above.

comparison to the portrait head, led to the conclusion that the buried man and the marble portrait were probably the same person.[119]

In my opinion, the dating and the depicted age of the marble portrait, the age of the dead man, his function as a priest of the imperial cult, and honorary burial in the city, all point to one man, namely, Aristion. If I am right, the search for the site of the original tomb of Aristion must begin at the lower Embolos. The sarcophagus is very large and weighs four to five tons. It probably was not transported over a long distance in order to bury it in the earth at the west side of the heroon. The careful placement of the head in the sarcophagus indicates an intentional action. Because the new religion of Christianity reviled the imperial cult, the grave and the statue of a priest of this cult must have been in danger of being destroyed and was therefore piously hidden away.

For the tomb of Aristion I suggest one highly hypothetical site: the eastern side of the Octagon. Excavators at the beginning of the century interpreted this monument as a heroon or tomb. In late antiquity it was reused as a workshop. The ruin allows reconstruction of a closed grave chamber, which was necessary for the unfinished sarcophagus, and a kind of pronaos with columns and bases for statues. Further archaeological investigation of the substructure and a search for the unknown architectural remains are therefore on the agenda for the coming years.

119. For the anthropological results, see Egon and Susanne Reuer, n. 105 above.

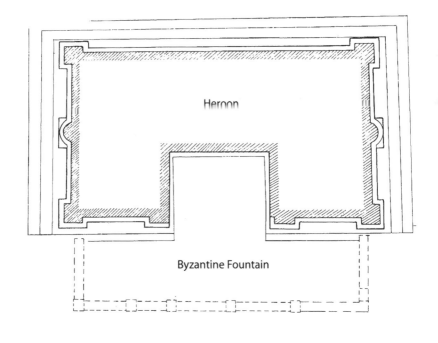

FIGURE 1   Floor plan of the Heroon of Androklos

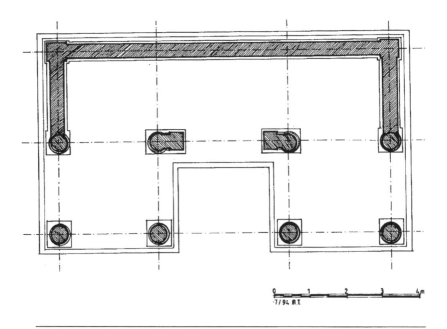

FIGURE 2   Second floor of the Heroon of Androklos

View from the North

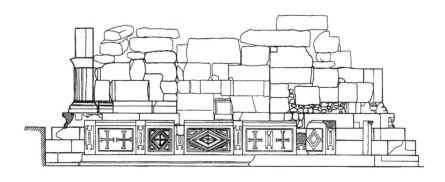

View from the West

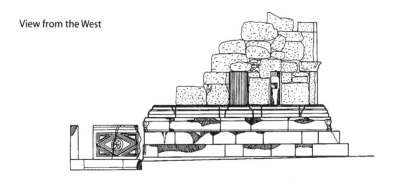

View from the East

Fig tree   Doric cornice

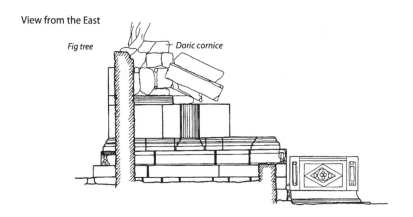

FIGURE 3   The ruin of the Heroon of Androklos with the
Byzantine fountain basin

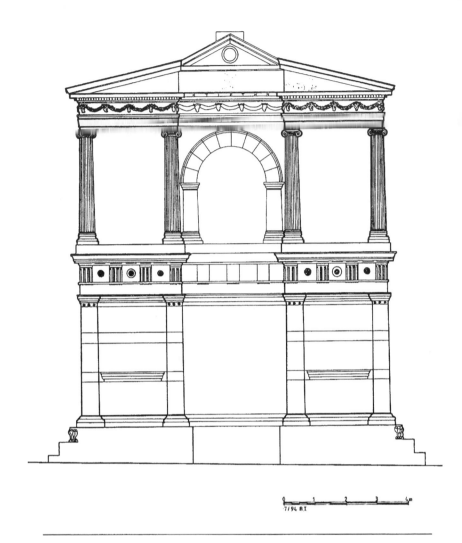

F I G U R E 4   The Heroon of Androklos reconstructed, view from the
north

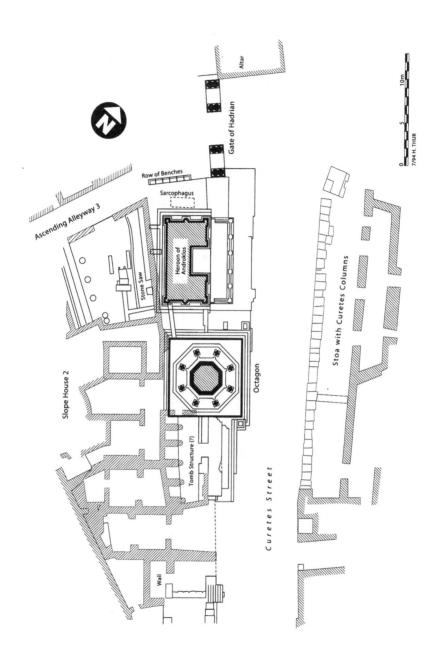

FIGURE 5   Heroa – Lower Embolos

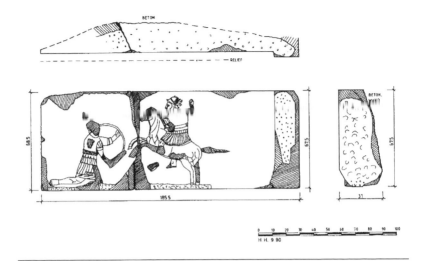

F I G U R E 6   Relief H377

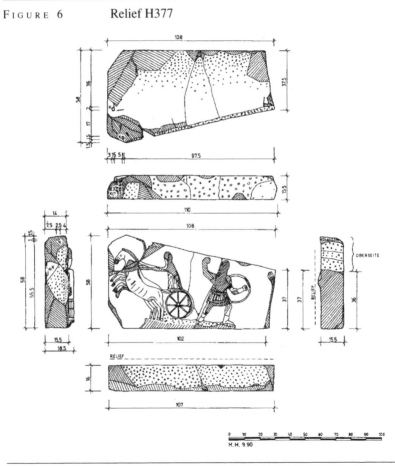

F I G U R E 7   Relief H374

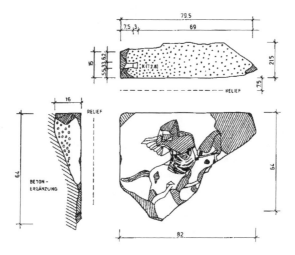

F I G U R E 8   Relief H376

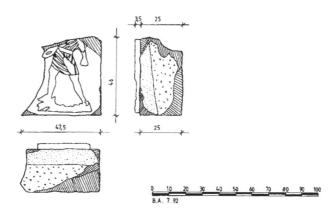

F I G U R E 9   Relief H390

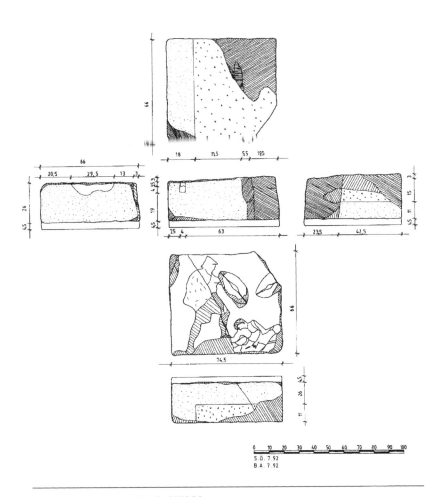

S.O. 7.92
B.A. 7.92

FIGURE 10   Relief H380

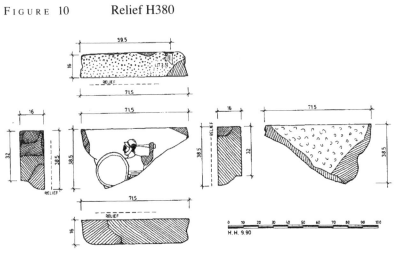

H.H. 9.90

FIGURE 11   Relief H375

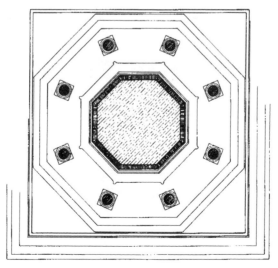

FIGURE 12   Wilberg's reconstruction of the Octagon
(drawn by Max Theuer)

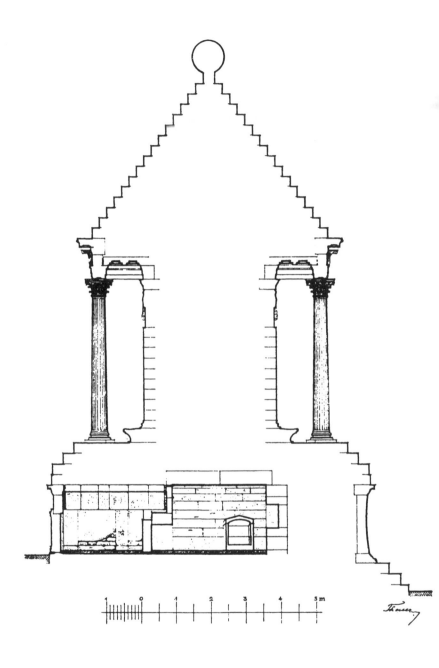

F I G U R E 13   Section through the Octagon with the burial chamber of Arsinoë IV (?)

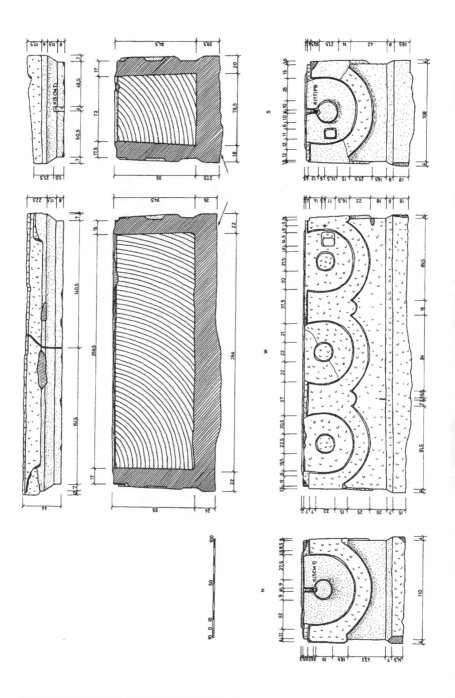

F I G U R E 14   The sarcophagus of Aristion (?)

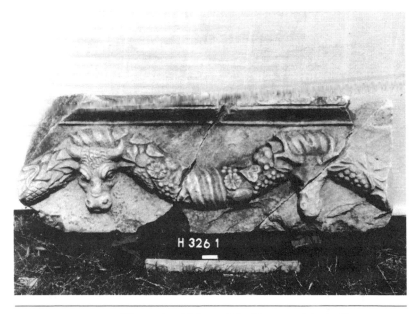

P L A T E 1   The garland frieze of the Heroon of Androklos

P L A T E 2   Relief H376, Androklos (?)

P LATE 3   Relief frieze with the boar hunt of Androklos from the so-called Temple of Hadrian

P LATE 4   Statue base with a dedication to Androklos and a view to the Heroon of Androklos

Preliminary Views of the Ephesian Harbor

Heinrich Zabehlicky
Österreichisches Archäologisches Institut

The importance of the harbor for the ancient metropolis of Ephesos can hardly be overestimated. The position of Ephesos as both a center of trade and commerce and a link between an important east-west land route and the Aegean Sea was one of the most significant factors in the growth and development of the city.[1] This study presents current research on the topographical, archaeological, and historical features of the harbor. Scholars believe that the harbor was located at three different sites in the early history of the city[2]; the silting up of each harbor forced the city to move, since its wealth and

1. For the benefits of the location of Ephesos, despite the technical problems of the harbor, see Strabo *Geog.* 14.1.24 (see below). Regarding roads, see Dieter Knibbe, "Ephesos," PWSup 12 (1970) 270; Lionel Casson, *The Ancient Mariners* (2d ed.; Princeton: Princeton University Press, 1991) 161–62.

2. Otto Benndorf, *Zur Ortskunde und Stadtgeschichte*, 9–110; Josef Keil, "Zur Geschichte und Topographie von Ephesos," *JÖAI* 21/22 (1922–24) 96–112. I am indebted to my colleagues, whose constrislutions grace this volume, for their counsel and assistance.

importance depended upon the accessibility of the harbor. The positions of these early harbors are not exactly known. The position of the berth, discussed recently,[3] is outside the region that the map covers.

The oldest settlement and its landing site, called the "holy port" (ἱερὸς λιμήν) in ancient and modern literature, were located in the area surrounding the Artemision (map no. 74).[4] Although ancient authors occasionally mentioned the position of the city and harbor in classical times, the information is somewhat ambiguous, since it was not written for the purpose of topographical interpretation. There have been suggestions that this settlement was located on the northern or eastern slope of Panayırdağ (Mount Pion, between map nos. 20 and 72). Based on the topographic situation in 1896, Benndorf and Schindler placed the Hellenistic port west of Panayırdağ at the site where a large *xystos* called the Halls of Verulanus was later discovered (map no. 10).[5] Their interior structures are early Hadrianic and the walls seem to have been built immediately before that,[6] although an earlier date is possible. Even before the beginning of the excavations, the large reed-covered area west of the visible remains was identified as a harbor.[7] In 1896, Otto Benndorf began excavations at the eastern edge of this area, which he called the Roman port. Although the high level of groundwater made the work difficult, excavations continued until 1902. By 1907, the ruins again became overgrown, and today they are almost unidentifiable.[8]

3. Recep Meriç, "Zur Lage des ephesischen Außenhafens Panormos," in Kandler, Karwiese, and Pillinger, *Lebendige Altertumswissenschaft*, 30–32.

4. Kreophilos cited in Athenaios *Deipnosophist.* 8 § 361e.; Benndorf, "Zur Ortskunde und Stadtgeschichte," 53 n. 2.

5. Otto Benndorf, "Vorläufiger Bericht über die Ausgrabungen in Ephesos," *JÖAI* 1 (1898) Beibl. 61 fig. 17.

6. Keil, *Führer*, 82. In personal communication with me (February 1994), Peter Scherrer said that he finds Keil's idea of an earlier phase unconvincing. The adjacent Harbor Baths were finished in 92/93 CE.

7. Wood, *Discoveries at Ephesos*. See also the plan of the ruins therein. See also the plan at the end of Ernst Curtius, *Ephesos* (Berlin: Hertz, 1874).

8. Preliminary reports: Benndorf, "Vorläufiger Bericht," Beibl. 53–72; Rudolf Heberdey, "Vorläufiger Bericht über die Ausgrabungen in Ephesos II," *JÖAI* 1 (1898) Beibl. 71–82; idem, "Vorläufiger Bericht über die Aus-

Three gates marked places where important roads reached the quay, which at this point was 10 m wide. The quay formed the eastern end of the basin next to the center of the city in polygonal design, which resulted in nonrectangular spaces where it met the rectangular road system. The southern gate (map no. 3) was reconstructed by George Niemann; the drawing clearly shows the problematic space in which the gate was constructed.[9] An inscription says that the rich Ephesian M. Fulvius Publicianus Nikephoros, who lived in Severan times, donated the funds for this gate. The central harbor gate (map no. 2) marks the end of the Arkadian Street. There is no epigraphic evidence on which to base the dating of this gate, which has therefore been subject to much debate.[10] George Niemann's reconstruction is based on the architectural decoration, and Hilke Thür and Peter Scherrer confirmed in personal communications that no convincing objection can be made to the Hadrianic date that Wilhelm Wilberg proposed.[11] Only a few architectural pieces were found at the northern gate (map no. 1), but an inscription indicates a date between the end of the second and the middle of the third century CE, similar to the southern gate.[12] If one accepts a Roman date for the central harbor gate and for the *xystos*, then no building existed northwest of the theater and the Tetragonos Agora in the Hellenistic period. The Hellenistic harbor therefore may have been situated where Benndorf first located it or at the easternmost part of the Roman and Byzantine harbor. Whether

---

grabungen in Ephesos III," *JÖAI* 2 (1899) Beibl. 37–50; idem, "Vorläufiger Bericht über die Ausgrabungen in Ephesos IV," *JÖAI* 3 (1900) Beibl. 83–96; idem, "Vorläufiger Bericht über die Ausgrabungen in Ephesos V," *JÖAI* 5 (1902) Beibl. 53–66; idem, "Vorläufiger Bericht 1904," Beibl. 37–56; Wilhelm Wilberg, *Torbauten am Hafen. Grabungsgeschichte* (*FiE* 3; Vienna: Hölder, 1923) 169–71.

9. Wilhelm Wilberg, *Der südliche Torbau*, (*FiE* 3; Vienna: Hölder, 1923) 172–88.

10. Heberdey ("Vorläufiger Bericht über die Ausgrabungen in Ephesos IV," 89) questioned an early Hellenistic or Hellenistic-Roman date. Wilhelm Wilberg (*Der mittlere Torbau. Bauschreibung und Datierung* [*FiE* 3; Vienna: Hölder, 1923] 213) supported a Hadrianic date. Alzinger (*Architektur*, 58) suggested the period of Tiberius to Nero.

11. Wilberg, *Der südliche Torbau*, 88.

12. Wilberg, *Torbauten*, 171.

and to what extent the earlier harbors were furnished with technical installations such as quays or jetties is unclear.

Literary and Epigraphic Evidence

Literary and epigraphic evidence from Hellenistic and Roman times repeatedly referred to the harbor. Strabo, writing at the time of Tiberius, referred to the time of Attalos II Philadephos (159–138 BCE):

> The city has both an arsenal and a harbour. The mouth of the harbour was made narrower by the engineers, but they, along with the king who ordered it, were deceived as to the result, I mean Attalus Philadelphus; for he thought that the entrance would be deep enough for large merchant vessels—as also the harbour itself, which formerly had shallow places because of the silt deposited by the Kaÿster River—if a mole were thrown up at the mouth, which was very wide, and therefore ordered that the mole should be built. But the result was the opposite, for the silt, thus hemmed in, made the whole of the harbour, as far as the mouth, more shallow. Before this time the ebb and flow of the tides would carry away the silt and draw it to the sea outside. Such, then, is the harbour; and the city, because of its advantageous situation in other respects, grows daily, and is the largest emporium in Asia this side of the Taurus.[13]

Between 54 and 59 CE, an inscription discusses the construction of a toll-house (τελωνεῖον) for fishing.[14] In 66 CE, the proconsul Barea Soranus provided for the opening of the Ephesian port (portui

13. Strabo *Geog.* 14.1.24 (LCL; trans. Horace L. Jones; 8 vols.; London: Heinemann and New York: Putnam, 1929) 6. 228–31; Ἔχει δ' ἡ πόλις καὶ νεώρια καὶ λιμένα· βραχύστομον δ' ἐποίησαν οἱ ἀρχιτέκτονες, συνεξαπατηθέντες τῷ κελεύσαντι βασιλεῖ. οὗτος δ' ἦν Ἄτταλος ὁ Φιλάδελφος· οἰηθεὶς γὰρ οὗτος βαθὺν τὸν εἴσπλουν ὁλκάσι μεγάλαις ἔσεσθαι καὶ αὐτὸν τὸν λιμένα, τεναγώδη ὄντα πρότερον διὰ τὰς ἐκ τοῦ Καΰστρου προσχώσεις, ἐὰν παραβληθῇ χῶμα τῷ στόματι, πλατεῖ τελέως ὄντι, ἐκέλευσε γενέσθαι τὸ χῶμα. συνέβη δὲ τοὐναντίον· ἐντὸς γὰρ ἡ χοῦς εἰργομένη τεναγίζειν μᾶλλον ἐποίησε τὸν λιμένα σύμπαντα μέχρι τοῦ στόματος· πρότερον δ' ἱκανῶς αἱ πλημμυρίδες καὶ ἡ παλίρροια τοῦ πελάγους ἀφήρει τὴν χοῦν καὶ ἀνέσπα πρὸς τὸ ἐκτός. ὁ μὲν οὖν λιμὴν τοιοῦτος· ἡ δὲ πόλις τῇ πρὸς τὰ ἄλλα εὐκαιρίᾳ τῶν τόπων αὔξεται καθ' ἑκάστην ἡμέραν, ἐμπόριον οὖσα μέγιστον τῶν κατὰ τὴν Ἀσίαν τὴν ἐντὸς τοῦ Ταύρου.)

14. *IvE* I 20, 1503. The reference to lagoon fishing is unconvincing.

Ephesiorum aperiendo).[15] Between 102 and 114 CE, T. Flavius Montanus gave seventy-five thousand denarii to outfit the port.[16] In approximately 105 CE, the prytanis C. Licinius Maximus Julianus gave two thousand five hundred denarii for the port and the new gymnasium.[17] In 129 CE, the emperor Hadrian was honored for making the harbor navigable and for diverting the Kaÿstros River, which had previously damaged the harbor.[18] Between 146 and 147 CE, the proconsul L. Antonius Albus ordered that timber should not be stored on the quay wall and that stones should not be cut on it; the weight of the timber would weaken the pillars of the wall and the emery from stonecutting would fill in the basin, both of which would make the quay inaccessible.[19] Between 222 and 238 CE, the prytanis M. Aurelius Artemidorus gave twenty thousand denarii for the purpose of cleaning the harbor.[20] Probably in the years between 254 or 268 CE, Valerius Festus was honored for making the harbor larger than even Kroisos had made it.[21]

These repeated references to the harbor demonstrate its importance, but they also require further commentary. Since sea fishing was free of tolls, mention of a tollhouse is puzzling. It may have been for a special local tax; this may also be an unorthodox use of the word τελωνεῖον to mean a fish market, perhaps under the control of the market authority. Moreover, the quotation from Tacitus referred not to the initial construction of the port, but rather to cleaning and dredging the bottom of the basin.

According to the inscriptions, building activities appear to have been concentrated in Trajanic and Hadrianic times. The diverting of the Kaÿstros was accomplished either by building a wall similar to the one that Attalos built some two hundred and fifty years before or

15. Tacitus *Annales* 16.23.
16. *IvE* VI 2061.
17. Ibid., VII 3066.
18. Ibid., II 274.
19. Ibid., I 23.
20. Ibid., VII 3071.
21. Dieter Knibbe and Bülent İplikçioğlu, "Neue Inschriften aus Ephesos IX," *JÖAI* 55 (1984) 130–31: "Die ephesischen Silberschmiede ehren Valerius Festus" ("The Ephesian silver casters honor Valerius Festus"). It is doubtful that the extent and outfit of the archaic harbor was known in the third century CE, although the text seems to state that.

by digging a new bed for the river. It is regrettable that the known text of the lost inscription is incomplete; the means by which he diverted the river is not recorded. If the river was diverted by a wall constructed in a more sophisticated way than that of Attalos, it is conceivable that some years later this quay wall had to be protected by Antonius Albus against inappropriate use. These efforts were successful for a hundred years, at which time the basin had to be cleaned again.

The dating and interpretation of harbor activities at the time of Emperor Gallienus are problematic; an early third-century date is possible. Valerius Festus is honored by the silver casters, for his financial support of many public works in Asia Minor and especially in Ephesos. He made the harbor larger (μεῖζων) than that of Kroisos. Whether this refers to the area of the basin itself or to a new and more beautiful restoration with halls and other buildings cannot be determined. As Dieter Knibbe has pointed out, the title κτίστης ("new founder") is also used in a similar case involving the Vedii Antonini in the midsecond century.[22] In approximately 140 CE, an earthquake struck Asia Minor and probably affected Ephesos, and in 262 CE another earthquake shook the town. Those who donated money to repair damages caused by such an event could well have been called "new founders." The use of this term in conjunction with Valerius Festus may therefore refer to the reconstruction of buildings along the quay walls after 262 CE.

Evidence from Excavations

Excavations from the years 1987 to 1989 uncovered new evidence regarding the Roman harbor.[23] A small slope along the southern side of the reed-covered area was expected to reflect the course of the quay wall. We therefore began to dig a trench perpendicular to this

22. Dieter Knibbe, "Ephesos (historisch)," *ANRW* 2.7.2 (1980) 787; idem, "Der Asiarch M. Fulvius Publicianus Nikephoros, die ephesischen Handwerkerzünfte und die Stoa des Servilius," *JÖAI* 56 (1985) 71–77.

23. Gerhard Langmann, the director of excavations during these years, initiated and directed the project. The local supervisors in 1987 were the late Erol Atalay and myself; in 1988 I was supervisor; and in 1989 Ulrike Vogler-Stangelmayer. Gerhard Langmann, "Ephesos 1987," *JÖAI* 58 (1988) Grabungen

line. In trench I, a slope-supporting wall of late antique or even medieval times was discovered. Many architectural spoils from different places and buildings were employed in the construction of this wall. At the surface lay a capital from the archaic Artemision.[24] We excavated a house from the first quarter of the fifth century CE and a pavement of stone slabs, corresponding to those typically found in Ephesos. West of this site, three column drums were visible above the ground. They stood on debris and were probably part of a slope-supporting construction.[25]

Installations for the port were found about 150 m west on the southern side of the port area, where a pond shows the deepest point of the marshy area. The installations included a quay that extended from the east in a curving line to a jetty that projected into the basin. West of the jetty, the quay turned back to the south and then bent westward. Pavement was found south of the quay; a building was later constructed on the rear edge of the quay (fig. 1).

On the water side, the top of the quay was made of immense slabs up to 1.5 m long and 1 m wide. The slabs were well laid and joined, but their surface was not carefully dressed. The irregular lower sides of the slabs were imbedded with mortar in masonry of smaller stones. The quay was 2.07 m wide, corresponding to seven Roman feet. The construction and appearance are consistent with what would be expected for such a quay. A massive solid wall on the top of the water side was protected by slabs to prevent damage caused by ships. Far from the center of the city, one would not expect a decorative appearance for the much-used wall. While the quay at the eastern end of the harbor was constructed of marble,[26] this part was made of limestone. Under the ancient surface, covered by debris, was a layer of clay,

1987, 8–9; idem, "Ephesos 1988," *JÖAI* 59 (1989) Grabungen 1988, 8–9; idem, "Ephesos 1989," *JÖAI* 60 (1990) Grabungen 1989, 31.

24. I thank Ulrike Muss, expert in Artemision architecture, for identifying the piece.

25. Beyond routine annual reports, only this part of the excavation is published. See Heinrich Zabehlicky, "Ein spätantiker Bau im südlichen Hafenbereich von Ephesos (Vorbericht)," in T. Bakir, A. Cilingiroglu, and E. Doger, eds., *Erol Atalay Memorial* (Arkeoloji Dergisi, Özel Sayi 1; İzmir: Ege Üniversitesi, 1991) 198–205.

26. Wilberg, *Torbauten,* 170.

which contained artifacts and could not, therefore, have been virgin soil. In addition to a pit, different floor levels were found, which may be the result of repairing activities.

A smaller wall, up to 1.3 m wide, was built on top of the quay in a series of straight paths that followed the curved line of the quay. Although the wall is in various states of preservation and in some places has altogether disappeared, it is probable that in antiquity it existed along the entire quay.

Most of the excavation work thus far has been concentrated on the jetty. At the head of the jetty, a water-eroded line on the front of the stones marks the ancient sea level. Visible under that line is a coating of shells, which typically develops immediately below the surface of the water. One characteristic technical detail is a hole drilled in an oblique direction through the edge of a slab that could have moored smaller vessels. Such mooring stones exist in other ancient ports as well, although they are generally much larger, stand vertically, and have horizontal perforations. At Ephesos, the juncture of the quay and jetty indicate that both parts were built at the same time; the horizontal slabs are set diagonally into the angle and could not have been inserted later. Because of its position under water, a four-edged piece of lumber, which may have been part of the scaffolding for the construction, was also preserved. The jetty is much more eroded than the quay, because it projected into the basin and was therefore more exposed to the waves. The amount of coating from shells is approximately equal on both the quay and jetty.

Despite difficult diving conditions, at the head of the mole excavators dug a trench to a depth of about 5 m below the usual summer water level. Much of the documentation is based on information from the divers. Black earth suspended in the water of the pond made work quite difficult, and since visibility was close to zero, the divers were forced to depend on tactile investigation. We were able to pump away the water and view the walls for short periods of time when working in depths of about two to three meters. The walls of the trench also had to be reinforced against the danger of collapse.

The top part of the jetty was constructed from approximately 0.5 m of the same slabs as the quay (fig. 2). Below these slabs lay stone masonry (1.5 m thick) placed over a step. More steps extended to 3.5 m below the top of the jetty; these steps were constructed from stones that were larger but less deliberately set. Excavations revealed rough blocks at the bottom of the stairs, which reached a depth of 6.3 m below the top of the jetty. The upper ends of wooden piles appeared at a depth of 4 m next to the stones. The types of material excavated changed at the depth of the top of the wooden piles. Above, it contained rubble and shell sand; underneath was loamy ground containing few finds.

These piles may have been part of a scaffold. In *De architectura*, Vitruvius described different methods of underwater construction.[27] If the water were pumped away, a caisson or a dam could be used to work on the dry or damp ground. Vitruvius recommended setting up piles of singed wood and a layer of charcoal to secure soft ground. Although we did not find these underneath the jetty, the rough blocks we found corresponded well to Vitruvius's recommendation of a foundation without mortar topped by elongated ashlars, much like the blocks found in the Ephesian harbor. Vitruvius preferred a construction that used hydraulic mortar with earth from Puteoli, but the Ephesian jetty followed the alternative construction, that of a caisson and regular mortar. The parts of the piles over the ground of the basin but under the surface of the water had to be removed at the end of construction, because if left in place, they would have damaged the ships' planking.

The basin was not very deep, as is confirmed by the problem of repeated silting. A large cargo vessel (400 to 500 gross register tons, with a length of about 30 m) was reconstructed according to a late antique wreck that was recovered at Pantano Longaroni in Sicily.[28] At the head of the jetty a loaded ship of this class would have had barely enough water under the keel.

A house had been built on the quay next to the jetty. Its level corresponds to the quay and pavement that lies some meters south of it. Inside the building some horizontally positioned stones marked the same level. If it had been part of the original plan, it would have blocked access to the mole and the jetty. Thus, it was undoubtedly constructed later than the quay (early second century CE) but earlier than the house in trench I (early fifth century CE).

27. Vitruvius *De architectura* 5.12.
28. Peter and Joan Throckmorton, "The Roman Wreck at Pantano Longaroni," *International Journal of Nautical Archeology and Underwater Exploration* 2 (1973) 258 fig. 16.

Near the quay, we found a well-preserved pavement that was similar to the pavement found in trench I. Both pavements were probably part of one road along the southern quay. It is striking that the edge of the terrain follows a curved line where the quay has now been excavated. The terrain edge continues eastwards for some 30 m and then goes straight to the eastern end of the harbor, which is again polygonal.

Design and History of the Harbor

Obviously, harbors of such huge dimensions needed to be constructed to conform to the coastline. Quay lines composed of circular lines and relatively regular polygons are, however, evident in more than one case. The northern quay of the port of Val Catena on the island of Brioni in present-day Croatia, for example, is composed of a long straight line and a circular projection set in polygonal parts.[29] This circular projection is caused by a temple that stood close by. These axial structures occur frequently in large-scale Roman architecture. We cannot say with any certainty whether a prominent religious or public building also was the cause for the circular projection of the quay at Ephesos. Two basins of Portus, the harbor of Rome next to Ostia, should be compared.[30] The outer harbor, dating from the time of Claudius, uses natural banks to enclose a nearly rectangular basin, while on the southeastern side, the quay line is formed in a more elaborate way by artificial dams. The inner basin, constructed under Trajan, is a regular hexagon linked with channels to the outer basin and the Tiber River. To develop a strict typology and chronology for installations that are as dependent upon natural conditions as harbors are would be presumptuous. Nevertheless, the part of the Ephesian harbor investigated from 1987 to 1989 can be compared to the Trajanic construction at Portus.

Wide-ranging design based upon simple geometric forms, such as circles and hexagons, can also be seen at other building sites of that time, such as the Forum of Trajan. These similarities in design con-

29. Anton Gnirs, "Forschungen in Istrien: I. Grabungen in Val Catena auf Brioni Grande," *JÖAI* 10 (1907) Beibl. 43–50.
30. D. J. Blackman, "Ancient Harbours in the Mediterranean. Part 2," *International Journal of Nautical Archaeology and Underwater Exploration* 11 (1983) 198 fig. 8.

tribute to the question of dating the port. Only a small number of find-spots provided well-stratified finds. Discoveries found under the pavement of the road south of the jetty were therefore crucial for this dating endeavor. Ulrike Outschar dated them between 50 and 125 CE, with the last figure providing a terminus post quem. Since the pavement and the quay correspond in level, they were probably parts of a common plan. Epigraphic evidence suggests building activities in Trajanic and Hadrianic times, such as the diversion of the Kaÿstros River and ancillary building (κατασκευή) in the harbor.

The rubble over the pavement and the quay offered many finds, mainly dating to the fourth to the seventh centuries. The building in trench I dates to the early fifth century; I propose a slightly earlier date for the building near the jetty. With only a few exceptions, the finds cannot be dated past the seventh century. Around that time, the Byzantine city wall, which did not include this part of the city, was constructed, and this quarter was abandoned.

A number of earthquakes in the fourth century in this part of the world are related to what geologists call the "early Byzantine tectonic paroxysm."[31] There is evidence at Ephesos of large-scale damage and destruction; it may be that the subsequent rubble was brought to the harbor area. I interpret the superimposed wall on the quay in relation to that. The effect of the movement of the crust at Ephesos has yet to be determined, but the land mass may have sunk in relation to the sea level, which would explain the flooding of the quay and the subsequent effort to heighten it.

Developing an exact stratigraphy was difficult. Indeed, beneath the murky water, it was only barely possible. We found rubble down to 4 m below the top of the jetty; the rubble presumably slipped down after the smaller wall on the quay was destroyed by the downhill pressure. Shell sand, which was found mixed up with this rubble, lay

31. Wolfgang Vetters, "Die Küstenverschiebungen Kleinasiens: eine Konsequenz tektonischer Ursachen," in Kandler, Karwiese, and Pillinger, *Lebendige Altertumswissenschaft*, 33–37; Paolo Antonio Pirazolli, "Sea Level Change and Crustal Movements in the Hellenic Arc. The Contribution of Archeological and Historical Data," in Avner Raban, ed., *Archaeology of Coastal Changes: Proceedings of the First International Symposium "Cities on the Sea—Past and Present"* (B. A. R. International Series 404; Oxford: British Archaeological Reports, 1988) 157.

at the bottom of the basin. When the port was in use, the movement of ships caused increased water motion, which in turn stirred up the ground and resulted in a mixing up of findings. In the middle of the pond an airlift was used for hauling the mud together with the finds from an underwater trench. The finds originate from the entire time in which the port was in use and the change from rubble to loamy ground suggested that the depth of the basin distant from the mole was 6 to 7 m.

Miscellaneous Finds

Some of the finds were well preserved because the absence of air reduced the oxidation of metals and the rotting of organic materials. Since the pressure of the water was less than that of the earth, we discovered ceramic finds that were nearly complete or consisted of large sherds, and a glass beaker that was nearly undamaged.

I shall mention only a few of the finds here. A lead model of an anchor (length 14.2 cm), dating to the third or fourth century CE, was found with all the parts of the model fully functioning (fig. 3). It may have been an offering, a decoration for a captain's room, or a tool to teach young sailors the function of the equipment. We also found a drawing on the shoulder of an amphora; a ship and, less clearly, a nearby crag or a rock are represented.

The greatest mass of the finds consist of sherds, either whole pieces or parts of amphorae, as one would expect at a shipping crossroads. The analysis of this vast material is only at the beginning stage; results concerning the inscriptions and the decorations are forthcoming. Late Hellenistic and early imperial types are rare among the finds; rather, the majority of finds are middle and late imperial types, especially Peacock Class 45.[32] This packing material gives evidence for the transport of wine, oil, and prepared fruit.

The Trade and Harbor at Ephesos

It is difficult to imagine a cargo that would not have been shipped to or from Ephesos. Dieter Knibbe proposes a close affiliation be-

---

32. D. P. S. Peacock and D. F. Williams, *Amphorae and the Roman Economy* (London: Longmans, 1986) 188–90 (class 45).

tween Ephesos and the writer of Revelation.[33] The list of wares found in Rev 18:12–13 may refer to one of the large luxury cargoes that John saw being bought and sold, loaded and unloaded, at this place. While it would exceed the scope of this paper to describe fully the high degree of activity in this harbor, I shall mention a few points of interest. Grain supply from Egypt was mentioned repeatedly,[34] and ceramic vessels were both imported and exported.[35] The busy shipping activity, however, was restricted in the wintertime; not many ships left or entered the port then due to storms in the Aegean. A list of travelers arriving or departing from the Ephesian harbor includes both the apostle Paul and Pliny the Younger, who regretted that his itinerary forced him to enter Asia at Ephesos, since he could have reached his destination, Bithynia, more directly by sea.[36]

Since we do not know much about the buildings along the quay and the street, we must depend upon other representations to visualize the appearance of the harbor. The Torlonia relief shows a ship sailing into the port of Ostia (Portus) and includes a scene featuring smaller vessels and loading activities.[37] This port was decorated with numerous statues and halls surrounded the quay and basin. A wall painting from Stabiae displays a smaller harbor with a jetty built on top of an arcaded substructure.[38] The Ephesian inscription that Antonius Albus set up also mentions pillars for the support of the quay. The ancient voyager arriving or leaving the Ephesian harbor may have observed an environment and architecture similar to that of the port of Ostia and undoubtedly would have witnessed a vital, busy place.

33. Dieter Knibbe, *(Ti. Claudius) Piso (Diophantus), 'Christus geboren aus Maria' und Johannes der 'Theologe'* (*BerMatÖAI* 7; Vienna: Schindler, forthcoming).

34. For example, *IvE* II 274, VII 3016.

35. In this volume, see the contribution of Susanne Zabehlicky-Scheffenegger; see also Ulrike Outschar, *Produkte aus Ephesos in alle Welt?* (*BerMatÖAI* 5; Vienna: Schindler, 1993) 47–52:

36. Pliny *Ep.* 10.17.

37. See Lionel Casson, *The Ancient Mariners* (2d ed.; Princeton: Princeton University Press, 1991) pls. following p. 2.

38. Mortimer Wheeler, *Römische Kunst und Architektur* (Munich/Zurich: Knaur, 1969) 199 fig. 185.

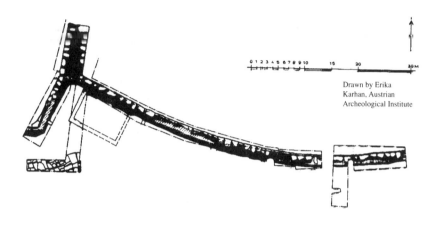

FIGURE 1   Plan of the quay, jetty, and pavement

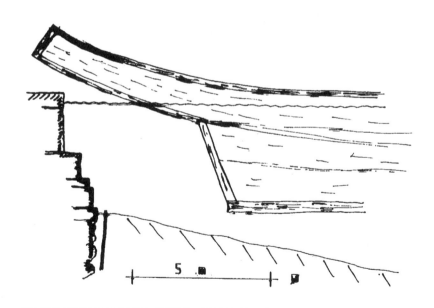

FIGURE 2   Sketch of the head of the jetty with a loaded ship of the
                  Pantano Longaroni type

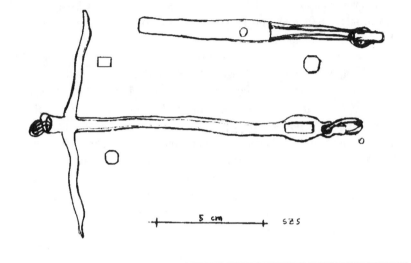

F I G U R E 3   Anchor model

Subsidiary Factories of Italian Sigillata Potters

THE EPHESIAN EVIDENCE

Susanne Zabehlicky-Scheffenegger
Vienna, Austria

Ancient ceramics of everyday use, such as the sigillata, a fine red-gloss Roman tableware, are not merely the remains of daily life and the personal artifacts of the Romans; because of the rapid change of taste and therefore the shapes of the vessels, sigillata plays an important role in dating archaeological sites. Due to its wide distribution throughout the ancient world and the custom of marking it with potters' stamps, sigillata contributes to an understanding of various historical problems, such as the pattern of trade in the Roman world and the social and economic history of the pottery industry.

The modern name "terra sigillata," which refers to both plain and relief-decorated red-gloss vessels, has been used by scholars since the late eighteenth century.[1] Pliny the Elder, in his *Natural History*, does not provide evidence of an ancient name:

1. Giuseppe Pucci, "Terra sigillata Italica," in *Enciclopedia dell'Arte Antica, Atlante delle forme ceramiche*, vol. 2: *Ceramica fine romana nel bacino mediterraneo* (Rome: Instituto della Enciclopedia Italiana, 1985) 365, 371.

The majority of mankind employs earthenware receptacles for this purpose. Among table services Samian pottery is still spoken highly of; this reputation is also retained by Arezzo in Italy, and, merely for cups, by Sorrento, Asti, and Pollenza, and by Saguntum in Spain and Pergamum in Asia Minor. Also Tralles in Asia Minor and Modena in Italy have their respective products, since even this brings nations fame, and their products also, so distinguished are the workshops of the potter's wheel, are carried to and fro across land and sea.[2]

The word *samia* generally means "pottery" and had already been used in that sense by Plautus in the third or second century BCE, long before sigillata existed.[3] Martial speaks about *arretina vasa,*[4] as do later authors.[5] Arretium, now Arezzo, is an Italian city situated near Florence in Etruria.

That these "Arretine vases" are identical with the sigillata can be seen from stamps inscribed ARRE, ARRETI, ARRETINA (scil. figlina), ARRETINVM (scil. vas), ARRET(inum) VER(um)[6] which are always impressed on non-Arretine products of southern or north-

2. Maior pars hominum terrenis utitur vasis. Samia etiam nunc in esculentis laudantur. Retinent hanc nobilitatem et Arretium in Italia et calicum tantum Surrentum, Hasta, Pollentia, in Hispania Saguntum, in Asia Pergamum. Habent et Trallis ibi opera sua et in Italia Mutina, quoniam et sic gentes nobilitantur et haec quoque per maria, terras ultro citro portantur, insignibus rotae officinis; Pliny *Hist. nat.* 35.160 (LCL; 10 vols.; trans. H. Rachman; Cambridge, MA: Harvard University Press, 1967–75) 9. 378–79.

3. Plautus *Bacchides* 2.2.24: Scis tu ut confringi vas cito Samium solet ("You know how quickly a Samian vessel is broken"); idem, *Captivi* 2.2.41: Ad rem divinam quibus est opus Samiis vasis utitur ("Sacrificing, he uses Samian vessels").

4. Martial *Epigrammata* 14.98: Arretina nimis ne spernas vasa monemus ("We remind you not to despise Arretine vessels").

5. Scholion to Persius *Satirae* 1.130: Arreti. . . ex Arretio municipio, ubi fiunt arretina vasa ("The people. . . of the city Arretium, where they produce the arretine vessels"); and 5.182: Rubrum fictile: quod est arretinum ("red earthenware: what is arretine"). Isidor of Sevilla *Etymologiae* 20.4.5: Arretina vasa: ex Arretio, municipio Italiae, dicuntur, ubi fiunt: sunt enim rubra ("Arretine vessels: named after the Italian city Arretium, where they were produced: the same are red").

6. August Oxé and Howard Comfort, *Corpus Vasorum Arretinorum: A Catalogue of the Signatures, Shapes and Chronology of Italian Sigillata* (Antiquitas 3.4; Bonn: Habelt, 1968) 38–39 no. 132.

ern Italian, Gallic, or Asiatic production. These stamps refer to the article, not the place of production. Thus, the use of the term "Arretine ware" for Italian-type sigillata, especially in books written in English, is correct in the ancient sense, but can mislead the reader. These sigillata vessels have not only been produced at Arezzo, but also elsewhere in Italy and even outside Italy, especially at Lyon (ancient Lugdunum).

Of the sigillata found at the Augustan legionary base at Haltern in northern Germany, for example, forty-eight percent was made at Lyon, while thirty-six percent came from Pisa. Only two percent came from Arezzo itself.[7] With the help of chemical analysis of the clays we are now able to distinguish between the different productions.[8] It is also possible, however, for a trained eye to distinguish between them by their appearance and texture, even if they bear similar potters' stamps.

In the late republic and early Augustan period, the earliest time of sigillata production in Italy, Arezzo was the dominant center of production. A quickly increasing market resulted from the military and commercial extension of the Roman empire, especially in a northern direction toward what were later established as Roman borders along the Rhine and Danube rivers. These regions demanded a large supply of sigillata. Shorter trade routes between the sites of production and consumption were sought for such fragile goods. Shipping across the sea or on rivers was preferred to cross-country trading or even to crossing mountains routes. Despite its location beside the small river Arno, Arezzo was poorly situated to take part in trade.

Northern Italy, Pisa, and Lyon

Small factories belonging to many different local potters had already produced large amounts of sigillata in northern Italy, in the so-called Padana. Arretine producers also established manufacting subsidiaries there. At Magdalensberg, a prominent excavation in the southern part of Austria, stamps with the names of well-known Arretine

---

7. Jacques Lasfargues and Maurice Picon, "Die chemischen Untersuchungen," in Siegmar von Schnurbein, ed., *Die unverzierte Terra Sigillata aus Haltern* (Bodenaltertümer Westfalens 19; Münster: Aschendorff, 1982) 16.

8. Ibid., 6–21; Gerwulf Schneider and Bettina Hoffmann, "Chemische Zusammensetzungen italischer Sigillata," in Ettlinger, *Conspectus*, 27–38.

potters (P. Attius, C. Sentius, A. Sestius, C. Sertorius Ocella, A. Titius) were found on vessels of Arretine as well as northern Italian manufacture.[9] The different colors and densities of the clays, their chemical analysis, and the distinct relationship of their chemical elements[10] facilitate easy identifications of their various production sites. Despite the different quality of the clay, the stamps and the shapes of the vessels are the same, indicating contemporaneous production.

At Pisa, west of Arezzo on the Tyrrhenian coast, factories by Arretine potters, especially Cn. Ateius, were also established. These supplied the western basin of the Mediterranean sea.[11]

Waste from sigillata production was found at two sites in Lyon; these remnants had Italian-type shapes and bore stamps from potters already known to have been working at Arezzo.[12] Prevalent potters' names include Ateius, Attius, Rasinius, Thyrsus, and C. Sentius.[13]

An analysis of molds found at Lyon proves that subsidiaries of the Arretine factories were established in Lyon. Two molds out of fourteen appear not to be made from local but from Arretine clay, which proves that the migrating potters took their tools along with them.[14]

As mentioned earlier, the great quantity of sigillata from Lyon used in the military bases along and near the Rhine demonstrates the commercial advantages of founding pottery factories in Gaul. The

9. Susanne Zabehlicky-Scheffenegger, "Frühe padanische Filialen einiger arretinischer Töpfereien," *Rei Cretariae Romanae Fautorum Acta* 29/30 (1991) 95–104.

10. I thank Marino Maggetti for the analyses. For corresponding analyses, see Marino Maggetti and Giulio Galetti, "Chemischer Herkunftsnachweis der 'Schwarzen Sigillata' vom Magdalensberg," in Hermann Vetters and Gernot Piccottini, eds., *Die Ausgrabungen auf dem Magdalensberg 1975 bis 1979* (Magdalensberg-Grabungsbericht 15; Klagenfurt: Geschichtsverein, 1986) 391–431.

11. Elisabeth Ettlinger, "Pisa und das Ateius-Problem," in idem, *Conspectus*, 7–8.

12. Siegmar von Schnurbein, "Die außeritalische Produktion," in Ettlinger, *Conspectus*, 19.

13. André Lasfargues, Jacques Lasfargues, and Hugues Vertet, "Les estampilles sur sigillée lisse de l'atelier augustéen de la Muette à Lyon," *Figlina* 1 (1976) 45–87; Schnurbein, *Die unverzierte Terra Sigillata*, 89–117.

14. Maurice Picon and Jacques Lasfargues, "Transfert de moules entre les ateliers d'Arezzo et ceux de Lyon," *Révue archéologique de l'Est et du Centre-Est* 25 (1974) 61–69.

dates and shapes of the pottery produced at Lyon indicate a relatively short production period, from approximately 10 BCE until 10 CE. The Arretine potter L. Gellius Quadratus provides an example of commercial genius and market specialization.[15] Having produced pottery at Arezzo and distributed it within Italy, Gaul, Spain, and Germany, L. Gellius also profited from a branch at Lyon. His partner L. Sempronius seems to have managed affairs there, as can be judged from the stamps: nearly all of the vessels stamped L.SEMPR/L.GELL (with Sempronius in the first line) are made at Lyon, while the vessels stamped L.GELL/L.SEMPR are made at Arezzo. The same is true for the stamps naming L. Gellius alone. The continued activity of the parent factory at Arezzo after the end of production at Lyon is proved by the fact that L. Gellius switched his marketing strategy to a northeastern direction after losing the northwestern market. He exported to northern Italy and the Danube provinces of Noricum, Pannonia, Dalmatia, and Moesia, as can be seen by the distribution of his vessels produced in the Tiberian and Claudian periods with stamps in footprint-frame.

Ephesos

Italian-type sigillata has been found at Ephesos, as well as in many other parts of the eastern Mediterranean, but only in a moderate quantity. The pieces date to the first century CE.[16] At the same time in the eastern Aegean, the local production of red-gloss tableware began. Named Eastern Sigillata B by Kathleen Kenyon,[17] it is characterized by a splintery or flaky cinnamon-colored clay with fine mica and a

15. Susanne Zabehlicky-Scheffenegger, "'Die Geschäfte des Herrn Lucius G.': Ein Arbeitsbericht," *Rei Cretariae Romanae Fautorum Acta* 21/22 (1982) 105–15.

16. Rudolf Heberdey, *Kleinfunde [vom Rundbau auf dem Panajirdagh]*, (*FiE* 1; Vienna: Hölder, 1906) 168–69; Veronika Mitsopoulos-Leon, *Die Basilika am Staatsmarkt in Ephesos: Kleinfunde*, vol. 1: *Keramik hellenistischer und römischer Zeit (FiE* 9.2.2; Vienna: Schindler, 1991) 123–30. Danica Beyll, *Terra Sigillata aus der Marienkirche in Ephesos: Erste Zwischenbilanz* (*BerMatÖAI* 5; Vienna: Schindler, 1993) 7.

17. Kathleen M. Kenyon, "Terra Sigillata," in idem, J. W. Crowfoot, and G. M. Crowfoot, *The Objects from Samaria* (Samaria-Sebaste; London: Palestine Exploration Fund, 1957) 283.

rather waxy or soapy orange-red gloss. This manufacture is distinct from Italian sigillata. Although the shapes of the vessels follow Italian models, they differ in some details. The strong link between Eastern Sigillata B and Italian sigillata can only be explained by an eastern dependence on the western sigillata. There is no evidence that Eastern Sigillata B ware was produced before the arrival of Italian sigillata in the east.

The earliest shapes of the Italian sigillata follow the tradition of former Italian black-gloss ware known as Campanian ware. In the late republic and early Augustan period in Italy, preference shifted from black-fired to red-fired vessels; for this period, the same shapes in black and red sigillata are found.[18] Since these earliest shapes of Italian red ware are not known in Eastern Sigillata B, it is probable that its production started at a later time, perhaps in the middle of the Augustan era. Italian potters probably founded or at least supported this production.[19] The earliest published example from a datable context comes from a late Augustan group found in the Athenian agora.[20] The beginning of the production of Eastern Sigillata B therefore coincides with the period of the extension of Italian sigillata potters to the west, to Lyon.

Eastern Sigillata B was distributed mainly in the Aegean, but was also transported as far as the Black Sea, North Africa, Italy, and Dalmatia, especially in its later phase, during the second half of the first century CE and the second century CE.[21] The exact location of the production of Eastern Sigillata B has long been debated. The micaceous clay and the main area of distribution point to the western coast of Asia Minor. Pliny, however, lists Tralles among the centers of sigillata production; Tralles, modern-day Aydın, is situated approximately thirty miles inland of Ephesos. Some stamps reading EKKAI/

18. Maria Schindler, "Die 'Schwarze Sigillata' des Magdalensberges 2: Neufunde seit 1965," in Vetters and Piccottini, *Die Ausgrabungen auf dem Magdalensberg 1975 bis 1979*, 362–63.

19. John W. Hayes, *Late Roman Pottery* (London: British School at Rome, 1972) 10; idem, "Sigillate orientali," in *Enciclopedia dell'Arte Antica*, 51.

20. Henry S. Robinson, *Pottery of the Roman Period, Chronology* (Athenian Agora 5; Princeton: American School of Classical Studies at Athens, 1959) 12, F 15.

21. Hayes, "Sigillate orientali," 52.

CAPHAΣ hint at this location.[22] Tralles was called Caesarea in early imperial times—the peak of Eastern Sigillata B production. Recent analyses of Eastern Sigillata B sherds and clays from the Aydın region offer proof for this theory, since the two have been found to have the same characteristics.[23]

During the 1988 excavations in the western part of the Tetragonos Agora at Ephesos, a small trench approximately 2 m square and 4 m deep was dug to determine the strata of an early Roman layer heaped up to raise the ground level for a rebuilding of the agora. This filling of earth and waste contained large amounts of pottery sherds, for the most part were Eastern Sigillata B—more than one thousand and two hundred sherds[24]—along with other contemporaneous pottery. Very little tableware in Eastern Sigillata A and Italian sigillata were discovered, but many platters or trays of different size and shape (round or rectangular) and different kinds of kitchenware and the typical "Ephesos lamps" were unearthed.

Most of the sherds of Eastern Sigillata B do not show the original brillant orange-red color, but are red-brown, brownish, or even black, mostly stained and of changing color within one vessel, an effect often caused by a damaging fire. Since the shapes and the stamps are extremely homogeneous and no traces of usage can be seen, this may be the debris of a merchant's shop which burned.

The shapes of the Eastern Sigillata B vessels resemble Italian sigillata shapes,[25] but show peculiar differences. The low ring foots are obviously different, as well as some exaggerations of projecting moldings and sharp angles. Rouletting is used to decorate forms that are not similarly decorated in Arretine ware. A few vessels are decorated with applied palmettes or have carved and painted decorations in the style of late Westslope ware.

22. Ibid., 49; Hayes, *Late Roman Pottery*, 9–10.

23. Ulrike Outschar together with R. Sauer and G. Schneider, expert petrographers and chemists, are currently carrying out these investigations in Vienna and Berlin.

24. Susanne Zabehlicky-Scheffenegger, "Der Italiener in Ephesos," *Alba Regia* 25 (1994) = *Rei Cretariae Romanae Fautorum Acta* 33 (forthcoming).

25. See Ettlinger, *Conspectus*, 54–139, 188 (form nos. 2, 5, 12, 14, 18, 20, 22, 31, 36, 37, 50 and jugs).

The stamps are divided into three groups: those written in Latin letters, those written in Greek letters, and those with ornamental stamps. Within the first group, the name of C. Sentius is prevalent. Other Latin stamps read ARRETINA, again a proof that stamps of this kind occur on vessels that are not of genuine Arretine provenance; the stamps indicate the type of article and not the location of manufacture. A third Latin stamp-type has been badly impressed and is therefore hard to interpret. It may read FVRTVNA, but no ready explanation of this word is available.

The Greek stamps name many potters, some of whom had several different stamp-types. For the most part the Greek stamps are written in two lines and give the potters' names in the nominative (this occurs six times) or in the genitive (this occurs seven times). The different writing of the letters epsilon and sigma in either the angular or rounded version is notable. Two angular or two rounded letters are always combined within one stamp.

The last group contains purely ornamental stamps, such as dots, rosettes, circles, and a dolphin. Scholars had speculated that these had not been produced before the second half or even the third quarter of the first century CE,[26] but this find now proves that these were also in use during the early production of Eastern Sigillata B, since the stamps are impressed on early shapes of vessels. The use of ornamental stamps continued into the second century. Name stamps were only used infrequently at that late date.

The most numerous stamps are those of the potter C. Sentius (sixty-four out of two hundred and forty-four), followed by ΠΟΘΟΥ (thirty-two), ΔΩΡΟΝ (twenty), ΕΡΜΗC/ΕΡΜΟΥ (nineteen), and ΔΑΜΑ (sixteen). All other stamps occur less than ten times.

That the lower and higher levels of filling represent only a brief period is demonstrated by the fact that the pottery sherds have the same shapes and stamps, and some sherds even fit together. Until now those shapes that have a vertical rim have been assumed to be of a later date, around the middle of the first century CE. As they are stamped by the same potters as the early ones, however, one should date the pottery earlier rather than extend the lifetime and the work-

---

26. Hayes, *Late Roman Pottery*, 10; idem, "Sigillata orientali," 51–52.

ing periods of the potters. Moreover, finds other than Eastern Sigillata B date within the mid-Augustan to perhaps early Tiberian periods. Nearly all of the Italian-shaped models are Augustan. As already mentioned, C. Sentius, a well-known Augustan Arretine potter, had subsidiaries in northern Italy and at Lyon. His stamps as well as those of many other potters have been found in the late Augustan to early Tiberian levels of the basilica on the north side of the so-called State Agora at Ephesos.[27] Here the stamps of the potter ΔΩPON are the most numerous, numbering twenty-two out of one hundred and twelve.

In the basilica of the State Agora, one hundred and twelve stamps on Eastern Sigillata B pottery have been found. On these were forty different names or ornaments in sixty-one different types. In the little trench in the Tetragonos Agora, in contrast, two hundred and twenty-four stamps with only twenty-five different names or ornaments in forty-four different types were found. This demonstrates that the material from the Tetragonos Agora is more homogeneous than that from the State Agora. The same stamps have been impressed on up to forty-two of the vessels, thus supporting the contemporaneity of these shapes and the homogeneity of the sherds' sources. This also lends strength to the theory that the filling from the Tetragonos Agora consisted of the debris of a burnt shop.

The sixty-four vessels stamped by C. Sentius share only three stamp-types, which is unusual. One would expect a far greater variety. Within that number, moreover, forty-two items were produced with one stamp-type. These name the potter in a typical abbreviated form: C.SENTI (with ENTI in ligature) or C.SENT (with a ligature of ENT) (see fig. 1). The synthesis of the vessel shapes is also disproportionate: there is only one plate and the foot of one large chalice, but there are sixty-two cups. This gives further credence to the theory that a special merchant's load was deposited here.

Robert Zahn was the first to recognize a single stamp of C. Sentius on Eastern Sigillata B found at Priene, some twenty miles south of Ephesos.[28] Zahn claimed that a subsidiary factory of C. Sentius ex-

27. Mitsopoulos-Leon, *Die Basilika am Staatsmarkt in Ephesos*, 94–122.

28. Robert Zahn, "Scherben von Sigillatagefässen," in Theodor Wiegand and Hans Schrader, *Priene: Ergebnisse der Ausgrabungen und Untersuchungen in den Jahren 1895–1898* (Berlin: Reimer, 1904) 437, 445.

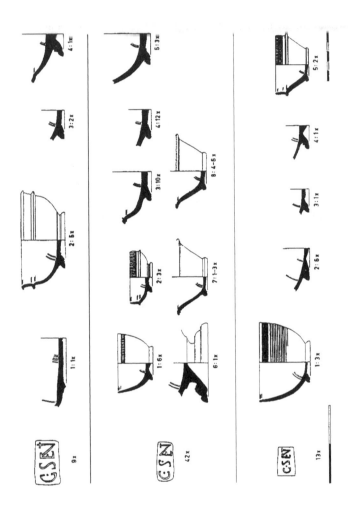

FIGURE 1   Types of stamps and vessel forms of C. Sentius on Eastern Sigillata B from Ephesos

isted in Asia Minor; his opinion was taken up by many scholars, although they lacked further evidence. Since 1904, only few more such stamps have been published: five from Ephesos, which included a fourth type, reading C. SE[29]; one is mentioned from Sardeis,[30] and some are known at Corinth.[31] There are altogether approximately ten to twenty pieces from C. Sentius, including some unpublished stamps that I have seen at other locations within Ephesos. The sixty-four new pieces therefore represent an exceptional find. Suddenly a more comprehensive view is available. The appearance of stamps of the Augustan Arretine potter C. Sentius suggests that the production of Eastern Sigillata B began as an eastern offshoot of the genuine Arretine factory. Dependence of eastern factories upon other Italian production centers is also supported by a similar stamp on Eastern Sigillata B found at Sardeis; this stamp names the potter Serenus, who is known to have worked in Puteoli in the Bay of Naples.[32] Without many complete vessels, one cannot determine whether Sentius produced the typologically earliest vessels. Nevertheless it seems likely that Sentius was one of the pioneers—if not the founder—of Eastern Sigillata B.

C. Sentius established factories in nearly all parts of the Roman world in which there was a demand for the production of sigillata. With the main production center situated at Arezzo, he founded subsidiaries in the Padana (although the exact location is uncertain), at Lyon, and in Asia Minor.[33] In contrast to the western subsidiary factories, such as Lyon, the eastern factory produced shapes that are not identical to the Italian ones, but rather have distinct forms. Despite the obvious dependence of Eastern Sigillata B on Italian sigillata, the

---

29. Heberdey, *Kleinfunde*, 168–69; Mitsopoulos-Leon, *Die Basilika am Staatsmarkt in Ephesos*, 97 and pl. 162, H 198.

30. James F. Wrabetz, "A New Serenus Stamping from Sardis and the Origins of the Eastern Sigillata B Ware," *HSCP* 81 (1977) 195.

31. Ibid.; John W. Hayes, "Roman Pottery from the South Stoa at Corinth," *Hesperia* 42 (1973) 468 n. 111; and personal communication from Kathleen Warner Slane (1992).

32. Wrabetz, "A New Serenus Stamping," 195–97.

33. See also Philip Kenrick, "Italian Terra Sigillata: A Sophisticated Roman Industry," *Oxford Journal of Archaeology* 12 (1993) 236–37.

eastern potters developed and altered the shapes. Sentius, or rather his proxy, respected the eastern fashion of shaping vessels when, together with local Greek potters, he worked in all probability at Tralles. From there the products were brought to the nearest great distribution center, Ephesos, from which they were shipped across the Aegean. It is my hypothesis that one load was destroyed by an accidential fire and the resulting garbage was used to raise the level for the new construction of the Tetragonos Agora.

In 1929, H. Comfort wrote skeptically: "I am not altogether convinced. . . by Zahn's attribution of an Asiatic factory to C. Sentius; the evidence is too slender for a dogmatic statement."[34] With this new discovery at Ephesos, however, the existence of a subsidiary factory linked to C. Sentius in the east is certain.

The Cult of the Roman Emperors in Ephesos

TEMPLE WARDENS, CITY TITLES, AND
THE INTERPRETATION OF THE
REVELATION OF JOHN

Steven Friesen
University of Missouri-Columbia

It has long been recognized that the worship of the emperors in some way constituted an important aspect of the relationships between the emperor and the cities of the Roman province of Asia. The importance of imperial cults in Asia is reflected in the city titles that permeate the epigraphic record. These titles tend to focus on the word "neokoros," which is often translated into English as "temple warden," because the term began as the title for an official who had special responsibilities related to the precincts of a deity. During the Roman imperial period, however, "neokoros" took on a specialized meaning. It became the technical term for a city where a provincial temple of the emperors was located. Thus, in the secondary literature the words "neokoros" and "neokorate" have become synonymous with provincial imperial cults.

This modern usage of neokoros as a term for all provincial temples is unfortunate. As Simon Price noted, in the provincial imperial cults this specialized use of the term neokoros only began in the late first century CE with the Temple of the Sebastoi at Ephesos.[1] During the second century, the term began to spread throughout the province and beyond. It is therefore anachronistic to use the term neokorate for provincial imperial temples if they were built before the late first century CE. More than linguistic precision is at stake here. The recognition of a clear historical moment at which Greek cities began to call themselves and each other by the title neokoros raises several issues, including the significance of this new metaphor. What ends were served by this rhetorical maneuver during the late first century?

In order to answer this question, I shall begin by examining the development and significance of the metaphor of the neokorate. Following a review of the work of scholars on civic competition and city titles, some implications for understanding developments in Asia will be discussed. Finally, I suggest that these conclusions, drawn from archaeological materials, should influence the way in which Revelation is interpreted.

Defining the New Metaphor

Before neokoros became a formal city title in Asia in the late first century, the term had evolved from a title for a temple official to a title for a benefactor and finally to a metaphor for a city. In its original sense, a neokoros was an individual with special responsiblities for the temple of a particular deity. This office could be filled by a female or a male, and there seems to have been a tendency for male neokoroi to serve in precincts of gods and females in precincts of goddesses.[2] The title neokoros could indicate a range of responsibilities, including guarding the temple precincts[3] or residing at the temenos.[4] Assistance in sacrificial activities was sometimes required,

1. Price, *Rituals and Power*, 65 n. 47.
2. Friesen, *Twice Neokoros*, 50–51.
3. *SIG* 3.981. This fourth-century BCE inscription comes from Amorgos.
4. Philippe Bruneau, *Recherches sur les cultes de Délos à l'époque héllenistique et l'époque impériale* (Paris: Boccard, 1970) 500–504. Mention of this practice is found in the Hellenistic period in Delos.

and the neokoros might receive payment from those making the offerings.[5] At the sanctuary of Delphi, the neokoros also served as a witness for manumission decrees.[6] References to neokoroi in the Roman period suggest that in most cases the title had come to reflect a different sort of office. In the common era, neokoroi tended to be benefactors rather than resident or attending officials. They paid for renovations or for regular maintenance of the facilities, and might serve for a limited time or for life.[7]

During the early imperial period, the first evidence emerges for the use of the term neokoros to refer to cities. An inscription from Kyzikos from the year 38 CE provides the earliest reference; it honors the benefactor Antonia Tryphaina for "restoring the ancient and ancestral city, (which is) neokoros of his [Gaius Caesar's] family."[8] At the time of this inscription, neokoros was not yet an official title for the city, for the term does not appear in other epigraphic or numismatic evidence from the city, and even this attestation is not found in a prominent part of the inscription. Rather, this seems to be an informal usage, occasioned by the genealogical, religious, and political ties between Tryphaina, Kyzikos, and the emperor Gaius.[9]

The next evidence for a city calling itself neokoros comes from Ephesos. A coin from 65/66 CE bears on its reverse the image of a temple and the inscription Ἐφεσίων νεωκόρων, "of the neokoros Ephesians."[10] Although there has been some discussion about the identification of the temple and the referent of the term neokoros, Josef Keil's arguments that the coin most likely refers to Ephesos as the neokoros of Artemis are convincing.[11]

5. *Die Altertümer von Pergamon* 8/2 (1890) §255.

6. G. Colin, "Epigraphie," in *Fouilles de Delphes* 3/2 (1909) 128, 215, 223.

7. *SIG* 2.898. Third-century CE inscription from Chalkis.

8. *SIG* 2.799 = *IG* IV 146.

9. Friesen, *Twice Neokoros*, 54–55.

10. Theodore E. Mionnet, *Description de medailles antiques, grecques et romaines* (7 vols.; 1806; reprinted Graz: Akademische Druck- und Verlagsanstalt, 1972) 3. 93 no. 253; Behrendt Pick, "Die Neokorien von Ephesos," in George Francis Hill, ed., *Corolla Numismatic: Essays in Honor of Barclay V. Head* (London: Frowde, 1906).

11. Josef Keil, "Die erste Kaiserneokorie von Ephesos," *Numismatische Zeitschrift* 12 (1919) 115–20.

Yet another reference to a city as the neokoros of a deity refers to Ephesos. Acts 19:35 describes Ephesos as the neokoros of Artemis:

> But when the town clerk had quieted the crowd, he said, "Citi zens of Ephesus, who is there that does not know that the city of the Ephesians is the temple keeper of the great Artemis and of the statue that fell from heaven?"

Since the precise date for Acts could be anywhere from the late first to the midsecond century CE, the appellation is at least accurate for the early second century CE. The author of Acts assumes that the metaphor is widely known, and, together with the coin described above, this suggests that the appelation was accurate already in the second half of the first century CE.

By the time that Asia established a provincial temple in Ephesos during the 80s of the first century CE, therefore, precedents existed for use of the term neokoros to describe a city's relationship to a particular deity. Moreover, Ephesos itself was already known as the neokoros of Artemis. The title was not yet official, as it was not used regularly in inscriptions or on coins; rather, it was a popular concept and its roots are difficult to trace before the first century CE.

On the occasion of the dedication of the Temple of the Sebastoi at Ephesos in 89/90, cities from all over Asia dedicated statues on inscribed bases for installation in the temple precincts. In these inscriptions, the term neokoros appears for the first time in what may be considered an officially sanctioned city title. Thirteen of these inscriptions have been found and published, providing in the public epigraphic record a history of the tensions between the cities as a result of the founding of the provincial imperial cult.[12] Specifically, they manifest an early and ultimately unsuccessful attempt to define how the metaphor neokoros would be understood. The texts of all thirteen existing inscriptions reflect one pattern which appears in two different variants: a longer form for free cities and a shorter form for subject cities. The pattern does not occur elsewhere in the inscriptions of Asia and was probably crafted by the city representatives in the *koinon*, or the provincial council of Asia, expressly for the dedication of the Temple of the Flavian Sebastoi.

---

12. *IvE* II 232–35, 237–42; V 1498; VI 2048.

The following inscription, commissioned by Aphrodisias, is an
example of the full pattern. It contains a dedication to Domitian,
which was partially erased after his death; a reference to the contemporaneous proconsul of Asia; a statement about the city that dedicated
the inscription, which includes the official name of the provincial
temple; an optional element naming Aphrodisian benefactors who presumably paid for the dedication; and the identitification of the high
priest of the temple. The inscriptions from subject cities did not include the statement about the dedicating city.

Αὐτοκράτορι ⟦Δομι-
2   τιανῶι⟧ Καίσαρι Σε-
βαστῶι ⟦Γερμανικῶι⟧
4   ἐπὶ ἀνθυπάτου Μάρκ[ου]
Φουλουίου Γίλλωνο[ς]
6   ὁ φιλοκαῖσαρ Ἀφροδεισι[έων]
δῆμος ἐλεύθερος ὢν κα[ὶ αὐ-]
8   τόνομος ἀπ᾽ ἀρχῆς τῆι τῶν Σε[βασ-]
τῶν χάριτι ναῶι τῶι ἐν Ἐφέσ[ωι]
10   τῶν Σεβαστῶν κοινῶι τῆς Ἀσί[ας]
ἰδίᾳ χάριτι διά τε τὴν πρὸς τοὺς [Σε-]
12   βαστοὺς εὐσέβειαν καὶ τὴν π[ρὸς]
τὴν νεωκόρον Ἐφεσίων [πό-]
14   λιν εὔνοιαν ἀνέστησαν
ἐπιμεληθέντος Ἀρίστω[νος τοῦ]
16   Ἀρτεμιδώρου τοῦ Καλλι. [ ]
ως ἱερέως Πλούτωνος [καὶ]
18   Κόρης καὶ νεοποιοῦ θεᾶ[ς]
Ἀφροδείτης, ἐπὶ ἀρχιερ[έως]
20   τῆς Ἀσίας Τιβερίου Κλαυδ[ίου]
Φησείνου ⟦   ⟧
⟦   ⟧
⟦   ⟧
⟦   ⟧

To Emperor ⟦Domitian⟧ Caesar Sebastos ⟦Germanicus⟧ when the
proconsul was Marcus Fulvius Gillo.
    The demos of the Aphrodisians, devoted to Caesar, being free
and autonomous from the beginning by the grace of the Sebastoi,

set up (this statue) by its own grace because of its reverence toward the Sebastoi and its goodwill toward the neokorate city of the Ephesians, (because of) Asia's common Temple of the Sebastoi in Ephesos. (This was) accomplished by Aristo[son] of Artemidoros of Kalli.[ ]os, priest of Pluto and Kore, and *neopoios* of the goddess Aphrodite, when the high priest of Asia was Tiberius Claudius Pheseinos ⟦three and one-half line erasure⟧.[13]

The word neokoros is embedded in the midsection of the inscription (line 13). Moreover, the phrase "the neokoros city of the Ephesians" is syntactically subordinated to the donor city because the title is placed within a prepositional phrase that is part of an adjectival construction describing the beneficence of the donor city toward Ephesos. The language of benefaction, evidenced by hierarchical terms such as εὐσέβεια ("reverence") and εὔνοια ("goodwill"), also plays a part in the effort to define the meaning of neokoros. The free cities represented themselves as the ones who had bestowed the provincial temple upon Ephesos, thereby placing the Ephesians in their debt.

In their effort to subordinate Ephesos, the major cities of the province drew upon their status as free cities to counter the new status of Ephesos as neokoros. In the classical and early Hellenistic periods, a free city was thought to have certain inalienable rights, which usually included political autonomy, immunity from taxation or tribute, and freedom from foreign garrisons.[14] Under the Hellenistic kings, however, such rights were often affirmed in theory, but restricted or ignored in practice. Constitutions that guaranteed ancestral rights could be amended, and newly "liberated" cities would of course require new troops to "protect" them from the old order.[15] By the late first century BCE, free status was no longer an inalienable right but a benevolent grant that could be accorded or removed by a ruler.[16] In

---

13. Ibid., 233. The erasure at the end of the inscription does not impinge on this discussion. It probably named an official from the municipal Ephesian Olympics established in Domitian's honor. See Friesen, *Twice Neokoros*, 137–40.

14. Magie, *Roman Rule*, 1. 56–67.

15. A. H. M. Jones, *The Greek City from Alexander to Justinian* (Oxford: Clarendon, 1940) 101–2.

16. Magie, *Roman Rule*, 1. 234–37; Mitchell, *Anatolia*, 1. 81, 198.

the imperial period, grants of freedom were fewer than the number of cities that lost their free status. This meant that the odds of gaining the status of a free city were slim and, simultaneously, that the potential benefits of autonomy and immunity from taxation were decreasing.[17]

This imperial definition of freedom as a benefaction, rather than as an ancestral right, is clearly articulated in the Aphrodisian inscription for the Temple of the Sebastoi, and it plays a part in the rhetorical strategy of subordinating Ephesos to the other free cities of the province. The text states that cities like Aphrodisias had been granted freedom and autonomy directly "by the grace of the Sebastoi" (lines 8–9). The free cities in turn acted by their own grace in the commissioning of the statue (lines 11–13), and by implication in the establishment of the Temple of the Sebastoi in Ephesos. These statements about grace and freedom indicate that the cities of the province were trying to keep Ephesos from claiming preeminence based on the Temple of the Sebastoi located there. Thus, the free cities defined neokoros in terms of the older meaning of a temple guardian in order to claim that Ephesos was dependent on them for its neokorate status. At the same time, the free cities portrayed themselves as connected directly to the emperors.

The effort to define neokoros in this way was not successful, however, and the meaning of neokoros as benefactor prevailed in the end. Before the end of the first century, Ephesos began to include the new title at the beginning of its municipal inscriptions. Soon other cities with provincial temples followed suit. Within a decade of the dedication of the Temple of the Sebastoi in Ephesos in 89/90 CE, the city of Pergamon began describing itself as neokoros.[18] Municipal inscriptions from 102 until 114 show that Pergamon amended its title and called itself the first neokorate city.[19] Residents of Pergamon apparently believed that the provincial temple to Roma and Augustus built over a century earlier allowed them to claim this title even though Ephesos was the first city to call itself neokoros. When Pergamon received a second provincial temple late in the reign of Trajan, it

17. Jones, *The Greek City*, 131.
18. *Die Altertümer von Pergamon* 8/2 (1890) §461.
19. Ibid., 8/1 (1890) §§438, 431.

began to use the title "first and twice neokoros" to emphasize both its primacy and its unprecedented second provincial cult.[20] Other qualified cities in the province also began to use the title, and use of the term neokoros soon spread beyond the confines of Asia. By the midthird century CE, cities from Macedonia to Samaria claimed neokorate status because of their provincial imperial temples. The latest known use of the title comes from Sardeis in the fifth century CE.[21]

Neokoros therefore became a coveted title in spite of early efforts in Asia to moderate its impact. The explosive spread of the term indicates not merely a new city title of local significance, but a fundamental shift in the identification of these cities—a shift in which the worship of the emperors played a crucial role. The innovation that began with Asia's Temple of the Sebastoi in Ephesos changed the public discourse of religion and identity in the eastern Mediterranean for centuries to come.

Civic Competition and City Titles in the Secondary Literature

The proliferation of city titles as part of a larger phenomenon of municipal competition has not yet been subjected to detailed scrutiny. T. Robert S. Broughton provided much data on these topics in his study on the economy and organization of Roman Asia Minor, but the material on city titles is found only in sections on honors and titles and is mostly in the format of a catalogue.[22] Little attention is given to making sense of the details in the catalogue, because Broughton did not approve of the municipal competition in the imperial period:

> Rivalry among several of the larger and more ambitious cities became intense, led to a great deal of *wasteful display*, and by the end of the second century resulted in a general increase in honorific titles until they bore little relation to the relative station and importance of the cities. *The virus spread* into smaller

20. Ibid., 8/1 (1890) §§395, 397, 520. See also ibid., 8/3 (1969) 158–61.
21. Barbara Burrell, "*Neokoroi*: Greek Cities of the Roman East," (Ph.D. diss., Harvard University, 1980) 248, 382, 405 no. 11.
22. T. Robert S. Broughton, "Roman Asia Minor," in Frank Tenney, ed., *An Economic Survey of Ancient Rome* (6 vols.; Baltimore: Johns Hopkins University Press, 1938) 6. 708–9, 740–44.

cities, so that we find Silandus and Temenothyrae both claiming to be the metropolis of Moccadene, and indication of rivalry between Olba and Diocaesareia of Cilicia.[23] (my emphasis)

For Broughton, city titles, like the worship of the emperors, were an unseemly display, an excessive concern for self-interest before which personal integrity gave way.

Magie offered slightly more discussion of civic competition but his perspective was not discernably different from that of Broughton. He mentioned city titles as one of the problems that the Romans needed to control in Asia during the Antonine period. Magie's opening sentence, indicating his opinion of the phenomenon, states, "Another source of trouble, in which the imperial government found it necessary to intervene, was the discord caused by the vanity and rivalry of the cities in the matter of rank and titles."[24] Magie briefly rehearsed the various titles used by cities, with the same two small cities capping the narrative of the folly: "So far was this absurd practice carried that even the former tribal centres Temenothyrae and Silanus assumed the title of Metropolis of Moccadene."[25] This is followed by a paragraph on the desire for the title neokoros, which was mostly intended "to gratify the cities' vanity."[26]

Not all commentators have been satisfied with declaring civic competition to be absurd or dismissing it as a mere vanity. Other darker motives have been read in the phenomenon. Anthony Macro wove the theme of vanity into a psychopolitical explanation of the phenomenon. The battles for city titles during the Roman period replaced political autonomy and the right to wage war, all three being manifestations of patriotism:

> Patriotism is an emotion that encourages excess: its consistent manifestations are warfare and ostentatious display. Among the independent poleis of Greece patriotic fervour had always been endemic. But the Roman imperium denied the Greek cities their habitual freedom to make war or to indulge in internecine feuds: political activity in its traditional form was stifled. . . . Warfare was now waged by propaganda and advertisement. This was

23. Ibid., 741.
24. Magie, *Roman Rule*, 1. 635.
25. Ibid. 1. 636–37.
26. Ibid., 1. 637.

usually trivial and expensive and, although it was not lethal, it was in the long run deleterious to the financial welfare of the cities.[27]

Most recently, Stephen Mitchell has adapted the theme of civic competition as an avenue for relatively independent political action; in doing so, he has made more explicit one last theme that surfaces in the literature—financial gain. The reason that political rivalry continued after the loss of autonomy, according to Mitchell, was that competition for material resources—not vanity or patriotism—was at the heart of both activities.

> These disputes over primacy were not merely disputes about titles. At major provincial festivals, seating and processional arrangements certainly made a city's position in the hierarchy clear for all to see. More important still, a city which acquired the right to celebrate an important festival, or to hold assizes, thereby gained a vital economic advantage for itself. Visitors on such occasions were an important source of local revenue.[28]

All of these factors need to be taken into account in a discussion of the phenomenon of city titles in Asia. Material resources and the desire for autonomy played a part in the emerging importance of city titles, and even the crude dismissals of "Greek vanity" in writers like Broughton and Magie point to the importance of honor and status in ancient Mediterranean societies. What is missing in these discussions, however, is a sense of the way in which competition related to the long term stability of the province and region. The rivalry of the cities cannot be reduced to vanity, emotional patriotism, or the desire for monetary gain.

Simon Price has provided an account of the competition between cities in Asia Minor that emphasizes both the tensions among the Greek cities and the framework within which this competition took place. On the one hand, the cities fought to preserve their status and titles in relation to the other cities of the region. The competition for resources was fierce. Cities often had to pressure wealthy citizens to undertake and underwrite municipal responsibilities, and the provin-

27. Anthony D. Macro, "The Cities of Asia Minor under the Roman Imperium," *ANRW* 2.7.2 (1980) 682–83.

28. Mitchell, *Anatolia*, 1. 206.

cial temples and high priesthoods of the emperors sometimes became the subject of heated debate in the province. "With the provincial cults the rivalry between cities was almost unbounded."[29] On the other hand, the institutions associated with the temples of the emperors provided ground rules for this competition. The cities of the province had to work together to request and build a provincial temple. Imperial festivals brought delegations and visitors from distant cities. Contributions from the whole province supported groups such as the choir for Roma and Augustus in Asia.[30] In all of this,

> the conflicts within the cities and between cities took place within a framework that was shared by all. The struggles of competitors to win at the imperial games, the fighting for honorific positions by the local élites and the concern for the standing of one's own city against other cities of the province all presupposed (and enhanced) the importance of the imperial cult. The cult. . . was a force for order rather than disorder, and consolidated the social and political hierarchies from which it arose.[31]

Price's approach is a clear advance over other attempts to explain civic competition. It recognizes a variety of material and emotional considerations, but it also allows us to appreciate the fact that in Asia civic competition and the jousting over the meaning of neokoros imagery took place within a given framework. Tension as well as consensus existed among the cities of Roman Asia. The neokoros imagery reminds us, however, that there were also novel developments in Asia Minor at this time.

Province, City Titles, and the Emperor

The metaphor of neokoros was not simply a new city title added to an existing public reservoir of honorable appellations. An examination of the inscriptions of Asia shows that the use of neokoros in Ephesian inscriptions marks the starting point of the phenomenon of city titles in the eastern Mediterranean. Prior to the building of the Temple of the Sebastoi at Ephesos, the cities of Asia began municipal inscriptions with a simple reference to the βουλή ("council") or the

29. Price, *Rituals and Power*, 64.
30. Ibid., 126–32.
31. Ibid., 132.

δῆμος ("people"), depending on the civic body responsible for setting up the inscription. With the advent of neokoros imagery, titles were placed at the beginning of municipal inscriptions.

The emergence of city titles in the late first century seems to have been targeted primarily at two audiences. In the case of Ephesos, the most immediate audience would have been Ephesians and other inhabitants of the city. Thus the use of titles in inscriptions and coins would have been one way of articulating an identity and self-understanding for the city.[32]

City titles, however, reached beyond the local populace. They also provided a way of positioning a city like Ephesos within the network of cities in its province and region. Individuals and delegations would be reminded of Ephesian claims at provincial festivals, meetings of the provincial council in Asia, and governmental proceedings. Such municipal maneuvering is evident in statements like those in the dedicatory inscriptions from the Temple of the Sebastoi discussed above.

The usefulness of titles becomes clearer when the specific terminology is examined.[33] While neokoros is used most frequently, the title of metropolis also occurs. In Asia, this term did not have the technical meaning of a regional capital as it did in Egypt.[34] Rather, several cities in Asia used the title metropolis to indicate that they were preeminent cities of the region. These included Pergamon, Smyrna, Ephesos, Kyzikos, and Sardes. Miletos, in contrast, used metropolis in the stricter sense of "mother-city" and named areas where the metropolis had founded colonies.[35] This use of municipal titles in coins and inscriptions suggests that the primary function of such titles was to influence perceptions of status and order among the larger cities, a theory that is well supported by an examination of the texts of the dedicatory inscriptions for the Temple of the Sebastoi. This conclusion calls into question two theoretical models for understanding the organization of the Roman Empire.

32. Rogers, *Sacred Identity of Ephesos*, 19–24.
33. A useful, although dated, list of titles in Asia Minor is found in Broughton, "Roman Asia Minor," 742–43.
34. Hans Wolfgang Helck, "Metropolis," *Der Kleine Pauly* 3.1284.
35. Philippe Le Bas and W. H. Waddington, *Voyage archéologique en Grece et en Asie Mineure* (Paris: Firmin Didot, 1870) 212.

The first is that of Fergus Millar, who has analyzed the functioning of the empire as a dialogue between the emperor and interested parties in the provinces.[36] Individuals or groups made appeals to the emperor and received responses from the imperial center of power. In this way, "the innumerable self-governing cities of the Empire had always lived within a common framework of rules issued from the centre. But, equally, the Emperor, in issuing his rulings, was subject to pressures from below," according to Millar.[37] While it is true that rulings from the emperor significantly impinged on the lives of people and communities in the provinces, the metaphor of dialogue cannot explain the relationships between the center and the provinces, much less the relationship between the cities and the emperor. The phenomenon of city titles allows us to affirm that the object of our scrutiny is not a dialogue but rather a complicated conversation involving many parties. In short, a provincial discourse is manifest in the epigraphic and numismatic record that required only occasional recourse to the emperor. Local and regional interests were at stake in the imagery of neokoros. The emperor played an important role, but not as adjudicator of contested issues; rather, the emperor played the important role of *theos*, of a god. Millar's approach does not take this religious factor seriously. Thus his major study, *The Emperor in the Roman World*, offers a bounty of valuable information and analysis, but has no sections devoted to the worship of the emperors.[38]

The study of municipal titles also raises questions regarding Glen Bowersock's model for understanding the interplay of imperial cults and civic titles. His explanation of the worship of the emperors in the Greek East is that the cults were essentially an extension of diplomacy. The Greek world was accustomed to dynastic cults for ruling families as well as cults for Roman magistrates. The cults of Augustus had their roots in those for Roman magistrates, but they took on the character of dynastic cults during the long reign of the first *princeps*,

---

36. Fergus Millar, "Empire and City, Augustus to Julian: Obligations, Excuses and Status," *JRomS* 73 (1983) 76–96.

37. Ibid., 95.

38. See Fergus Millar, *The Emperor in the Roman World (31 BC–AD 337)* (Ithaca, NY: Cornell University Press, 1977).

or emperor.[39] In this sense the "imperial cult belongs to that natural evolution which Augustus encouraged in Graeco-Roman affairs. Initiative from Rome was not required, only modification and adjustment."[40] This approach provides a broader context for understanding the role of the emperor and is thus preferable to that of Millar. Bowersock's model, however, reduces religious phenomena to political categories.[41] If diplomatic traditions explain the true nature of imperial cults, what explains the religious nature of diplomacy? Or, to put the question less polemically, why would a religious metaphor be appropriate for the origins of the phenomenon of city titles?

With the publication of Price's book on imperial cult in Asia Minor, Bowersock retracted his political interpretation of the worship of the emperors in favor of Price's anthropological approach.[42] Indeed, Price has taken imperial cults seriously as a religious phenomenon and related them to the political and community structures of their times. Price argued that modern interpretation of the worship of the emperors has been hampered by undue emphasis on the emotions of the individual as the primary criterion by which religious phenomena are judged to be authentic.[43] Thus, in dealing with imperial cults, interpreters have tended to ask whether the Greeks really believed that the emperor was a god.

Price, however, posed a different question. Drawing on ritual theory, he concluded that imperial cults were at base a way of representing power relationships. He stated, "I wish to develop the idea that imperial rituals too were a way of conceptualizing the world. I do not see rituals merely as a system of 'honours' addressed to the emperor but as a system whose structure defines the position of the emperor."[44] The need that gave rise to imperial cults as a representation of power, according to Price, was tension between Greek traditions of civic autonomy and the reality of Roman authority. Roman authority was

39. G. W. Bowersock, *Augustus and the Greek World* (Oxford: Clarendon, 1965) 113–21.

40. Ibid., 121.

41. See Price, *Rituals and Power*, 15–19.

42. G. W. Bowersock, "Divine Might," *New Republic* 192 (1985) 36.

43. Price, *Rituals and Power*, 10–11.

44. Ibid. 7–8.

foreign, but not completely alien to the Greek cities because of the precedent of the Hellenistic dynasties. The Greek world therefore used their traditional symbol systems to create an imperial cult, and thus incorporate Roman authority into their world. Price explained:

> The imperial cult, like the cults of the traditional gods, created a relationship of power between subject and ruler. It also enhanced the dominance of local élites over the populace, of cities over other cities, and of Greek over indigenous cultures. That is, the cult was a major part of the web of power that formed the fabric of society.[45]

According to Price, the Greeks arrived at a solution by placing the emperor at the focal point between human and divine. An intermediate position appropriate to the power of the emperor and the traditions of the Greeks was formed. Imperial cult thus became one of the ways that power relationships were articulated.[46]

Price's study can rightly be considered a breakthrough in the scholarly understanding of the worship of the emperors. He moved the discussion away from the question of what the Greeks believed or felt, and toward the question of how these cults functioned in their historical and cultural settings. He took the cults seriously as religious phenomena and attempted to show how they were involved in the political process.

Price's framework, however, needs some amendments. Elsewhere, I have questioned his handling of the topic of imperial statues in the precincts of other deities, and the alleged tension between sacrifice to the emperor and sacrifices to deities on behalf of the emperor.[47] More important for this study is Price's choice to treat the imperial cult as a phenomenon with a relatively stable structure and function. Price did not ignore historical developments,[48] but he presupposed static civic institutions in order to describe the imperial cult as a phenomenon.[49] As a result, in his theory the function of imperial cults remains frozen in time, as if Roman authority remained foreign and was

45. Ibid., 247–48.
46. Ibid., 233.
47. Friesen, *Twice Neokoros*, 73–74, 146–50.
48. Price, *Rituals and Power*, 245–47.
49. Ibid., 5.

always in need of rationalization through ritual. By the time the Temple of the Sebastoi was built, however, Roman authority was not in question in the province of Asia; the social system was founded on this authority. In order to understand the use of the metaphor of neokoros and the proliferation of city titles after the late first century CE, one must recognize the dynamic nature of such cults. Each cult institution could have distinctive characteristics and functions. These cults constituted arenas where questions of local, regional, and imperial relationships could be negotiated, shaped, and proclaimed.

The use of the imagery of neokoros in the provincial cults of the emperors beginning in the 80s of the first century suggests four developments regarding social context at that time. First, the cities of Asia had come upon a new way of expressing both their cohesion and their competition; the imagery of neokoros provided new ways to debate and revise their relationships to each other and the imperial center. As Price reminds us, however, the competition took place in a regulated framework and served the purposes of order in the province. The metaphor affirmed the provincial network, even as the participants elbowed for position within that network. Second, these new developments were articulated in terms of the worship of the emperor. Other images, such as the notion of a free city, were available in the late first century for these purposes, but it was precisely the provincial worship of the emperors that provided the necessary symbolic resources.

Third, the Temple of the Sebastoi and the related institutions did not simply introduce a new rhetoric; they also initiated a host of new activities and relationships. There were new responsibilities and honors for the élite sectors of the province. From the thirteen extant dedicatory inscriptions for the temple, a picture of the possible kinds of involvement emerges. At the highest level were those who served as high priests for the Temple of the Sebastoi: the Ephesian Tiberius Claudius Aristio, who also served as the neokoros of the temple in 90/91; Tiberius Claudius Pheseinos of Teos; and Tiberius Julius Dama Claudianus. Not quite so prestigious, although certainly noteworthy, were the honors that accrued to the other men mentioned in the inscriptions as representatives of their cities: from Aizanoi, Claudius Menandros, an archon; Aphrodisias, Aristio, son of Artemidoros, priest of Pluto and Kore and *neopoios* ("temple trustee") of Aphrodite;

Keretapa, Glykon, son of Agathokles, superintendent of public works; Klazomenoi, Tiberius Claudius Kleandros, strategos; Silandros, Marcus Claudius Agrippa, strategos; Makedones Hyrkanioi, the archons Timothy and Metrodoros, and the superintendents Menophilos, Menogenos, and Menokratos; and Tmolos, Aulos Leibios Agro, city secretary, treasurer of the city council, honored as a son of the city council, and priest and neokoros for life in a local cult for Domitian, Domitia, the imperial house, and the Roman Senate. Clearly, the proliferation of provincial cults and city titles meant more than just a new phrase on coins and inscriptions. The activities and public profiles of the wealthy and powerful were being transformed.

Asia was blazing a path that would be followed by others. The Temple of the Sebastoi was Asia's third provincial temple. At this time, no other province had more than one such provincial cult, and several had none. In the late first century, Asia was on the cutting edge of the worship of the emperors.

Implications for the Study of Revelation

The issues that I have raised with regard to religion and identity in the late first and early second century in western Asia Minor impinge upon the study of early Christianity in several ways. The topic of interest here, however, is the relationship of these issues to Revelation.

The fact that the Temple of the Sebastoi and Revelation both appeared at approximately same time has occasioned comment in the secondary literature. An extended discussion of the date of Revelation is not necessary at this point; it is sufficient to note that the majority of scholars now support a date in the Domitianic period rather than an earlier date at the time of Nero.[50] Most scholars even specify the years 95 to 96 for the writing of Revelation, based on Irenaeus's statement that the book first appeared at the end of Domitian's reign.[51] While this precise date would suggest a direct correlation between the Temple of the Sebastoi and Revelation, it is

---

50. For a summary of recent scholarship, see Adela Yarbro Collins, "Revelation, Book of," in David N. Freedman, ed., *Anchor Bible Dictionary* (1st ed.; 6 vols.; New York: Doubleday, 1992) 5. 694–708.

51. Irenaeus *Adv. haer.* 5.30.3.

probably not wise to place full confidence in the precision of Irenaeus's testimony. Revelation should rather be dated more generally in the Domitianic period or simply in the last two decades of the first century. The connection between the temple and the text, then, is to be found in their differing evaluations of larger trends in imperial cults in Asian society during the late first and early second centuries.

Most interpreters of Revelation address this question at some point, and there is currently no consensus regarding the status of imperial cults in Asia at the time of the production of Revelation. The views of three prominent scholars—Elisabeth Schüssler Fiorenza, Adela Yarbro Collins, and Leonard Thompson—represent the range of views on this issue.

Elisabeth Schüssler Fiorenza's understanding of imperial cults in Asia in the late first century serves as an introduction to the views of most scholars. Schüssler Fiorenza argues that under the Flavians, and especially under Domitian, imperial cults were enthusiastically promoted. Domitian himself demanded to be acclaimed as "our Lord and God." In this situation, the Christians in Asia came under increasing pressure to participate in imperial cult activity or suffer the ultimate punishment.[52] The author of Revelation wrote in order to alienate the churches from imperial cult and traditional Greek cults by creating a symbolic universe that reinterpreted reality. This symbolic universe gave the churches the strength to decide whether "to worship the anti-divine powers embodied by Rome" or "to worship God."[53] Schüssler Fiorenza injects new factors into the understanding of Revelation by framing the discussion in terms of rhetorical criticism and arguing that the author was competing with another prophetic Christian sector in the Asian churches.[54] The interpretation of Revelation as a response to the situation that Domitian's extravagant religious policies produced is one with which most scholars agree.

Adela Yarbro Collins stakes out a different and somewhat ambivalent position in her book *Crisis and Catharsis: The Power of the*

---

52. Elisabeth Schüssler Fiorenza, *The Book of Revelation: Justice and Judgment* (Philadelphia: Fortress, 1985) 193–94; idem, *Revelation: Vision of a Just World* (Minneapolis: Fortress, 1991) 54.

53. Schüssler Fiorenza, *The Book of Revelation*, 191.

54. Revelation refers to this group as Nikolaites, children of Jezebel, and

Apocalypse, as well as in later articles.[55] She neither portrayed Revelation as a response to the imperial cult nor denied its relationship to the cult. According to Yarbro Collins, Domitian did not persecute Christians or initiate any new practices in the area of imperial cults. Certain flatterers may have heightened the rhetoric and practice of imperial cults, but this was not a crucial factor for the author and audience of Revelation.[56] The imperial cult was actually one of several factors that would produce a crisis for Asian Christians. John foresaw the severity of the coming crisis, which included such factors as the growing hostility between traditional Jews and followers of Jesus; increasing tensions between Christians and pagans; severe strains between rich and poor in Asia Minor in late first and early second centuries, and certain experiences of trauma such as the destruction of the Jerusalem temple, persecutions under Nero, the offensiveness of imperial cult to some Christians, the execution of Antipas (Rev 2:13), and John's own banishment.[57] In pointing out the effects these growing problems might have in the future, John's Revelation was more a product of Christian faith than a mere response to social conditions. Thus, while Revelation was not written because of imperial cults, without imperial cults it would have been different, or perhaps it would not have been written at all.[58] The genius of Revelation, according to Yarbro Collins, is that it clarified and objectified an incipient conflict through the creation of a new linguistic world. This did not allow for the resolution of the real sources of conflict, but it controlled feelings of frustration and aggression on the part of Christians in Asia Minor.[59]

With regard to the relationship of imperial cults to Revelation, Leonard Thompson's contribution to the discussion represents the opposite end of the interpretative spectrum from that of Schüssler

---

those who hold the teachings of Balaam; see ibid., 195; Schüssler Fiorenza, *Revelation: Vision of a Just World*, 55–56.

55. Adela Yarbro Collins, *Crisis and Catharsis: The Power of the Apocalypse* (Philadelphia: Westminster, 1984); see also idem, "Revelation," 5. 694–708.

56. Yarbro Collins, *Crisis and Catharsis*, 69–77.

57. Ibid., 84–107.

58. Ibid., 104–5.

59. Ibid., 161.

Fiorenza. He concludes that imperial cults played no role in the book's production or theology. Domitian, according to Thompson, was no mad tyrant; on the contrary, he was an able administrator who tried to improve the lot of the provincials of the empire.[60] The imperial cult was probably objectionable to some Christians during his reign, but no more so than during the reign of anyone else. Imperial cults preceded Domitian and outlived him.[61] There were no innovations, no exaggerated claims to divinity, but only a prosperous province of Asia in which Christians for the most part lived quiet lives without disturbance.[62] According to Thompson, "John reports surprisingly few hostilities toward Christians by the non-Christian social world. He anticipates conflict, but conflicts stemming from his fundamental position that church and world belong to antithetical forces. In other words John encourages his audience to see themselves in conflict with society; such conflict is a part of his vision of the world."[63]

According to Thompson, the author of Revelation did not simply reject the world. He did not create an alternative symbolic universe as Schüssler Fiorenza maintains, nor a literary world as Yarbro Collins proposes. Rather, he established an encompassing vision that explained the whole world, including everyday life in western Asia Minor.[64] This wholeness of vision indicates that Revelation should not necessarily be located in the social situation of a persecuted conventicle— the situation was more complex than that. The author's attempt to speak to the public order from the apocalyptic perspective required him to have an ambivalent relationship with the Roman world. He both rejected that order and attempted to absorb it into his vision. The result was an apocalyptic text that did not require its hearers to withdraw from the world into a sectarian social setting; they only needed to be willing to engage that world as an enemy from a particular Christian perspective.[65]

This brief review of the three important contributions to the study of Revelation leads to several observations. Many scholars argue for

60. Leonard Thompson, *The Book of Revelation: Apocalypse and Empire* (New York: Oxford University Press, 1990) 96–115.
61. Ibid., 158–67.
62. Ibid., 116–32.
63. Ibid., 174.
64. Ibid., 74.
65. Ibid., 195–97.

the significance of Revelation by addressing three issues: the general sociopolitical situation in Asia, the particular situation of Christians in Asia, and the status of imperial cults in Asia. Together, these factors lead to diverse readings of the significance of John's Revelation. One's conclusions about the practice of imperial cults in the late first century in Asia will therefore affect how one reads Revelation.

Schüssler Fiorenza's stance on imperial cults, which maintains that Domitian stood at the center of the Roman world, making demands that radiated out to the provinces, has weakened with time. The traditional view of the mad emperor has been questioned as a piece of later propaganda. Here, Yarbro Collins's view is somewhat more promising since it shifts the attention from the imperial center to the provinces. The characterization of imperial cults as insincere flattery, however, is also weak, as earlier arguments in this paper have shown. Thompson, by utilizing newer literature on Domitian, on the sociopolitical situation in Asia,[66] and on the worship of the emperors in general, demonstrates convincingly that society in Asia Minor was relatively stable in the late first and early second centuries CE, and that imperial cults were an integral part of that society rather than a foreign intrusion into that world. He incorrectly concludes, however, that nothing new occured with regard to the worship of the emperors at the time of Revelation. As this was manifestly not the case, the question remains: How do the developments in late first century Asia affect one's reading of Revelation?

Three conclusions lead us to an answer to this question. First, when John denounced imperial worship, he was not attacking a marginal socioreligious phenomenon. The developments in provincial worship of the emperors that are manifested in the Temple of the Sebastoi indicate that the worship of the emperors played an increasingly important role in society at many levels. Municipal identities, regional cohesion and competition, and imperial authority were brought together in this religious phenomenon. These trends appeared first in Asia, and other areas soon followed the province's example. John was combatting a serious, and growing, phenomenon.

Second, the rapid spread of the title of neokoros throughout the eastern Mediterranean shows that the worship of the emperors had a wide base of support. As always, the question about the depth of that

66. See Mitchell, *Anatolia*, 1. 206.

support arises. Even if imperial cults were found throughout wide regions, which sectors of society were in agreement with them? Were imperial cults simply the playing field of the élite? These are questions that cannot be answered inductively from a historically distant vantage point. When the range of imperial cult phenomena is taken into account, however—including worship, processions, festivals, delegations, sports, governance, inscriptions, and coinage—the burden of proof lies with those who claim that the majority of first-century Asians disapproved of such cults. This in turn suggests that John, in critiquing imperial worship, did not speak for the masses.[67] In Asia at least, he did not speak for an oppressed majority. He spoke as a minority in his society, and perhaps even as a minority in the churches.

Third, an appreciation of the municipal and regional dynamics of imperial cults draws one's attention not to Rome but to the provinces. John's critique was therefore directed more at local enemies than at the distant emperor. Outmoded views of imperial cults that focused on the role of the emperor resulted in a misinterpretation of Revelation. Certainly John railed against the emperor, but was the emperor his primary audience or even his primary opponent? In the late first century in Asia, a denunciation of imperial cults constituted a denunciation of city efforts to define themselves, a rejection of proper legal decisions of the *koinon*, and a sarcastic commentary on the public religious activities of the wealthy and of many others. John not only prophesied against imperial power; he also declared illegitimate the presuppositions of the local élite's claim to authority and condemned the general population for their compliance. If the author's trip to Patmos was punishment, it occured because John was a nuisance to the province rather than the empire.

The Book of Revelation must be understood in its local setting as part of a clash of religious ideologies, for it represents an assault on fundamental issues of social organization in late first-century Asia. The text was seditious not because it attacked the emperor, but because it indicted the emerging social order in Asia as a blasphemous force that deceived all people and spilled the blood of the saints.

---

67. See Richard Bauckham, *The Theology of the Book of Revelation* (Cambridge: Cambridge University Press, 1993) 36.

Sculptures of Gods and Heroes from Ephesos

Maria Aurenhammer
Österreichisches Archäologisches Institut

Because of the many years of excavations at Ephesos, an exceptionally large amount of free-standing and relief sculpture has been unearthed in and around the city. These pieces are now housed in five different museums in Turkey, Vienna, and London. In the eighties, Hermann Vetters initiated a project to cover this vast material and present a systematic catalog. The author works on this project together with colleagues from the Kunsthistorisches Museum, Vienna, and the Efes Müzesi, Selçuk. The majority of extant Ephesian sculptures dates to the Hellenistic and Roman imperial periods, since excavations have been concentrated mainly within the boundaries of the Hellenistic-Roman city, where few earlier structures have been discovered. With the exception of the Artemision, which will not be dealt with here, archaic and classical sculptures, as well as free-standing Hellenistic sculptures, have been found only rarely in Ephesos; the bulk of sculpture is Roman imperial. This paper will focus on the sculptural repertoire of the Hellenistic-Roman city.

I present here a selection of Ephesian ideal sculpture—that is, sculptures of gods, goddesses, and heroes.[1] Ephesos is considered the city of Artemis, but many other major and minor deities were worshipped there, as Dieter Knibbe and Richard Oster have elaborated in their studies of literary, epigraphic, and numismatic evidence.[2] Two multifigured bands of reliefs on a large Hellenistic votive block found in a wall near the Temple of Domitian (map no. 53) may reveal just how manifold the Ephesian pantheon was.[3]

Since the publication of Robert Fleischer's basic volume, *Artemis of Ephesos*, and his subsequent articles,[4] other fragments of replicas of the cult image have been found at Ephesos, all of them small and some even miniature. They adhere to the well-known iconography of the goddess.[5] An interesting piece of evidence concerning the cult of Artemis Ephesia is embodied in a fragment of sculpture from Slope House 2 (fig. 1; map no. 45).[6] It is a small fragment of a right hand,

1. See Maria Aurenhammer, *Die Skulpturen von Ephesos: Idealplastik 1* (*FiE* 10.1; Vienna: ÖAW, 1990), which presents the sculptures of gods and heroes. Aurenhammer, *Die Skulpturen von Ephesos: Idealplastik 2* (Vienna: ÖAW, forthcoming) will present the sculptures of goddesses. In this paper, each cited piece of sculpture is documented by a bibliographical reference or, if the piece has not yet been published, by the inventory number of the museum. The illustrations chosen for this paper show a variety of sculptures of Ephesian goddesses from the Austrian excavations.

2. See Dieter Knibbe, "Ephesos, nicht nur die Stadt der Artemis," 2. 489–503; Richard E. Oster, "Ephesus as a Religious Center," 1661–1726. For numismatic evidence, see Stefan Karwiese, "Ephesos C. Numismatischer Teil," PWSup 12 (1970) 297–364, 353–61 (indices of coin motifs). Since this paper does not attempt to present the entire Ephesian pantheon, but focuses on the extant Ephesian ideal sculpture, some of the important gods venerated in the city, such as the gods of the Prytaneion, will not be discussed here.

3. Erol Atalay, "Un nouveau monument votif hellénistique à Éphèse," *RArch* 1985/2, 195–204.

4. See Robert Fleischer, *Artemis von Ephesos*; idem, "Artemis Ephesia," *LIMC* 2 (1984) 755–63; idem, "Artemis und verwandte Kultstatuen aus Anatolien und Syrien. Supplement," in Şahin, *Studien zur Religion und Kultur Kleinasiens*, 324–41. See also Lynn R. LiDonicci, "The Images of Artemis Ephesia and Greco-Roman Worship: A Reconsideration," *HTR* 85 (1992) 389–415.

5. All of these will be published in Aurenhammer, *Skulpturen 2*.

6. Selçuk, Efes Müzesi P 1/80. This piece was found on the threshhold between the atrium H 2/36 and the basilica privata H 2/8 of C. Fl. Furius

which is larger than life-size, holding a statuette of Artemis Ephesia, of which only the base, feet, and lowest part of the dress are extant. Similar, better-preserved sculptures from Aphrodisias and Iasos show that this motif of hand and statuette was probably used with the bust or statue of a priest of the city's main goddess, or of a priest of the imperial cult, as is the case in the statue of Iasos.[7] Several Ephesian coin types, however, show various deities and personifications holding a statuette of Artemis Ephesia; thus this fragment could be interpreted as, for example, Tyche holding the image of the city's main goddess.[8]

The Hellenistic-Roman cult image of Aphrodite of Aphrodisias is attired in a fashion similar to the image of Artemis Ephesia.[9] Aphrodite's stiff body is wrapped in a tight ependytes adorned with several bands of reliefs featuring busts of gods and Hellenistic motifs such as the three graces, Aphrodite on a sea ram, and three putti. Aphrodite of Aphrodisias was also venerated in Ephesos, as shown by several fragments of small replicas of her cult image. The two largest fragments, found in different places in Ephesos, probably come from the same statue.[10] In 1988, the base with the lowest part of the dress of a small

---

Aptus's flat. For the complete plan of Slope Houses 1 and 2, see Vetters, "Vorläufiger Grabungsbericht 1984 und 1985," fig. 28a. For basilica H 2/8, see Hermann Vetters, "Ephesos. Vorläufiger Grabungsbericht 1978," *AnzWien* 113 (1979) 496–500. For atrium H 2/36, see idem, "Vorläufiger Grabungsbericht 1980," 143–44. With regard to the luxurious apartment of C. Flavius Furius Aptus, see below nn. 55 and 95.

7. With regard to Aphrodisias, see Kenan T. Erim, "Recent Work at Aphrodisias 1986–1988," in idem, and Charlotte Roueché, eds., *Aphrodisias Papers: Recent Work on Architecture and Sculpture* (Journal of Roman Archaeology suppl. 1; Ann Arbor: Editorial Committee of the Journal of Roman Archaeology, 1990) 15–18 fig. 9. With regard to Iasos, see Sebastiana Lagona, "Statua panneggiata dalla Stoa di Artemis Astias a Iasos," *ASAtene* 46 (1984) 141–49 figs. 1–3.

8. For examples of Zeus, Mount Pion, and Tyche holding an image of Artemis Ephesia, see Stefan Karwiese, "Ephesos C," 332, 334, 343, 346 (Zeus); 341 (Pion); 343 (Tyche); for Pion, see also Stefan Karwiese, "Pion," *LIMC* 7 (1994) 411.

9. See Robert Fleischer, "Aphrodite von Aphrodisias," *LIMC* 2 (1984) 151–54.

10. See Fleischer, *Artemis von Ephesos*, 153–54 cat. nos. A 24, 26; pls. 70, 72.

replica of an image of Aphrodite was found in the harbor excavations.[11] This is the only example of a base found in Asia Minor that shows a relief of the two doves—sacred birds of Aphrodite—holding a garland in their beaks.[12] In Aphrodisias, doves were protected, as an inscription of the first century CE testifies.[13] The motif of the relief on the base—doves with garlands of vittae—recalls, for example, the frieze of doves adorning an architrave from the precinct of Aphrodite Pandemos on the Athenian acropolis.[14]

In Ephesos, the goddess Artemis was also represented as huntress, in the usual Greek style. The major extant work of this type is an almost completely preserved Artemis, smaller than life-size, which was set up in late Roman times in a niche of the so-called room of Socrates in Slope House 2, probably in its third phase of display (fig. 2).[15] The statue, representing the girlish Artemis striding to the right, gripping her dress with her right hand and originally brandishing the bow in the left, follows an early Hellenistic type labelled "Artemis Louvre-Ephesos." The Ephesian replica is the only one to have preserved the head with its melon coiffure.[16] Fleischer and Simon dated

11. Selçuk, Efes Müzesi 45/54/88.

12. For a parallel piece in Rome, see Fleischer, *Artemis von Ephesos*, 152 cat. no. A 20; pl. 69. See also the piece, perhaps restored, in a private Swiss collection, ibid., 151 cat. no. A 17.

13. Joyce Reynolds, *Aphrodisias and Rome: Documents from the Excavation of the Theatre at Aphrodisias* (JRomS Monograph Series 1; London: Society for the Promotion of Roman Studies, 1982) 172 no. 4.

14. See Luigi Beschi, "Contributi della topografia ateniese," *ASAtene* 45/46 (1967/68) 521–26 fig. 7.

15. Robert Fleischer, "Artemisstatuette aus dem Hanghaus II in Ephesos," *JÖAI* 2 Beih. (1971) Beibl. 172–88 figs. 7–14. Lily Kahil, "Artemis"; and Erika Simon, "Artemis/Diana," *LIMC* 2 (1984) 646 no. 270, 807–8 no. 31a, respectively.

16. Barbara Vierneisel-Schlörb (*Glyptothek München: Katalog der Skulpturen II. Klassische Skulpturen des 5. und 4. Jhs.* [Munich: Beck, 1979] 301 n. 39) links this head with postpraxitelean heads from around 300 BCE; for a similar dating—as ascertained by comparison of the style of Artemis's dress—see Wilfred Geominy, *Die Florentiner Niobiden* (Ph.D. diss., Rheinische Friedrich-Wilhelms-Universität Bonn, 1984) 279. For a different chronology based on the position of the braids encircling the melon coiffure, see John J. Herrmann, Jr., *In the Shadow of the Acropolis: Popular and Private Art in Fourth Century Athens* (2d ed.; Salt Lake City: Utah Museum of Fine Arts, 1988) 22 no.

the Ephesian statue to late Hellenistic times.[17] Most of the other Ephesian images of Artemis in these series also adhere to classical or Hellenistic types.[18] One monument which stands out of this series is an under life-size statuette originally set up in a private lararium in Slope House 2 (fig. 3).[19] It is a Roman pasticcio of Hadrianic date; it is not a singular work, but member of a typological group of peplophoroi. It combines archaic elements, in particular the stance and tight dress of the lower part, with early classical traits, such as the overfall of the peplos. The rather plump arms contrast with the delicate hybrid head.

Two other venerable goddesses, Meter and Hekate, share some aspects with Artemis. The old Phrygian mother goddess was called "Phrygian mother, mother of the mountains, ancestral mother, chaste mother" (Μήτηρ φρυγίη, ὀρίη, πατροίη, ἀγνή) in Ephesos and worshipped in a precinct on the northeastern slope of Panayırdağ (Mount Pion; map no. 72).[20] Some of the votive reliefs, which were placed into rock-cut niches or inserted in slits cut into the rock, were found in situ; one can still be seen there, carved in the rock. Meter was venerated in this precinct together with Zeus, Apollo, and Hermes, according to inscriptions on the reliefs and carved in the rock[21]; the

---

11. According to this chronology, the braids over the top of the head indicate an earlier date in the age of Alexander.

17. Fleischer, "Artemisstatuette," 187–88; Simon, "Artemis/Diana," 807 no. 31a.

18. Compare, for example, the early imperial replica of a head of the Artemis Colonna type, which is of good quality, from the Scholastikia Baths (Bammer, Fleischer, and Knibbe, *Führer*, 70–71 no. 708).

19. Atalay, *Gewandstatuen*, 15 cat. no. 1, 57–58, 114, fig. 1; Enrico Paribeni, "Di Diana Nemorensis e di Artemide Efesia," *Dialoghi di Archeologia* 3 (1981) 42–48 fig. 8; Simon, "Artemis/Diana," 797 no. 3; Mark D. Fullerton, *The Archaistic Style in Roman Statuary* (Mnemosyne suppl. 110; Leiden: Brill, 1990) 17–18, 21–22 cat. no. I A1, 36 fig. 2.

20. See, for example, Josef Keil, "XII. vorläufiger Bericht," Beibl. 256–61; Knibbe, "Ephesos, nicht nur die Stadt der Artemis," 490–91; Friedrike Naumann, *Die Ikonographie der Kybele in der phrygischen und griechischen Kunst* (IstMit suppl. 28; Tübingen: Wasmuth, 1983) 214–16, pl. 32; Oster, "Ephesus as a Religious Center," 1687–88; Maarten J. Vermaseren, *Corpus Cultus Cybelae Attidisque* (EPRO 50; 7 vols.; Leiden: Brill, 1987) 1. 184 no. 612.

21. *IvE* II 101–4, 107–9; IV 1203, 1214–27; V 1576.

sanctuary was frequented from classical to Roman imperial times. The votive reliefs of the characteristic and enduring "Ephesian type" feature the enthroned or standing goddess in the center, with lions and tympanum, flanked by an old bearded god (probably Zeus) and a young god clad in chiton or chlamys, sometimes with an additional petasos and equipped with an oinochoe.[22] The young god, who appears often, is ambiguous; according to his iconography, he may be Hermes or Apollo. Both interpretations are supported by inscriptions. There is no real evidence that the young god is Attis,[23] although the existence of a cult of Attis in Ephesos is clearly attested by an early Hellenistic mold representing the figure of Attis as a dead, bandaged infant.[24]

The oldest of the free-standing images of Meter-Kybele is one of the rare archaic sculptures found in Ephesos. The exact find spot is unknown.[25] This late archaic sculpture represents the goddess enthroned with flanking lions—only scant traces of them are still extant—and a tympanum is in her left arm.

Most of the other Ephesian Kybele statuettes of Hellenistic and Roman date follow the style of the votive reliefs, showing the god-

22. For the votive reliefs, see, for example, Naumann, *Die Ikonographie*, 218–29; Vermaseren, *Corpus Cultus Cybelae*, 184–87 cat. nos. 613–18, 188 cat. no. 622, 189–90 cat. nos. 632–33, 190–91 cat. nos. 634–37, 192–93 cat. nos. 641–45, 194–96 cat. nos. 649–55, 196–98 cat. nos. 659–65, 199–200 cat. nos. 669–73, 200–202 cat. nos. 675–84.

23. For the interpretation of the two male gods on the reliefs, see Naumann, *Die Ikonographie*, 220–22. For an interpretation of the younger god as Attis or Hermes-Kadmilos, see Bammer, Fleischer, and Knibbe, *Führer*, 166 no. 55; Knibbe, "Ephesos, nicht nur die Stadt der Artemis," 490–91.

24. Stefan Karwiese, "Der tote Attis," *JÖAI* 49 (1968–71) 50–51 fig. 1; Vermaseren, *Corpus Cultus Cybelae*, 191 cat. no. 639. For other monuments featuring Attis, see Aurenhammer, *Skulpturen 1*, no. 110. Vermaseren presents a monument that features Attis (*Corpus Cultus Cybelae*, 119 cat. no. 638), but his other Attis monuments (nos. 635, 636) must be excluded for reasons of iconography; regarding no. 635, see Schneider, *Bunte Barbaren*, 125–28, 135, 204 cat. no. SO 27; and Vermaseren, *Corpus Cultus Cybelae*, 191 cat. no. 636, see Antoine Hermary, "Eros," *LIMC* 3 (1986) 855–56 no. 5.

25. See Bammer, Fleischer, and Knibbe, *Führer*, 163–64 no. 148, pl. 25; Naumann, *Die Ikonographie*, 130, 136, 303 cat. no. 65; Vermaseren, *Corpus Cultus Cybelae*, 200 cat. no. 674, pl. 151.

dess according to the pattern of the classic Attic image of Kybele: she is enthroned in chiton and himation, with a tympanum in her left arm and a cup in her right hand, the lions arranged in various positions (see fig. 4).[26] One of the earliest Ephesian representations of this type, a terra-cotta of the fourth century BCE, was found some years ago buried in a well of the late classical settlement below the Tetragonos Agora (map no. 30).[27] One of the Kybele statuettes was modelled after a Hellenistic type.[28]

Besides these rather unpretentious pieces of sculpture, primitive examples have also been found. In addition to a roughly hewn block, excavated in 1993, which shows an early stage of a Kybele sculpture,[29] a primitive idol of the goddess was found in a late antique stratum in the western stoa of the Tetragonos Agora (see fig. 5).[30] The idol consists of the veiled head and the blocklike torso of the goddess without limbs; a small lion is crouching on the protruding lower part of the block. A necklace adorns the plump neck of the goddess. Such primitive representations of the mother goddess can be found throughout Asia Minor. A monument, originally found at Sille and now in the museum of Konya, provides a parallel to the form of this image: here Kybele's figure is incorporated into the middle part of a tall Roman stele, with a niche hewn in its lower part.[31]

Literary, epigraphic, and archaeological evidence testify to the existence of the cult of Hekate in Ephesos.[32] Strabo cited the Hekatesion

26. Selçuk, Efes Müzesi 1907 from the nympheion ("Fontäne"), map no. 66; this will be published in Aurenhammer, *Skulpturen 2*. Regarding the fountain, see Wilhelm Alzinger, "Ephesos," PWSup 12 (1970) 1606. Kybele statuettes from Ephesos already cited in this paper include Bammer, Fleischer, and Knibbe, *Führer*, 164 no. 53 = Vermaseren, *Corpus Cultus Cybelae*, 199 cat. no. 668, pl. 148; in the latter work, 196 cat. no. 658 is not from Ephesos, but from Aydın, according to Naumann *(Die Ikonographie*, 330 cat. no. 298; see also 324 cat. no. 247).

27. Feristah Soykal, *Eine spätklassische Terrakottastatuette der Kybele aus Ephesos (BerMatÖAI* 5; Vienna: Schindler, 1993) 53–56 figs. 1–4.

28. Selçuk, Efes Müzesi 2256. Compare Vermaseren, *Corpus Cultus Cybelae*, 194 no. 647, pl. 141.

29. Austrian excavation, no. P 31/93; this piece was found in the theater.

30. Selçuk, Efes Müzesi 31/27/84.

31. Vermaseren, *Corpus Cultus Cybelae*, 235 no. 783, pl. 170.

32. See Oster, "Ephesus as a Religious Center," 1696.

of a certain Thrason in Ephesos.[33] According to Pliny, a highly praised, shining image of Hekate was set up in the temenos of Artemis (in templo Dianae post aedem).[34] Hekate's worship is also attested in the precinct of Meter on Panayırdağ.[35] Hekate's images were still intact in late antiquity, as the magic rites that the Ephesian sophist Maximos performed with an image of this goddess demonstrate.[36] Hekate is protectress of Ephesian crossroads. She exercises this function twice at the Triodos, the important crossroad in the center of the city, the meeting place of the Processional Way along the Tetragonos Agora, Curetes Street, and the way to Ortygia (near map no. 36).[37] A clumsy inscription in the eastern passage of the southern gate of the Tetragonos Agora (map no. 34) calls Hekate to avenge the forbidden act of urinating there.[38] Above this inscription an image of the goddess herself is scrawled, single-bodied, holding short torches in her hands. Her image in the western passage of the same gate—a very shallow, partially destroyed relief—features the goddess in the usual triple-bodied form, here with three *poloi* (typical headgear of goddesses) and six arms with torches.[39]

A better-preserved, gabled votive relief for Hekate is stored in the Kunsthistorisches Museum in Vienna.[40] The goddess is flanked by stags in shallow relief—a hint of her kinship to Artemis—and she probably held snakes in her lowest arms. The main, frontal figure of the goddess features a characteristic combination of shifted stance and archaistic dress. Roman reliefs representing the triple-bodied goddess with a mixture of archaistic and stylistically "freer" traits and

33. Strabo *Geog.* 14.1.23.¡
34. Pliny *Hist. nat.* 36.23.
35. *IvE* IV 1233.
36. Eunapius *Vit. Soph.* 50.
37. Regarding the Triodos, see Knibbe, *Parthermonument*, 6; idem, *Via Sacra I*, 55.
38. *IvE* II 567. Helmut Engelmann and Dieter Knibbe, "Aus ephesischen Skizzenbüchern," *JÖAI* 52 (1978–80) 40 no. 54. For the single-bodied type, compare Hekate's image on the frieze of the gods at the so-called Temple of Hadrian; see Fleischer, "Fries des Hadrianstempels," 27 fig. 17 D10, 47–48.
39. Knibbe, *Parthermonument*, 16 fig. 1.
40. Vienna, Kunsthistorisches Museum I 914. The exact find spot is unknown. Elpis Mitropoulou, *Triple Hekate Mainly on Votive-Reliefs, Coins, Gems and Amulets* (Athens: Pyli, 1978) 46 no. 60, fig. 76.

with a number of various attributes are prevalent in Thrace, but are also found in Asia Minor.[41]

The extant small-sized Hekataia of Ephesos were found in the peristyle courts of the apartment blocks, in official buildings, and along streets. Most of them adhere to the simple archaistic type, showing the goddess clad in the high-girdled archaistic dress with a prominent fold between the legs and triangular over-fall (see fig. 6 for an example).[42] There is also an example of the Hellenistic type of Hekataion encircled by the three dancing Charites.[43] Like Meter, Hekate was commemorated in form of very primitive monuments, either a small column with three single relief figures of the goddess, accompanied by dogs, or a simple peg, with figures in relief, to be inserted into the ground directly by a tenon.[44] The Kybele statuettes and Hekataia, which follow a long-standing pattern, are difficult to date precisely, but may be grouped according to workmanship.

Exceptional in this mass of simple monuments is an under life-size head of the triple-bodied Hekate, found in the cryptoporticus of the Temple of Domitian.[45] The three heads of the goddess are crowned by diadems and a single-turreted *polos*, a link with Tyche. Like the famous Hekataion in Leiden,[46] this Ephesian Hekate shows classicizing, masklike facial features.

41. Compare ibid., 34–40 nos. 11–32, 46 no. 58; Haiganuch Sarian, "Hekate," *LIMC* 6 (1992) 1001–2 nos. 160–65 for reliefs from Asia Minor.

42. Fig. 6 displays one side of the three-sided Hekataion (Selçuk, Efes Müzesi 132/59/80 from the peristyle court of apartment 7 in Slope House 2). For the simple archaistic type in general, see Sarian, "Hekate," 998–1000, 1015. All the Hekataia cited here will be published in Aurenhammer, *Skulpturen 2*.

43. Selçuk, Efes Müzesi 2/1/88, from excavations in the Church of St. John. For the style, see Sarian, "Hekate," 1004 nos. 217–20.

44. The column (Selçuk, Efes Müzesi 2089) is from the East Gymnasium. Compare Sarian, "Hekate," 1002, no. 166. The peg (Selçuk, Efes Müzesi 51) is from early excavations; the exact location of the find is unknown. Compare Mükkerem Anabolu, "Izmir arkeoloji müzesi'nin deposunda bulunan yedi hekataion," in *Festschrift Ekrem Akurgal = Anadolu (Anatolia)* 22, 1981–83 (1989) 329, 333–34 fig. 5 a–c.

45. Selçuk, Efes Müzesi 10/37/72.

46. Theodor Krause, *Hekate* (Heidelberg: Winter, 1960) 155, pls. 19.1–3, 21.1; Sarian, "Hekate," 1000 no. 139.

Miniature images of the goddess were also set up, as a fragment in the Kunsthistorisches Museum in Vienna shows. The uppermost part of a prismatic Hekate herm does not reach a height of 10 cm (fig. 7).[47] Similar images from Delos preserve the complete form.[48] The heads of this Ephesian herm are softly modelled in a delicate Hellenistic style.

In terms of sheer numbers, images of the Greek-styled Aphrodite hold first place in Hellenistic-Roman ideal sculpture from Ephesos. At this time, over one hundred statues, statuettes, and torsos of this goddess have been found, excluding the numerous unidentified female heads. These images of Aphrodite must be explored according to their setting.[49] While not abundant, literary and epigraphic evidence concerning the cult of Aphrodite in Ephesos reflects continous veneration of the goddess.[50] A temenos of Aphrodite and a temple of Aphrodite Hetaira are testified.[51] In the harbor excavations, a decree of a merchant's guild (κοινὸν τῶν Ἀφροδισιαστῶν) was found; it referred to the seat of their corporation in the harbor area, which was also a sanctuary of their goddess.[52] Moreover, two altars for the goddess are extant; one was set up for Aphrodite Daitis.[53]

Without presenting examples of all the well-known types of Aphrodite from Ephesos, I want to point out some interesting examples of sculptural decoration related to Aphrodite which are found in private and public buildings in Ephesos. One small-size, half-naked

47. Vienna, Kunsthistorisches Museum I 892; the exact find spot is unknown.

48. Jean Marcadé, *Au musée de Délos* (Bibliothéque des écoles françaises d'Athènes et de Rome 215; Paris: Boccard, 1969) pl. 59A, nos. 6020, 6022–23. See also Sarian, "Hekate," 1003–4 nos. 196–205.

49. See Hubertus Manderscheid, *Die Skulpturenausstattung der kaiserzeitlichen Thermenanlagen* (Monumenta Artis Romanae 15; Berlin: Mann, 1981) 32–33. See review by Richard Neudecker in *Gnomon* 57 (1985) 174–75.

50. See Knibbe, "Ephesos, nicht nur die Stadt der Artemis," 493 n. 3; Oster, "Ephesus as a Religious Center," 1667–68.

51. Polyainos *Strategika* 5.18; Athenaios *Deipnosophist.* 13.573a.

52. Knibbe, Englemann, and İplikçioğlu, "Neue Inschriften aus Ephesos XII," 125–26 no. 17.

53. *IvE* IV 1202. Compare Josef Keil, "Aphrodite Daitis," *JÖAI* 17 (1914) 145–47; Kurt Latte, "Aphrodite in Ephesos," *ARW* 17 (1914) 678–79. Knibbe and İplikçioğlu, "Neue Inschriften aus Ephesos VIII," 147 no. 164.

Aphrodite of Roman date, which is modelled after a late Hellenistic type, Aphrodite of Agen, was used as a fountain adornment in Slope House 1 (map no. 46). Water spurted through a hole in her right breast (see fig. 8).[54] C. Flavius Furius Aptus, who was priest of Dionysos and owner of the luxurious apartment 6 in Slope House 2 in the late second century CE, set up two statues of Aphrodite. Obviously presents to the generous host, they flanked the staircase leading from the atrium to the private basilica, according to the inscriptions on the bases, which alone remain.[55] This is a rare example in which the exact position of sculptural decoration in the Slope Houses can be located. Statues of Aphrodite also abound in public buildings. The façade of the Fountain of C. Laecanius Bassus (map no. 60) was decorated with a series of Aphrodisian sculptures, all modelled after Hellenistic types.[56] This fountain boasted an especially rich sculptural program, including, among others, a pair of copies of a Hellenistic version of the Louvre-Naples type and a single statue with a head shaped after yet another Hellenistic model.[57] An iconographically in-

54. Selçuk, Efes Müzesi 1909. Regarding Aphrodite of Agen, see Angelos Delivorrias, "Aphrodite," *LIMC* 2 (1984) 79–80 no. 707. Another fountain sculpture of Aphrodite—water spurted from her breasts—is from Carthage; see Balazs Kapossy, *Brunnenfiguren der hellenistischen und römischen Zeit* (Zürich: Juris, 1969) 14 under the heading "Varia, Bardo, Musée Alaoui."

55. Hermann Vetters, "Vorläufiger Grabungsbericht 1980," 144, 146 figs. 13–18; idem, "Nochmals zur basilica privata," *Römische Historische Mitteilungen* 23 (1981) 210–11; Knibbe and İplikçioğlu, "Neue Inschriften aus Ephesos VIII," 132–33 no. 140. For other evidence concerning C. Flavius Furius Aptus, see *IvE* II 502, 502A; III 675, 834; IV 1099, 1267, 1932A; VII 3064. For statuary pendants, see Elizabeth Bartmann, "Decor and Duplicatio: Pendants in Roman Sculptural Display," *AJA* 92 (1988) 211–25.

56. See Elizabeth Fossel and Gerhard Langmann, "Das Nymphaeum des C. Laecanius Bassus"; and Robert Fleischer, "Skulpturenfunde," *JÖAI* 50 (1972–75) Grabungen 301–10, 421–32, respectively. Regarding the sculptural program, see the latter article.

57. For copies of the Louvre-Naples type, see Bammer, Fleischer, and Knibbe, *Führer*, 423–25, figs. 3, 4; 50–51 nos. 1580, 1583; Robert Fleischer, "Doppelte Nemesis-Aphrodite?" in *Festschrift Ekrem Akurgal*, 132 nos. 13–14, 136 (for an interpretation of this last piece as the dual Nemesis of Smyrna, see below p. 264 and n. 69). Regarding the statue of Aphrodite with the head, see Fleischer, "Skulpturenfunde," 425–26 fig. 6; Bammer, Fleischer, and Knibbe, *Führer*, 51–52 no. 1582.

teresting and qualitatively far better statue, modelled after the Aphrodite Capua type, was set up in the Baths of Vedius (see fig. 9)[58]; it is fully clad in chiton and himation, and an octopus lies at her feet. Originally, she balanced a small figure of Eros on her left upper thigh; a small right hand on her left breast and the fragment of a right foot at her left upper thigh testify to this.

Like the images of Aphrodite, images of Eros appear in great number in Ephesos. Numerous statues of Eros were set up in the theater (map no. 26).[59] Outstanding among the sculptures that feature putti engaged in various activities are two monuments of Hadrianic date. A copy of the head of Lysippos's Eros bending the bow, which is from the State Agora (map no. 56), is of good quality. A typologically interesting Eros as *promachos* from Slope House 2 features an early classical pattern of movement. It may have been a member of a group.[60]

The goddess Athena plays a part in the foundation myth of the city of Ephesos. Androklos, the founder of Ephesos, was thought to be a son of Athen's mythical king Kodros; a sanctuary of Athena was installed near the foundation of the first settlement.[61] Athena's sanctuary, which by Strabo's time was situated outside of town, has not yet been located. In Hellenistic and Roman times Athena probably played a minor role; inscriptional evidence regarding her is scanty.[62] Statues of Athena were set up in Roman Ephesos mostly as members of the sculptural decoration of official buildings such as baths or the theater. Because of its good quality, I shall mention here a larger than life-size late Hadrianic replica of a head of the Athena Medici type, which was found immured in one of the Byzantine structures cover-

58. Atalay, *Gewandstatuen*, 29–30 cat. no. 20; 84–86 figs. 47–49.

59. For Eros in Ephesos, see Oster, "Ephesus as a Religious Center," 1696 n. 276c. For statues in the theater, see *IvE* III 724; for statues in the State Agora, see *IvE* VII 3015.

60. Aurenhammer, *Skulpturen 1*, nos. 64 and 65.

61. Regarding Athena's sanctuary, see Athenaios *Deipnosophist.* 8 §361e and Strabo *Geog.* 14.1.21. Regarding Androklos, son of Kodros, see Strabo *Geog.* 14.1.3–23. For Androklos, see below pp. 271–72 and n. 117.

62. See Knibbe, "Ephesos, nicht nur die Stadt der Artemis," 492; Oster, "Ephesus as a Religious Center," 1671. Regarding Athena Pammousos, see *IvE* I 33 lines 10 and 20. Rogers, *Sacred Identity of Ephesos*, 37 n. 111, 180–81 lines 465–67.

ing Slope House 2 (fig. 10).[63] A small Roman variation of another Athena type of the fifth century BCE, the Athena Ince, was found aside the busts of Tiberius and Livia in a niche of apartment 7 in Slope House 2, surely a late Roman arrangement (fig. 11).[64] Only a bronze statuette of Athena, grouped with images of Sarapis and Isis Panthea and a small incense burner, can be cited as evidence of private worship in Slope House 2.[65]

Of the minor goddesses and cult personifications, I shall mention only Nemesis, who was venerated in the Ephesian theater (map no. 26) and stadium (map no. 21), as well as at the Magnesian Gate (map no. 70).[66] An inscription from the third century CE, found in a wall of the northern parodos of the theater, mentions the restoration of a pronaos of the Nemeseion.[67] A statuette of the goddess, excavated in the debris of the scene, is consistent with this evidence.[68] She is

63. Maria Aurenhammer, "Athena Medici in Ephesos," in Kandler, Karwiese, and Pillinger, *Lebendige Altertumswissenschaft*, 212–15, pl. 25.

64. See Vetters, "Vorläufiger Grabungsbericht 1980," 149–50, pl. 28. For the Athena Ince type, see Paulina Karanastassis, "Untersuchungen zur kaiserzeitlichen Plastik in Griechenland II," *MDAI.A* 102 (1987) 360–69. For the portraits of Livia and Tiberius, see Maria Aurenhammer, "Römische Porträts aus Ephesos," *JÖAI* 54 (1983) Beibl. 105–25, 144–46. For the bronze snake, see Vetters, "Vorläufiger Grabungsbericht 1980," 149–50, pls. 24, 27; idem, "Ein weiterer Schlangengott in Ephesos," in Brinna Otto and Friedrich Ehrl, eds., *Echo. Beiträge zur Archäologie des mediterranen und alpinen Raumes. Johannes Trentini zum 80. Geburtstag* (Innsbrucker Beiträge zur Kulturwissenschaft 27; Innsbruck: Institut für Sprachwissenschaft der Universität Innsbruck, 1990) 315–20.

65. See Fleischer, "Skulpturenfunde," Grabungen 461–62 fig. 35. See also below p. 270.

66. See Knibbe, "Ephesos, nicht nur Stadt der Artemis," 499; Oster, "Ephesus as a Religious Center," 1697. See Michael B. Hornum, *Nemesis, the Roman State, and the Games* (EPRO 117; Leiden: Brill, 1993) 46, 49, 58–59, 287–88 for the epigraphical evidence from the theater and the stadium. See Robert Fleischer, "Eine neue Darstellung der doppelten Nemesis von Smyrna," in Margreet B. de Boer and T. A. Edridge, eds., *Hommages à Maarten J. Vermaseren* (EPRO 68; 3 vols.; Leiden: Brill, 1978) 1. 396, pl. 79.2 for the relief from the Magnesian Gate.

67. *IvE* IV 2042; Hornum, *Nemesis*, 287–88 no. 239.

68. This piece is now at the Ephesos Museum in Vienna (I 931). Bernhard Schweitzer, "Dea Nemesis Regina," *JdI* 46 (1931) 208–9 fig. 9. Alfred Bernhard-

equipped with numerous attributes: a griffin and an ell are at her right
side; a cornucopia, globe, and probably a rudder are at her left side;
a turreted crown is apparently on her head. The iconography of the
rudder and crown establish a link with Tyche, and the statue can be
dated to the late second or early third century. In Smyrna, Nemesis
was venerated in Roman times in a dual form. A miniature replica of
this Smyrnaean image, found in Slope House 2,[69] represents the winged
goddesses performing the characteristic gesture with her right hand,
equipped with ell, wheel, and griffin, and clad in archaistic dress.

Most of the male gods of the Greek pantheon receded into the
background in a city dominated by a mighty goddess. Veneration of
Zeus as Patroios on Panayırdağ, however, is attested since the fifth
century BCE.[70] Worship of his different aspects—such as Keraunios,
Hyetios, and Meilichios—is documented by epigraphic and numismatic evidence and in a few votive reliefs.[71] Very few free-standing
images of Zeus have been found in Ephesos; most of these are small
statuettes representing the god in the usual enthroned form.[72] Volker

---

Walcher, in Oberleitner, *Funde aus Ephesos und Samothrake*, 109–10 no.
146. Hornum, *Nemesis*, 41, 49, 65, 79, 88, pl. 17.

69. For the Nemesis of Smyrna, see Fleischer, "Eine neue Darstellung,"
393–96; for the statuette from Slope House 2, see 392–93, 396, pl. 77 (compare also the relief from the Magnesian Gate on p. 396, pl. 79.2). For the
interpretation of the two variations of the Louvre-Naples type from the Fountain of Laecanius Bassus as the dual Nemesis, see above n. 57. Hornum,
Nemesis, 10–14, 64–65, 327–30.

70. *IvE* II 101–4.

71. Knibbe, "Ephesos, nicht nur Stadt der Artemis," 491–92; Oster, "Ephesus
as a Religious Center," 1691–95. Regarding the votive reliefs, for Keraunios,
see Bammer, Fleischer, and Knibbe, *Führer*, 156 no. 45; for Meilichios, see
Hermann Vetters, "Der Schlangengott," in Şahin, *Studien zur Religion und
Kultur Kleinasiens*, 977, pl. 227.6; and *IvE* IV 1241. For the worship of Zeus
Olympios and the Olympieion, see also Stefan Karwiese's and Hilke Thür's
contributions in this volume.

72. See Aurenhammer, *Skulpturen 1*, nos. 2–4. The enthroned Zeus in the
British Museum will be published by Ulrike Muss, who is dealing with sculpture found in the area of the Artemision. See Arthur H. Smith, *A Catalogue
of Sculpture in the Department of Greek and Roman Antiquities* (British Museum;
3 vols.; London: n.p., 1894–1904) 2 no. 1236. Salomon Reinach, *Répertoire
de la statuaire grècque et romaine* (4 vols.; Paris: Leroux, 1904–20) 3. 6 fig.
3.

Strocka has recently grouped the head of Zeus and the colossal figure of a reclining, armed youth from the Flavian reshaping of the Monument of Pollio (map no. 59) and has presented a convincing new interpretation of the reclining youth as the river god Marnas.[73] From numismatic, epigraphic, and archaeological evidence, it is now certain that this image of Marnas, together with a companion sculpture of the river god Klaseas (extant only in fragments),[74] flanked the statue of Zeus. The latter was an imitation of the image of Jupiter Optimus Maximus Capitolinus, which was restored in Rome under Domitian. These three sculptures adorned the terminus of the water conduit fed by these two rivers; this fountain was restored in 92/93 CE by Calvisius Riso (map no. 59).[75]

Apollo Patroios and Hermes were both venerated at Meter's side on Panayirdağ.[76] According to Kreophilos (ca. 400 BCE), cited in Athenaios, Apollo had once pointed out the place of the settlement to the founders of Ephesos, who then installed his sanctuary at the harbor.[77] Apollo appears in several aspects that are testified by epigraphic and numismatic evidence[78]; in a newly discovered metric poem singing his sister's praise, he is named the oracle god and brother of Artemis.[79] Only one extant fragment of a votive relief depicts Apollo at Artemis's side.[80] At the lower end of the sacred way, leading to the Prytaneion, a votive base that Poplius Karsidius Krispinus set up in the second century CE groups the images of Apollo (embodied by

73. Volker Michael Strocka, "Zeus, Marnas und Klaseas. Ephesische Brunnenfiguren von 93 n. Chr.," in Nezih Başgelen and Mihin Lugal, eds., *Festschrift für Jale İnan* (Istanbul: Arkeoloji ve Sanat Yayinlari, 1989) 77–92, pls. 39–40 figs. 1–5 (Marnas), pl. 40 figs. 6–7 (head of Zeus). See also Aurenhammer, *Skulpturen 1*, nos. 1 and 117.

74. See Strocka, "Zeus, Marnas und Klaseas," 81–82, pl. 41 figs. 8–9.

75. Ibid., 78–79, 83–85.

76. *IvE* II 101, 102 (Apollo Patroios); see above p. 255–56.

77. Kreophilos, cited in Athenaios *Deipnosophist.* 8 §361e.

78. Knibbe, "Ephesos, nicht nur die Stadt der Artemis," 493–95; Oster, "Ephesus as a Religious Center," 1668–69.

79. Dieter Knibbe, *Anhang: Orakel Apollons (BerMatÖAI* 1; Vienna: Hölder, 1991) 14–15; idem, Engelmann, and İplikçioğlu, "Neue Inschriften aus Ephesos XII," 130–32 no. 25.

80. Bammer, Fleischer, and Knibbe, *Führer*, 158 no. 245.

tripod and omphalos) and Hermes.[81] The free-standing Roman images of both gods occur mainly as decoration of public buildings: the head of Hermes from the Harbor Gymnasium (map no. 9),[82] for example, modelled after Polykleitos's Herakles, according to Roman taste of the second century CE, or copies of Hellenistic Apollo types.[83] In addition, the Roman city was adorned with the usual number of simple and double herms.[84]

Epigraphic evidence attested that a sanctuary of Asklepios was already extant in early Hellenistic times. Votives for Asklepios and Hygieia are common.[85] A votive relief found in an unknown location groups the two healing gods with Kybele, who is identified by her extant attributes, the lion and tympanum.[86] Under Nero's reign, the rich freedman Stertinius Orpex, together with his daughter, donated statues of Asklepios, Hygieia, and Hypnos "in the gymnasium" (ἐν τῷ γυμνασίῳ).[87] Statues of Asklepios and Hygieia have survived as decoration of baths: in the main hall of the Vedius Gymnasium (map no. 19), an under life-size Asklepios was grouped with an over life-size statue of Hygieia modelled after the Sappho type,[88] a combination which was not unusual in Roman times. In Ephesian private

81. Franz Miltner, "XXI. vorläufiger Bericht über die Ausgrabungen in Ephesos," *JÖAI* 43 (1956–58) Beibl. 38–40 figs. 21–24; *IvE* IV 1248.

82. Aurenhammer, *Skulpturen 1*, no. 7 and photograph on the cover.

83. See, for example, ibid., no. 11 (Apollo from Daphne), no. 13 (Apollo from Cyrene).

84. See, as a famous example, the copy of Alkamenes' Hermes from the Vedius Baths, which is now in İzmir. Josef Keil, "XIV. vorläufiger Bericht ü ber die Ausgrabungen von Ephesos," *JÖAI* 25 (1929) Beibl. 31–32. Camillo Praschniker, "Der Hermes des Alkamenes in Ephesos," *JÖAI* 29 (1935) 23–31. Dietrich Willers, "Zum Hermes Propylaios des Alkamenes," *JdI* 82 (1967) 39–40, 42–44 no. 1 figs. 1–4. For the barrier of herms at the fountain in the peristyle of the domus in Slope House 1, see Bammer, Fleischer, and Knibbe, *Führer*, 67–68 no. 1575; Hermann Vetters, "Zur Baugeschichte der Hanghäuser," in Volker Michael Strocka, *Die Wandmalerei der Hanghäuser in Ephesos* (*FiE* 8.1; 2 vols.; Vienna: ÖAW, 1977) 17 fig. 17.

85. Knibbe, "Ephesos, nicht nur die Stadt der Artemis," 493; Oster, "Ephesus as a Religious Center," 1669–70.

86. Selçuk, Efes Müzesi 253.

87. *IvE* IV 2113.

88. These statues are new in the museum in İzmir. Manderscheid, *Die Skulpturenausstattung*, 45, 89 cat. nos. 175 and 176.

quarters a few small images of Hygieia were found, as well as miniature Asklepios statuettes of Hellenistic and Roman date, mostly in the popular Giustini type.[89] Dionysos clearly dominated the male part of the Ephesian pantheon, even before Roman times[90]; the festival of the Dionysia is attested since the late classical or early Hellenistic age. The *katagogia*, festival of the return, is described in the *Acts of Timothy*, who was the first Ephesian bishop and who may have been a martyr.[91] Sanctuaries of Dionysos must have been abundant in and around Ephesos. One was situated in the quarter of the Koressitai; in Roman times an association (guild) of σακηφόροι μύσται ("sack-bearing initiates") assembled there.[92] Other sanctuaries were installed out of town, such as the place of worship for Dionysos Phleus—where he was venerated with Demeter πρὸ πόλεως ("before the city"); Dionysos Oreiogyadon; and Dionysos Oreios Bakchios πρὸ πόλεως.[93] The Embolos was a center of the worship of Dionysos, as Helmut Engelmann has recently demonstrated.[94] Inscriptions in Slope House 2 refer to the mountain-dwelling god. In an inscription in the peristyle court of luxurious apartment 6, the owner, C. Flavius Furius Aptus, presented himself as

89. See Aurenhammer, *Skulpturen 1*, nos. 17–22, 24–29 for small Asklepios statuettes. The miniature statuettes of Hygieia will be published in Aurenhammer, *Skulpturen 2*. For a statue of Hygieia from the East Gymnasium, see Manderscheid, *Die Skulpturenausstattung*, 91 cat. no. 192.

90. See Knibbe, "Ephesos, nicht nur die Stadt der Artemis," 495–96; Oster, "Ephesus as a Religious Center," 1673–76.

91. Regarding the Dionysia, see Rudolf Heberdey, "Inschriften," in idem, Niemann, and Wilberg, *Theater*, 99 no. 3. Regarding the *Acts of Timothy* and the *katagogia*, see Richard C. Kukula, *Literarische Zeugnisse über den Artemistempel* (*FiE* 1; Vienna: Hölder 1906) 257–58 no. 272; and Josef Keil, "Zum Martyrium des heiligen Timotheus in Ephesos," *JÖAI* 29 (1935) 82–92. For further literature concerning the *Acta S. Timothei*, see Oster, "Ephesus as a Religious Center," 1674–75 n. 98.

92. *IvE* II 293.

93. Regarding Dionysos Phleus, see Reinhold Merkelbach, *Die Hirten des Dionysos* (Stuttgart: Teubner, 1988) 19–20 nn. 16, 17. Regarding Dionysos Oreiogyadon, see *IvE* II 106; and Helmut Engelmann, "Statue und Standort," in *Festschrift für Arthur Betz* (Vienna: Gesellschaft für Klassische Archäologie, 1985) 252 and n. 6. For Dionysos Oreios Bakchios, see below n. 95.

94. Engelmann, "Statue und Standort," 251–54.

venerator of Dionysos Oreios Bakchios; he also set up a statuette of the god, which is now extant only in fragments.[95] A central point of the quarter, the street corner of Marble Street and Curetes Street (map nos. 27, 29), was marked by a dionysiac statue group with a satyr, which was set up in Flavian times.[96] Generally, Dionysiac elements in the decoration of the private and public buildings abound along Curetes Street. The worshippers of Dionysos rushed down from Bülbüldağ (Lepre Akte) and swept Curetes Street where, in early Christian times, Bishop Timothy confronted them "in the middle of the Embolos."[97]

The majority of Dionysiac sculptures features the god alone or grouped with members of his thiasos—such as the Dionysos of the Fountain of Trajan (map no. 49), modelled in late Antonine fashion after an early classical Apollo type,[98] or a common group with Dionysos and a satyr—such as an element of the decoration of the late antique fountain house in front of the stadium (map no. 21).[99] Dionysos's popularity is apparent, too, in the wealth of table legs and herm busts featuring dionysiac motifs; many of these adorn the apartments of Slope House 2.[100] Standing out from these monuments, which all follow common sculptural types, is an apparently singular Dionysos statue, which is part of the primary decoration of the Fountain of Trajan (the aforementioned naked Dionysos was added to the fountain two decades later).[101] The god appears here richly clad in an actor's long-sleeved dress, a long chiton, and pardalis, holding a shawl-like himation and the thyrsos in his left arm. His facial features are ef-

95. *IvE* IV 1267. See Hermann Vetters, "Vorläufiger Grabungsbericht 1979," 259 fig. 18. For the stucco ceiling of the annex to the basilica in this flat, which features Dionysiac motifs, see also idem, "Ein Stuckraum in Ephesos," in Alzinger and Neeb, *Pro Arte Antiqua*, 2. 335–39.

96. Engelmann, "Statue und Standort," 249–51, 252–53; *IvE* II 507.

97. See Keil, "Zum Martyrium," 87–92; Engelmann, "Statue und Standort," 252 n. 14.

98. Aurenhammer, *Skulpturen 1*, no. 41.

99. Ibid., no. 46.

100. See, for example, the bronze table legs adorned with figures of young satyrs in Friederike Harl-Schaller, "Figürliche Gerät-und Möbelfüße," *JÖAI* 51 (1976/77) 45, 46 figs. 1–4, 47, 51, 55 cat. no. A IV 24. Compare the table legs with figures of Dionysos in Bammer, Fleischer, and Knibbe, *Führer*, 9–10 no. 1552; 138 no. 7.

101. Aurenhammer, *Skulpturen 1*, no. 31.

feminate and resemble a matron's. The Roman sculptor followed Hellenistic trends in the statue's proportions and elaborate dress.

One of the Ephesian Dionysiac mysteries also incorporated the worship of Pan; according to myth, he, too, nourished Dionysos.[102] Achilles Tatius mentions a grotto with a syrinx behind the Artemision, a hint of Pan's presence.[103] A terra-cotta of the dancing Pan from John T. Wood's excavation may testify to an early period of the cult in Ephesos.[104] An early imperial votive block, unearthed by the English excavators, features Pan as god of war.[105] The extant free-standing images of Pan, which date to the Roman period, are all decorative elements that probably adorned public buildings. For example, the group in the Kunsthistorisches Museum in Vienna[106] shows Pan with the infant Dionysos, a rare combination in such Roman kourotrophos groups. Dionysos's other companions were also favorites in the sculptural decoration of public buildings; examples include the original Flavian head of a satyr crowned by a stone pine wreath, which is from the Scholastikia Baths (map no. 40), and a reclining satyr modelled after famous motifs of Pergamene sculpture, which is from the Fountain of Trajan.[107] The figure of a silenus acted as support in the construction of the skene of the Odeion (map no. 63), balancing a basket on his head as *kistaphoros* ("bearer of the sacred basket") or *liknophoros* ("bearer of the winnowing fan").[108] The statue's support features interesting details: crowning the bulging vessel on top of the tripod is a *liknon*-shaped basket containing a phallos and a crescent; these last items were also formed into amulets.

In this volume, James Walters elaborates the rich evidence for the cult of Egyptian gods in Ephesos.[109] Their popularity climaxed in the

102. *IvE* V 1600 line 48. For the worship of Pan in Ephesos, see Oster, "Ephesus as a Religious Center," 1697 n. 288.

103. Achilles Tatius *Leucippe et Clitophon* 8.6.

104. Klaus Tuchelt, "Pan und Pankult in Kleinasien," *IstMit* 19–20 (1969–70) 225, 233 no. 6.

105. Ibid., 234 no. 17, 226, pl. 43.3.

106. Aurenhammer, *Skulpturen 1*, no. 58.

107. For the head of a satyr, see ibid., no. 49; for the reclining satyr, see no. 51.

108. Ibid., no. 56.

109. See James Walters's contribution in this volume. Knibbe, "Ephesos, nicht nur die Stadt der Artemis," 500–501; Günther Hölbl, *Zeugnisse ägyptischer*

second and third centuries CE, a period in which most of their images, made of marble and bronze, were produced. As mentioned in the first part of this paper, bronze statuettes of Sarapis and Isis Panthea, together with a statuette of Athena and an incense burner, formed a kind of lararium in Slope House 2.[110] This Sarapis bronze, like the Sarapis of black stone in the Ephesos Museum in Vienna, follows the typical enthroned image of Sarapis in Alexandria.[111] The statuette in Vienna is unfinished, as details in the workmanship show. The spherical attribute at the god's right side may be interpreted as a globe; normally, Sarapis is accompanied by Kerberos in this type. The Isis bronze represents a typically syncretistic image of the universal goddess, mingling symbols of Isis, Artemis, Athena, and Nike.[112]

Two torsos clad in a typical dress of Isis and her servants—the so-called palla, tied in knots—have been found in Ephesos, one in the area of the *Felsspalttempel* ("rock-crack temple"; map no. 16).[113] These images should probably be interpreted as the goddess herself. In a multibanded Roman relief,[114] Isis appears in the same dress and is accompanied by Harpokrates, a fragmentary female goddess with paredros—probably Aphrodite and Eros—and a Kybele featuring syncretistic symbols.

Two free-standing sculptures of Harpokrates represent the Greco-Roman type, which assimilates the iconography of Eros. The small head from the western gate of the Tetragonos Agora[115] (map no. 30)

Religionsvorstellungen für Ephesos (EPRO 73; Leiden: Brill, 1978); Oster, "Ephesus as a Religious Center," 1677–81.

110. See above p. 263 and n. 65.

111. For the Sarapis bronze, see Fleischer, "Skulpturenfunde," 460–61 fig. 34; Hölbl, *Zeugnisse*, 64–65, pl. 8.2. For the black stone of Sarapis, see Aurenhammer, *Skulpturen 1*, no. 79.

112. For the Isis bronze, see Fleischer, "Skulpturenfunde," 459–60 fig. 33; Hölbl, *Zeugnisse*, 59–64, pl. 8.1a, b.

113. Selçuk, Efes Müzesi 96 (from the rock-crack temple). For this type of sculpture, see Johannes Eingartner, *Isis und ihre Dienerinnen in der Kunst der römischen Kaiserzeit* (Mnemosyne suppl. 115; Leiden: Brill, 1991) 8–25. For the rock-crack temple, see Karwiese, "Koressos," 2. 215–19.

114. Vermaseren, *Corpus Cultus Cybelae*, vol. 1, no. 633, pl. 135.

115. Aurenhammer, *Skulpturen 1*, no. 81 (now in Vienna).

clearly portrays the god performing the characteristic gesture, with his fingertip on his lower lip. A sun disk is attached to his mop of hair, alluding to Harpokrates as sun god. Another puttolike god,[116] part of the decoration of the late antique fountain house, is equipped with a mask with a spout conveying water and a crocodile dangling from his right hand; he may represent Harpokrates as conqueror of crocodiles.

Of the Ephesian heroes, I shall discuss only Androklos, the mythical founder of the city.[117] In her paper, Hilke Thür has unfolded a fascinating thesis of a heroon for the mythical founder in the center of the city (map no. 43).[118] A founding myth presents Androklos as a boar hunter, and this image of him can be found on the late antique frieze of the so-called Temple of Hadrian (map no. 41) and on Ephesian coins minted beginning with Hadrian's reign.[119] The monuments feature the hero grouped with the boar, as well as alone, brandishing a spear and accompanied by a dog. Two free-standing sculptures of hunters, both elements of the decoration of public buildings, have also been associated with Androklos. The hunter of the Fountain of Trajan,[120] which is part of the original decoration of the building, is modelled after the famous Meleager type of Skopas (fourth century BCE). The other figure of a hunter, which was set up in the main room of the Vedius Baths, was clearly part of a boar-hunting group; extant are the hunter himself, the figure of a dog attached to the trunk support, and a fragment of a dog's paw on the boar's bristles.[121] A second trunk support found nearby may have belonged to the same group; the

116. See ibid., no. 82.

117. Regarding Androklos, see Oster, "Ephesus as a Religious Center," 1682–84; and Hilke Thür's contribution in this volume. Regarding his iconography, see Marie-Louise Bernhard, "Androklos," *LIMC* 1 (1981) 765–67.

118. See Thür's contribution in this volume.

119. For the frieze, see Fleischer, "Fries des Hadrianstempels," 25 fig. 14 A4, 26, 35 (boar hunt) and 27 fig. 17 D6, 35–36, 45–50 (Androklos in the frieze of the gods). Bernhard, "Androklos," 765 nos. 2, 3. For the coins, see Stefan Karwiese, "Ephesos C," *PWSup* 12 (1970) 334–35, 340, 346; Bernhard, "Androklos," 765 nos. 2, 3.

120. Aurenhammer, *Skulpturen 1*, no. 104.

121. Ibid., no. 105. Bernhard, "Androklos," 766 no. 7.

group was longer than the intercolumnar space of the main room of the baths.[122] Androklos's torso is modelled after an early classical *promachos* type, while the head is a typical Roman creation, calling to mind but not reproducing accurately Antinoos's portrait.[123] This is a fine example of the popular midsecond-century CE combination of a classicist ideal torso combined with a head inspired by Antinoos's portrait. This *ktistes* ("founder") figure, moreover, is linked to P. Vedius Antoninus, the sponsor of the baths, who was celebrated as "founder of the city."[124] Apart from the images of boars, which hint at Androklos, literary and epigraphical evidence speaks of two other sculptures of him. Thür deals with these in her paper: one was set up in the center of the city; the other, a sculpture of an armored man, was set on top of the hero's *mnema* ("monument or tomb").[125] Mention of the figure of Androklos amid the crowded, multifigured frieze of gods on the so-called Temple of Hadrian is a fitting conclusion to this survey of Ephesian gods and heroes.[126] In this frieze, which is dated to the end of classical antiquity, the whole Ephesian pagan pantheon is once more presented in a row of stereotyped frontal figures.

In conclusion, I want to emphasize some of the problems that one must tackle when studying ideal sculpture found in Ephesos. The scholar is confronted with a wide range of material, in terms of the workmanship, chronology, function, and setting of the sculptures. Because of the long period of use of private quarters and public buildings in Ephesos and due to the reshaping of the town in late Roman times, many sculptures were added to the ones that had been

122. See Aurenhammer, *Skulpturen 1*, 128 no. 105. This trunk support is mentioned in the excavation diary of 1927; it is probably identical with a trunk found in the Vedius Baths, which is now in İzmir (Basmane Müzesi 252).

123. Aurenhammer, *Skulpturen 1*, 128, pl. 74, a, b.

124. Regarding P. Vedius Antoninus, see *IvE* III 727; IV 2065; VII 3075.

125. See Hilke Thür's contribution in this volume. Pausanias (7.2.8–9) mentioned Androklos's *mnema* with an armored man on top. See Engelmann and Knibbe, "Aus ephesischen Skizzenbüchern," 47 no. 81; and *IvE* II 501; III 647 (statue of Androklos in the center of the city).

126. See Fleischer, "Fries des Hadrianstempels," 27 fig. 17 D6, 35–36, 45, 50. Bernhard, "Androklos," 765 no. 4.

set up earlier, and many were reused in a new context. As examples I want to call to mind the statue of the striding Artemis as huntress in Slope House 2, which is a case of multiple reuse (fig. 2),[127] and the late Roman arrangement of the portraits of Tiberius and Livia, the bronze snake, and a statuette of Athena (fig. 11) in a niche of Slope House 2.[128] With regard to the public buildings, one recalls the naked Dionysos that was added to the richly clad one in the Fountain of Trajan.[129] This reuse of sculpture of course affects the question of original decoration programs. Several studies have already dealt with the sculptural decoration of Ephesian public buildings, focusing on the original decoration.[130] Checking the early excavation reports has brought to light further information about the exact position of some of the statues set up in the baths. Similar studies should be applied to the sculptural programs of all the fountains (especially the Fountain of C. Laecanius Bassus, which is particularly rich),[131] the theater, and the Slope Houses. The latter two present a further problem: due to the large amount of debris piled high on the terraces, the exact position of the free-standing sculpture in the Slope Houses can rarely be reconstructed. I consider the setting of sculpture to be of great importance, but for the systematic catalogue as well as for this study, I have nevertheless chosen to classify according to iconography, owing

127. See above pp. 254–55 and fig. 2.
128. See above p. 263 and n. 64.
129. See above p. 268 and nn. 98 and 101. For the sculptural program of Fountain of Trajan, see Robert Fleischer, "Zwei eklektische Statuen aus Ephesos," in Alzinger and Neeb, *Pro Arte Antiqua*, 1. 123–24.
130. See Manderscheid, *Die Skulpturenausstattung*, 44–45, 86–88 cat. nos. 155–71 (Harbor Gymnasium), 88–91 cat. nos.173–91 (Vedius Baths), 91–93 cat. nos.192–206 (East Gymnasium). For further studies concerning the sculptural programs of Ephesian public buildings, see Fleischer, "Zwei eklektische Statuen," 123–24; and Werner Jobst, "Ein spätantiker Strassenbrunnen in Ephesos," in Otto Feld and Urs Peschlow, eds., *Studien zur spätantiken und byzantinischen Kunst, Friedrich W. Deichmann gewidmet* (3 vols.; Römisch-Germanisches Zentralmuseum Monographien 10.1; Bonn: R. Habelt, 1986) 1. 57–60 (late antique fountain).
131. See Fossel and Langmann, "Das Nymphaeum des C. Laecanius Bassus," 301–10 (Fountain of Bassus; see Fleischer, "Skulpturenfunde," 421–32, for the sculptures found there).

to the extensive reuse of sculpture and the large number of sculptures for which there is no record of the original find spot. Finally, with regard to the workmanship of ideal sculpture found in Ephesos, one encounters a wide range of material, from rather unpretentious monuments set up for private or public worship to high-quality Roman replicas of Greek prototypes set up in private quarters and public buildings. An "Ephesian style" can be detected in the reliefs of Meter which are characteristic to Ephesos and its surroundings.[132] The small statuettes of Kybele and Hekate are also typical for this area, as demonstrated by similar examples that one finds in the museum in İzmir.[133] For large-scale Roman copies of Greek ideal sculpture, special workshops were obviously engaged for the original sculptural decoration of public buildings, as documented by the homogenous style of sculptural programs, such as the sea thiasos of the Fountain of C. Laecanius Bassus.[134] An overall view of the ideal sculpture found in Ephesos compared with the Roman portraits produced there will provide more information on both the style and the workshops where these sculptures were produced. A future project will deal with the analysis of marbles used for Ephesian sculptures.

132. See above pp. 255–56.
133. Regarding the Hekataia, compare Anabolu, "Izmir arkeoloji müzesi'nin deposunda bulunan yedi hekataion," 329–35, figs. 1–10.
134. See Fleischer, "Skulpturenfunde," 421–24; and Aurenhammer, *Skulpturen 1*, nos. 84–85, 88–92.

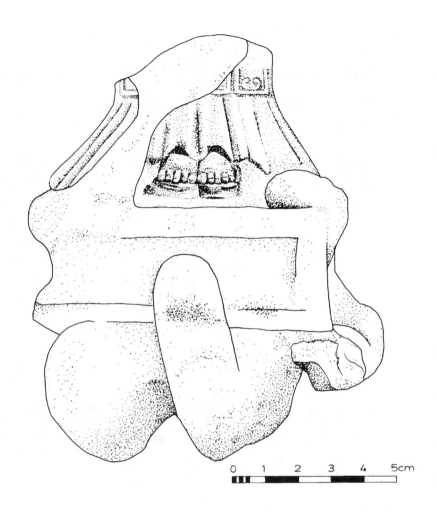

Fragment of a hand holding a statuette of Artemis
Ephesia from Slope House 2. *Drawing by Maria
Aurenhammer and Isabella Benda.*

FIGURE 2
Striding Artemis from Slope House 2.
Photo Franz Xaver Prascsaits.

FIGURE 3
Eclectic Artemis from Slope House 2.
*Photo Österreichisches
Archäologisches Institut.*

F I G U R E   4   Kybele from the southern nympheion of the State Agora.
Photo Thomas Römer.

F I G U R E   5   Kybele idol from the Tetragonos Agora.
Photo Maria Aurenhammer.

FIGURE 6   Archaistic Hekataion from Slope House 2.
                  Photo Thomas Römer.

FIGURE 7   Head of miniature Hekate herm.
                  Photo Maria Aurenhammer.

FIGURE 8   Aphrodite as fountain sculpture from Slope House 2.
Photo Thomas Römer.

FIGURE 9   Aphrodite with Eros from the Vedius Baths.
Photo Erol Atalay.

FIGURE 10   Head of Athena Medici. *Photo Ulrike Outschar.*

FIGURE 11   Athena statuette from Slope House 2.
Photo Ulrike Outschar.

Egyptian Religions in Ephesos

James C. Walters
Hanover, NH

Dieter Knibbe is certainly correct in his rather provocative title of a 1978 essay, "Ephesos—Not Only the City of Artemis: The 'Other' Ephesian Gods," that Artemis was not the only deity in Ephesos.[1] Updating the earlier survey of Ephesian deities by Ludwig Bürchner,[2] Knibbe presents evidence for Meter Oreia, Zeus, Athena, Aphrodite, Asklepios, Apollo, Hephaistos, Dionysos, Demeter, Hestia and the Prytaneion deities, Leto, Nemesis, Sarapis, Isis, Tyche, and Poseidon, not including Judaism, Christianity, and imperial and hero cults. Although with less significance or attestation, to these could be added Theoi Pantes, the Kabiroi, Enedra, Ge Karpophoros, Hekate, Herakles, Theos Hypsistos, Pan, Pluto, Concordia, Pion the mountain god, and several river deities.[3] If one excludes local indigenous cults, traditional Greek and Roman cults, the imperial cult, Judaism, and Christianity, the worship of Isis and Sarapis remain the

1. Knibbe, "Ephesos, nicht nur die Stadt der Artemis," 2. 489–503.
2. Ludwig Bürchner, "Ephesos," PW 5 (1905) 2773–822.
3. See Dieter Knibbe, "Ephesos: A. Historisch-epigraphischer Teil," PWSup 12 (1970) 281–87, and Oster, "Ephesus as a Religious Center, 1662–1728.

only well-attested foreign religions in Ephesos. This prompted Richard Oster to write:

> Prominent Syrian and Phrygian deities and the Mithraic cults exerted virtually no influence in the [imperial] period. This dearth of eastern cults in Ephesus vividly points out the fact that even though Ephesus was an eastern city geographically, its religious ethos was not. Unlike Rome, it apparently did not drink heavily from the Orontes.[4]

Extant evidence makes it appear that Christianity and the Egyptian cults were the only religions from the East—even the only foreign religions depending on how one defines foreign—that made significant inroads into the religious life of Ephesos.

The focus of this article will be the Egyptian cults in Ephesos. Contemporary analyses of Egyptian cultic materials are greatly indebted to a number of important publications that have appeared in the past quarter century. Ladislaus Vidman's important catalogue of Isis and Sarapis inscriptions was published in 1969.[5] In the following year, Vidman published an analysis of these cults based on the epigraphical materials.[6] In the early 1970s, several broad-based investigations of Egyptian religions appeared in the *Études préliminaires aux religions orientales dans l'empire Romain* series, which Maarten Josef Vermaseren edited: Regina Salditt-Trappmann's study of the temples of the Egyptian gods in Greece and western Asia Minor[7]; Wilhelm Hornbostel's study of Sarapis[8]; G. J. F. Kater-Sibbes' catalogue of Sarapis monuments[9]; and Françoise Dunand's study of the Isis cult.[10] Each of these works involves the interpretation and distil-

4. Oster, "Ephesus as a Religious Center," 1727.

5. Ladislaus Vidman, *Sylloge inscriptionum religionis Isiacae et Sarapiacae* (Berlin: de Gruyter, 1969).

6. Ladislaus Vidman, *Isis und Sarapis bei den Griechen und Römern* (Berlin: de Gruyter, 1970).

7. Regina Salditt-Trappmann, *Temple der ägyptischen Götter in Griechenland und an der Westküste Kleinasiens* (EPRO 15; Leiden: Brill, 1970).

8. Wilhelm Hornbostel, *Sarapis* (EPRO 32; Leiden: Brill, 1973).

9. G. J. F. Kater-Sibbes, *Preliminary Catalogue of Sarapis Monuments* (EPRO 36; Leiden: Brill, 1975).

10. Françoise Dunand, *Le culte d'Isis dans le bassin oriental de la Méditerrané* (EPRO 26; Leiden: Brill, 1973).

lation of a huge volume of evidence from a multitude of sites, scattered over large geographical areas and spanning several centuries. The benefits of the kind of comparative work represented by such volumes is indisputable; the accuracy of their comparisons and those of their successors, however, depends to a great extent on local site work and publications that are based more narrowly on individual sites. Data of this kind provide the essential parameters for grouping evidence and constructing accurate analogies.[11]

Two notable studies that have focused solely on the Egyptian materials from Ephesos are Josef Keil's "Denkmäler des Sarapiskultes in Ephesos,"[12] and Günther Hölbl's *Zeugnisse ägyptischer Religions-vorstellungen für Ephesus*.[13] Hölbl's monograph incorporates the evidence and results of previous studies on Ephesos as well as broader publications like those noted above.

Building on these studies, this article will present the evidence for Egyptian cultic activity in Ephesos, describe and weigh evidence for the complexes that have been commonly identified as Egyptian temples, and conclude by discussing briefly the convergence of the spread of Egyptian religions in Ephesos with that of Christianity.

Evidence of Egyptian Cultic Activity

Isolated artifacts bear witness to Egyptian presence in Ephesos as early as the seventh century BCE.[14] These objects, however, tell us more about the influence of Egyptian art than they do about the prac-

---

11. For a catalogue of publications where the majority of the Ephesian materials have appeared, see Oster, "Ephesus as a Religious Center," 1662 n. 2. For a fuller bibliography of Ephesian studies, see idem, *A Bibliography of Ancient Ephesus* (ATLA Bibliography Series 19; Metuchen, NJ: Scarecrow, 1987).

12. Josef Keil, "Denkmäler des Sarapiskultes in Ephesos," *AnzWien* 91 (1954) 217–29.

13. Günther Hölbl, *Zeugnisse ägyptischer Religionsvorstellungen für Ephesus* (EPRO 73; Leiden: Brill, 1978).

14. The bulk of these materials were foundation deposits at the Artemision. Their dating has been difficult. Recent excavations, however, indicate that they belong to the Kroisos temple (Wilhelm Alzinger, "Ephesos Archäologischer Teil," PWSup 12 [1970] 1657).

tice of Egyptian religion in Ephesos.[15] It is not until the Hellenistic period that evidence of widespread Egyptian religious activity appears in Asia Minor and Ephesos.[16]

In the third century BCE, through both commercial relations and military power, Egypt extended her influence into the islands and cities of western and southwestern Asia Minor. Along with Egypt's merchant and military presence came the worship of its gods. Ephesian evidence for this emerging religious presence comes from an inscription dated to the first half of the third century BCE. Constructed partly of stone, the alter was dedicated to "Sarapis, Isis, Anubis, temple-sharing gods," (Σαράπ[ιδι], Ἴσιδι, Ἀνούβιδι, Θεοῖς συννάοι) and was set up "according to a command" (κατὰ πρόσταγμα). If Θεοῖς συννάοις is read as an appositive, as seems preferable, the dedication is to Sarapis, Isis, and Anubis, who are identified as Θεοὶ συννάοι.[17] The formula κατὰ πρόσταγμα is most common in dedications to Isis and Sarapis and reflects the role of dreams in the cults—the person making the dedication was commanded to do so in a dream—as well as the universal power and lordship that worshippers ascribed to these deities.[18] Although neither the text of the inscription nor its association with an altar is sufficient evidence for postulating a temple for the Egyptian gods in Ephesos, it does establish their worship in the city early in the Hellenistic period.

15. Hölbl, *Zeugnisse*, 5. On the phenomenon of Egyptian influence in this period in Ephesos and beyond, see Walter Burkert, *The Orientalizing Revolution* (Cambridge, MA: Harvard University Press, 1992) 53–54.

16. A 12 cm tall statuette of Harpokrates, however, taken from sarcophagus 9 in the late-archaic necropolis under the State Agora, may indicate religious activity prior to the Hellenistic period. It was found with Attic ceramic materials of the early fifth century BCE (Gerhard Langmann, "Eine spätarchaische Nekropole unter dem Staatsmarkt," *JÖAI* 48 [1967] Beibl. 117–20).

17. *IvE* IV 1231(= Vidman, *Sylloge*, 296). On the combination of Sarapis, Isis, and Anubis, see Dunand, *Le cultes d'Isis*, 3. 335; Arthur Darby Nock, "ΣΥΝΝΑΟΣ ΘΕΟΣ," in idem, *Essays on Religion and the Ancient World* (2 vols.; ed. Zeph Stewart; Oxford: Clarendon, 1972) 1. 202–51; and Vincent Tran Tam Tinh, "État des études iconographiques relatives à Isis, Sérapis et Sunnaoi Theoi," *ANRW* 2.17.3 (1984) 1710–38.

18. Nock, "Studies in the Graeco-Roman Beliefs of the Empire," in idem, *Essays*, 1. 45.

The introduction of the Egyptian cults in Asia Minor coincides with the extension of Egyptian rule in the region beginning with Ptolemy I Soter in 309 BCE.[19] Although many of the cities he acquired were subsequently lost to Demetrios Poliorketes, much of the territory was subsequently regained. According to Theokritos, the son of Ptolemy I, Ptolemy Philadelphos, ruled over "all the Pamphylians and the spear-bearing Cilicians, the Lycians, the Carians, lovers of war, and the islands of the Cyclades."[20] Ptolemy Philadelphos appointed a Ptolemaic governor over Ephesos who was either a son of Arsinoë II and Lysimachos, or an illegitimate son of Philadelphos.[21] His rule of Ephesos ended when he allied himself with Timarkos, the tyrant of Miletos, against Philadelphos and was murdered by his own soldiers. This allowed Antiochos II to intervene and annex Ephesos.[22] During the third Syrian war between Seleukos II and his brother Antiochos Hierax (ca. 240 BCE), however, Ephesos was once again under Ptolemaic control. The transfer back to Ptolemaic rule may have occurred when Sophron, who commanded the Egyptian fleet at the battle of Andros, abandoned the city to the generals of Ptolemy III Euergetes.[23] A decree of Athens, passed soon after 222, praised Ephesos for its "good will" (εὔνοια) to the "Athenians and King Ptolemy" and coins of Berenike, wife of Ptolemy III, were issued at Ephesos.[24] According to Polybios, Ephesos still had an

---

19. David Magie, "Egyptian Deities in Asia Minor in Inscriptions and on Coins," *AJA* 57 (1953) 163.

20. Theocritus 17.88–89; my translation.

21. Evidence of Egyptian cultic activity in Ephesos during the rule of Philadelphos is found in a recent revision of an Ephesian inscription (*IvE* II 199) dedicated to the ruler, his wife Arsinoë, and Sarapis:

[Βασιλεῖ Πτ]ολεμαίῳ [ι]	To [King Pt]olemy
[Βασιλί]σσηι Ἀρσι[νόηι]	To [Que]en Arsi[noë]
[Σ]αράπι Δικαι[ ]	To [S]arapis the just[ ]
[ ].[ ]	[ ].[ ]

The name(s) of the person(s) making the dedication would have begun on the third line after Δικαι. The revision is published in *JÖAI* 59 (1989) 235.

22. Hölbl, *Zeugnisse*, 18.

23. Magie, *Roman Rule*, 2. 936.

24. Hölbl, *Zeugnisse*, 18.

Egyptian garrison in 221 and the city remained Ptolemaic until 197 BCE when Antiochos III seized control of it.[25]

Although the expansion of Egyptian cults in the region coincides with the extension of Egypt's political influence, the relationship be-tween the two has been debated. At one time the dominant interpreta-tion was that the Ptolemaic rulers sponsored the spread of the Egyptian cults—especially Sarapis as the official cult of the Ptolemies—in the territories it acquired by using their political leverage.[26] The so-called "imperialistic theory," however, is seldom advanced in contemporary studies.[27] Research has shown that Egyptian cults were no more popu-lar in territories controlled by the Ptolemies than elsewhere. For ex-ample, in Rhodes the evidence for the Egyptian cults is both early and plentiful, even though the island was never politically dependent on Egypt. Because Rhodes and Egypt were the two great maritime powers in the Aegean in the third century BCE, close interaction was inevi-table. Spontaneous expansion, which commerce and trade facilitated, coupled with the related desire of cities to show friendliness to the Ptolemies—often communicated through adopting the Alexandrian de-ity—accounts for the wide dissemination of the Egyptian cults in the Aegean basin in the third century BCE.[28]

Two additional inscriptions and a water clock that was used to time cultic activities have also been put forward as evidence for

25. Polybios 5.35.2.

26. P. M. Fraser notes ("Two Studies on the Cult of Sarapis in the Helle-nistic World," *Opuscula Atheniensia* 3 [1960] 20) that this view was the stan-dard textbook interpretation from Lafaye (1884) to Nilsson (1950). Its proponents also included Rusch, Cumont, Weinrich, Wilchen, and Kornemann.

27. Pierre Roussel (*Les cultes égyptiens à Délos* [Nancy: n.p., 1915]) persistently argued against the imperialistic interpretation.

28. Fraser ("Two Studies," 32, 37, 49) presents evidence from the Aegean islands and Asia Minor as well as other territories stretching from the main-land of Greece to Syria. Thomas A. Brady (*The Reception of the Egyptian Cults by the Greeks* [Columbia: University of Missouri Press, 1935]) broad-ened the basis of the imperialistic theory but his explanation still depends substantially on the sponsorship of the Ptolemaic rulers. Arthur Darby Nock (*Conversion* [Oxford: Oxford University Press, 1933] 54–55) and Magie ("Egyp-tian Deities in Asia Minor," 170–71) read the evidence more like Fraser. Nock's synopsis (*Conversion*, 54) reflects the current consensus: "The intro-duction of the cult [of Sarapis] into a city was no doubt generally due to

Egyptian cult activity in Ephesos during the Hellenistic period. The first, a recently published inscription, is found on a white marble stele that was set up for Sarapis and Isis:[29]

Σαράπιδι ῎Ισιδι	To Sarapis, Isis
Φιλιστίων	Philistion
᾿Αρτεμιδώρου	son of Artemidoros
ἀνέθηκε	erected it

The second, a fragment of a building inscription dated to the period of Ptolemaic rule, refers to the construction of a hieron (ἱερό[ν]), a naos (νάος), and a temenos (τέμενος) built "according to the command of God."[30] Because the formulas "according to a command" (κατὰ πρόσταγμα) and "having been commanded by God" (τοῦ θεοῦ προστάξαντος) are especially typical of dedications to Sarapis and Isis, this inscription may provide evidence of a temple for the Egyptian gods in Ephesos during the Hellenistic period. The association of the inscription with the Egyptian cults, however, is not certain because the formulas also appear in dedications to other deities.[31]

In excavations of the Tetragonos Agora in Ephesos, fragments of an Egyptian water clock were unearthed.[32] The water clock, along with other debris, was used as fill during the Roman renovation of the area in the last half of the first century CE. Analysis of the clock fragments and correlations with the evolution of the Egyptian calen-

---

immigrants. . . sometimes to the action of the city. This action has been thought to be inspired by political considerations, in fact by Ptolemaic influence. . . but the Ptolemies did nothing about it during their period of influence at Delos, where the cult emerges under Antigonid suzerainty. At the same time, while the Ptolemies did nothing from above, it was natural that the cities should take action of their own to win favor."

29. The inscription was published in *JÖAI* 62 (1993) 133. The location where the stele was discovered is apparently unknown since it is not mentioned. The Hellenistic date is presented as "probable."

30. *IvE* IV 1246 (= Vidman, *Sylloge*, 297).

31. Nock (*Essays*, 45–46) has collected a large number of dedicatory inscriptions that use these or similar formulas in dedications to numerous deities.

32. The clock fragments were uncovered 36.1 m north of the agora's southwest corner. For details regarding the discovery of the clock, see Gerhard Langmann, "Die ägyptische Wasserauslaufuhr aus Ephesos. I. Fundgeschichte und Fundort," *JÖAI* 55 (1984) Beibl. 1–6.

dar have shown that the clock was constructed during the time of Ptolemy II.[33] The water clock, the nineteenth known example of this type, was probably brought from Egypt to Ephesos for the purpose of timing cultic events in a Hellenistic Sarapeion. Because of an adjustment in the Egyptian calendar enacted in approximately 280 BCE, the water clock became obsolete and was eventually discarded.[34]

Other evidence of Egyptian cultic activity does not surface until the first century BCE. The only extant inscription from this period is an orthostatic plate of white marble used secondarily as a paving stone in front of the Library of Celsus. The dedication simply reads "set up for Sarapis" (Σαραπιδί ἀνέθηκεν).[35] Further indications of Egyptian cultic activity in Ephesos during the first century BCE, however, may be found in a series of cistophoric coins with representations of the headdress of Isis. Cistophoric coins were struck in Ephesos from 88 until 48 BCE. According to Hölbl, this coin issue indicates that the general population knew and possibly understood the symbolic and iconographic elements of Isis religion.[36] Magie thinks that coins with representations of the headdress of Isis not only indicate the awareness of Isis in the issuing city, but also cultic activity. He reached this conclusion by analyzing the overlap between cities that issued coins depicting the headdress of Isis with cities where epigraphical evidence for Isis cults is extant.[37]

It is widely assumed that Antony and Cleopatra left their religious mark on Ephesos at the end of the Roman republic.[38] After the vic-

33. For the date of the clock, see Günther Hölbl, "Die ägyptische Wasserauslaufuhr aus Ephesos. III. Die ägyptische Wasseruhr Ptolemäos' II," *JÖAI* 55 (1984) Beibl. 40–45. For a technical analysis of the astronomical assumptions implicit in the design of the clock, see Maria G. Firneis, "II. Astronomische Bestimmung der geographischen Breite aus den Markierungen einer ägyptischen Wasseruhr," *JÖAI* 55 (1984) Beibl. 7–20.

34. Christine Thomas, "Egyptian Waterclock," in Helmut Koester and Ann Brock, eds., *Archaeological Resources for New Testament Studies* (Valley Forge, PA: Trinity, 1995) vol. 2, Ephesos A 27, 28.

35. *IvE* II 298 (= Vidman, *Sylloge*, 298).

36. Hölbl, *Zeugnisse*, 20.

37. Magie, "Egyptian Deities in Asia Minor," 57.

38. The identification of the temple foundation on the State Agora as an Isis temple constructed during the late republic under the influence of Antony and Cleopatra is discussed below.

tory of the triumvirate, Mark Antony crossed over to Asia Minor to take command of the East. He entered Ephesos in triumph and was honored by the Ephesians as the incarnation of Dionysos.[39] He spent the winter of 41/40 BCE with Cleopatra in Alexandria, where his transformation from Roman general to oriental monarch began.[40] His breach with the West began with his marriage to Cleopatra in the early winter of 37/36 BCE and widened after the campaign in Armenia. In connection with a triumphal celebration in Alexandria after the campaign, he declared Cleopatra's son Caesarion to be the lawful son of Julius Caesar and made him the co-ruler of Egypt with his mother. Moreover, he divided Roman lands from Armenia to the Hellespont among his heirs and appointed himself supreme ruler of the inhabited world. When news of this reached Rome, it aroused great indignation and provided fuel for the propaganda necessary for Octavian to prepare for battle.

In the winter of 33/32 BCE, while preparations for war were being made, Antony and Cleopatra located their military headquarters at Ephesos.[41] In the spring they moved their headquarters to Samos while preparations for battle continued. In September of 31 BCE, Antony's fleet finally met Octavian's off the promontory of Actium, and Antony and Clepatra's direct influence over Ephesos ended. Although the potential for Egyptian religious influence was great during this period, no clear evidence of its effect has yet been discovered in Ephesos.

There is therefore a gap in the epigraphic evidence for Egyptian cultic activity in Ephesos that spans over two centuries: from the late republic until the middle of the second century CE.[42] Four inscriptions dating from this period through the third century CE, however, have been found. Cyriacus and Wood recorded the first of these inscriptions, which is now missing. According to their notes, Cyriacus saw

---

39. Plutarch *Anton.* 24. On the association of Antony with Osiris and Dionysos and Cleopatra with Isis, see Reginald Eldred Witt, *Isis in the Graeco-Roman World* (Ithaca, NY: Cornell University Press, 1971) 147.

40. Magie, *Roman Rule*, 1. 430.

41. See Plutarch *Anton.* 56; Dio Cassius *Hist.* 50.2.

42. It is interesting that this corresponds to Robert Wild's findings ("The Known Isis-Sarapis Sanctuaries of the Roman Period," *ANRW* 2.17.4 [1984] 1834–35) regarding the periods when the Egyptian cults were most popular.

the inscription on a marble base at the Harbor Baths while Wood saw it at the Theater Gymnasium.[43] Of particular interest in this epigraph is the dedication to Isis and Sarapis of a phiale and a spondeion, indicators of cultic activity because they would have been used as libation vessels. Apuleius mentions that libations were performed in the Isis cult and that both milk and water were used in purification rituals.[44] This epigraph also mentions two Ephesian men, Lykidas and Charidemes, who served as ναυβατοῦντες, ceremonial sailors who helped to consecrate and launch a new ship during the annual nautical festival (πλοιαφέσια).[45] The ship, moreover, was sacred to Isis and, according to Apuleius, was offered as "first-fruits of a new year's navigation."[46] That this particular festival would be celebrated in an important harbor city like Ephesos comes as no surprise. It was a festive event that would have presented the cult before the city in a positive way.[47]

The second imperial inscription is on a fragment of an architrave block discovered in 1926 in the rubble of the gate structure of the large temple complex west of the lower agora (map no. 33). The 0.59 m block was broken at both ends leaving only the letters ιστολοσκαιν. Keil restored the inscription to read [ἀρχ]ίστολος καὶ ν[εωκόρος] ("keeper of the sacred vestments and temple warden").[48] The association of the inscription with Egyptian cults depends on the first term because neokoroi are commonly found as temple functionaries in both Greek and Egyptian cults. *Stolistai*, however, were functionaries of Egyptian cults charged with the care of the cult statue. Their respon-

43. *IvE* IV 1213 (= Vidman, *Sylloge*, 302). Keil, "Denkmäler," 224.

44. Apuleius *Met.* 11.10, 20.

45. See Vidman, *Isis und Sarapis*, 83.

46. Apuleius *Met.* 11.16–17; see commentary in John Gwyn Griffiths, *The Isis Book* (Leiden: Brill, 1975) 31–47.

47. That another Isis festival was celebrated in Ephesos may be indicated by a number of lamps that have been found with iconography associated with the Egyptian cults. For a discussion of the festival, called a λαμπαδεία, and a description of three lamps that have been published, see Hölbl, *Zeugnisse*, 67–69.

48. *IvE* IV 1244 (= Vidman, *Sylloge*, 299). Josef Keil, "Das Serapeion von Ephesos," in *Memoriam Halil Edhem* (Ankara: Türk Tarih Kurumu Basimev, 1947) 189.

sibilities included the washing, anointing, decorating, and clothing of the statue.[49] Although the particular form ἀρχίστολος is nowhere else attested, a similar form, ἀρχιστολιστής, is extant.[50] Furthermore, the extant appellation ὑπόστολοι provides a useful parallel. If the prefix ὑπό was attached to signify persons who assisted the ἱερόστολος (Egyptian priest who had charge of the sacred vestments)—the most natural interpretation of ὑπόστολοι—it is quite plausible that the prefix ἀρχι- was used as an honorary title for certain ἱερόστολοι.[51] Keil's claim that this epigraph is part of a dedicatory inscription that was erected by an ἀρχίστολος of the Egyptian cults in Ephesos seems well founded.[52]

From the time of Antoninus Pius (137–61 CE), there is a dedication that belonged to an Isis statue with an altar. Although the statue represented Isis, the dedication was to Ephesian Artemis, the emperor, and the city.[53] The statue was also dedicated to those conducting business at the customs house (τελώνιον) for tolls on fishing. From the inscription one cannot determine whether the statue stood in the customs house, but it was found in the harbor area. Dunand may be correct in his proposition that the customs house of fishermen (τὸ τελώνιον τῆς ἰχθυϊκῆς) was an association that gathered under the patronage of Isis.[54] The relationship of Isis to fishermen is already indicated by the nautical festival mentioned above.[55]

49. Dunand, *Le culte d'Isis*, 3. 153–54.
50. LSJ, suppl. 24; LSJ, 253.
51. For a discussion of these functionaries and the relevant inscriptions, see Dunand, *Le culte d'Isis*, 3. 69; 2. 24–25, 47–48.
52. Keil, "Das Serapeion von Ephesos," 188–89.
53. *IvE* V 1503 (= Vidman, *Sylloge*, 301). This dedication may provide inscriptional evidence from Ephesos of the interchangeability of the names of Isis and Artemis as reflected in Xenophon's romance, the *Ephesiaka*, and elsewhere (Witt, *Isis*, 149, 249–50). Witt emphasizes that the association of Isis with Artemis was common. In fact, he writes, "Isis and Artemis were temple associates more often than any other pair of goddesses" (p. 151).
54. Dunand, *Le Culte d'Isis*, 3. 71. The symbolic significance of the fish in the Isis cult may provide some further rationale for Dunand's speculation (Hölbl, *Zeugnisse*, 52).
55. In Apuleius *Met.* 11.8, a fisherman in Kenchreai is noted as one of the persons taking part in the procession honoring Isis. It is possible that the woman who dedicated the Isis statue, Kominia Junia, was a patron of the

An inscription on a statue base with a dedication to the emperor Caracalla has survived but is poorly preserved.[56] The base was found near the propylon steps leading to the large temple precinct on the west side of the Tetragonas Agora. According to Keil's reading of the inscription, the person who set up the imperial statue did so "for those who sacrifice to Sarapis in the presence of my Nile god" (τοῖς ἐπὶ θεοῦ μου Νείλου Σεράπιδι θύουσι).[57] Caracalla was an enthusiastic promoter of the Sarapis cult who took part in processions of the cult and even served in an official cultic capacity.[58] The temple he built for Sarapis on the Esquiline in Rome further indicates that he earned the apellation "lover of Sarapis" (*philosarapis*). The Sarapis cult enjoyed a period of expansion during the rule of Caracalla and his predecessors, Commodus and Septimius Severus.[59] As Witt notes, however, the worship of Egyptian gods reached its zenith under Caracalla.[60]

---

fishing association, although this would be more likely if such a patronship were advertised in the dedication. It is more likely that she had a familial relationship to members of the association. See the discussion in G. H. R. Horsley, ed., *New Documents Illustrating Early Christianity* (5 vols.; North Ryde, N.S.W.: Ancient History Documentary Research Centre, Macquarie University, 1981) 5. 105–7.

56. *IvE* IV 1230 (= Vidman, *Sylloge*, 303). Keil, "Das Serapeion von Ephesos," 183.

57. Keil, "Denkmäler," 225.

58. Vidman, *Isis und Sarapis*, 170.

59. A dedicatory inscription on a white marble plate (*IvE* IV 1247 = Vidman, *Sylloge*, 304), probably from the third century CE, has a dedication beginning with the phrase "great is the name of the god" (Μέγα τὸ ὄν[ο]μα τοῦ θεοῦ). This phrase is often, but not exclusively, used of Sarapis. The inscription refers to "the council of servants" (τό συνέδρ[ιον] λατρευτ[ῶν]). Because λάτρις is used of an Isis priest in a second- or third-century epitaph from Megalopolis (Vidman, *Sylloge*, 42), some have found in the term further reason to identify the inscription with Egyptian cults. There is no way, however, to limit to the use of this term to Egyptian cults. Because of the ambiguity of both connections, the association of this inscription with Egyptian religion must be regarded as tenuous. I am aware of one other relevant inscription, a fragment of a white marble base has an inscription that includes the name of Isis (*IvE* VI 2912); it was found in the Church of St. John, but I have seen no attempts to date the stone.

60. Witt, *Isis*, 237.

Numerous Homonoia coins with representations of Egyptian dieties, usually with Artemis, as well as a ceramic relief, were issued under Gordian III. They testify to the special relationship that existed between Ephesos and Alexandria.[61] This Homonoia is evidence for a level of commercial interaction that would have brought numerous merchants and shipping personnel to Ephesos. The coins issued under Gordian III do not require one to assume, however, that the level of commercial traffic was substantially greater at that time than under the earlier reigns of Macrinus and Caracalla. This is true whether the Homonoia relationship can be traced back to their reigns based on numismatic evidence or not.[62] The coins issued under Gordian III do not so much inaugurate a new relationship as they recognize an existing one.[63]

Temples

The identification of Ephesian temple remains with the Egyptian cults has been problematic. Suggestions have been made, however, regarding two structures that may have been used for Egyptian cultic activity: the temple foundation on the State Agora and the large temple complex on the west side of the Tetragonas Agora.

The foundation of a canonical Greek peripteral temple was discovered on the western side of the State Agora in 1970 (map no. 58). The peripteros was 6 by 10 columns and the crepidoma was probably four steps (see fig. 1).[64] It has been dated to the second half of the first century BCE on the basis of ceramic finds. One approached the temple from the east and entered a small pronaos by passing through a porch that was two columns deep. The cella was almost square (6.22 m by 5.92 m). The foundation of the entire structure, including the peripteros, was 14.5 m by 22.2 m. An almost square shaft (50 cm by 55 cm) 5 m deep was found on the northwest side of the foundation outside the

61. A number of these are described in Hölbl, *Zeugnisse*, 71–77.
62. Ibid., 24–25.
63. For Ephesos's dependence on Egyptian grain, see Michael Wörrle, "Ägyptisches Getreide für Ephesos," *Chiron* 1 (1971) 325–40.
64. For a detailed description of the material remains with dimensions, diagrams and photos, see Elisabeth Fossel, "Zum Tempel auf dem Staatsmarkt in Ephesos," *JÖAI* 50 (1971–75) 212–19.

cella but within the colonnade. The shaft was filled with amphora fragments.

There are no remains of an altar, but a water basin (1.2 m by 1.5 m by 18 cm deep) was found on the same level as the temple and positioned exactly on the temple's axis. It was 12.5 m in front of the temple and may have served as an ablution facility for those entering the sacred area.[65] It has both a feed line and a drain. Although the basin appears to belong to the temple, it was added later, perhaps in the late second or third century CE. Robert Wild does not find this basin to be typical of those associated with temples for the Egyptian gods. He claims, however, that the shaft at the northwest corner of the building is located exactly where temple basins—apparently for priestly ablution rituals—are often found in Isis and Sarapis temples. Although the excavation reports give no indication that the shaft held water, Wild believes that it was more than "a place to deposit broken ritual vessels."[66]

The small finds that initially raised the question of the temple's association with Egyptian cults are the head of a small statue of Amon-Re; an Alexandrian terra-cotta statue, which is unpublished and too battered to identify; and a small bronze bell, now lost, which could have belonged to a sistrum. In addition, a colossal portrait head—possibly of Antony—was unearthed in a trench nearby.[67]

There are, however, a number of problems with the identification of this temple with Egyptian cults. The small finds were discovered in rubble at a level above the temple foundations; the contents of this layer reach into the Byzantine period.[68] Furthermore, the Greek style of the temple does not correspond to any known examples of Egyptian temples from the first century BCE within or outside of Egypt.[69] Finally, the function of the shaft is unclear, the water basin is late, and the portrait head's identification is disputed.[70]

65. Robert Wild, *Water in the Cultic Worship of Isis and Sarapis* (EPRO 87; Leiden: Brill, 1981) 1775.

66. Ibid., 1776.

67. Hölbl, *Zeugnisse*, 29.

68. Werner Jobst, "Zur Lokalisierung des Sebasteion-Augusteum in Ephesos," *IstMit* 30 (1980) 249.

69. Hölbl, *Zeugnisse*, 30.

70. Jobst, "Lokalisierung," 249–50.

Hölbl sought to resolve some of these difficulties by following up on a suggestion he attributes to Stefan Karwiese, emphasizing the Greek character of the structure, that the site originally may have been dedicated to a Greek deity.[71] Because of the date of the temple, the portrait head's possible representation of Antony, and Antony's association with Dionysos, Hölbl thinks that the temple originally may have been built for Dionysus. He then posits that sometime later, because of the association of Osiris and Dionysos, Egyptian deities found a place in the sanctuary, resulting in the eventual addition of the ablution basin after 200 CE.[72]

Jobst has criticized this scenario because, in his view, it depends on an uncritical identification of the portrait head with Antony, as well as an undemonstrated assumption that the head was associated in some way with the temple.[73] Jobst's interpretation of the temple foundation is different. He has argued convincingly that the foundation is more likely that of a temple for Augustus (and perhaps Dea Roma) and that the State Agora is in fact an Augustus forum.[74]

The other edifice in Ephesos often associated with Egyptian cults is the large temple complex on the southern end of the west side of the Tetragonas Agora (map no. 33). Because the precinct is built on the slope of Bülbüldağ (Lepre Akte), it stands at a level higher than that of the agora. The site was excavated in 1913 by the Austrian Archaeological Institute, and there has been a long-standing disagreement over the identification of the building.[75] Keil assigned a second century CE date to the building, while Alzinger thought it probably belonged to the beginning of the third century.[76] The structure has

71. Hölbl, *Zeugnisse*, 31 n. 99.

72. Ibid., 30–31.

73. Jobst, "Lokalisierung," 249.

74. Ibid., 251. See also Price, *Rituals and Power*, 254.

75. Preliminary results of more recent work on this site are reported by Gerhard Langmann and Peter Scherrer in *JÖAI* 61 (1991/92) Beibl. 6–8 and *JÖAI* 62 (1993) Beibl. 14–16.

76. Keil, "Denkmäler," 225; Alzinger, "Ephesos Archäologischer Teil," 1653. Peter Scherrer (Harvard Divinity School, Cambridge, MA, 25 March 1994) suggested a date during the reigns of Domitian or Trajan on the basis of column capitals used in the structure, which match datable capitals from the Harbor Bath complex.

been interpreted as a nympheion, imperial temple, and Sarapeion. I shall describe the building, survey the evidence for its association with Egyptian cults, and consider whether the peculiarities of the structure are best explained in light of Egyptian cult practices. The precinct consists of a 73 m by 106 m space defined by a 7 m deep colonnaded hall that opened to the inside (see fig. 2).[77] The main structure was positioned against the south wall of the enclosure, leaving a large courtyard in front of the building. One gained access to the north side of the temenos by means of a propylon near the west gate of the agora. Steps ascended to the propylon from the south colonnade of the street, which ran from the west gate of the agora toward the harbor. The appearance of the building is that of a prostyle temple on a high podium whose relation to the courtyard is typical of Roman temple complexes. Keil rejected early interpretations of the structure as a nympheion, because the building did not correspond to any known nympheia in Asia Minor.[78] Furthermore, Keil's detection of the temenos wall undermined this interpretation since such a wall, although characteristic of temple complexes, would have restricted access to a fountain.[79]

The temple's dimensions are 29.2 m by 37 m (see fig. 3). The pronaos is 8.2 m deep, leaving an almost square cella (17.15 m by 20.1 m). The temple was approached by means of a monumental stairway (29.2 m wide), which was divided into three intervals with uneven numbers of steps. Eight large monolithic columns sitting on Attic bases, which are in situ, and carrying Corinthian capitals adorned the front of the temple. The distance between the columns was 2 m, except for the two columns in the center that were 3.35 m apart. The bases are 1.9 m in diameter while the columns are 1.6 m. Based on common ratios, the columns would have been 14 to 15 m tall and must have weighed close to 50 tons each. Large fragments of these columns can still be seen on the site.

---

77. This description is based largely on Salditt-Trappmann, *Tempel der ägyptischen Götter*, 26–32, and the author's personal analysis of the site in the summer of 1994.

78. Josef Keil, "Ephesische Funde und Beobachtungen," *JÖAI* 18 (1915) Beibl. 286.

79. Idem, "XII. vorläufiger Bericht," 266.

The façade of the temple was decorated with four pilasters, two on either side of the large entrance door. They were positioned on an exact line with the second and third and sixth and seventh columns, respectively. The entry was 5.3 m wide and carried a door that was probably 12 m tall. The door opened to the inside in two leaves, as indicated by semicircular grooves in the floor that were cut by the rollers on which the two leaves of the door travelled. The 12 ton lintel block that spanned the opening can be seen among the ruins.

On the basis of the height of the columns, one can assume that the cella walls were 14 to 15 m tall. With the exception of the south wall, the walls were constructed of limestone blocks that were faced with marble revetment. The south wall was mostly constructed with bricks, although some limestone blocks were also used. The cella carried a barrel-vault roof structure—indicated by fragments found within the main room—which was supported by the inside walls 2.4 m thick. There were also outside walls of the same thickness that were 1.2 m removed from the inside walls. The inner walls probably carried the vault, while the outer walls may have helped to compensate for the horizontal thrust produced by the vault. The east and west inside walls contain six niches each. The height of the niches cannot be determined, but they were 1 m deep and 2 m wide and the bottom of each niche was about 3 m above the floor level.

A large rectangular apse measuring 7.22 m by 6.3 m occupies the middle of the south wall of the main room. Its floor level is approximately 1 m higher than that of the cella; moreover, a low wall separated the apsidal room from the cella. Niches were also located on the south wall, one on either side of the rectangular apse. Although similar in size, these two niches were somewhat wider than those on the long walls.

Niches are also found in the two passageways that the spaces between the inside and outside walls on the east and west sides of the temple created. Five niches were evenly spaced in each passageway on the outside walls. The width of these niches corresponds to those in the main room, but they are .2 m deeper. In contrast to the niches in the cella, these niches extend to the level of the floor so that they appear as indentions into the outside wall. If statues stood in these niches, therefore, they would probably have rested on bases. One gains access to these passageways through openings in front of the first niche on the east and west walls, respectively. When the passageways reach the south wall they turn at right angles toward the apse and rise sharply by means of stairways identical to the east and west. Unfortunately, their destination cannot be determined from the extant materials because only the lower portions of the structure have survived.

One other conspicuous characteristic of the building is its water system, which caused Rudolf Heberdey to identify it as a nympheion.[80] Water entered the cella at each of the niches in the main room. The water must have reached the niches from pipes which conducted water to the upper portion of the niches. Unfortunately, there are no architectural remains from a level high enough to observe how the upper niche structures were constructed. Centered under each of the niches in the main room, however, one can still observe cuttings for drain pipes which conducted water from the niches to a shallow rectangular basin in front of the apse on the south wall.[81] The water made its way from the niches to the rectangular basin through shallow troughs in the floor, which ran along the walls. Water was also supplied to the large apse on the south wall. Although the supply pipe is no longer extant, a vertical channel in which the water pipe was embedded can be observed in the center of the south wall.

It is surprising that the temple had no building inscription. Continuing debates over the identification of this temple with the Egyptian cults stem from ambiguities regarding the relationship between the temple and the material evidence discovered in the temple's prox-

80. Rudolf Heberdey, "II. vorläufiger Bericht über die Grabungen in Ephesos 1913," *JÖAI* 18 (1915) Beibl. 84–88.

81. Salditt-Trappmann (*Tempel der ägyptischen Götter*, 30–31) mistakenly imagines that water flowed out of the lower half of the niches where it could have poured down on initiates. I surveyed the niches carefully in August of 1994. The only wall cuttings that are visible are below the niches, a position that indicates drain pipes rather than supply pipes. Because the water was conducted to the shallow troughs in the floor through drain pipes below each niche, it could not have poured down on initiates. In fact, the water in the niches would not have been visible unless it was seen pouring down from above. This cannot be observed in the archaeological remains, however, since the upper portions of the niches have not survived.

imity and from the interpretation of the building's unusual architectural features.

Keil based his conclusion that the structure was a Sarapeion primarily on two inscriptions found within the temple precincts: the architrave block with the inscription [ἀρχ]ίστολος καὶ ν[εωκόρος] and especially the statue base dedicated to Caracalla that was set up for τοῖς ἐπὶ θεοῦ μου Νείλου Σεράπιδι θύουσι.[82] The architrave block was not found in situ; rather, it was discovered in the rubble of the propylon complex that provided access to the temenos area on the north side of the temple.[83] Although it is possible that, as Keil claims, the block belonged to one of the structures of the temple complex, the connection is not certain. The statue base was found in situ in front of the steps of the propylon, but the base was not in its original position. Rather, it was reused in this location to support an unstable column. It is a reasonable conjecture, however, that the gate complex was repaired by those who used the precincts and that they utilized stones from the temenos that were no longer valued in the position where they were originally set up. This view is strengthened somewhat by the discovery of a second column base that was also reused in the renovation of the gate complex. Although no Egyptian cultic activities are reflected on this stone, Egypt is mentioned twice in the inscription.[84]

Attempts to connect the building with Egyptian religions on the basis of its architecture have focused primarily on the niches, water system, and passageways. If one assumed that the structure was in

---

82. *IvE* IV 1244 (= Vidman, *Sylloge*, 299) and *IvE* IV 1230 (= Vidman, *Sylloge*, 303), respectively. As evidence for the connection, Keil ("Das Serapeion von Ephesos," 183) also includes a fragment of a statue made from Egyptian granite that was found in front of the temple.

83. Ibid., 189.

84. For the text of the inscription, see Keil, "XII. vorläufiger Bericht," 268–70. The Hellenistic Egyptian water clock, mentioned earlier in the paper, may provide further circumstantial evidence for this location as a center for Egyptian cultic activity. If the clock was discarded because changes in the cultic calendar made it obsolete, it was probably discarded before the building of the Roman Sarapeion. It may have been found adjacent to the Roman Sarapeion, because the Roman Sarapeion was built on the site of its Hellenistic predecessor.

fact a temple for the Egyptian gods, how would these features be explained? Undoubtedly the niches held statues of various deities, presumably Egyptian gods, although other deities could have been included.[85] At Delos, for example, there were dozens of deities who were invoked and received dedications along with the Egyptian gods. The list includes Aphrodite, Astarte, Asklepios, Artemis, Demeter, Dionysos, Mater Deum, Hygieia, Hermes, Pluto, Herakles, Nike, Agathodaimon, Agathe Tyche, and Zeus Soter.[86] A dedication from Pergamon dated to the first century CE indicates that two "bearers of holy vessels" (ἱεραφόροι) offered statues or reliefs of Sarapis, Isis, Anubis, Harpokrates, Osiris, Apis, Helios, Ares, and the Dioskouroi, by order of Isis.[87] Since the passageways between the walls each contain five niches and since the pathways do not seem to have been interconnected, it is a reasonable conjecture that both passages may have held statues of Sarapis, Isis, Anubis, Harpokrates, and Apis.[88] The apse must have held a large statue of the deity to whom the temple was dedicated, presumably Sarapis, or even a statue group. Why fourteen other niches were included in the design of the cella is a mystery.[89]

The water system was clearly designed for ritual purposes, although its exact function remains unclear. Salditt-Trappmann thinks that the small water course in front of the niches may have been designed for a decorative effect. She compares them to the basins in the colonnaded courtyard of the Sarapeion at Pergamon.[90] I believe that the water flowing from these fourteen niches, each of which probably held statues of different deities, to a position just in front of the

85. The names Isis and Harpokrates appear in an inscription on a relief fragment found in the vicinity of the Varius Baths which also included other deities (*IvE* IV 1245). The fragmentary form of the inscription does not permit the other names to be read, but introductory language and space for other gods indicates their presence in the complete inscription.

86. Vincent Tran Tam Tinh, "Sarapis and Isis," in Ben Meyer and E. P. Sanders, eds., *Jewish and Christian Self-Definition*, vol. 3: *Self Definition in the Greco-Roman World* (Philadelphia: Fortress, 1982) 106.

87. Vidman, *Sylloge*, 313.

88. Hölbl, *Zeugnisse*, 35.

89. Hölbl (ibid., 37) offers a few possibilities, but none is compelling.

90. Salditt-Trappmann, *Tempel der ägyptischen Götter*, 31.

temple statue may have been an architectural depiction of the universal lordship of Sarapis.[91] Although the small water course that collected the water from the niches surrounding the cella may have served only a decorative function, the larger basin in front of the apse seems more likely to have been used for ablution rites. Only a few ancient sources detail the sort of purification practices conducted in Isis and Sarapis cults. Most significant are the passages in Apuleius because they offer information regarding how at least some of the rituals were conducted. In book eleven of the *Metamorphoses*, Lucius experiences a number of purification rituals in a variety of settings: the sea, the public baths, and the Isis temple.[92] Wild does not think that shallow ablution basins located within sacred areas were used by everyone who entered, or even initiates. Rather, he suggests they were used by the priests of the sanctuary and their attendants, who were required to wash or sprinkle themselves before entering certain areas of the temple or before engaging in certain ceremonies.[93] A relief from the eighteenth dynasty shows the purification of a priestess and a priest; they stand in low, flat basins and have water poured or sprinkled on their heads. The scene is thought to be indicative of priestly purification practices in Egyptian cults.[94] Because of the shallow basin's position in front of the cult statue, I think that it was used for similar rituals. Nonetheless, initiates and others desiring to approach the god in prayer or worship—as Lucius did in the *Metamorphoses*—were no doubt required to submit to ablutions that may have occurred here as well.

Although this facility does not correspond precisely to the canons that Wild established, the variety of the settings for the ablutions in Apuleius's account, coupled with the variety of basin types in excavated temples, should caution interpreters against prematurely rejecting this temple as a site for Egyptian cultic activity. Salditt-Trappmann

91. Tinh emphasizes ("Sarapis and Isis," 108) this characteristic of Sarapis when he writes, "Sarapis (like Isis) unites in his person all the powers of the gods." The design of the Sarapeion thus depicts what an inscription from Rome states: "The unique Zeus Sarapis Helios, invincible, master of the world" (Vidman, *Sylloge*, 389).

92. Apuleius *Met.* 11.1, 7, 11.20, 23.

93. Wild, *Water*, 146.

94. Ibid.

thinks that the apse on the south side of the building could have included a Nile water container in addition to providing the setting for the temple statue. She thinks that the water pipe in the rear wall would have been hidden by the statue, making the appearance of the water somewhat mysterious.[95] Again, while the installation is not typical of the fixed water containers that Wild analyzed, he has only three fixed containers of Roman period construction with which to compare it.[96]

On the basis of the water system and architecture, Hölbl thinks the Sarapeion at Ephesos was used for initiations.[97] If so, the apse water container would be the likely location for the initiation rites. Here the initiate may have stood in the basin while water from the apse plumbing poured over his or her head. Although the complex water system that was designed for this building is open to a variety of interpretations, it has more in common with water installations in Egyptian temples than it does with those of any other Greco-Roman cult.

At Ephesos, unlike Pergamon, excavators have discovered no underground passages for priestly entrances or symbolic underworld journeys, but the passageways between the inside and outside walls have intrigued scholars because of their statue niches and the mystery of their destination along the south wall.[98] Salditt-Trappmann speculates that they were in fact used for rituals in which initiates would have passed through the dark passages, where they would have observed the statues of the gods illuminated in the niches by oil lamps.[99] Describing the initiation experience, Apuleius says that Lucius "came to the boundary of death," "travelled through all the elements and

95. Salditt-Trappmann, *Tempel der ägyptischen Götter*, 31.
96. Wild, *Water*, 155.
97. Hölbl, *Zeugnisse*, 39.
98. The passageway on the eastern side of the temple has been excavated, but the western passageway has never been uncovered. Plans of the temple assume that the western passageway is a mirror of the one on the opposite side of the building. This conclusion is supported by two features: a doorway corresponding to the one that leads into the passageway on the eastern side can be observed on the western side; and excavators have uncovered a portion of the stairway on the southwestern corner of the building that corresponds to the one on the opposite side.
99. Salditt-Trappmann, *Tempel der ägyptischen Götter*, 31.

returned," and "came face to face with the gods below and the gods above and paid reverence to them from close at hand."[100] Salditt-Trappmann speculates further that the huge piers in the southeast and southwest corners of the building could have contained rooms at a higher level, which were reached by the stairs at the end of the passageways in the south wall. Other initiatory activities would have taken place in these rooms before the initiates returned to the cella.[101] Hölbl adds that an opening in the passageway leading to the rooms may have allowed the initiate to see the face of the cult statue in the apse.[102]

Such theories are obviously highly speculative due to the fragmentary nature of the evidence, but other explanations of the passageways have proved untenable. It is unlikely that they provided a rear exit, since this exit would have increased the temple's vulnerability to theft. For the same reason, it is not likely that they provided an alternate entrance for the priests. The theory that the passageways were a means by which the priests could make sudden, surprise entrances to enhance cultic activities—as one finds at Pergamon and other Egyptian cult sites—fails because the entrances to the passages are plainly visible at the front of the cella.

Although interpretations of the structure—particularly its niches, water system, and passageways—are admittedly speculative, no other identification for the temple provides a more reasonable context for these unique features than a Sarapeion or an Iseion. Correlations with Apuleius's account are suggestive, but should not be pressed too far. Even though the detailed pictures of Lucius's experiences in book eleven of the *Metamorphoses* are unparalleled in other ancient sources, they still provide only a sketchy view of the relationship between those experiences and the architecture of an Isis temple.[103] On the basis of Apuleius's account and the architecture of known temples for

100. Apuleius *Met.* 11.23; my translation.
101. Salditt-Trappmann, *Tempel der ägyptischen Götter*, 31.
102. Hölbl (*Zeugnisse*, 42). This would have allowed the initiates to see the god "face to face" (Apuleius *Met.* 11.23).
103. This is true whether one concludes that Apuleius used the Kenchreai sanctuary as his context in a strict sense or whether his description was intended to correspond to Isis sanctuaries in a more general way. See Dennis Smith, "The Egyptian Cults at Corinth," *HTR* 70 (1977) 209.

the Egyptian gods (especially at Pergamon), it seems likely, however, that water, a sacred journey, and encounters with various gods played a central role in initiations into the cults of the Egyptian gods.[104]

Conclusion

While the evidence for Egyptian cultic activity in Ephesos is not extensive, it does suggest that the Egyptian gods were worshipped in the city at least from the early third century BCE through the fourth century CE. Ephesos was probably home to at least one temple for the Egyptian gods during the Hellenistic period. One should recall, however, that domestic space and cultic space were not as separated in antiquity as they often are in the minds of modern scholars.[105] Because these cults spread primarily through the personal initiative of interested parties, personal residences often provided cultic space, as the evidence from Delos shows. In fact, the record from Delos reminds us that even the building of a temple did not necessarily mean that the Egyptian gods were no longer worshipped in private homes.[106]

In his study of Isis and Sarapis sanctuaries of the Roman period, Wild found that building activities peaked during the third and second centuries BCE, and especially during the second century CE.[107] There was a notable lull in the building of temples for the Egyptian gods during the first century BCE and during the first century CE. Comparing the building pattern with the epigraphic record to determine whether there was any correlation, Wild found that the concentration of Isis

104. At the conclusion of his study of Isis and Sarapis sanctuaries, Wild notes ("Known Isis-Sarapis Sanctuaries," 1837) that "a large number of Sarapis sanctuaries from both Hellenistic and Roman times have the cult statue facing either S-SE or its opposite, N-NW." Whether or not this feature is to be explained by the gathering of worshippers in front of the cult statue to receive the *salutatio Solis* ("greeting of the sun"), as Wild suggests, it may be worth noting that the temple adjacent to the Tetragonas Agora is oriented in this way, while the one on the State Agora is not (ibid.).

105. See Michael White, *Building God's House in the Roman World: Architectural Adaptation among Pagans, Jews, and Christians* (Baltimore, MD: Johns Hopkins University Press, 1990).

106. On the developments at Delos, particularly the use and adaptation of private space, see ibid., 32–40.

107. Wild, "Known Isis-Sarapis Sanctuaries," 1834.

and Sarapis inscriptions was substantially higher in the second century BCE and the second century CE.[108]

It is interesting that, although limited, the evidence from Ephesos appears to fit this general pattern. From the period of the late republic through the early imperial period no evidence of cultic activity has been discovered at Ephesos. Beginning in the second century CE, however, the cult seems to regain prominence. A monumental temple was built in the center of the city in close proximity to the theater, the agora, and the Embolos. Moreover, four inscriptions that firmly attest cultic activity have survived from the second and third centuries CE.[109]

It seems that during the period of Christian expansion in Ephesos, the Egyptian cults also experienced something of a resurgence. Because of the relative absence of evidence for other foreign religions in Ephesos, particularly mystery cults, the metropolis of Asia may be a unique site where the contextualiztion of these two religions and their special appeal during this period could be jointly analyzed.[110] In Ephesos, to an even greater extent than other sites, these cults may provide helpful and important commentary on one another.[111] Why

108. See the table of epigraphic material in ibid., 1835.

109. A variety of sculptures, gems, and coins from Ephesos also reflects Egyptian influence during the period, but their reflection of cultic activity is more difficult to assess. For a catalogue with brief descriptions of these materials, see Hölbl, *Zeugnisse*, 54–78.

110. Oster writes ("Ephesus as a Religious Center," 1727): "The strength of Egyptian religious influence, dating from the Hellenistic and imperial period, was an anomaly in Ephesos since other external eastern influences were noticeably absent in imperial Ephesus' religious life. . . . Except for Christianity and Judaism, there were few independent eastern religions present in Roman Ephesus."

111. If Peter Scherrer's plans for a campaign to reexcavate the Sarapeion at Ephesos are realized, the potential for a fruitful comparison will be greatly extended. There is a relative abundance of literary and nonliterary Christian materials; the Egyptian materials, however, are still limited. The *Ephesiaka* of Xenophon of Ephesos purports to tell the reader about Egyptian cults in Ephesos. It is doubtful, however, whether the details contained therein reflect awareness of the actual situation at Ephesos. Reinhold Merkelbach (*Roman und Mysterium in der Antike* [Munich: Beck, 1962] 92) has shown that Xenophon uses Artemis of Ephesos only as a *Deckname* ("cover name") for Isis, while John Gwyn Griffiths ("Xenophon of Ephesus on Isis and Alexandria," in

did these two particular cults thrive in Ephesos during the second and third centuries CE?[112] Looking back from the vantage point of Christianity's triumph over paganism, the conclusion of Witt's book emphasized how much the early Christ's message and expansion owed to its "fore-runner," the Egyptian cults: "The time has come for Christian churches to acknowledge that the roots of the 'new' religion. . . were abundantly watered not just by the Jordan but also by the Nile."[113] Prior to Christianity's triumph, however, especially during the second and third centuries CE, it appears that both the Jordan and the Nile were flowing freely into the Kaÿstros Valley.

Margareet B. de Boer and T. A. Edridge, eds., *Hommages à Maarten J. Vermaseren* [3 vols.; EPRO 68; Leiden: Brill, 1978] 1. 409–37) has argued that the name of the city of Ephesos was used as a surrogate for Alexandria. On the general question of the use of the romances for evidence of Egyptian cultic activity in Ephesos, see Hölbl, *Zeugnisse*, 79–86, and Christine M. Thomas's contribution to this volume.

112. With both the Sarapis cult and Christianity one encounters a "new" cult that developed from ancient roots in an ethnic religion but which moved outside its original ethnic and nationalistic limitations. This may provide a good beginning point for analyzing their context and appeal. This is briefly noted by both Nock (*Conversion*, 41) and Tinh ("Sarapis and Isis," 105). For more detail on this aspect of the Egyptian cults, see esp. John Gwyn Griffiths, "The Great Egyptian Cults of Oecumenical Spiritual Significance," in A. H. Armstrong, ed., *Classical Mediterranean Spirituality* (New York: Crossroad, 1986) 39–65.

113. Witt, *Isis*, 280.

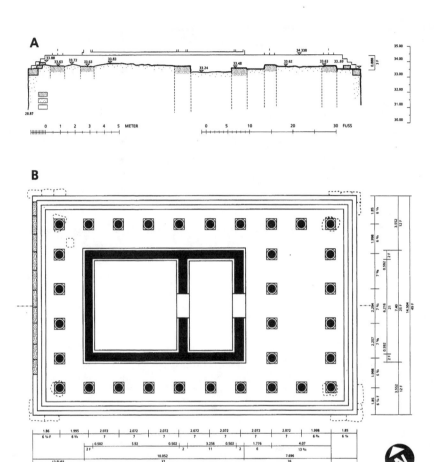

FIGURE 1   Plan of the temple on the State Agora. *Drawing by E. Fossel.*

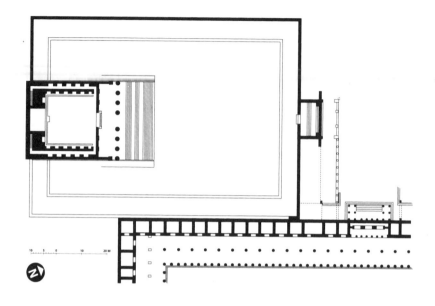

F ɪ ɢ ᴜ ʀ ᴇ 2   Sarapis Temple Precincts. *Drawing by Joseph Keil.*

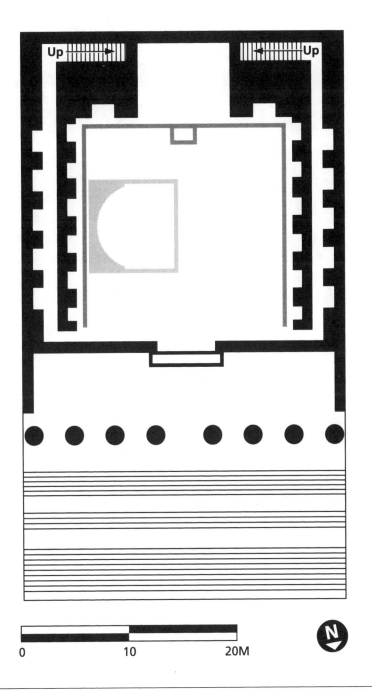

F i g u r e 3   Sarapis Temple

The Church of Mary and the Temple of Hadrian Olympius

Stefan Karwiese
Österreichisches Archäologisches Institut

The Austrian excavation of the long building in the northwest of Ephesos (map nos. 13 and 14) had resulted in its identification as the famous Church of Mary, where the Third Ecumenical Council was held in 431. In 1932, Josef Keil and F. Knoll gave an extensive preliminary report in *Forschungen in Ephesos*, describing a sequence of four building phases: First, the original Roman building, a 265 m long three-aisled stoa or basilica with an apse at both ends and with peculiar chambers and niches in its outer walls, was identified as the epigraphically attested Mouseion, or Temple of the Muses. Second, the first church was built into its western half, with its great apse just in the center of the stoa; it was again a three-aisled basilica on columns (*Säulenkirche*) with a huge atrium to the west front, from which people passed through the exonarthex and esonarthex. To the north of the atrium, an octagonal baptistery was added. It was alleged that this complex was founded in the time of Constantine I. In the third phase, according to Keil and Knoll, the basilica was replaced by a shorter building (which excluded the east part with the apse), built completely of bricks and with a vaulted roof (*Kuppelkirche*). This was said to have happened in the seventh century, perhaps after a fire. Keil and Knoll envisioned the fourth and final stage of the complex in this way: After the collapse of the vaulted church the old east part with apse was reused, but now had pillars instead of columns (*Pfeilerkirche*).[1]

This sequence and its interpretations have become commonplace and have been included in reference and handbooks. Only in the case of the Mouseion have some scholars suggested different identifications, such as a house of the medical boards,[2] an Asklepieion,[3] or a *deigma* ("stock exchange").[4] With regard to the building phases of the church, F. Fasolo believed he had found evidence enough to divide the first phase into four subphases, and the datings became controversial.[5]

In the end uncertainty remained; for this reason, in 1984 the late Professor Hermann Vetters asked me to begin a new archaeological investigation. On the second day of work, the understanding of the building was revolutionized. In a trench outside the church wall, secure evidence was found in the foundation ditch proving that the church was not built as early as the period of Constantine nor even in 431, but several decades later. After eight years of painstaking research (1984–1986 and 1990–1993), we now possess much information that explains a part of Ephesos where many important clues to the city's history may lie.

Recent geological deep drilling in this area has shown that as late as the Augustan era a coastal swamp still existed relatively close to the foot of Panayırdağ (Mount Pion); only in about 100 CE did the Ephesians fill this area in order to wrestle new land from the sea. Thus, the hill towering above the church was originally a peninsula reaching out into the gulf; until now, this hill has only partially been

1. Reisch, Knoll, and Keil, *Die Marienkirche.*
2. *IvE* V 1161–63.
3. Wilhelm Alzinger in Hermann Vetters, *AnzWien* 110 (1973) 180.
4. Reisch, Knoll, and Keil, *Die Marienkirche,* 2.
5. F. Fasolo in Wilhelm Alzinger, "Nachträge: Ephesos B," PWSup 12 (1971) 1679.

explored. I have tentatively identified it as the old Ionian acropolis.[6] It appears that from the beginning the new ground was intended for a single purpose—the giant foundations of a new sanctuary, consisting of a huge temple and a surrounding precinct.

The foundations for this temple (map no. 15) were built according to the high standards of Roman building art: two rectangular rings of precisely set high block walls (stereobates) were enclosed by opus cementitium, together forming a secure base for the large marble superstructure of a peripteros temple. The peristasis has a length of 60 m, and a height of about 23 m for the overall vertical extension can be reconstructed. Although only a few damaged pieces of the architecture have been found, it is certain that the building was decorated in the Corinthian order. Since this building, which dates to the Hadrianic period, was pulled down in about 400 CE, and its marble was burnt to limestone, we can infer that the building was associated with the official imperial Roman cult, which was loathed by the Christians. Other Ephesian buildings that were equally destroyed— and even literally uprooted—are the Temple to Domitian (Vespasian) and the small templet opposite it, incorrectly identified as the Temple of Isis. A church was also built in the center of what has been perhaps wrongly identified as the Sarapeion.

Pausanias aids in the identification of this giant temple, which was deliberately founded in the most prominent region available in Ephesos. In one of his few references to Ephesos, he states that on his way from the Temple of Artemis to the Magnesian Gate he passed by the Olympieion.[7] This reference has usually led to the opinion that the Olympieion was situated east of—that is, behind—Panayirdağ, where the shortest route between temple and gate was assumed to be. As this route was constructed by the famous Damianus at the end of the second century, however, Pausanias must have entered the city by the Koressian Gate not far from the stadium. The huge temple under consideration here should therefore be identified as Pausanias's Olympieion. This must have been the temple the Ephesians built in honor of Hadrian for their long desired second neokorate, that is, the second imperial cult established in Ephesos. Since Hadrian, like

6. Karwiese, "Korressos," 2. 218.
7. Pausanias 7.2.9.

Domitian before him, deigned to be worshipped as Zeus Olympios, almost all of Hadrian's temples were Olympieia and as such of Olympian dimensions. According to numismatic and inscriptional evidence,[8] the title of twice neokoros was conferred to Ephesos between the years 130 and 132. Along with the new imperial cult the Adrianeia, the Hadrianic Games, were established. Unlike the restored Domitianic Olympia, Adrianeia were celebrated every five years.

The temple was surrounded by a large open area enclosed by four porticoes, of which only the southern has been excavated and explored. According to the latest finds, this portico is none other than the long stoa in which the Church of Mary was later built, for it is connected to both lateral porticoes and represents the only possible border of the temenos, or precinct, to the south. Surprisingly, this stoa was built after the Hadrianic era, as the sherds found in the strata belonging to the stoa show. It would not be unusual to find that all the stoas here were built after the temple itself, as the latter was of course consuming so much funds and labor that further building activity was delayed. The south stoa, which is longer than the width of the temenos, provided the main entrance to the sanctuary and was itself a prominent and important building. The revision of its dating to approximately 200 CE provokes new questions.

I have already pointed out that the plan of the long stoa clearly fell into two halves, each containing an apsidal exedra, perhaps an indication of cultic activities. This information favors the theory that the Ephesians established here the proper building frame for the third neokorate, won from the joint rulers Caracalla and Geta in 211. Ceramic evidence further supports this date. Searching for the temple by which the city became thrice neokoros, archaeologists wrongly identified the Sarapeion as this temple. The epigraphical data for the much older Sarapeion names only Caracalla[9]; the neokorate had to be cancelled after Caracalla murdered Geta. Yet another fact favors the interpretation that the stoa was built for the third neokorate. Like its founder, Septimius Severus, the rulers of the Syrian dynasty regarded themselves as Baal, that is, Helios. Subsequently Caracalla and Geta

---

8. For example, *IvE* II 218 and 430.
9. *IvE* IV 1230.

were titled *neoi helioi* ("new suns"), and as such were similar to Zeus Olympios, according to the Syrian understanding.

Another piece of evidence determines with even more certainty that the Ephesian Olympieion became the home of all new imperial cults. A peculiar coin scene dedicated to Emperor Macrinus in 217 shows a group of Ephesians leading a bull to an altar in front of what is clearly an imperial temple. All persons raise their arms to the figure in the temple, who must be the emperor. What is striking here is that the Latin word *vota* ("vows") appears in Greek as *BΩTA* either on the temple pediment or in the coin exergue. This indicates that this was a votive temple. The word cannot refer to the annual imperial *vota*, as has been recently alleged by Simon R. F. Price,[10] since these would also have been reflected elsewhere on coinage. A similar reverse scene on a coin of Macrinus shows two agonistic shields enscribed with *Adrianea* and perhaps *Ephesia*, set alongside the temple. Although the legend is damaged, it can be derived that, apart from the word *Oly]mp. . .* , a neokorate—which does not appear on any other coin of 217/218—was also mentioned. The evidence suggests that another neokorate cult might have been established for Macrinus, perhaps in the Olympieion. Therefore, we may be fairly certain that underneath the inconspicuous surface of the temple's precinct, more buildings are buried. These may include altars and stoas belonging to the first half of the third century. In 1986 and 1992, excavation on one of these began.

The Olympieion, or the temple itself, was levelled to the ground in about 400 and then covered by erosion. A century later it became a quarry, when its block foundations were dismantled in order to plunder the iron clamps and the leaden dowels that held the blocks together, rather than the building material in general.

The new exploration of the Church of Mary has not so much revealed new evidence and unknown information, but has rather begun to adjust and increase evidence. Archaeological evidence from sherds and coins has proven beyond doubt that the lateral walls, consisting of huge limestone blocks which might have come from the foundations of the Olympeion, were not erected before about 500. Since

---

10. Price, *Ritual and Power.*

these walls closed the open sides of the Roman stoa, they belong to the time when the church was founded. The Constantinian date apparently had been proposed because of the shape of the great apse, the masonry of which had been taken from its Roman predecessor. It must be rejected, however, and instead a date in the reign of Anastasius I must be employed.[11] Similarly, it is clear that the block walls did not replace older church walls, since there is no evidence of this. The dates of the baptistery and narthexes have not yet been verified.

In 1985 and 1986, many skeleton graves were discovered inside and outside the church; unfortunately, those found during the early excavation in the 1920s were not documented. A whole cemetery, which covers the ground within the vaulted portion of the building, has come to light. Those graves alongside the northern and southern walls seem to extend further to the west. In the latter group of graves, glazed sherds which appear to belong to the late medieval period were discovered. This means that the church was still considered holy ground in the time of the tolerant Seljuks (1307–1390), who allowed the Christians to use their old centers of worship.

It has not yet been possible to date the beginning of the burial tradition within the Church of Mary. While some assumed that this occured in the sixth century, the evidence now indicates a later date.[12] In 1993, a twelfth-century coin was found on top of one of the usually well-sealed graves. This suggests that all these burials are medieval, and also indicates that the building—in particular the vaulted portion—was still standing at that time. Whether the graves date to a time when there was still a cult going on in the church cannot be ascertained, but the fact that the graves (usually in a shallow position) were sealed suggests that this was the case. A bronze cross found in 1993 in one of the chests suggests the burial of a priest, which in turn indicates that a priest was in office here. Other graves, which do not have solid lids, may date to a later period when the church was no longer in use.

Finding any evidence regarding the date of the vaulted church was difficult, for its foundations were cut into the Roman strata without an extra ditch, which might have yielded finds helpful for dating. In

11. The latest excavation results have shown that the great apse was not built before 431.

12. Stefan Karwiese, *JÖAI* 63 (1994) Grabungen 1993, 15

1993, we succeeded in spotting a short ditch from which we unearthed the remnants of a glazed pot dating to the early Byzantine
time. Corroborating this evidence, a sherd that fits into the pot was
found in one of the sealed graves, again revealing that these graves
are more recent. It had been thought improbable that the Church of
Mary could have lasted or have been in use longer than the
episkopeion, which will be described later. All former ideas concerning the end of the Church of Mary, which experienced a grandiose
rebuilding at a time when the Church of St. John (map no. 78) on the
Selçuk castle hill had long been the episcopal see, must be disre-
garded. As the Church of St. John was turned into a stable by Pauli-
cians in 867/868, it is possible that the ensuing destruction or damage
caused by this militant Armenian sect necessitated a temporary re-
moval of the see to the Church of Mary, which might have been long-
abandoned or neglected. In this case, there would have been an
important reason to rebuild the Church of Mary after the seventh
century.

In 1986, the eastern part of the Roman stoa was recovered from
the overgrowth in which it had been concealed. Keil and Knoll, who
had excavated it together with the church, did not properly recognize
the building that was later built into the stoa. It had a central peristyle
court around which the rooms were located and thus looked like any
of the typical palace-like Ephesian peristyle houses. The fact that it
is built into the same complex as the church, however, suggests an
identical owner—the Christian community. Perhaps it can be identified as the episkopeion or bishop's palace, which archaeologists formerly had located in the rooms adjoining the great apse. As there was
no standard rule for bishops' palaces, the identification of the rooms
is uncertain, apart from a triklinon or "reception room" and possibly
a skeuophylakion or "treasury." Some minor objects, such as a bronze
thymiaterion or "incense burner," a leaden ampoule, and even a glass
bottle with the depiction of the menorah, indicate the Christian character of this house. Its interpretation as episkopeion is also corroborated by the discovery of an adjoining private bath complex; a fine
comparable example exists at Ravenna.[13]

13. Clementina Rizzadi, "Note sull'ántico episcopio di Ravenna: Formazione
e Suiluppo," in *Actes du XIe congrés international d'archéologie chrétienne*
(3 vols.; Rome: École française de Rome, 1989) 1. 725 and passim.

Fifty-six coins, dating between 359 and 548 CE, lay scattered on the floor of the treasury; as well as the aforementioned objects that belong to the sixth century, they date the destruction of the episkopeion. The youngest coin found on the floor, however, dated to 615. All these must have been overlooked during the raid that occurred here after 615 and that was probably the first Arabian plundering expedition into Byzantine areas by the later caliph Muʿāwiya. The raid probably occured in 654/655.

After this time, the episkopeion was abandoned, which means that the archbishop of Ephesos left the city and moved to the Church of St. John. This in turn indicates that the see and the *kathedra*, or bishop's throne, were removed. Although this shift was final, the latest evidence has shown that the Church of Mary was later used not only as a location for pilgrimage and hallowed burial ground, but also as a center where masses were again performed, at least for some time in the eighth or ninth century.

The council of 431 raises further questions about the Church of Mary, as there appears to be a discrepancy between the archaeological account and certain textual passages in the acts of the Council.[14] According to these, the sessions were held in a church named after Mary and in the adjoining episkopeion. Apart from the fact that these must be buildings we do not yet know, as those excavated are of a clearly later date, the terms used here for the church are curious. Although the Greek καλουμένη ("so-called") and ἐπίκλην ("named") are not uncommon in this context—together they seem to mean "with the second name of"—the terms indicate that Mary would have been merely an additional saint at the episcopal church. These terms differ from the official language, preserved in the inscription of the archbishop Hypatios during the reign of Justinianus I and found in the Church of Mary. Here, the juridically correct formula states "the most holy church of the famous all saintly and ever virginal Mary."[15] It therefore seems possible that the original metropolis, or seat of the bishop, had another patron saint—one would expect a local martyr,

---

14. Eduard Schwartz, ed., *Acta conciliorum oecumenicorum* (Berlin: de Gruyter, 1927) passim.

15. *IvE* VII 4135. This sixth-century inscription reads ἁγιωτάτη ἐκκλησία τῆς παναγίας ἐνδόξου θεοτόκου καὶ ἀειπαρθένου Μαρίας.

and at Ephesos one would expect John himself, whoever he actually was. Mary was linked to this saint for the occasion of the council, since the most important subject was the nature of Christ and thereby also the nature of his mother. Her new name of Theotokos ("she who gave birth to God") in the acts of the Council is proleptic and shows later editing.

The Church of Mary was built at the same time as the Church of St. John on the Selçuk castle hill, in about 500, which may indicate something peculiar. For reasons unknown to us—perhaps a quarrel between factions over the *proteia*, the priority of saints—the old see was split in two. The bishop moved with Mary to a new place, while the Church of St. John was transferred to the location of his—or some other John's—tomb.

The Council of Ephesos

THE DEMISE OF THE SEE OF EPHESOS AND
THE RISE OF THE CULT OF THE THEOTOKOS

Vasiliki Limberis
Temple University

Generations of church historians recount that the Council of Ephesos defined how Mary the mother of Jesus could be called the Theotokos, the God-bearer. From the physical and cultural evidence of the period, it is clear that the cult of the Virgin Mary grew tremendously between 400 and 451. This evidence is manifest in the rapid building of new churches to her all over the Mediterranean, the most famous of which are the churches built by Empress Pulcheria in Constantinople, all begun in the 430s. The church of the Blachernae housed the Virgin's robe; the church of Hodegetria housed the icon of the Virgin believed to have been painted by Luke. This icon was sent to Constantinople by Pulcheria's sister-in-law, the empress Eudokia, wife of Emperor Theodosios II. The third church, the Chalkoprateia, housed the Virgin's cincture.[1] In other cities of the

1. Raymond Janin, *Les églises et les monastères de Constantinople* (Paris: Institut français d'études byzantines, 1953) 177, 208, 246; and Kenneth Holum, *Theodosian Empresses* (Berkeley: University of California Press, 1982) 142, 221. Cyrus, who was both praetorian prefect and prefect of the city from 438

Mediterranean, only the church of Santa Maria Maggiore, built in
Rome in the late 430s by Pope Sixtus, was contemporaneous with
these three churches. The church of Santa Maria Trastevere is indeed
a fourth-century building, but it was not dedicated to the Virgin until
the seventh century. Santa Maria Kosmedin dates to the sixth century,
Santa Maria Antiqua and Santa Maria Aquiro to the seventh.[2] The
church to the Virgin in Thessaloniki, the ἀχειροποίητος ("not made
by hands"), dates roughly from the period between 450 and 470.[3] In
the 480s, the emperor Zeno built a church on Mount Gerazim to the
Virgin.[4] There is also the Church of Mary in Ephesos.[5] Moreover,

---

to 441, built the famous Theodosian walls and the first church to the Virgin
in Constantinople. Janin claims that it must have been built before 438. For
the legend surrounding the building, see Nikephoros Kallistos *Hist. eccl.* 13.46;
and Hesychios *Patria* 3.3.111 (ed. Theodore Preger; New York: Arno, 1975)
252.

2. Richard Krautheimer, *Corpus Basilicarum Christianorum Romae* (2 vols.;
Citta del Vaticano: Ponitifico instituto di archeologia cristiana, 1937–77) 2.
2–3, 249–74, 275–76, 277–307; 3. 1–60, 65–71.

3. Richard Krautheimer, *Early Christian and Byzantine Architecture*
(Harmandsworth, England: Penguin, 1986) 99. See also Charles Diehl, Marcel
le Tourneau, and Henri Saladin, *Les monuments chrétiens de Salonique* (2
vols.; Paris: Leroux, 1918) 1. 35–58. I thank James Skedros for reminding me
of this church.

4. Krautheimer, *Early Christian and Byzantine Architecture*, 75.

5. Much has been written about this church from an archaeological stand-
point, yet its date is still debated. See Reisch, Knoll, Keil, *Die Marienkirche*,
27–30. The Council Church, also known as the Church of the Virgin Mary,
was built on an older structure measuring 85.34 m. The long narthex and
atrium added another 58.83 m. Reisch believed that the old foundation was a
commercial building, and that the assignment of the church to Mary was a
result of the council (pp. 27–30). Both Carlo Cechelli (*Mater Christi* [4 vols.;
Rome: Ferrari, 1946] 1. 191–93) and Holum (*Empresses*) say that this second
opinion is unfounded. Veronika Mitsopoulou-Leon ("Ephesus," *Princeton
Encyclopedia of Classical Studies* [Princeton: Princeton University Press, 1976]
309) equivocates about the date—"about the fourth century A.D." Krautheimer
(*Early Christian and Byzantine Architecture*, 498 n. 13) faults Keil for not
giving reasons for dating the remodeling of the second-century structure into
a church at 350. He also criticizes F. W. Deichmann for proposing that the
church was built sometime in the early decades of the fourth century. Krautheimer
proposes judiciously, "Until further proof is forthcoming, it might be best to
withhold judgement."

wonderful hymns, extolling the Virgin in emotional, hyperbolic language, were written by prominent bishops of the day. Legends concerning her death began to appear in the fourth century. This study will focus on the Council of Ephesos, particularly as it relates to the Virgin Mary. In studying the acts of the Council of Ephesos, one may be astonished to find that the council had little to do with Mary and a great deal to do with conflict over episcopal hierarchy. The following question therefore arises: How do these conflicts regarding hierarchy relate to the cult of the Theotokos? In considering this question, it is important to keep in mind two facts that are clear even from a cursory study of this period. First, from 400 until 451, Ephesos lost to Constantinople the prestige and power it had had as an ancient apostolic see. Second, the legends that locate Mary's life and death in Jerusalem, not Ephesos—legends that became popular during this period—are consistent with Constantinople's claims over the Mary cult.

In addition to the many churches dedicated to Mary, other evidence points to the proliferation of her cult. Beautiful hymns were written in her honor, and stories called *Transitus Mariae* legends detailed Mary's later life and miraculous death. The account of Mary's relics in the *Euthymiac History*, as it is preserved in John of Damascus,[6] is also a significant example of the increasing impact of the

6. John of Damascus *In dormitionem Mariae homilia* (PG 96.748–52). The *Euthymiac History* is not extant. John of Damascus' homily includes a small section which describes the fate of Mary's relics; most scholars consider this to be an interpolation. Martin Jugie (*La mort et l'assumption de la sainte Vièrge* [Studi e testi 114; Vatican City: Biblioteca Vaticana, 1944] esp. 688–707) has written that the legend is an invention of the ninth century. Antoine Wegner agreed with Jugie only that the story was apocryphal and unhistorical, but since he found the *Euthymiac History* in MS Sinaiticus 491, he held that the legend could be dated back to 750; see Antoine Wegner, *L'Assomption de la S. Vièrge dans la tradition byzantine de VIe au Xe siècle* (Paris: Institute français d'étude byzantines, 1955) 137. Ernest Honigmann, ("Juvenal of Jerusalem," *DOP* 5 [1950] 211–77, esp. 268–70) disagreed with Jugie's assessments and gave a more nuanced account of the dating, meaning, and importance of the *Euthymiac History*. I am convinced by Honigmann that the *Euthymiac History* was written sometime after 518 and was interested in the "glorification of Juvenal" (p. 270). I believe, however, that it could have been circulating orally for fifty years before that, given the ecclesiastical politics and Marian building projects of the mid- to late fifth century.

cult of Mary. In considering this evidence, it is important to remember that whenever cult becomes important, physical sites of holiness in regions and cities gain great significance. This trend explains the importance placed upon the location of Mary's later life on earth and the city of her death. The *Akathistos Hymn*, the oldest extant hymn to the Theotokos still in liturgical use today in the orthodox church, dates to the period of the proliferation of the cult of Mary.

> Hail, to you, who conducts the opposites to unity. Hail to you, who has woven maidenhood into motherhood. Hail to you, through whom transgression was loosened. Hail to you, through whom paradise was opened. Hail, O key of Christ's kingdom. Hail, O hope of eternal blessings. Hail, O bride unwedded (Χαῖρε, νύμφη, ἀνύμφευτε).
>
> Hail, O unshakable tower of the church. Hail, O impregnable wall of the kingdom. Hail to you, through whom trophies of victory are assured. Hail, to you, through whom enemies are vanquished. Hail to you, who are the healing of my body. Hail to you, who are the salvation of my soul. Hail, O bride unwedded (Χαῖρε, νύμφη, ἀνύμφευτε).[7]

A similar hymn was written by Bishop Proclus; it so angered Bishop Nestorius that the resulting bitter conflict over the term "Theotokos" eventually forced Emperor Theodosius II to convene the Third Ecumenical Council at Ephesos. It reads:

> Hail, full of grace, you who weave without hands the crown for creation. Hail, full of grace, you are the return for those who fled the world. Hail, full of grace, you are the undepletable treasury of the starving world. Hail, full of grace, the joy from you, Holy Virgin, is infinite. Hail, full of grace, you are adorned with virtue-bearing light, an inextinguishable light brighter than the sun.[8]

7. *Akathistos Hymn* 15, 23 (PG 92. 1335–48).

8. Proclus of Constantinople (PG 61. 737–38). In the Migne edition, this hymn is listed as part of the *spuria* under Chrysostom. Recent scholarship has given evidence that it is by Proclus. F. J. Leroy, *L'homilétique de Proclus de Costantinople* (Citta del Vaticano: Biblioteca Apostolica Vaticana, 1976) 267–70; and Robert Caro, *La Homiletica mariana griega en el siglo V* (Dayton: University of Dayton, 1972) 308–24; S. A. Campos, ed., *Corpus Marianum Patristicum* (4 vols.; Burgos: Ediciones Aldecoa, 1976) 1. 35, 61–63.

Evidence for the increasing popularity of the Mary cult comes not only from hymns, but also from legends of the *Transitus Mariae*, or the falling asleep of Mary, of which there are eight extant versions. The legend, most scholars agree, dates from the fourth century. There are four Coptic versions, one Greek, two Latin, and one Syriac.[9] They all basically agree on the contents of the legend, which can be condensed into seven elements. First, Jesus entrusted Mary to the care of John. In some versions, both Mary and John continued to live in Jerusalem; in others, John departed for Ephesos, after ensuring that his family, which lived on the side of Mount of Olives, would watch over Mary's welfare in Jerusalem. All versions stress, however, that she lived in her own house with three virgin servants. No version says that she went to Ephesos, let alone died there. Second, the angel Gabriel announced her impending death. Third, she begged for all the apostles to be present at her death. They were spirited back to Jerusalem on clouds from each of the cities in which they were evangelizing, and, of course, John arrived from Ephesos. Fourth, topological conflicts with the Jews and subsequent conversion miracles occurred. Fifth, some versions maintain that Mary was buried in Gethsemane, some in the valley of Jesephat. Sixth, after anywhere from three to two hundred and six days, depending on the version, her body was taken to heaven and only her shroud and robe remained. Seven, all the apostles witnessed her empty tomb.

Another version of the legend is found in the *Euthymiac History*, which is no longer extant. Scholars believe that the legend circulated in written form during the midsixth century, but could easily have been circulating orally fifty years earlier. This legend about the Virgin's relics is contained in one of the eighth-century sermons of John of Damascus.[10]

The *Euthymiac History* reports that at the Council of Chalcedon in 451, Empress Pulcheria and Emperor Marcion, her husband in name

9. J. K. Elliott, *The Apocryphal New Testament* (Oxford: Clarendon, 1993) 691–93, 694–723.

10. John of Damascus *In dormitionem Mariae homilia* (PG 96. 748–52). Walter J. Burghardt, *The Testimony of the Patristic Age Concerning Mary's Death* (Westminster, MD: Newman, 1961) 35, 55 n. 116.

only, approached Bishop Juvenal of Jerusalem and said that they had heard that the Theotokos had been buried in Gethsemane. They asked him if they might have the remains and take them back to Constantinople. Juvenal, replying that indeed the Virgin died and was buried there, recounts the entire *transitus Mariae* story, how the apostles were spirited back to Jerusalem, and how they found Mary's tomb empty. Juvenal eagerly complies with Pulcheria's request, and the robe of the Theotokos is solemnly put into her new and magnificent Blachernae church. The Virgin then takes up residence in the church in Constantinople, the most beloved and sacred place in the imperial city. Although I shall analyze in more detail how these legends functioned, what is important now is that all this evidence—the church buildings, the *transitus Mariae* legends, and the *Euthymiac History*—specifically locate Mary's life and death in Jerusalem and connect her relics to imperial auspices.

Evidence that Mary was in Ephesos is meager, but probably proliferated in popular circles with the quick growth of the cult of the Virgin at the end of the fourth century. Epiphanius expressed earnest concern regarding this in his *Panarion*. He details three major heresies concerning the Theotokos: the Kollyridians, who worshipped Mary as a goddess and who had a female priesthood; the Antidikomarianites, who, conversely, said she was a normal woman who had conjugal relations with her husband Joseph and gave birth to many other children.[11] These first two heresies do not concern us here. The third heresy does, however. Epiphanius records that there was too much speculation circulating concerning the death of Mary. He reports that some said she was killed with a sword, some that she died, and some that she continues to live. In his desire to urge people to stop this useless speculation, he cautions them that they should keep silent as he chooses to do. He also says that the scriptures are absolutely silent about Mary's fate:

> Even though John was preparing for the journey to Asia, it says nowhere that he brought the holy Virgin with him, on account of

11. Epiphanius *Pan.* 3.78–79; 3.78.13–17 (Antidikomarianites); 3.79.109 (Kollyridians).

the awesomeness of the miracle, in order that the wonder would not lead the minds of humans to terror (or into dementia).[12] Here Epiphanius provides a rare and valuable clue that there was a tradition of Mary and John in Asia; and, as discussed above, John was associated specifically with Ephesos. By pointing out that the scriptures are silent about Mary's accompanying John to Asia, Epiphanius reveals precisely the story that was being bandied about, and the fact that many were connecting Mary's place of death to Ephesos.

The only other evidence of a tradition of Mary in Ephesos comes from two scant references in the acts of the Council of Ephesos. One finds them among the polemic details of the raucous proceedings of the council. In a letter that Cyril sent home to Alexandria, he says the "holy council met in the city's great church which some call Mary Theotokos."[13] The second is a general letter of the council to the church and laity in Constantinople. It read, "Whence Nestorius, the instigator of the doubly impious heresy, having arrived in the city of the Ephesians, wherein. . . John the theologian, and the Virgin Mother of God holy Mary."[14] These two references are the sum of the ancient contemporaneous evidence for Mary in Ephesos.

With regard to the more intricate political situation of the court of Constantinople and the Council of Ephesos, for some time scholars have realized and taken into account how the volatile personalities of

12. Ibid., 3.78.11; ζητήσωσι τὰ ἴχνη τῶν γραφῶν, καὶ εὕρωσιν ἂν οὔτε θάνατον Μαρίας οὔτε εἰ τέθαπται οὔτε εἰ μὴ τέθαπται, καίτοι γε τοῦ Ἰωάννου περὶ τὴν Ἀσίαν ἐνστειλαμένου τὴν πορείαν· καὶ οὐδαμοῦ λέγει ὅτι ἐπηγάγετο μεθ᾽ ἑαυτοῦ τὴν ἁγίαν παρθένον, ἀλλ᾽ ἁπλῶς ἐσιώπησεν ἡ γραφή, διὰ τὸ ὑπερβάλλον τοῦ θαύματος, ἵνα μὴ εἰς ἔκπληξιν ἀγάγῃ τὴν διάνοιαν τῶν ἀνθρώπων. ἐγὼ γὰρ τὴν τολμῶ λέγειν, ἀλλὰ διανοούμενος σιωπὴν ἀσκῶ.

13. *Cyril of Alexandria* "Letter 24," in Johannes Domininus Mansi, ed., *Sacrorum Conciliorum* (41 vols.; Florence: n.p., 1760) 4. 1241; ἡ ἁγία σύνοδος γέγονεν ἐν τῇ Ἐφέσῳ, ἐν τῇ μεγάλῃ ἐκκλησίᾳ τῆς πόλεως, ἥ τις καλεῖται Μαρία θεοτόκος.

14. Ibid.; ὅθεν καὶ Νεστόριος, [ὁ τῆς δυασεβοῦς αἱρέσεως ἀνακαινιστὴς] φθάσας ἐν τῇ Ἐφεσίων, ἔνθα ὁ θεολόγος Ἰωάννης, καὶ ἡ θεοτόκος ἡ ἁγία Μαρία.

Cyril of Alexandria and Nestorius affected ecclesiastical politics of the Christological controversy. W. H. C. Frend characterizes Nestorius as "tactless and loquacious."[15] Until the past few decades, however, tow realized the extent of the empress Pulcheria's power in these political and ecclesiastical intrigues. Older sister of Emperor Theodosius II, the empress directed political and ecclesiastical policy for the empire for the first half of the fifth century. From the beginning of the 420s until her death in 453, she politicized and institutionalized in Constantinople her intense devotion to the Virgin. Emperor Theodosius II did not always agree with her; their lives were marked by periodic breaches and subsequent reconciliations. One of these breaches occurred as a result of Theodosius's personal decision to invite an Antiochene monk, Nestorius, to become bishop of Constantinople in 428. Pulcheria and Nestorius soon found each other utterly odious. Much to Pulcheria's dismay, not only did Nestorius efface her own image above the altar in the great church that she had set up to instruct the people; he also barred her from the receiving communion inside of the altar, as had been her custom at Easter. Moreover, he did not allow her robe to be used as an altar covering.[16] The enmity between Nestorius and Pulcheria—who as an Augusta[17] had directed the ecclesiatical pageantry in Constantinople—was deeply personal.[18] The worst affront, however, was Nestorius's refusal to call Mary

15. W. H. C. Frend, *The Rise of Christianity* (Philadelphia: Fortress, 1984) 754.

16. Holum, *Empresses*, 77.

17. Pulcheria was proclaimed an Augusta in 414 and would proceed to exercise all the power bequeathed to her in that title. See Kenneth Holum, *Theodosian Empress* (Berkeley: University of California Press, 1982) 97. In my book I argue that Pulcheria redirected the powers of her *imperium* to establish public, institutionalized veneration of the Theotokos. "All of Pulcheria's efforts to establish public veneration of the Theotokos in Constantinople she accomplished as an Augusta creating new civic religious ceremonies. In addition by doing so she created new ecclesiastical rituals based on traditional civic ceremonies" (Vasiliki Limberis, *Divine Heiress, The Virgin Mary and the Creation of Christian Constantinople* [London: Routledge, 1994] 59–60).

18. The texts describing the fight between Nestorius and Pulcheria are preserved in Barḥadbeshabbā Arbāyā *La première partie de l'histoire de Barḥadbešabba 'Araïa; text syriaque* (PO 33.2; trans. François Nau; Paris: Firmin-Didot, 1913) 565–66; see also Holum, *Empresses*, 153–54.

"Theotokos," or God-bearer. He preached long, rousing sermons in the great church on the theological reasons why Mary should only be called Χριστοτόκος or Θεοδόχος—"God-vessel."[19] Pulcheria had her own bishops in residence, Proclus of Cyzicus and Eusebius of Dorylaeum, who because of endless political battles could not take up the bishoprics in their own cities. Instead, they helped Pulcheria to muster popular support against Nestorius, preached sermons in honor of the Theotokos, and delivered panegyrics to Pulcheria.[20]

At this time, Cyril of Alexandria heard from his spies in Constantinople what Nestorius was preaching.[21] Cyril had been instrumental in John Chrysostom's demise[22] and took any opportunity to chastise the church in Constantinople. The church there was an imperial see, not an ancient apostolic one, and Cyril could not abide its claims to a second position of honor next to Rome. This new claim had been pronounced in 381 at the Second Ecumenical Council, and had effectively demoted Alexandria to third place, Antioch to fourth, Jerusalem to fifth, and Ephesos to sixth.[23] After Cyril informed Pope Celestine of Nestorius's deeds and presented Nestorius with ultimatums, the pope excommunicated Nestorius, appointed Cyril his representative, and gave Cyril the power to carry out the decisions of the Roman synod.[24] Cyril delayed carrying out the pope's wishes, however, and sent his own ultimatum to Nestorius, along with twelve anathemas against him. He also unwisely angered the emperor by writing letters to Pulcheria and her sisters and Empress Eudokia, who then further badgered Theodosius about getting rid of Nestorius. In November 430, Theodosius preempted Cyril and Pope Celestine by convoking an ecumenical council in Ephesos. Theodosius wrote an angry letter to Cyril, ordering him to act in a conciliatory and colle-

19. Karl Joseph von Hefele, *A History of the Councils of the Church* (5 vols.; Edinburgh: T. & T. Clark, 1883–96) 3. 23–24.
20. Proclus of Constantinople (PG 64. 787–89); see Holum, *Empresses*, 138; and Limberis, *Divine Heiress*, 51.
21. Hefele, *History*, 3. 23–24.
22. Frend, *Rise of Christianity*, 752–55.
23. Ibid.; Raymond Janin, "Ephèse," *Dictionnaire d'histoire et de géographie écclésiastique* 15 (1963) 556.
24. Hefele, *History*, 3. 25.

gial manner at the proceedings and to stop meddling in the affairs of the imperial family.

Cyril's conduct at the council was less than exemplary. During the hot summer of 431, some two hundred and forty-five bishops from all over the empire met in Ephesos. Notable absences were Pope Celestine, who sent three presbyters, Augustine of Hippo, who was invited but had died, and Emperor Theodosius, who sent two military counts, Candidian and Irenaeus. Candidian's job was to police the area and keep the Alexandrian monks from rioting and mugging their enemies, and Irenaeus's mission was to be Nestorius's bodyguard.[25]

John of Antioch, friend and fellow Antiochene of Nestorius, arrived three weeks late, and found that Nestorius had already been excommunicated by Cyril and his council. John set up a countersynod of forty-three like-minded eastern bishops.[26] During the entire summer, Nestorius could not leave his house due to violence. Cyril's greatest ally at the council, Bishop Memnon of Ephesos, had monks and local clergy sack Nestorius's residence and abuse his friends. Memnon also closed the Church of John to the Nestorians and then barred them from all Ephesian churches.[27] Count Candidian soon retaliated and cut off food supplies to the Cyrillian synod, and made sure imperial guards abused and harrassed those bishops. Indeed, several bishops died that summer, and by July most were begging to go home.[28] Horrendous reports from both sides were reaching Constantinople and the emperor: Cyril wrote to the emperor and laity in the city, and Candidian sent his own version of how Nestorius was essentially being convicted without a trial. Pulcheria was simply content that Nestorius was out of her city and her churches. The people, moreover, supported her, not her brother.[29]

By the end of July, Theodosius had Bishops Memnon, Cyril, and Nestorius arrested, and he declared by imperial edict that no one could leave Ephesos. The city had been turned into an episcopal

25. Ibid., 3. 24, 41; and Mansi, *Sacrorum Conciliorum*, 4. 1109, 1110.
26. Hefele, *History*, 3. 358.
27. Ibid., 3. 53.
28. Ibid., 3. 59–61; Mansi, *Sacrorum Conciliorum*, 4. 1444–45.
29. Holum, *Empresses*, 170–71.

prison.[30] Theodosius further ordered that representatives from both sides come to Constantinople and explain their cases, but so many anti-Nestorian riots ensued that Theodosius told the envoys to wait for him in Chalcedon.[31] Among those representing the Cyrillian side was Bishop Juvenal of Jerusalem, who through the absence of John of Antioch and the jailing of Cyril was next in episcopal order. This plan for a meeting before Theodosius still did not resolve the situation. Finally, in late September, weary from the Constantinople riots and petty disputes, Theodosius agreed to depose Nestorius and dissolved the council. Nestorius was deposed and exiled to a monastery in Antioch. Bishops Memnon and Cyril were released from jail and allowed to resume their episcopal duties, although Cyril had already managed to escape back to Alexandria. Theodosius, however, was not convinced of their so-called orthodox position. The imperial edict reads: "At the same time we also give it to be known that, as long as we live, we shall not condemn the orientals, for they have not been confuted in our presence."[32]

Two more years would pass before bishops and theologians of the Antiochene school would accept the title Theotokos and Cyril's twelve anathemas would be dropped. Pulcheria believed that her point of view had triumphed as soon as Nestorius had vacated Constantinople. An aged bishop, Maximian, was ordained in the capital, and in only two and a half more years Proclus would become bishop of Constantinople.[33]

This cursory overview reveals that the council was not concerned with mariology. Cyril's Christological definition—"one nature of God

30. Mansi, *Sacrorum Conciliorum*, 4. 1444–45; "This is the reason that we have been guarded like prisoners. Everything that is being reported to the most pious Emperor is brought up against us falsely. The garrison-like watch against us is tremendous, and a huge war is resulting." αἴτιον δὲ τοῦ οὕτως ἡμᾶς φρουρεῖσθαι, τὸ πάντα τὰ καθ᾽ ἡμᾶς ψευδῶς τως εὐσεβεστάτῳ βασιλεῖ ἀναφέρεσθαι. . . . ἡ πολλὴ καθ᾽ ἡμῶν φρουρά, καὶ ὁ πολὺς γίνεται πόλεμος. This unsigned letter addressed the clergy of Constantinople, pleading for an end to the council.

31. Hefele, *History*, 3. 99.

32. Ibid., 3. 110.

33. Frend, *Rise of Christianity*, 763.

incarnate" (μία φύσις τοῦ θεοῦ σεσαρκωμένη)—entered into broad usage. It allowed Mary to be called Theotokos in a derivative way, or more precisely through the growing theological principle of *communicatio idiomatum.*[34] Cyril's expositions are thoroughly Christological; in his most famous exposition on Mary, seventeen of the nineteen paragraphs deal with the union of the two natures of Christ and with the definition of hypostasis. Only one paragraph deals with Mary.[35] Cyril's language, moreover, is so vague and imprecise that the Monophysites would later use him as their source. It would take the Council of Chalcedon in 451 to hone the language of the two natures of Christ, and also establish the cult of the Virgin in Constantinople and permanently subject the see of Ephesos to a powerless status, which in some respects was a necessary consequence of Constantinople's bid for power and legitimacy. These conclusions, which were reached only twenty years after the Council of Ephesos, must nevertheless be traced to two important canons of the earlier council. First, the Council of Ephesos established a new system of episcopal hierarchy—archmetropolitans, who became known as patriarchs.[36] The only four sees granted this status of patriarchate at the council were—in this order—Rome, Constantinople, Alexandria, and Antioch. Furthermore, the patriarchs were defined separately from their suffragans and were required to sign separately from their suffragans at the council.[37] This would have fatal consequences for Ephesos, since

34. *Communicatio idiomatum* is a theological hermeneutic that derives from the Christological formulations of the fifth century. Since Christ is one divine hypostasis with two natures, one divine and one human, he has a single source of existence. His human and his divine actions are united in his divine personhood. Christ's divine hypostasis "communicated to the human nature characteristics that normally belong only to divinity, and reciprocally, the Word (Logos) assumes a human mode of existence" (John Meyendorff, *Christ in Christian Thought* [Crestwood, NY: St. Vladimir's Seminary Press, 1975] 170). By the principle of *communicatio idiomatum*, whatever can be posited of the divine nature can also be posited of the human nature; the principle legitimates the "deification of the flesh" with reference to Christ's body and the use of the appellation "Theotokos" for Mary, since she gave birth to one divine person, the Logos incarnate (p. 24).

35. Cyril Alex. *St. Cyril of Alexandria*, vol. 1: *Letters 1–50* (FC 76–77; trans. John I. McEnerney; Washington, DC: Catholic University Press, 1985) letter 17. 80–92 (pp. 80–92); Limberis, *Divine Heiress*, 109.

36. Frend, *Rise of Christianity*, 761.

37. Anna Crabbe, "The Invitation List to the Council of Ephesus and Metropolitan Hierarchy in the Fifth Century," *JTS* 32 (1981) 395–400. Suffragan

its only claim to power was the important western Asia Minor regions it ruled.[38] A second important event was Juvenal of Jerusalem's stellar rise to power at the council.[39]

The decision to make distingushed archmetropolitans separate from their suffragans had far-reaching repercussions. Ephesos had been recognized as an apostolic see by the First Ecumenical Council in Nicea, since it could boast apostolic visits from Paul, Timothy, and John. The sixth canon of that council recognized that Ephesos had jurisdiction over Asia proconsularis, the eleven provinces that formed Asia; it was head of the diocese of the two Asias, Caria, Lycia, Lydia, the two Pamphylias, the two Phrygias, the Hellespont, and Bithynia.[40] This division was based on the Diocletian reorganization of the government into dioceses. The second canon of the Second Ecumenical Council of 381 affirmed the Council of Nicea's decision that Ephesos ruled over western Asia Minor.[41] The third canon of this council, however, began the gradual eclipse of Ephesian power. As the new imperial see, Constantinople sought honor and legitimacy, and the third canon asserts that the see of Constantinople was second in the empire after Rome, effectively displacing Alexandria, Antioch, Jerusalem, and Ephesos.[42] Constantinople's justification for the new precedent was the "prestige of the city and imperial dignity."[43] Roman popes chose to ignore this claim and its justification for the next seventy years until 451, since technically the canons had not been

---

bishops are under an archbishop or metropolitan and may be summoned at any time to provide services for their superior. Crabbe makes the point that all the bishops at the council were stripped of the voting power of their suffragans. For those sees designated as patriarchates this was not crippling. But for the bishop of Ephesos to be stripped of his many suffragan bishops and not to become a patriarchate was a double blow to the city's power and prestige.

38. Frend, *Rise of Christianity*, 761.

39. Ernest Honigmann, "Juvenal of Jerusalem," *DOP* 5 (1950) 211–77; Frend, *Rise of Christianity*, 759–60; Hefele (*History*, 3. 107) states, "In many ways Juvenal of Jerusalem had been guilty of presumption."

40. Janin, "Ephèse," 557.

41. Ibid.

42. Ibid.

43. Francis Dvornik, *The Idea of Apostolicity in Byzantium and the Legend of the Apostle Andrew* (Cambridge, MA: Harvard University Press, 1958) 54 n. 41.

submitted to Rome for ratification.[44] Rome, Ephesos, and many other cities stressed apostolic foundation as the criterion for honor, precedence, and position. Apostolicity, however, was less important or awe-inspiring in the East than in the West.[45] According to the Acts of the Apostles and the various apocryphal acts, the apostles had visited many eastern cities, and thus the claim to apostolic favor held much less lustre. Ephesos's continued claim to apostolicity would have little effect. Significantly, at the Council of Ephesos, Memnon of Ephesos was the only eastern bishop who acknowledged the Roman legates' claim to apostolic foundation.[46] It was too late, however, to control the growing power of Constantinople.

Beginning in 381, the church in Constantinople infringed upon Ephesian sovereignty. John Chrysostom, bishop of Constantinople in approximately 400, was instrumental in closing the temple of Artemis, and also began to trespass upon the Ephesian bishop's territorial jurisdiction, intervening in his affairs.[47] In 400, Chrysostom called a local synod in the capital to hear seven articles of grievance against Bishop Antoninus of Ephesos. Although Antoninus had died by the time that Chrysostom reached Ephesos, Chrysostom proceeded with his investigation, holding a council of seventy bishops from the provinces of Asia, Lydia, and Caria. Together they consecrated Heraclides bishop of Ephesos and then deposed six bishops for simony.[48] On the way home, Chrysostom meddled in Phrygia, rooting out Novationists and Quartodecimani.[49] Chrysostom had begun the precendent of usurping the power of the Ephesian see, especially by consecrating the bishop, whose "claim to archepiscopal status was as good as, or better than, his own."[50] The foundation had been laid for the Ephesian see's enmity toward the see of Constantinople.

44. Ibid., 52–56. Dvornik maintains that the third canon was intended to break the stronghold that Alexandria had over Constantinople, and that Rome regarded this as an eastern conflict.

45. Ibid., 48.

46. Ibid., 66.

47. Clive Foss, *Ephesus after Antiquity* (Cambridge: Cambridge University Press, 1979) 30; Frend, *Rise of Christianity*, 750–51.

48. Frend, *Rise of Christianity*, 751.

49. Ibid.

50. Ibid., 750.

From the acts of the Council of Ephesos it is clear that Bishop Memnon squandered his chance to gain favor with the imperial court. He may have promoted the correct teaching regarding the Theotokos, but he had been placed under house arrest in his own city, since he attached himself too closely to the rabble-rouser Cyril, whose own antipathy to the see of Constantinople was never disguised. In more than one sense, Memnon's fateful actions in combination with the Council of Ephesos had doomed the see of Ephesos in terms of prestige and authority. It was only a matter of time before Constantinople would completely rob it of its territories and dignity.[51] The council's decision that a bishop could be a patriarch separate from the regions he ruled was catastrophic for Ephesos. Without his administrative subordinates, the bishop of Ephesos was rendered less important; and the decision effectively rendered the Ephesian see unprotected with regard to Constantinople's designs. Edward Schwartz correctly explained, "It was from the imperial chancellery"—rather than from an episcopal council—"that the new orders emanated."[52]

Juvenal of Jerusalem was the final link in the story of the demise of the see of Ephesos and the simultaneous rise of the cult of the Theotokos under Constantinopolitan control. Juvenal, a Latin by birth and language, enjoyed a long tenure as a bishop, from 422 until 458. Characterizing Juvenal's career, Ernest Honigmann stated, "Juvenal's chief object was the elevation of the see of Jerusalem from its subordinate position to Antioch and Caesarea, to the status and power of full archmetropolitan."[53] Juvenal's main enemy was therefore John of Antioch, whose territories were adjacent to Juvenal's. Conveniently, Juvenal theologically opposed John's more Nestorian position,[54] and at times Juvenal's vituperations in defense of orthodoxy and against John masked blatant displays of ambition. Although Juvenal sided closely with Cyril and the supporters of Theotokos, Cyril did not support Juvenal's political ambitions. At the council, Cyril discovered

51. Janin, "Ephèse," 557.
52. Crabbe, "Invitation List," 400. Edward Schwartz, *Über die Bischofslisten der Synoden von Chalkedon, Nicaea und Konstantinopel* (SBAW.PPH n.f. 13; Munich: Verlag der Bayerischen Akademie der Wissenschaften, 1937) 15.
53. Honigmann, "Juvenal," 211.
54. Ibid., 213.

that Juvenal had applied to the pope to get Antiochene territories under his Jerusalem provenance; indeed, because of John's tenuous heretical position at the council, Juvenal was able to rule over some of the Antiochene territories for a time. Cyril and the pope did not agree with Juvenal's claim.[55] After the council, however, Juvenal's territorial expansion program found favor with Constantinople. When Bishop Proclus was elected patriarch of Constantinople, he sent warm greetings to Juvenal.[56] Knowing of Juvenal's close ties with the court in the later 430s, Cyril wrote to Abbot Gennadius of Palestine, who would not submit to Juvenal and foresake Antioch; Cyril encouraged him to have patience, tolerate Juvenal's overblown pretensions, and not sever relations with Proclus.[57] Honigmann has shown that before the council in 431, Emperor Theodosius had conferred wider territorial rights on Juvenal, although these imperial edicts are not extant.[58] Juvenal's close ties with the imperial court infuriated Cyril, and neither Cyril nor the pope would acknowledge Juvenal's new rank.[59]

Although Juvenal remained an ardent supporter of the Cyrillian side, he managed to remain in the favor of the court, even when Emperor Theodosius unleashed his wrath against Cyril and Memnon. After the council, at the emperor's bidding, Juvenal was able to go to Chalcedon to represent the theology of the Theotokos.[60] Juvenal's power continued unabated for the next fifteen years. For example, during the Robber Council, the Latrocinium, of 449, which supported monophysite Christology, Juvenal's strong alliance with the new Alexandrian bishop, Dioskouros, convinced Theodosius of the council's orthodoxy.[61] In 450, moreover, a local Constantinople synod gave

55. Ibid., 217; Hefele, *History*, 77.
56. Honigmann, "Juvenal," 217..
57. Ibid.
58. Ibid.
59. Ibid., 217, 221.
60. Ibid., 224.
61. Ibid., 234–38. Leo named the council "Latrocinium" because of the way in which Dioskouros seized power, not even allowing his *Tome* to be read in the council. Leo wrote the *Tome* in 449 to set forth a balanced theological corrective to Eutyches and others who misunderstood Cyril's Christological language. Cyril's language was so ambiguous that it easily lent itself to monophysite Christology, which Eutyches espoused. Leo's tome has since

Juvenal three provinces that he coveted—Arabia and two Phoenician provinces; he also gained the goodwill of the emperor.[62]

Juvenal's triumphs were not to last, however. For some time, Pulcheria had been estranged from her brother and the court because he was under the primacy of the chamberlain Chrysaphios, an ardent supporter of Bishop Dioskouros.[63] Early in 450, Theodosius finally learned of some of Chrysaphios's illegal activities and quickly exiled him.[64] With Chrysaphios's departure, Pulcheria immediately returned in full power to the court. She strongly disagreed with the monophysite Christology of Juvenal and Dioskouros and wrote to Pope Leo about the impious error.[65] As an answer, Leo prepared his famous *Tome*, which arrived in the capital in the fall of 450.[66] In July, however, Emperor Theodosius died in a riding accident. Pulcheria recognized this opportunity to seize power. Even though she was a virgin dedicated by a vow to God, she wisely chose a husband who would respect her vow. Although her consort Marcian was the emperor, she successfully reigned until her death in 453.

In 451, Pulcheria convoked a council at Chalcedon to rid the empire of the latest heresy. Pope Leo's *Tome* against monophysite Christology was sent to all the bishops. Juvenal had two choices: he could sign in agreement with Pope Leo, or go into exile with Dioskouros.[67] At the council he was essentially on trial, and for all his previous bravado, claimed that he had had only a small role in the Robber Council. He switched his theology and was rewarded by reinstatement with status as a patriarch, although he lost three of his six newly acquired provinces.[68]

Those under his jurisdiction, who included strongly monophysite Palestinian monks, revolted at his reinstatement; not only did they

---

been credited as the foundation of Chalcedonian Christology. For the English text, see James Stevenson, ed., *Creeds, Councils, and Controversies* (New York: Seabury, 1966) 315–24.

62. Ibid., 238.
63. Holum, *Empresses*, 191–202.
64. Ibid., 206–7.
65. Hefele, *History*, 267–74, Honigmann, "Juvenal," 239.
66. Honigmann, "Juvenal," 240.
67. Ibid.; Hefele, *History*, 330.
68. Honigmann, "Juvenal," 240–47.

refuse to allow him to return to Jerusalem, but they also elected their own bishop. Using his exile well, Juvenal lived in Constantinople and won the friendship and respect of Empress Pulcheria and Marcian.[69] To his advantage, moreover, Pulcheria's sister in law, the Empress Eudokia, whom Pulcheria had grown to dislike bitterly in later years, supported the Palestinian monks against Juvenal. For the past thirteen years, Eudokia had effectively been exiled in the Holy Land for alleged infidelity to Theodosius, thanks to the machinations of Chrysaphios. Pulcheria gladly supported Juvenal against her sister-in-law.[70]

By 453, Juvenal was able to return to Jerusalem, accompanied by a military troop which ensured his safety. Marcian and Pulcheria wrote separate letters to most of the important clergy in Palestine, declaring that Juvenal was "saved by the Holy Trinity," and he should be honored since he was bishop of Jerusalem, the throne of the "thrice-holy James."[71] At the Council of Chalcedon, Juvenal was restored to the episcopacy and an enlarged territory through his favor with Pulcheria and Marcian.

Another important result of the Council of Chalcedon was its twenty-eighth canon, which stated that along with Pontus and Thrace, Asia proconsularis—that is, territories under the see of Ephesos—would thereafter be under the jurisdiction of the patriarchate of Constantinople.[72] Ephesos, as well as Rome, strongly protested, but to no avail. Ephesos was effectively reduced to a provincial diocese with absolutely no power; as a result, Constantinople used Ephesos as a pawn in its bid for patriarchal dignity and power. Ephesos allied itself even more strongly with Alexandria, Constantinople's most virulent competitor.[73]

In 474, Paul, then patriarch of Alexandria, restored to Ephesos its ancient rights in a council he held in Asia. All Ephesian territories were reestablished and its third place of honor, after Rome and Alex-

69. Ibid.

70. Holum, *Empresses*, 184–94.

71. Honigmann, "Juvenal," 251–56 as he quotes *Marciani Imp. Epist. ad Macarium espiscopos et monachos in m. Sina ACO* 2. 1, pars 3, p. 132.1–2 [491.1–2]; and p. 133.27–28 [492.27–28].

72. Janin, "Ephèse," 556; Hefele, *History*, 410–20.

73. Janin, "Ephèse," 556–57.

andria, was reinstated.[74] This did not take effect, however. In fact, during the reign of Justinian the Ephesian see was further effaced by being acknowledged as a "second level metropolitanate," after Caesarea in Cappadocia.[75] As I have argued, however, this devolution had begun with the Council of Ephesos.

To summarize, from the time of the Second Ecumenical Council, Constantinople embarked on a program of legitimating its imperial see and gaining power in ecclesiastical politics. Constantinople was not vengeful toward Ephesos; Ephesian territories were simply adjacent to Constantinople, as were Pontus and Thrace. Moreover, Ephesos allied itself too closely with Alexandria, which was most injured by Constantinople's ascendency and forever lost its battles with Constantinople. Ephesos was merely a victim of its location, as apostolicity did not matter to the capital.

I have stressed that Constantinople's usurpation of Ephesos's jurisdictions and its effective disempowerment were neither punitive nor "personal"; after all, Constantinople had already taken the bones of Timothy from Ephesos in 356.[76] Such moves were ploys to gain legitimacy and power. The location of the Virgin's tomb was just such a ploy; there is no doubt that one of Pulcheria's goals was to sacralize Constantinople. She brought the relics of a dozen saints and forty martyrs to the city; for many of these she built magnificent churches. Above all, she spent her life in devotion to the Theotokos and was at the forefront of those who wanted publically and liturgically to institute the cult of the Virgin in Constantinople. The close political alliance of Bishop Juvenal and Pulcheria represents a convergence of piety, politics, and the creation of legends. Whether Juvenal gave Pulcheria the Virgin's relics is not the central issue; rather it is significant that the predominant legends of the Virgin's death in Jerusalem and subsequent transfer of relics became the accepted version throughout the empire. Moreover, these legends corroborate the political alliance between Juvenal and the imperial court. The Jerusalem legends proliferating at this time overshadow the weaker legend tradition that Mary died in Ephesos and serve as propaganda for both Constantinople and

74. Ibid., 557.
75. Ibid.
76. Foss, *Ephesus*, 36.

Jerusalem. It is significant that in 474 Emperor Zeno built a church to Mary on Mount Gerizim and that in 532 Bishop Hypatios of Ephesos denied the validity of the legend associating Juvenal and Pulcheria with the Virgin's relics.[77] It is clear that Ephesos was not in political favor in either Constantinople court circles or ecclesiastical circles.

The legend relating that Juvenal gave the relics to Pulcheria rewarded his loyalty to the court against the mounting threat of Alexandrian monophysitism and gave honor to the Jerusalem see forever. Most of all, the *Transitus Mariae* legends and the legend in the *Euthymiac History* accomplished four things. First, they legitimated the cult of the Virgin and dispelled any notion of bodily relics. Second, they legitimated a particular version of her death: she was not martyred, but she died in Jerusalem while John was in Ephesos. This effectively dispelled Epiphanius's concerns regarding the dangerous speculations surrounding Mary's death. Third, the legends gave Constantinople exclusive rights to Mary's relics, further sanctifying and legitimating the new Rome with the holiest of all presences. Fourth, because Mary's death and assumption were located once and for all in Jerusalem, Ephesos lost its claim to her presence and holiness.

In the events surrounding the Council of Ephesos, "we see a civilization unembarrassed by its belief in the immanence of the metaphysical in the realm of the mundane"[78]—a society that operated all the while by the principles of *Realpolitik*.

77. Honigmann, "Juvenal," 268.

78. Anthony Cutler, *Transfigurations: Studies in the Dynamics of Byzantine Iconography* (University Park: Pennsylvania State University Press, 1975) 119.

Glossary

abacus: The uppermost part of a column capital, carrying the architrave.

aedile: A Roman official with responsibilities concerning public works.

agonothetes: Originally the judge of a contest; also the sponsor and/or president of games and athletic contests.

agora: A market, political center, and meeting place of a Greek city, usually composed of public and sacred buildings with one or more stoas, framing an irregularly shaped open space. Unlike the Roman agora (forum), the Greek agora was normally not entirely enclosed.

agoranomos: A clerk of the market, in charge of regulating business transactions there.

akroterion: Statuary or other decorations made of marble or terracotta, supported by blocks resting on the vertex and lower extremities of the pediment.

amphora: A tall jar for oil or wine with a narrow mouth and two handles.

antae: The projecting walls of the cella of a temple forming the pronaos and opisthodomos; two columns are usually placed between the antae (described as "columns in antis").

anthemion: An ornamental band consisting of alternating palmettes and lotus flowers, decorating the frieze of a wall or the uppermost part of a column.

archierea, archiereus: High priestess; high priest.

archiiatros: Chief physician; court or official physician.

archisynagogos: Leader of a synagogue.

architrave: The lowest portion of the entablature, which rests directly on the column capitals.

arris: The sharp edge between the concave moldings of the flutes of a Doric column (see fillet).

ashlar: Masonry technique in which dressed rectangular slabs are fitted together without mortar.

asiarch: High official in the province of Asia; the religious and/or political functions of this office are not well known.

astragal: A type of decorative molding which often combines bead-and-reel motifs with egg-and-dart.

atrium: An entrance hall or inner court of a building (a house or a court of a church), usually open-air, often surrounded by colonnaded porticoes.

baldachin: An ornamental canopy which projects from the wall or is supported by columns, especially over an altar or seat of honor. See also ciborium.

basilica: A roofed hall of a secular or religious building with two internal colonnades which divide the hall into one central and two side aisles. Major Christian churches may have as many as four internal colonnades. In the early Christian period, any Christian assembly hall could be designated as a basilica.

bead-and-reel: Type of decorative molding with an alternating pattern of one larger circle and two much smaller circles. Often found just below egg-and-dart decoration.

boukranion: A bull's head or skull, carved in frontal view, used in ornamental design and found especially on altars and sometimes tombs and friezes, often in combination with garlands which recall the bulls garlanded for sacrifice.

boule: The council of a city, composed of elders or elected or appointed representatives. It is distinct from the demos (the assembly of all citizens), and the prytaneis (the presiding officers of the city government).

bouleuterion: Meeting hall for the city council.

cardo: A central street, which usually ran north-south, perpendicular to the main thoroughfare, or decumanus.

cavea: The rounded, often semicircular, section of the theater or amphitheater containing seats for the spectators.

caveto: A concave molding having a curve that roughly approximates a quarter circle.

cella: Central part of a temple in which the temple statue is placed. See naos.

cenotaph: An honorary tomb or monument for persons whose remains are kept or buried elsewhere as, for example, soldiers who died in foreign wars.

chalcidicum: A partially or completely roofed annex to a basilica or other public building.

chiton: A full-length tunic worn by Greek women; a knee-length tunic worn by Greek men.

chlamys: A short mantle fastened on the right shoulder.

ciborium: A baldachin or canopy, usually supported by four columns, over a sacred object or martyr's relics.

coffer: A recessed panel in a ceiling, vault, or soffit.

colonnade: A row of columns along a street or building (see stoa).

Corinthian order: Closely related to the Ionic order with respect to the columns and entablature. The capitals of its columns and pilasters are decorated with acanthus leaves.

cornice: The projecting, upper part of the entablature below the sima.

crepidoma: (also crepis) The upper part of the stereobate, resting on the foundations, usually consisting of three steps, of which the uppermost is the stylobate.

cryptoporticus: A porch under the main level of a building or agora.

cuirass: A piece of armor covering the body from neck to hips with a breastplate and a back piece.

decuma: The tenth person, day, or hour; tithe; tenth part of booty.

decumanus maximus: The main road in a Roman settlement, usually running east-west, perpendicular to the cardo.

decurion: Member of the city council in cities of Roman or Italian constitution.

demos: The assembly of all citizens of a city who were qualified to vote (see boule).

dentils: Small rectangular cuttings which extend down from the lower edge of the cornice.

Doric order: Doric columns stand directly on the stylobate without a base. The columns have sixteen to twenty flutes which are separated by sharp arrises. The column capitals consist of two parts: a square abacus, which rests upon a bell-shaped echinus. The entablature is composed of (from bottom to top): an architrave of undecorated stone beam, a frieze with alternating triglyphs and metopes, and a cornice or geison which usually projects outward.

echinus: The lower part of a Doric capital. See Doric order.

egg-and-dart: A type of molding decoration characteristic of the Ionic order. The pattern consists of repeated egg shaped ovals with dart-like decorations between each of them.

eirenarch: A police magistrate.

entablature: The upper part of a building which rests on a wall or columns, consisting of architrave, frieze, and cornice, and which carries the pediment and roof of the building. See Doric order, Ionic order.

ependytes: Clothing or ornaments that are worn over other garments.

epistyle: The architectural components above the columns of a building, consisting of architrave, frieze, and geison (see entablature).

façade: The front of a building which is given special, often superficial, architectural treatment.

fasciae: The three, or sometimes two, lightly projecting bands of the architrave of the Ionic and Corinthian orders.

fillet: Narrow projecting vertical strip on an Ionic column which separates its concave flutes.

finial: Usually floral detail or ornament crowning the peak of a conical roof, corresponding to the akroterion on a pediment.

flute: The vertical channel on a column; flutes are separated from one another by an arris (Doric order) or by a fillet (Ionic order).

forum: The Roman counterpart of the Greek agora, usually a rectangular, open-air building, enclosed on all sides and including shops, temples, and public buildings, often with porticoes on all four sides.

frieze: Part of the entablature above a colonnade or the uppermost part of a wall, usually decorated with reliefs. Decorated friezes also appear on the top of the walls of peripteros temples inside the colonnades.

geison: See cornice.

grammateus: Scribe; in Ephesos the scribe of the demos was the most important political official.

herm: A square pillar surmounted by a sculpted head. Male genitals (often an erect phallus) are the only sculptures on the pillar itself. Herms were commonly used as boundary markers, but were also incorporated into household worship and were often used as decorative statues and memorials for famous persons.

heroon: A cenotaph shrine or funerary monument to a hero or heroine.

hexastyle: A temple with a row of six columns in front of its cella.

himation: A heavy mantle worn by Greek women and men.

insula(e): One of the rectangular plots defined by the street grid of a town; a block of shops or houses.

Ionic order: Each Ionic column stands on a base, consisting of plinth, spira, and torus which is set upon the stylobate. The columns have twenty to twenty-four flutes which are separated by blunt fillets. The capitals consist of an egg-and-dart band, volutes, and a narrow abacus. The entablature is composed of the architrave (normally consisting of three fasciae), the frieze (often decorated with an uninterrupted band of reliefs), and the cornice or geison with a band of egg-and-dart and a band of dentils.

koinon: Provincial council of Asia.

komarchia: Leadership of a band of revellers, especially in the cult of Dionysos.

kosmeteira: Female magistrate in Ephesos with functions in the cult of Artemis.

kourotrophos: Epithet of Artemis and other goddesses, meaning "nourisher of youths."

lintel: The horizontal architectural piece above a door or other opening.

martyrium: The place, either a separate (sometimes octagonal) building, chapel, or a crypt inside a church under the altar or apse, where the relics of a martyr are kept.

metope: In Doric architecture the square or nearly square field between two triglyphs in the entablature, often decorated with sculptures in low relief.

molpoi: A guild of musicians.

naiskos: A little naos; a small temple or shrine. See naos.

naos: (also cella) The shrine or innermost part of a temple in which the temple statue was placed.

narthex: The entrance hall of a Christian basilica, situated between the atrium and the church, usually rectangular. From the narthex, one enters the main sanctuary, or nave and aisles, of the basilica, usually by means of three doorways.

nave: The central aisle in a basilica (public hall or church), usually higher and wider than the two side aisles, extending from the rear wall to the apse or screen of the altar. In a cruciform church, it does not include the transept.

neokoros: Temple warden. Used in early times for priestly officers of high rank; under the Roman emperors, the term became a title of dignity for cities which had received permission to erect temples for the imperial cult and were regarded as guardians of the official provincial cult of the emperor.

neopoios: Official in charge of the temple-fabric.

odeion: A roofed concert or lecture hall, generally much smaller than open-air theaters.

opisthodomos: The rear chamber of a peripteros or double antae temple, corresponding to the pronaos on the opposite side, often used as a treasury.

opus cementicium: Roman concrete composed of rubble aggregate laid in lime mortar.

opus incertum: Irregular wall made of stones of different sizes, often also with cement.

orchestra: Originally meant "the space where the chorus danced." A circular or semicircular area between the front row of the cavea and the skene.

ovolo: A rounded convex molding that in Roman work is usually a quarter circle in sections and in Greek work is flatter.

panegyriarch: Leader of a festal assembly.

pardalis: Leopard.

paredros: Assessor or coadjutor of a chief magistrate; an assisting deity.

parodos: The entryway into the Greek theater, one on each side between the wing of the cavea and the skene, through which the chorus processed into the orchestra. Gates were often built at the entrance to the orchestra.

pediment: The triangular space in the gable of a building above the entablature, including the tympanum and geison, usually decorated with sculpture in high relief.

peplos: A heavy garment worn by Greek women, fastened at both shoulders.

peripteros: A temple in which the cella is surrounded on all sides by one row of columns with two columns in antis in the pronaos and opisthodomos.

peristyle: The covered colonnade around a building (such as a temple) or the colonnades that surround the inner court of a house.

pilaster: A rectangular pier projecting from a wall with a base and capital; it is treated like a column according to the appropriate architectural order of the building to which it belongs.

plinth: The square block which serves as the bottom of an Ionic or Corinthian column base; also refers to the lowest portion of a pedestal.

polos: Headdress worn by a goddess.

portico: See stoa.

portorium: Tariff charged at ports for goods in transit.

promachos: Champion; often of a god who leads in a battle.

pronaos: The front chamber of a temple, through which the cella is accessible, usually with two columns in antis.

propylon: A gate or entrance building to a market or an enclosed sacred district, often with interior columns.

prostyle: A temple with a row of columns in front of its cella and two columns in antis in its pronaos.

prytaneion: The building in which the acting magistrates had their office; sometimes the sacred hearth was located here.

prytanis: Usually an acting magistrate of a Greek city; in Ephesos the chief supervisor of the cult of Artemis.

pulvinus: Part of the decoration of the Ionic capital.

quaestor: A Roman financial officer in charge of public monies; also a public judge or prosecutor in criminal trials.

revetment: The facing of a wall of a building with stones or other materials; e.g., marble revetment of a brick wall.

sebastophant: Priest of Augustus; *flamen Augusti.*

sekos: The unroofed inner cella of a large dipteros temple; a small naiskos for the temple statue is built inside against the back wall of the sekos.

sima: The gutter of a building attached to the geison; its spouts are often sculpted as animals' (often lions') heads.

skene: The entire stage building of a theater or odeion.

spoils: (spolia) Building materials which have been previously used.

stele: A stone pillar or slab carved with a legal, political, or commemorative inscription.

stereobate: The substructure of a colonnade or wall, consisting of: (1) the undressed or roughly dressed foundations which lie under the ground level; (2) the euthynteria, or the dressed uppermost course of the foundations; and (3) the crepidoma, the stepped platform of dressed stones above the ground level.

stoa: (also portico) A long covered colonnade or arcade, either freestanding or alongside a building.

stylobate: The uppermost step of the crepidoma which carries the columns or the column bases.

syrinx: Pan's pipe; the hollow part of the hinge.

tabula ansata: A "double-eared" plaque, either of metal or imitated in sculpted relief, usually bearing an inscription. Its shape is rectangular, with an equilateral triangle projecting horizontally from each of its vertical sides.

technitai: Members of an association of artisans.

temenos: A sacred precinct, cut off from common usage and dedicated to a god. It usually consists of the land immediately surrounding a temple, often marked by a low wall.

thiasos: Religious association.

torus: Convex molding, usually found as the upper part of a column base, above the spira.

triglyph: An ornament of a Doric order frieze consisting of a projecting rectangular tablet with two vertical channels. The triglyphs are usually located above each column, with one or two (or even three) in the spaces between the columns.

tympanum: The recessed triangular space of the pediment, above the cornice; also the space within an arch above a lintel. It is usually decorated. A drum or similar instrument.

uguentarium: Vessel for perfume or ointment.

volute: An ornamental motif in the form of a spiral curve, typical of Ionic capitals.

xoanon: A rudely-carved wooden image of a deity. In many ancient religions, the xoanon was the cult statue (distinct from the temple statue) that was decorated and carried in processions.

xystos: A long portico used for athletic exercises and training, especially for running and therefore of the same length as a stadium.

Index